arihant

AF819703

# Ignite

## Topicwise MCQs

*"Give Fire to **Your Prelims Prep**"*

# Environment & Ecology

For **Civil Services** & **State PCS**
Preliminary Examination

MentorsHut

arihant
SUCCESS AND NOTHING LESS

**ARIHANT PUBLICATION (INDIA) LIMITED**



**卐 Administrative & Production Offices**

**Regd. Office**

'Ramchhaya' 4577/15, Agarwal Road, Darya Ganj, New Delhi -110002
Tele: 011- 47630600, 43518550

**卐 Head Office**

Kalindi, TP Nagar, Meerut (UP) - 250002 Tel: 0121-7156203, 7156204

**卐 Sales & Support Offices**

Agra, Ahmedabad, Bengaluru, Bareilly, Chennai, Delhi, Guwahati, Hyderabad, Jaipur, Jhansi, Kolkata, Lucknow, Nagpur & Pune.

卐 **PRICE**: ₹ 275.00

卐 **PO No :** TXT-XX-XXXXXXX-X-XX

Published by Arihant Publications (India) Ltd.

For further information about the books published by Arihant, log on to www.arihantbooks.com or e-mail at info@arihantbooks.com

Follow us on

# Preface

The *Ignite Series* is more than just a resource - it's your ultimate guide to conquering one of the toughest examinations in India. With nearly **10 lakh aspirants** filling the forms for the UPSC Civil Services Preliminary Examination each year and **only around 15,000 qualifying for Mains**, the success rate stands at a staggering **1.5%**. Designed by the authors of the bestselling *Pulse Handwritten Notes for Prelims*, this series is meticulously crafted to transform your preparation and significantly enhance your chances of success.

What truly sets the *Ignite Series* apart is its ability to **bridge the gap between rote learning and deep conceptual understanding**. Packed with over **6,000+ carefully designed MCQs**, the series offers comprehensive coverage of the Prelims syllabus, ensuring no topic is left unexplored. Each question is strategically designed to challenge your knowledge and sharpen your problem-solving skills.

In an exam where every mark counts, **standing out isn't optional - it's essential**. To equip you for this challenge, the *Ignite Series* introduces a **three-tiered evaluation system**, testing your knowledge at **Factual, Conceptual and Analytical levels**. This innovative approach mirrors the demands of the UPSC, ensuring you are thoroughly prepared to tackle its dynamic and unpredictable nature. Additionally, **topic-wise Previous Years' Questions (PYQs)** included at the end of each chapter provide valuable insights into trends and patterns, helping you craft a data-driven strategy.

Understanding concepts is important, but **retaining and applying them under pressure** is the key to success. To make this process seamless, every question in this series is accompanied by **detailed explanations**, enriched with **infographics, tables and maps** that simplify complex topics.

Recognizing the importance of self-assessment, the series offers **free access to 3 All India Mock Tests**. These simulated tests replicate real exam conditions, allowing you to benchmark your performance, identify areas of improvement, and refine your preparation strategy. By offering a clear picture of where you stand, these tests ensure that you are not just prepared but **exam-ready**.

With the *Ignite Series*, you're not merely preparing for an exam - you're gearing up to outshine the competition and achieve your dreams. Let this book be the tool that empowers you to break into the top **1.5%** and take a giant step toward becoming a civil servant.

This masterpiece wouldn't have been possible without the **tireless efforts of the entire MentorsHut family**, who dedicated countless hours to creating a resource that truly serves aspirants.

To our daughter, **Prisha Mangtani**, your unwavering patience and love have been our greatest source of strength throughout this journey. Thank you for your sacrifices and for inspiring us to give our best.

We at MentorsHut remain committed to excellence and continuous improvement. Your feedback is invaluable to us. If you have suggestions or ideas to make this series even better, please don't hesitate to reach out to us at **info@mentorshut.com**.

Here's wishing you the very best for your preparation - may this series **ignite the spark of excellence within you** and guide you toward achieving your goals.

**Amit Mangtani,**
**CA Shalini Wadhwani**
Founders, MentorsHut

# Contents

## Topical PYQ Trend Last 8 Years'

| Section | 2024 | 2023 | 2022 | 2021 | 2020 | 2019 | 2018 | 2017 |
|---|---|---|---|---|---|---|---|---|
| Ecosystem | 0 | 1 | 2 | 6 | 0 | 1 | 1 | 0 |
| Environmental Pollution | 3 | 2 | 5 | 4 | 2 | 4 | 0 | 3 |
| Biodiversity and Conservation | 7 | 9 | 6 | 3 | 7 | 6 | 1 | 5 |
| Climate Change and Mitigation Strategies | 0 | 2 | 0 | 0 | 2 | 2 | 2 | 2 |
| International Conventions, Treaties, Funds and Organisations | 0 | 1 | 2 | 2 | 0 | 1 | 2 | 2 |
| National Organizations, Funds, Acts and Policies | 1 | 1 | 3 | 0 | 2 | 4 | 2 | 2 |
| Sustainable Development: Energy and Agriculture | 3 | 2 | 2 | 4 | 5 | 1 | 2 | 3 |
| **Total** | **14** | **18** | **20** | **19** | **18** | **19** | **10** | **17** |

**Section-wise Weightage (Average): Environment & Ecology**
**Last 8 Years' PYQ Trend**

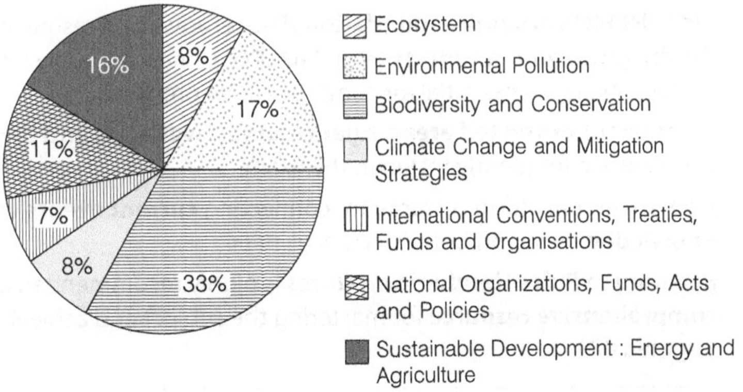

## Overall PYQ Trend Last 8 Years'

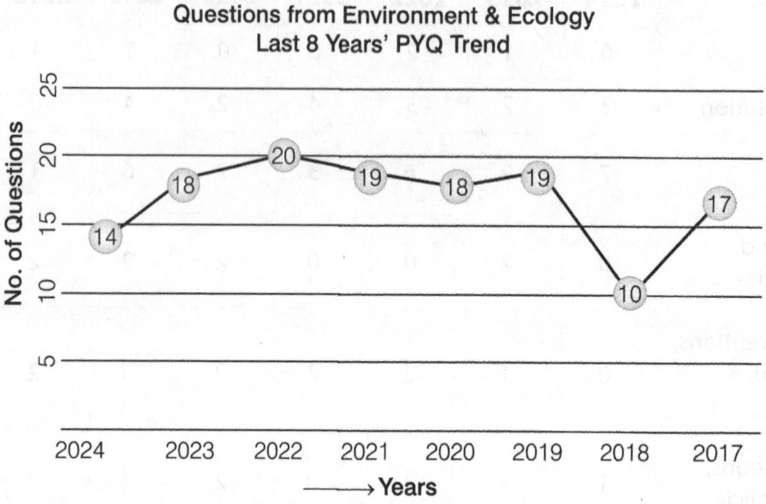


**Key Learnings from the PYQs of 'Environment and Ecology'**

1. The **Environment section** consistently holds prominence in the UPSC Prelims, with **16-19 questions** regularly appearing.
2. Questions test **interdisciplinary knowledge**, linking the **environment to science, agriculture and international relations.**
3. **Cross-referencing** is key, as many questions require an integrated understanding of ecology, policies and geography, such as linking species to their habitats or legislation to practices.
4. While **NCERTs provide a foundational base**, advanced resources like **Pulse Books, government reports (e.g., MOEFCC)**, international treaties and current affairs are essential for comprehensive preparation.
5. Locations of **protected areas, tiger reserves, wetlands and biosphere reserves** are frequently tested in the exam.
6. **Analytical reasoning** is crucial for connecting **current events with static knowledge**, ensuring better accuracy.
7. Referring to **Pulse Handwritten Notes** is highly recommended as a **comprehensive resource** for mastering the subject and achieving the targeted 80% accuracy.

CHAPTER 01

# Ecology and Ecosystem

## Assessment Round

**1.** Identify the type of ecosystem service based on the following characteristics:

1. This service includes nutrient cycling and soil formation.
2. It is fundamental for maintaining the conditions necessary for life and underpins other types of ecosystem services.
3. It also includes the maintenance of biodiversity, which supports all other ecosystem services.

Choose the correct answer from the options given below:

(a) Provisioning service
(b) Regulating service
(c) Supporting service
(d) Cultural service

**2.** Which of the following statements best defines the concept of 'Standing State' in an ecosystem?

(a) It is the total biomass present in an ecosystem, representing the living matter at a given time.
(b) It refers to the concentration of inorganic nutrients that determine the ecosystem's productivity and varies seasonally.
(c) It describes the balance between living organisms and their physical environment, highlighting energy flow.
(d) It indicates the cumulative effects of biogeochemical cycles within a specific habitat.

**3.** Which of the following options best describes an 'Ecocline'?

(a) It refers to a specific type of ecosystem boundary where distinct species from neighbouring biomes coexist due to shared environmental conditions.
(b) It denotes a gradual change in certain species traits across geographical regions in response to varying physicochemical factors like salinity and pH.
(c) It is a transition zone where organisms adapted to entirely different environments begin interbreeding due to proximity.
(d) It represents a sudden shift in vegetation appearance along geographic borders, generally due to sharp climatic variations.

**4.** Consider the following statements regarding the process of decomposition in ecosystems:

1. Decomposition occurs at an accelerated rate in humid tropical regions due to optimal temperature and moisture conditions.
2. The presence of high lignin content in detritus is positively correlated with the rate of decomposition.
3. Soil microbes are primarily responsible for the breakdown of organic matter, and their activity is influenced by environmental and chemical factors.
4. In colder climates, even with adequate moisture, the rate of decomposition can be significantly hampered.

Which of the above statements are correct?

(a) 1 and 3 only (b) 2 and 4 only
(c) 1, 3 and 4 only (d) 1, 2, 3 and 4

**5.** Which of the following statements regarding the levels of organisation in ecology is/are correct?

1. An organism represents the basic unit of ecological study and includes interactions with both biotic and abiotic factors in its environment.
2. A population is defined as a group of individuals belonging to different species that inhabit the same geographic area and interact with one another.
3. A community encompasses all living populations within a specific area, along with their interactions, and is considered synonymous with an ecosystem.
4. A biome characterised by distinct climatic conditions and types of vegetation, consisting of multiple ecosystems with similar environmental conditions.

Choose the correct answer from the options given below:

(a) 1 and 4 only
(b) 2 and 3 only
(c) 1 and 3 only
(d) 1, 2 and 3

**6.** Which of the following statements best describes 'ecosystem accounting'?

(a) Ecosystem accounting is solely concerned with tracking the economic value of environmental assets without integrating measures of human activities.
(b) Ecosystem accounting is a framework that integrates measures of ecosystems and the flows of services from them with measures of economic and other human activity, building upon the System of Environmental-Economic Accounting (SEEA) Central Framework.
(c) Ecosystem accounting focuses only on measuring individual environmental resources like water and soil without considering their interactions within a broader system.
(d) Ecosystem accounting is a method for recording historical data on the usage of natural resources but does not account for the impacts of human activities.

**7.** With regard to ecosystem productivity, which of the following statements is/are incorrect?

1. The Net Primary Productivity (NPP) of an ecosystem is always lower than its Gross Primary Productivity (GPP).
2. Primary productivity is influenced by the photosynthetic capacity of plants.

Choose the correct options from the codes given below:

(a) 1 only (b) 2 only
(c) Both 1 and 2 (d) Neither 1 nor 2

**8.** In the context of ecology, which of the following statements most correctly describes the term 'ecophene'?

(a) It is a phenotype exhibited by an organism after living in a new environment for an extended period.
(b) It refers to a population that cannot exchange genes with other populations of the same species.
(c) It denotes a structural change in chromosomes that alters the genetic makeup, leading to the development of new ecological races.
(d) It is the initial phenotype an organism displays when it encounters a new environment, characterised by temporary and reversible changes.

**9.** Which of the following best describes Ecological Fiscal Transfers (EFT)?

(a) EFTs are a type of payment made from local governments to national governments based on ecological indicators.
(b) EFTs involve transferring public revenue from higher to lower levels of government based on ecological indicators, such as protected areas or watershed management areas.
(c) EFTs are used to penalise governments that do not meet environmental conservation targets by withholding funds.
(d) EFTs distribute funds from international organisations directly to local conservation groups based on their ecological performance.

**10.** Consider the following characteristics related to ecotypes:

1. Genetic distinctness
2. Adaptation to specific environmental conditions
3. Presence of a significant atmospheric component
4. Geographic distribution in specific habitats

Which of the characteristics listed above are associated with ecotypes?

(a) 1, 2 and 4 only
(b) 1, 2 and 3 only
(c) 2 and 4 only
(d) 1 and 3 only

**11.** Which of the following statements correctly describes the types of feedback loops involved in homeostasis within an ecosystem?

(a) A positive feedback loop stabilises the ecosystem by reducing food supply, leading to more deaths.
(b) A negative feedback loop amplifies population changes, leading to more births and further population increase.
(c) A positive feedback loop amplifies changes in the population, leading to more births and a larger population.
(d) A negative feedback loop increases the population, resulting in more births and a larger population.

**12.** Consider the following statements about food chains:

1. A food chain represents the sequence in which organisms feed upon each other.
2. Food chains exist within the populations of a species.
3. A food chain shows the number of organisms at each level that are consumed by others.

Which of the statements given above is/are correct?

(a) 1 only (b) 1 and 2 only
(c) 1, 2 and 3 (d) None

**13.** The following passage describes a crucial ecological concept:

'It encompasses a complex network of trophic interactions, showcasing the multitude of energy and nutrient transfers among various organisms and species within a given ecosystem.'

Choose the correct answer from the options given below.

(a) Trophic Cascade
(b) Energy Flow Diagram
(c) Nutrient Cycle
(d) Food Web

**14.** In a pond ecosystem, consider the following statements regarding the food chain and its dynamics:

1. The food chain in a pond ecosystem consists of Algae, Water Fleas, Stickleback, and Pike in that order.
2. Removing the Pike from the ecosystem will lead to an immediate population increase of Stickleback, followed by a subsequent decline due to resource depletion.
3. A food web with fewer links is more resilient to the removal of a species compared to a complex food web with many links.

Which of the statements above is/are not correct?

(a) 1 only
(b) 1 and 2 only
(c) 3 only
(d) 1, 2 and 3

**15.** Consider the following statements regarding habitats and ecosystems:

1. A habitat is always defined by the presence of multiple species, making it inherently a shared environment.
2. The terms 'habitat' and 'environment' are interchangeable and refer to the same concept in ecology.
3. A habitat can exist independently of any organism, relying solely on its physical characteristics.

How many of the statements above is/are correct?

(a) Only one
(b) Only two
(c) All three
(d) None

**16.** Which of the following statements best describes antibiosis in ecological interactions?
(a) It is a positive interaction where both organisms benefit from the relationship.
(b) It involves competition between organisms of the same species for resources.
(c) It is a negative interaction where one organism produces harmful secretions that adversely affect another.
(d) It refers to a symbiotic relationship that enhances survival for both species.

**17.** Consider the following statements regarding food chains in ecosystems:
1. Grazing food chains begin with green plants as producers and primary consumers are typically herbivores.
2. Detritus food chains start with detritus and are mainly found in the soil or sediments of aquatic ecosystems.
3. Supplementary food chains in ecosystems include parasites and scavengers.

Which of the above statements is/are correct?
(a) 1 and 3 only (b) 1 and 2 only
(c) 2 and 3 only (d) 1, 2 and 3

**18.** Which of the following statements correctly describes how various factors can impact the stability of food chains :
1. Habitat destruction and fragmentation can reduce available resources and alter predator-prey dynamics.
2. Pollution and contamination have no impact on food chain stability as they only affect individual species.
3. Overharvesting of species can disrupt food chain balance by depleting predator or prey populations.
4. Climate change can shift species distributions and alter predator-prey interactions within food chains.
5. Diseases and parasites can spread through food chains, affecting the health and success of multiple species.

Choose the correct answer from the options given below:
(a) 1, 3, 4 and 5 only
(b) 1, 2, 3 and 4 only
(c) 2, 4 and 5 only
(d) 1, 2, 3, 4 and 5

**19.** Consider the following organisms found in a desert food chain:
1. Desert Willow
2. Desert Hare
3. Snake
4. Falcon
5. Coyote

Which of the following correctly lists these organisms in the sequence of the desert food chain, from the primary producer to the apex predator?
(a) Desert Willow → Desert Hare → Snake → Falcon → Coyote
(b) Desert Hare → Desert Willow → Snake → Falcon → Coyote
(c) Desert Willow → Desert Hare → Falcon → Snake → Coyote
(d) Desert Hare → Desert Willow → Falcon → Snake → Coyote

**20.** Which of the following statements about ecological pyramids is/are not correct?
1. The pyramid of energy is always upright because energy is lost as heat when it flows from one trophic level to the next.
2. The pyramid of numbers can sometimes be inverted, such as in the case where a large number of small producers support a few larger consumers.
3. The pyramid of biomass in aquatic ecosystems is generally upright because the biomass of phytoplankton typically exceeds that of fish.

Choose the correct answer from the options given below:
(a) 1 only (b) 3 only
(c) 1 and 2 only (d) 1, 2 and 3

**21.** Consider the following types of ecological pyramids:

1. Pyramid of numbers
2. Pyramid of biomass
3. Pyramid of energy

Which of the above pyramids can never be inverted in shape?

(a) Only one (b) Only two
(c) All three (d) None

**22.** Consider the following statements about the anaerobic decomposition process:

1. Anaerobic decomposition happens in the absence of oxygen and produces a significant amount of energy.
2. Anaerobic decomposition is effective in killing weed seeds and pathogens in the waste.

Which of the above statements is/are correct?

(a) 1 only (b) 2 only
(c) Both 1 and 2 (d) Neither 1 nor 2

**23.** Consider the following pairs:

| | Term | Definition |
|---|---|---|
| 1. | Ecotype | A phenotype of an organism adapted permanently due to changes in genes. |
| 2. | Ecophene | Temporary, reversible phenotype changes in response to new environmental conditions, without gene changes. |
| 3. | Ecospecies | Permanent, genetically distinct variations due to long-term environmental separation of ecotones. |

How many of the above pairs is/are correctly matched?

(a) Only one
(b) Only two
(c) All three
(d) None

**24.** Consider the following statements regarding ecological succession:

1. The pioneer stage is characterised by the establishment of the first colonisers in a barren or disturbed area.
2. The climax stage represents a dynamic phase where species composition is constantly changing.
3. The seral stage involves a transition period between the pioneer and climax stages, with increasing species diversity and interactions.

How many of the statements given above is/are correct?

(a) Only one
(b) Only two
(c) All three
(d) None

**25.** In the context of species interactions, what is the difference between commensalism and predation?

(a) In commensalism, one species benefits while the other is harmed, whereas in predation, one species benefits and the other is unaffected.
(b) In commensalism, both species benefit, whereas in predation, only one species benefits, and the other is harmed.
(c) In commensalism, one species benefits without affecting the other, while in predation, one species benefits by directly harming or consuming the other.
(d) In both commensalism and predation, both species are equally benefited, though one may be less affected.

**26.** Consider the following statements about primary and secondary productivity in ecosystems:

1. The annual net primary productivity of the oceans is approximately 55 billion tonnes, covering about 70% of the Earth's surface.
2. Secondary productivity measures the rate at which consumers convert the organic matter they consume into new biomass.
3. The primary productivity of oceans is high due to the abundance of sunlight throughout the water column, promoting photosynthesis.

Which of the statements above is/are correct?

(a) 1 only (b) 1 and 2 only
(c) 2 and 3 only (d) 1, 2 and 3

**27.** With regard to ecosystem productivity, which of the following statements is/are incorrect?

1. The Net Primary Productivity (NPP) of an ecosystem is always lower than its Gross Primary Productivity (GPP).
2. Primary productivity is influenced by the photosynthetic capacity of plants.

Choose the correct answer from the options given below:

(a) 1 only
(b) 2 only
(c) Both 1 and 2
(d) Neither 1 nor 2

**28.** Consider the following statements about trophic cascades:

1. A trophic cascade involves the direct effects of changes in predator-prey relationships on the entire ecosystem.
2. The removal of a top predator can lead to a decrease in the abundance of its prey, which then negatively impacts plant communities.
3. Trophic cascades are always short-lived and have minimal long-term effects on ecosystem structure.

Which of the above statements is/are correct?

(a) 1 and 2 only (b) 2 and 3 only
(c) 1 and 3 only (d) 1 only

**29.** What is a key distinguishing factor between competition and commensalism among species?

(a) In competition, one species benefits at the expense of another, while in commensalism, both species are negatively impacted.
(b) In competition, the fitness of both species is reduced due to resource sharing, whereas in commensalism, one species benefits without affecting the other.
(c) In commensalism, one species benefits while the other is harmed, whereas, in competition, neither species benefits, and both are unaffected.
(d) In competition, both species benefit equally, while in commensalism, one species is unaffected, and the other faces reduced fitness.

**30.** Which of the following statements correctly describes a density-dependent limiting factor?

(a) Climate change impacts populations by affecting their growth and distribution, regardless of population density.
(b) Natural disasters reduce population size by causing widespread habitat destruction, independent of the population density.
(c) Competition among individuals within a population intensifies as population density increases.
(d) Mutualism benefits both interacting species and is considered a limiting factor that affects population growth based on their density.

**31.** Which of the following services provided by ecosystems are classified as 'Supporting Services'?

1. Recreation and Tourism
2. Production of Food
3. Carbon Sequestration
4. Maintenance of Genetic Diversity

Choose the correct answer from the options given below:

(a) Only one
(b) Only two
(c) Only three
(d) All four

**32.** Consider the following statements regarding the process of speciation:

1. Speciation occurs when new species form from existing ones due to evolutionary changes.
2. Geographic isolation, behavioural isolation, and genetic isolation are factors that contribute to speciation.
3. Once reproductive isolation is established, the isolated populations can no longer interbreed and produce fertile offspring.

Which of the statements given above is/are correct?

(a) 1 and 2 only
(b) 2 and 3 only
(c) 1 only
(d) 1, 2 and 3

**33.** Consider the following about the survival strategy of organisms with its corresponding environmental condition or mechanism.

1. Hibernation - Escaping cold temperatures by entering a state of reduced metabolic activity.
2. Aestivation - Entering a state of suspended development to avoid extreme heat and desiccation.
3. Diapause - Entering a state of reduced metabolic activity to avoid cold temperatures.
4. Migration - Moving to different environments to escape unfavourable conditions.

Which of the above pair(s) are correctly matched?

(a) 1, 2 and 4 only (b) 1, 3 and 4 only
(c) 2, 3 and 4 only (d) 1, 2 and 3 only

**34.** Which of the following statements about ecological succession is/are correct?

1. A sere refers to the entire sequence of communities that successively change in a given area.
2. Secondary succession occurs more rapidly than primary succession.
3. Xerarch succession occurs in wet environments.

Choose the correct answer from the options given below:

(a) 1 and 2 only (b) 2 and 3 only
(c) 1 and 3 only (d) 1, 2 and 3

**35.** Which of the following statements correctly describes ecological succession?

(a) Primary succession occurs in areas previously occupied by a community, while secondary succession occurs in barren areas lacking topsoil.
(b) In primary succession, pioneer species such as lichens and mosses colonise initially barren areas, whereas secondary succession happens more quickly in previously disturbed areas with existing soil.
(c) The climax community is the initial stage of succession, and each transitional community is referred to as a climax community.
(d) In all ecosystems, the climax community is dominated by grasses, regardless of the type of ecosystem.

**36.** Consider the following statements regarding ecotones:

1. Ecotones are transition areas between two distinct biomes, such as mangrove forests between marine and terrestrial ecosystems.
2. Ecotones always have lower productivity compared to the adjacent natural ecosystems.
3. The edge effect describes the phenomenon where species richness and population density are higher at the boundary of two different habitats.
4. Edge species are those that thrive specifically in the ecotone rather than in either of the adjoining ecosystems.

Which of the statements given above are correct?

(a) 1 and 3 only
(b) 2 and 4 only
(c) 1, 2 and 3 only
(d) 1, 3 and 4 only

**37.** Which of the following ecological pyramids are inverted?

1. Pyramid of numbers in a parasitic food chain
2. Pyramid of biomass in grassland
3. Pyramid of biomass in a pond

Select the correct answer from the options given below:

(a) 1 only
(b) 2 and 3 only
(c) 1 and 3 only
(d) 1 and 2 only

**38.** Which of the following statements correctly describes the concept of edge effects in ecological contexts?

1. Edge effects refer to the ecological changes and variations that occur at the boundaries between two distinct ecosystems or habitat types, known as ecotones.
2. The edge effect typically results in environmental conditions that are similar to those found in the interior of the adjacent ecosystems.
3. Species composition in ecotones often includes a unique mixture of species adapted to both of the adjacent ecosystems, potentially increasing biodiversity.

Which of the above statements is/are correct?
(a) 1 only
(b) 1 and 3 only
(c) 2 and 3 only
(d) 1, 2 and 3

**39.** Examine the following statements about species diversity:

1. Species evenness refers to how abundance is distributed across species within a community.
2. Species richness indicates the total number of species present in a given area.

Which of the above statements is/are correct?
(a) 1 only (b) 2 only
(c) Both 1 and 2 (d) Neither 1 nor 2

**40.** In the context of ecological succession, which of the following parameters generally increases during the successive seral stages?

1. Total biomass
2. Number of organisms
3. Number of species

Select the correct answer from the options below:
(a) 1 and 2 only (b) 2 and 3 only
(c) 3 only (d) 1, 2 and 3

**41.** Consider the following statements regarding energy flow in ecosystems:

1. Except for deep-sea hydrothermal ecosystems, the Sun is the only source of energy for all ecosystems on Earth.
2. Plants in a terrestrial ecosystem capture approximately 1% of the sunlight energy that falls on their leaves and convert it into food energy.
3. The average energy transfer efficiency from one trophic level to the next is about 10%, which significantly limits the number of trophic levels that can be supported in an ecosystem.
4. An energy pyramid is always upright due to the continuous availability of energy at each trophic level, reflecting the laws of thermodynamics.

Which of the above statements are correct?
(a) 1 and 2 only
(b) 3 and 4 only
(c) 2 and 3 only
(d) 1, 2 and 4 only

**42.** Which of the following are the primary consumers in an ecosystem?

1. Ants 2. Deer
3. Fox 4. Tiger

Select the correct answer from the options given below:
(a) 1 and 2 only
(b) 2 and 3 only
(c) 1, 2 and 3 only
(d) 2, 3 and 4 only

**43.** Consider the following statements regarding ecological succession:

1. Pioneer species are the first to colonise a disturbed or newly formed habitat and begin the process of normalising the environment.
2. A seral community is an intermediate stage in ecological succession that occurs between the pioneer stage and the climax community.
3. A climax community represents a stable community that is in near equilibrium with the environment, resulting from gradual and predictable changes in species composition.

Which of the above statements are correct?
(a) 1 and 2 only
(b) 2 and 3 only
(c) 1 and 3 only
(d) 1, 2 and 3

**44.** Consider the following statements regarding bioaccumulation and biomagnification:

1. Bioaccumulation refers to the increase in concentration of a pollutant from the environment to the first organism in a food chain.
2. Biomagnification occurs when there is an increase in the concentration of a pollutant as it moves from one trophic level to the next in a food chain.
3. For biomagnification to occur, the pollutant must be long-lived, mobile, soluble in fats, and biologically active.

Which of the above statements are correct?

(a) 1 and 2 only (b) 1 and 3 only
(c) 2 and 3 only (d) 1, 2 and 3

**45.** Which one of the following statements is correct regarding biomagnification?

(a) Biomagnification refers to the tendency of pollutants to increase in concentration as they move from one trophic level to the next in a food chain.
(b) Pollutants that dissolve in water are more likely to biomagnify as they are retained by organisms for a long time.
(c) Short-lived pollutants are the primary concern in biomagnification as they accumulate quickly in organisms.
(d) In mammals, pollutants are typically measured in lean tissue, as fat-soluble pollutants do not pose a threat to the organism.

**46.** What is the fundamental difference between a food chain and a food web?

(a) A food chain consists of multiple interlinked pathways of energy flow within an ecosystem, whereas a food web follows a single, linear pathway of energy flow.
(b) A food chain is generally more complex than a food web, as it includes various trophic levels linked to multiple organisms.
(c) In a food chain, a disturbance at any trophic level disrupts the entire system, whereas in a food web, such disturbances have minimal impact due to interconnected pathways.
(d) A food chain is a graphical model of interconnected relationships within an ecological community, while a food web shows a linear pathway of organismal energy flow.

**47.** Consider the following statements regarding ecological dominance:

1. Ecological dominance occurs when one or more species exert major control over other species in a community due to factors such as their size, productivity, or abundance.
2. Tidal swamps in tropical regions are usually dominated by species of mangroves.
3. In temperate bogs, the dominant vegetation typically includes species of Sphagnum moss.
4. Some seafloor communities are dominated by brittle stars.

How many of the above statements is/are correct?

(a) Only one (b) Only two
(c) Only three (d) All four

**48.** What is the difference between a biome and an ecological niche?

(a) A biome refers to a specific region classified by its plants and animals, while an ecological niche describes the role and function of a species within its community.
(b) A biome focuses on the functional role of a species in its environment, whereas an ecological niche describes a large geographical area with distinct climates and ecosystems.
(c) A biome and an ecological niche are interchangeable terms, both referring to the area where a species lives and interacts with others.
(d) A biome determines the food chain of an ecosystem, while an ecological niche explains the geographical range of a species.

**49.** Arrange the phases of ecological succession as proposed by Clements in the initial to final sequence:

1. Nudation
2. Invasion
3. Competition
4. Reaction
5. Climax

Choose the correct sequence from the codes given below:

(a) 1-2-3-4-5 (b) 1-3-2-4-5
(c) 2-1-4-3-5 (d) 1-4-2-3-5

**50.** Consider the following pairs regarding types of species interactions:

| Interaction Type | Description |
|---|---|
| 1. Amensalism | One species is inhibited, while the other species is unaffected. |
| 2. Predation | One species benefits while the other is harmed or inhibited. |
| 3. Parasitism | One species benefits while the other species is harmed, as the parasite depends on the host for nourishment. |
| 4. Competition | Both species are adversely affected due to limited resources. |
| 5. Commensalism | Both species benefit from the interaction, often forming a close association. |
| 6. Mutualism | One species benefits, while the other species is neither harmed nor benefited. |

How many of the above pairs are correctly matched?

(a) Only two pair (b) Only three pairs
(c) Only four pairs (d) All six pairs

**51.** Consider the following nutrient cycles:

1. Nitrogen cycle
2. Sulfur cycle
3. Carbon cycle
4. Phosphorus cycle

How many of the above is/are gaseous nutrient cycles?

(a) Only one (b) Only two
(c) Only three (d) All four

**52.** Consider the following pairs related to the nitrogen cycle:

1. Nitrogen Fixation - Conversion of gaseous nitrogen to ammonia
2. Nitrification - Conversion of nitrogenous waste into ammonia
3. Ammonification - Conversion of ammonia to nitrates or nitrites
4. Denitrification - Conversion of nitrates to gaseous nitrogen

How many of the pairs given above is/are correctly matched?

(a) Only one (b) Only two
(c) Only three (d) All four

**53.** Consider the following statements regarding eutrophication:

1. Eutrophication is caused by the leaching of nitrates and phosphates from agricultural lands into aquatic ecosystems.
2. The growth of algae during eutrophication improves oxygen levels in the water.
3. Algal blooms can lead to the suffocation of aquatic organisms due to decreased oxygen availability.

Which of the above statements is/are correct?

(a) 1 and 2 only (b) 1 and 3 only
(c) 2 and 3 only (d) 1, 2 and 3

**54.** Which of the following processes is not part of the phosphorus cycle?

(a) Weathering of rocks
(b) Atmospheric deposition
(c) Plant uptake
(d) Decomposition

**55.** Which of the following statements correctly describes the sedimentary nutrient cycle?

(a) Most sedimentary cycles are generally considered perfect cycles with no significant losses or gains of nutrients.
(b) The reservoir for sedimentary nutrient cycles primarily includes the Earth's crust, while the atmosphere and hydrosphere are less significant.
(c) The sedimentary nutrient cycle involves reservoirs in the Earth's crust, atmosphere, and hydrosphere, but it is not typically considered a perfect cycle due to nutrient losses.
(d) Sedimentary nutrient cycles are perfect cycles with reservoirs limited to the atmosphere and hydrosphere, not including the Earth's crust.

**56.** Which of the following statements correctly describes the sources of nitrogen in the atmosphere?

1. Atmospheric precipitation contributes nitrogen primarily in the form of nitrates.
2. Geological sources refer to nitrogen released from rock formations that have undergone weathering.
3. Agricultural land is a significant contributor to nitrogen levels due to runoff from fertilizers.
4. Livestock, particularly ruminants, release nitrogen compounds through enteric fermentation and manure.
5. Urban waste contributes nitrogen to the ecosystem mainly through the breakdown of organic materials.

Select the correct answer using the codes given below :

(a) 1, 3, and 4 only
(b) 2, 3 and 5 only
(c) 1, 3, 4 and 5 only
(d) 1, 2, 3, 4 and 5

**57.** Consider the following statements regarding the Sedimentary Nutrient Cycle:

1. Most sedimentary cycles are generally considered perfect cycles.
2. The phosphorus cycle is sedimentary.
3. The reservoir of sedimentary nutrients is located in the Earth's crust.

Which of the above statements is/are incorrect?

(a) 1 only
(b) 1 and 2 only
(c) 1 and 3 only
(d) 2 and 3 only

**58.** In which one of the following biogeochemical cycles, the weathering of rocks is the main source of the release of nutrients to enter the cycle?

(a) Carbon cycle
(b) Nitrogen cycle
(c) Phosphorus cycle
(d) Sulfur cycle

**59.** With reference to Social Forestry, consider the following statements:

1. The term 'Social Forestry' was first introduced by the National Commission on Agriculture in 1976.
2. Social Forestry involves the plantation of trees in and around agricultural fields, along roadsides, and on village common lands to reduce pressure on natural forests.
3. The main goal of Social Forestry is to clear forest land for agricultural use.

How many of the above statements is/are correct?

(a) Only one
(b) Only two
(c) All three
(d) None

**60.** Consider the following pairs of Sacred Groves and their names in different states:

| | Sacred Grove Name | State |
|---|---|---|
| 1. | Sarna | Bihar |
| 2. | Kavu | Himachal Pradesh |
| 3. | Devarakadu | Karnataka |

Which of the above pairs are correctly matched?

(a) 1 and 2 only (b) 1 and 3 only
(c) 2 and 3 only (d) 1, 2 and 3

**61.** With reference to Atmospheric Rivers (AR), consider the following statements:

1. Atmospheric Rivers (AR) are long, narrow regions in the atmosphere that transport water vapour from the tropics to the poles.
2. ARs are part of extratropical cyclones and are typically located within low-level jet streams.
3. Atmospheric Rivers are responsible for transferring 50% of moisture from the tropics to the poles.

Which of the statements given are correct?

(a) 1 and 2 only
(b) 2 and 3 only
(c) 1 and 3 only
(d) 1, 2 and 3

**62.** With reference to the Gross Environment Product Index (GEPI) launched by Uttarakhand, which of the following statements is correct?
1. GEPI is designed to evaluate the ecological impact of human interventions on the environment.
2. The four pillars of GEPI include air, soil, trees and water.
3. GEPI quantifies the contribution of natural ecosystems to the economy and overall welfare.

Select the correct answer from the options given below:
(a) 1 and 2 only
(b) 2 and 3 only
(c) 1 and 3 only
(d) 1, 2 and 3

**63.** What is the difference between allelopathy and amensalism?
(a) Allelopathy involves one organism benefiting while another is harmed, whereas amensalism occurs when both organisms are equally affected.
(b) Allelopathy refers to one organism producing chemicals that influence other organisms, while amensalism occurs when one organism is harmed and the other is unaffected.
(c) In allelopathy, both organisms benefit from the relationship, whereas in amensalism, both organisms suffer.
(d) There is no difference between allelopathy and amensalism as both involve the exchange of nutrients between species.

**64.** Which of the following statements correctly describes epiphytes?
(a) Epiphytes grow on other plants for nutrients and often harm their host.
(b) Epiphytes derive moisture and nutrients from their host plant, similar to parasites.
(c) Epiphytes grow on the surface of other plants but obtain nutrients from the air and rain, not from the host.
(d) Epiphytes are parasitic organisms that negatively affect their host plant.

**65.** The Himalayan range is known for its extraordinary species diversity. Which of the following is the most appropriate reason for this phenomenon?
(a) The region experiences high rainfall, supporting lush vegetative growth.
(b) The Himalayas serve as a confluence of various bio-geographical zones, resulting in diverse habitats.
(c) Exotic and invasive species have not been introduced in the region, preserving its biodiversity.
(d) The region has experienced minimal human interference, allowing ecosystems to flourish.

**66.** Which of the following best describes Humboldt's Enigma?
(a) It refers to the mystery of why biodiversity only increases in tropical regions but not in mountainous areas.
(b) It is a theory that explains why coastal regions have less biodiversity than inland areas.
(c) It refers to the observation that both tropical areas and mountainous regions have high biodiversity, despite the general trend of biodiversity decreasing with latitude.
(d) It describes how deserts maintain biodiversity through unique geological and climate processes.

**67.** In the context of a circular economy, which of the following actions aligns with the principles of waste elimination and resource efficiency?
1. Composting biodegradable waste to return nutrients to the soil.
2. Recycling non-biodegradable materials, such as plastics and metals, for future use.
3. Manufacturing products designed for single-use only, followed by immediate disposal.
4. Utilising renewable energy in production processes to reduce reliance on fossil fuels.

Select the correct answer using the code given below:
(a) 1, 2, and 3 only (b) 2 and 3 only
(c) 1, 2, and 4 only (d) 1 and 4 only

**68.** With reference to Red Snow, consider the following statements:

1. Red Snow is caused by the algae species Chlamydomonas nivalis, which contains a red carotenoid pigment called astaxanthin.
2. Chlamydomonas nivalis is a cold-loving (cryophilic) algae that thrives in freezing water.
3. Chlamydomonas nivalis exists in snow in tropical and temperate regions and uses a red pigment to protect itself from predators.

How many of the statements given above is/are not correct?

(a) Only one (b) Only two
(c) All three (d) None

**69.** Consider the following statements regarding 'Red Tide' :

1. 'Red Tide' is primarily caused by the blooming of certain phytoplankton species containing pigments.
2. Red Tide phenomena are always associated with harmful effects on marine life.
3. The term 'Red Tide' correctly describes the phenomenon, as the water is always red during these blooms.

Which of the above statements is/are correct?

(a) 1 only (b) 1 and 2 only
(c) 1 and 3 only (d) None of these

**70.** Consider the following pairs related to ecological principles:

| | Ecological Principle | Description |
|---|---|---|
| 1. | Allen's Rule | Larger animals are found in colder climates |
| 2. | Bergmann's Rule | Variation in body shape based on temperature |
| 3. | Gloger's Rule | Darker pigmentation in humid environments |
| 4. | Shelford's Law of Tolerance | The range of environmental conditions affects survival |

How many pair/pairs given above is/are correctly matched?

(a) Only one (b) Only two
(c) Only three (d) All four

**71.** With regard to Gloger's Rule, consider the following statements:

1. Animals in colder and drier climates typically exhibit lighter pigmentation.
2. Gloger's Rule applies universally without exception across all species.
3. The rule helps explain pigmentation differences in animals within the same species across different geographical ranges.

How many of the above statements is/are correct?

(a) Only one
(b) Only two
(c) All three
(d) None

**72.** With reference to the characteristics of freshwater ecosystems, consider the following statements:

1. Freshwater ecosystems are classified into static (lentic) and running (lotic) water.
2. Freshwater ecosystems have low salt content, which distinguishes them from marine systems.
3. Temperature variations in freshwater ecosystems range from tropical to polar regions, affecting biodiversity and biological processes.
4. The availability of light is crucial for aquatic plant growth and overall ecosystem productivity.

How many of the above statements is/are correct?

(a) Only one (b) Only two
(c) Only three (d) All four

**73.** Consider the following statements regarding the tundra biome:

1. Tundra is characterised by severe environmental conditions, and is classified into Arctic and Alpine types.
2. Typical vegetation in the Arctic tundra includes cotton grass, sedges and lichens.
3. Tundra animals have adaptations such as large body size and thick fur for insulation.

How many of the above statements is/are incorrect?

(a) Only one (b) Only two
(c) All three (d) None

**74.** Identify the type of forest based on the following statements:
1. Annual rainfall exceeds 250 cm.
2. Trees are evergreen and do not shed their leaves simultaneously.
3. Dominant species include mahogany, white cedar and bamboo.
4. Found on the Western side of the Western Ghats and in the Andaman and Nicobar Islands.
5. The annual temperature is about 25°-27°C.

Select the correct answer from the options given below:
(a) Tropical Dry Evergreen Forest
(b) Tropical Semi-evergreen Forest
(c) Tropical Dry Deciduous Forest
(d) Littoral and Swamp Forest

**75.** Identify the forest type based on the following statements:
1. This forest is characterised by tall, straight evergreen trees.
2. It is predominantly found in the Western Ghats and North-Eastern regions.
3. Common trees include jackfruit, betel nut palm and mango.

Which forest type is being correctly described in the above statements?
(a) Tropical Semi-evergreen Forest
(b) Tropical Moist Deciduous Forest
(c) Tropical Wet Evergreen Forest
(d) Tropical Thorn Forest

**76.** Identify the forest type based on the following statements:
1. This forest is a mix of wet evergreen trees and moist deciduous trees.
2. It has a dense canopy filled with a variety of tree species.
3. Found primarily in the Western Ghats and Eastern Himalayas.

Which forest type is being correctly described in the above statements?
(a) Tropical Dry Evergreen Forest
(b) Tropical Semi-evergreen Forest
(c) Tropical Dry Deciduous Forest
(d) Littoral and Swamp Forest

**77.** Identify the type of forest based on the following characteristics:
1. Annual rainfall is less than 75 cm.
2. Trees are low (6 to 10 meters maximum) and widely scattered, with prominent Acacias and Euphorbias.
3. Found in regions such as South-Western Punjab, Western Haryana, Kutch and neighbouring parts of Saurashtra.
4. The mean temperature is 25°-30°C.

Choose the correct answer from the options given below:
(a) Tropical Dry Deciduous Forest
(b) Tropical Moist Deciduous Forest
(c) Littoral and Swamp Forest
(d) Tropical Thorn Forest

**78.** Which of the following statements regarding Equatorial Rainforest Climates is/are correct?
1. Equatorial rainforests receive annual rainfall exceeding 2500 mm and maintain high humidity levels throughout the year.
2. The soil in equatorial rainforests is typically rich in nutrients, supporting diverse vegetation without the need for specialised adaptations.
3. Equatorial rainforests support a vast array of vegetation, including numerous epiphytes and lianas, contributing to high biodiversity.
4. These forests are primarily distributed between 0 and 10 degrees latitude in both hemispheres, covering regions such as the Amazon basin, Congo basin and South-East Asia.

Select the correct answer using the codes given below:
(a) 1 and 3 only (b) 2 and 4 only
(c) 1, 3 and 4 only (d) 1, 2, 3 and 4

**79.** Arrange the following states in descending order of their forest cover as a percentage of their total geographical area, as per the India State of Forest Report 2021:

1. Meghalaya
2. Manipur
3. Arunachal Pradesh
4. Mizoram
5. Nagaland

Choose the correct answer from the codes given below:

(a) 4 - 3 - 1 - 2 - 5 (b) 4 - 3 - 5 - 1 - 2
(c) 3 - 4 - 1 - 2 - 5 (d) 4 - 1 - 2 - 3 - 5

**80.** Arrange the following states in descending order of their forest cover, as reported in the India State of Forest Report 2021:

1. Maharashtra
2. Arunachal Pradesh
3. Chhattisgarh
4. Madhya Pradesh
5. Odisha

Choose the correct sequence from the codes given below:

(a) 4 - 3 - 2 - 5 - 1
(b) 2 - 4 - 3 - 5 - 1
(c) 4 - 2 - 3 - 5 - 1
(d) 3 - 4 - 2 - 1 - 5

**81.** Which of the following are surveyed but not categorised as forests in the State of Forest Report 2021?

1. Very Dense Forests
2. Moderately Dense Forests
3. Open Forests
4. Scrubs

Select the correct answer from the codes given below:

(a) 1 and 2 only (b) 1, 2 and 3 only
(c) 4 only (d) 2 and 4 only

**82.** Consider the following initiatives related to forests:

1. Forest cover assessment in tiger reserves
2. Forest carbon stock assessment
3. Scrub area assessment

Which of the above initiatives was/were introduced in the State of Forest Report 2023?

(a) 1 only (b) 2 and 3 only
(c) 1 and 3 only (d) 1, 2 and 3

**83.** Identify the report based on the following statements:

1. It is the first global scientific assessment of greenhouse gas emissions and sequestration by forests in UNESCO World Heritage Sites.
2. It is published by UNESCO in collaboration with the World Resources Institute and IUCN.

Choose the correct answer from the options given below:

(a) Global Forest Resources Assessment
(b) State of the World's Forests
(c) World Heritage Forests Report
(d) Global Biodiversity Outlook

**84.** Which of the following are common characteristics of the cold desert regions of India?

1. Mean annual rainfall less than 400 mm
2. Temperature drops to –50°C during winter
3. Rich organic soil content
4. Home to the Asiatic Ibex and Snow Leopard

Select the correct answer from the codes given below:

(a) 1 and 4 only
(b) 1, 2 and 3 only
(c) 2 and 4 only
(d) 1, 2 and 4 only

**85.** Which of the following plants are typically found in the cold desert regions of India?

1. Juniperus
2. Oak
3. Birch
4. Pine

Select the correct answer from the options given below:

(a) 1 and 3 only
(b) 2 and 4 only
(c) 1, 3 and 4 only
(d) 1, 2, 3 and 4

**86.** Which of the following statements correctly describes the process of desertification in India?

1. Desertification is primarily caused by climatic changes and droughts.
2. Increased agricultural activities contribute to desertification.
3. The total area undergoing land degradation in India is 105.48 million hectares.

Select the correct answer from the codes given below:

(a) 1 only
(b) 2 and 3 only
(c) 1 and 2 only
(d) 2 and 3 only

**87.** Arrange the following groups of aquatic organisms in the correct order based on their position in the aquatic ecosystem from the surface to the bottom:

1. Nekton
2. Neuston
3. Benthos
4. Plankton

Choose the correct order from the codes given below:

(a) 2-4-1-3
(b) 2-1-4-3
(c) 4-1-2-3
(d) 1-4-2-3

**88.** Consider the following statements regarding eutrophication:

1. Eutrophication is caused by the leaching of nitrates and phosphates from agricultural lands into aquatic ecosystems.
2. The growth of algae during eutrophication improves oxygen levels in the water.
3. Algal blooms can lead to the suffocation of aquatic organisms due to decreased oxygen availability.

Which of the above statements are correct?

(a) 1 and 2 only (b) 1 and 3 only
(c) 2 and 3 only (d) 1, 2 and 3

**89.** Consider the following statements regarding the phosphorus and sulfur cycles:

1. Phosphorus primarily enters ecosystems through the process of weathering and erosion, as it originates from phosphate rocks and minerals.
2. Unlike nitrogen, phosphorus has no significant atmospheric component in its cycle and is mainly a sedimentary cycle.
3. The sulfur cycle involves both sedimentary and gaseous phases, with sulfur entering the atmosphere through volcanic eruptions and the combustion of fossil fuels.
4. Sulfur enters terrestrial and aquatic ecosystems in the form of sulfates and passes through the food chain as part of sulfur-bearing amino acids.

Which of the above statements are correct?

(a) 1 and 2 only
(b) 3 and 4 only
(c) 1, 2 and 3 only
(d) 1, 2, 3 and 4

**90.** Consider the following statements regarding tropical moist deciduous forests and tropical dry deciduous forests:

1. Tropical moist deciduous forests are found throughout India except in the Western and North-Western regions and are dominated by species like sal, teak and mango.
2. Tropical dry deciduous forests are found throughout the Northern part of India except in the North-East, and they commonly feature species like sal, acacia, and bamboo.
3. Trees in tropical moist deciduous forests generally do not shed their leaves, while those in tropical dry deciduous forests lose their leaves in the dry season.

Which of the above statements are correct?

(a) 1 and 2 only
(b) 2 and 3 only
(c) 1 and 3 only
(d) 1, 2 and 3

**91.** Consider the following statements regarding the Thar desert:

1. The Thar desert experiences scanty and irregular rainfall, with a climate marked by excessive drought.
2. The winter rains of Northern India often penetrate the Thar desert, providing moisture to the region.
3. From November to March, the desert exhibits extreme temperature variations, with temperatures frequently dropping below freezing at night.
4. The relative humidity of the atmosphere is always low, and the climate is hostile to vegetation, allowing only plants and animals with special adaptations to survive.

How many of the statements given above is/are correct?

(a) Only one (b) Only two
(c) Only three (d) All four

**92.** Consider the following statements regarding the kelp ecosystem:

1. Kelp forests are found in coastal waters of the Southern Hemisphere, particularly in tundra regions.
2. Kelp is harvested and used for the production of soda ash in various industries.

Which of the above statements is/are correct?

(a) 1 only (b) 2 only
(c) Both 1 and 2 (d) Neither 1 nor 2

**93.** With reference to mangroves, consider the following statements:

1. Mangroves thrive mainly in tropical areas and do not thrive on polar coasts.
2. Pneumatophores and stilt roots are adaptations that help mangroves survive in low-oxygen environments.
3. Tamil Nadu has mangrove forests in Pichavaram.

How many of the above statements is/are correct?

(a) Only one (b) Only two
(c) All three (d) None

**94.** Which of the following correctly describes the zonation of the oceans?

(a) The littoral zone extends to a depth of 1,000 m.
(b) The neritic zone extends from the coast to the continental shelf, where the ocean is about 200 m deep.
(c) The hadal zone is the surface layer of the ocean, extending to 200 m in depth.
(d) The bathypelagic zone is located between the surface and 200 m of the ocean. Abyssal Zone: From 4,000 m to 6,000 m.

**95.** Consider the following statements regarding coral bleaching:

1. Coral bleaching occurs when there is a significant decline in the density of zooxanthellae or a decrease in their photosynthetic pigments.
2. Corals that experience bleaching can regain their symbiotic zooxanthellae if the stress-causing conditions subside in time.
3. Coral bleaching is irreversible, and all affected corals eventually die due to prolonged zooxanthellae loss, regardless of environmental recovery.
4. High temperatures above 30°C can impair the photosynthesis pathways in zooxanthellae, leading to the disassociation of the coral-algal symbiosis.

Which of the above statements are correct?

(a) 1, 2 and 4 only (b) 1 and 3 only
(c) 2 and 4 only (d) 1, 2, 3 and 4

**96.** Consider the following statements regarding xenobiotics and their impact on coral bleaching:

1. Xenobiotics such as copper (Cu), herbicides, and oil can cause the loss of zooxanthellae in corals when present in elevated concentrations.
2. Bleaching caused by xenobiotics is typically widespread and long-lasting due to the low concentration of these contaminants required to induce zooxanthellae loss.
3. Since high concentrations of xenobiotics are necessary to cause zooxanthellae loss, bleaching resulting from such sources is usually extremely localised and/or transitory.

Which of the following statements is/are correct?

(a) 1 and 2 only (b) 2 and 3 only
(c) 1 and 3 only (d) 1, 2 and 3

# OMR SHEET

**Assessment Round**

| | | | | | | | | | | | | | | | | | | | |
|---|---|---|---|---|---|---|---|---|---|---|---|---|---|---|---|---|---|---|---|
| 1 | a | b | c | d | 31 | a | b | c | d | 61 | a | b | c | d | 91 | a | b | c | d |
| 2 | a | b | c | d | 32 | a | b | c | d | 62 | a | b | c | d | 92 | a | b | c | d |
| 3 | a | b | c | d | 33 | a | b | c | d | 63 | a | b | c | d | 93 | a | b | c | d |
| 4 | a | b | c | d | 34 | a | b | c | d | 64 | a | b | c | d | 94 | a | b | c | d |
| 5 | a | b | c | d | 35 | a | b | c | d | 65 | a | b | c | d | 95 | a | b | c | d |
| 6 | a | b | c | d | 36 | a | b | c | d | 66 | a | b | c | d | 96 | a | b | c | d |
| 7 | a | b | c | d | 37 | a | b | c | d | 67 | a | b | c | d | 97 | a | b | c | d |
| 8 | a | b | c | d | 38 | a | b | c | d | 68 | a | b | c | d | 98 | a | b | c | d |
| 9 | a | b | c | d | 39 | a | b | c | d | 69 | a | b | c | d | 99 | a | b | c | d |
| 10 | a | b | c | d | 40 | a | b | c | d | 70 | a | b | c | d | 100 | a | b | c | d |
| 11 | a | b | c | d | 41 | a | b | c | d | 71 | a | b | c | d | 101 | a | b | c | d |
| 12 | a | b | c | d | 42 | a | b | c | d | 72 | a | b | c | d | 102 | a | b | c | d |
| 13 | a | b | c | d | 43 | a | b | c | d | 73 | a | b | c | d | 103 | a | b | c | d |
| 14 | a | b | c | d | 44 | a | b | c | d | 74 | a | b | c | d | 104 | a | b | c | d |
| 15 | a | b | c | d | 45 | a | b | c | d | 75 | a | b | c | d | 105 | a | b | c | d |
| 16 | a | b | c | d | 46 | a | b | c | d | 76 | a | b | c | d | 106 | a | b | c | d |
| 17 | a | b | c | d | 47 | a | b | c | d | 77 | a | b | c | d | 107 | a | b | c | d |
| 18 | a | b | c | d | 48 | a | b | c | d | 78 | a | b | c | d | 108 | a | b | c | d |
| 19 | a | b | c | d | 49 | a | b | c | d | 79 | a | b | c | d | 109 | a | b | c | d |
| 20 | a | b | c | d | 50 | a | b | c | d | 80 | a | b | c | d | 110 | a | b | c | d |
| 21 | a | b | c | d | 51 | a | b | c | d | 81 | a | b | c | d | 111 | a | b | c | d |
| 22 | a | b | c | d | 52 | a | b | c | d | 82 | a | b | c | d | 112 | a | b | c | d |
| 23 | a | b | c | d | 53 | a | b | c | d | 83 | a | b | c | d | 113 | a | b | c | d |
| 24 | a | b | c | d | 54 | a | b | c | d | 84 | a | b | c | d | 114 | a | b | c | d |
| 25 | a | b | c | d | 55 | a | b | c | d | 85 | a | b | c | d | 115 | a | b | c | d |
| 26 | a | b | c | d | 56 | a | b | c | d | 86 | a | b | c | d | 116 | a | b | c | d |
| 27 | a | b | c | d | 57 | a | b | c | d | 87 | a | b | c | d | 117 | a | b | c | d |
| 28 | a | b | c | d | 58 | a | b | c | d | 88 | a | b | c | d | 118 | a | b | c | d |
| 29 | a | b | c | d | 59 | a | b | c | d | 89 | a | b | c | d | 119 | a | b | c | d |
| 30 | a | b | c | d | 60 | a | b | c | d | 90 | a | b | c | d | 120 | a | b | c | d |

## Calculate Your Score

| | |
|---|---|
| **Correct (✓)** | |
| **Incorrect (✓)** | |
| **Unattempted** | |
| **Total Score** | |
| **Accuracy (%)** | |

## Reasons for Incorrect Answers?

| | |
|---|---|
| 1. Lack of Knowledge/Existing Source Insufficient | |
| 2. Lack of Multiple Revision | |
| 3. Common Sense Mistakes | |

**Note :**

1. Calculate total score as correct answers carry 2 marks each 1/3rd marks will deducted for **Incorrect** Answers.
2. Calculate Accuracy (%) by dividing the number of correct answers to the total number of attempted questions.

## Past Learning

**1.** With reference to the role of biofilters in Recirculating Aquaculture System, consider the following statements : **(2023)**

1. Biofilters provide waste treatment by removing uneaten fish feed.
2. Biofilters convert ammonia present in fish waste to nitrate.
3. Biofilters increase phosphorus as nutrient for fish in water.

How many of the statements given above is/are correct?

(a) Only one (b) Only two
(c) All three (d) None

**2.** 'If rainforests and tropical forests are the lungs of the Earth, then surely wetlands function as its kidneys.' Which one of the following functions of wetlands best reflects the above statement? **(2022)**

(a) The water cycle in wetlands involves surface runoff subsoil percolation and evaporation.
(b) Algae form the nutrient base upon which fish, crustaceans, molluscs, birds, reptiles and mammals thrive.
(c) Wetlands play vital role in maintaining sedimentation balance and soil stabilisation.
(d) Aquatic plants absorb heavy metals and excess nutrients.

**3.** Which of the following are nitrogen-fixing plants? **(2022)**

1. Alfalfa 2. Amaranth
3. Chickpea 4. Clover
5. Purslane (Kulfa) 6. Spinach

Select the correct answer using the codes given below:

(a) 1, 3 and 4 only
(b) 1, 3, 5 and 6 only
(c) 2, 4, 5 and 6 only
(d) 1, 2, 4, 5 and 6

**4.** In the nature, which of the following is/are most likely to be found surviving on a surface without soil? **(2021)**

1. Fern
2. Lichen
3. Moss
4. Mushroom

Select the correct answer using the codes given below.

(a) 1 and 4 only (b) 2 only
(c) 2 and 3 only (d) 1, 3 and 4 only

**5.** What is blue carbon? **(2021)**

(a) Carbon captured by oceans and coastal ecosystems.
(b) Carbon sequestered in forest biomass and agricultural soils.
(c) Carbon contained in petroleum and natural gas.
(d) Carbon present in atmosphere.

**6.** Which of the following have species that can establish symbiotic relationship with other organisms? **(2021)**

1. Cnidarians
2. Fungi
3. Protozoa

Select the correct answer using the codes given below.

(a) 1 and 2 only (b) 2 and 3 only
(c) 1 and 3 only (d) 1, 2 and 3

**7.** Which of the following are detritivores? **(2021)**

1. Earthworms 2. Jellyfish
3. Millipedes 4. Seahorses
5. Woodlice

Select the correct answer using the codes given below.

(a) 1, 2 and 4 only (b) 2, 3, 4 and 5 only
(c) 1, 3 and 5 only (d) 1, 2, 3, 4 and 5

**8.** In case of which one of the following biogeochemical cycles, the weathering of rocks is the main source of release of nutrient to enter the cycle? **(2021)**

(a) Carbon cycle (b) Nitrogen cycle
(c) Phosphorus cycle (d) Sulfur cycle

**9.** Consider the following kinds of organisms: **(2021)**

1. Copepods
2. Cyanobacteria
3. Diatoms
4. Foraminifera

Which of the above are primary producers in the food chains of oceans?

(a) 1 and 2 only
(b) 2 and 3 only
(c) 3 and 4 only
(d) 1 and 4 only

**10.** Why is there a great concern about the microbeads that are released into environment? **(2019)**

(a) They are considered harmful to marine ecosystem.
(b) They are considered to cause skin cancer in children.
(c) They are small enough to absorbed by crop plants in irrigated fields.
(d) They are often found to be used as food adulterants.

**11.** Which of the following leaf modification occur(s) in the desert areas to inhibit water loss? **(2018)**

1. Hard and waxy leaves
2. Tiny leaves
3. Thorns instead of leaves

Select the correct answer using the codes given below :

(a) 2 and 3 only (b) 2 only
(c) 3 only (d) 1, 2 and 3

**12.** Why is a plant called Prosopis juliflora often mentioned in news? **(2018)**

(a) Its extract is widely used in cosmetics.
(b) It tends to reduce the biodiversity in the area in which it grows.
(c) Its extract is used in the synthesis of pesticides.
(d) None of the above

**13.** Recently, our scientists have discovered a new and distinct species of banana plant which attains a height of about 11 metres and has orange-coloured fruit pulp. In which part of India has it been discovered? **(2016)**

(a) Andaman Islands
(b) Anaimalai Forests
(c) Maikala Hills
(d) Tropical rain forests of North-East

**14.** With reference to bio-toilets used by the Indian Railways, consider the following statements: **(2015)**

1. The decomposition of human waste in the bio-toilets is initiated by a fungal inoculum.
2. Ammonia and water vapour are the only end products in this decomposition which are released into the atmosphere.

Which of the statements given above is/are correct?

(a) 1 only
(b) 2 only
(c) Both 1 and 2
(d) Neither 1 nor 2

**15.** Which one of the following is the best description of the term 'ecosystem'? **(2015)**

(a) A community of organisms interacting with one another.
(b) That part of the Earth which is inhabited by living organisms.
(c) A community of organisms together with the environment in which they live
(d) The flora and fauna of a geographical area

**16.** In India, in which one of the following types of forests is teak a dominant tree species? **(2015)**

(a) Tropical moist deciduous forest
(b) Tropical rain forest
(c) Tropical thorn scrub forest
(d) Temperate forest with grasslands

**17.** If you travel through the Himalayas, you are likely to see which of the following plants naturally growing there? **(2014)**

1. Oak
2. Rhododendron
3. Sandalwood

Select the correct answer using the codes given below.

(a) 1 and 2 only (b) 3 only
(c) 1 and 3 only (d) 1, 2 and 3

**18.** Lichens, which are capable of initiating ecological succession even on a bare rock, are actually a symbiotic association of **(2014)**

(a) Algae and bacteria
(b) Algae and fungi
(c) Bacteria and fungi
(d) Fungi and mosses

**19.** Which of the following have coral reefs? **(2014)**

1. Andaman and Nicobar Islands
2. Gulf of Kutch
3. Gulf of Mannar
4. Sunderbans

Select the correct answer using the code given below.

(a) 1, 2 and 3 only (b) 2 and 4 only
(c) 1 and 3 only (d) 1, 2, 3 and 4

**20.** Which of the following adds/add carbon dioxide to the carbon cycle on the planet Earth? **(2014)**

1. Volcanic action
2. Respiration
3. Photosynthesis
4. Decay of organic matter

Select the correct answer using the codes given below.

(a) 1 and 3 only (b) 2 only
(c) 1, 2 and 4 only (d) 1, 2, 3 and 4

**21.** Which one of the following is the correct sequence of a food chain? **(2014)**

(a) Diatoms-Crustaceans-Herrings
(b) Crustaceans-Diatoms-Herrings
(c) Diatoms-Herrings-Crustaceans
(d) Crustaceans-Herrings-Diatoms

**22.** Which one of the following is the process involved in photosynthesis? **(2014)**

(a) Potential energy is released to form free energy
(b) Free energy is converted into potential energy and stored
(c) Food is oxidised to release carbon dioxide and water
(d) Oxygen is taken, and carbon dioxide and water vapour are given out

**23.** Consider the following **(2014)**

1. Bats
2. Bears
3. Rodents

The phenomenon of hibernation can be observed in which of the above kinds of animals?

(a) 1 and 2 only
(b) 2 only
(c) 1, 2 and 3
(d) Hibernation cannot be observed in any of the above

**24.** With reference to the food chains in ecosystems, which of the following kinds of organism is/are known as decomposer organism/organisms? **(2013)**

1. Virus 2. Fungi
3. Bacteria

Select the correct answer using the codes given below.

(a) 1 only
(b) 2 and 3 only
(c) 1 and 3 only
(d) 1, 2 and 3

**25.** Which one of the following is the correct sequence of ecosystems in the order of decreasing productivity? **(2013)**

(a) Oceans, lakes, grasslands, mangroves
(b) Mangroves, oceans, grasslands, lakes
(c) Mangroves, grasslands, lakes, oceans
(d) Oceans, mangroves, lakes, grasslands

**26.** In the grasslands, trees do not replace the grasses as a part of an ecological succession because of **(2013)**

(a) Insects and fungi
(b) Limited sunlight and paucity of nutrients
(c) Water limits and fire
(d) None of the above

**27.** Which one of the following terms describes not only the physical space occupied by an organism, but also its functional role in the community of organisms? **(2013)**

(a) Ecotone (b) Ecological niche
(c) Habitat (d) Home range

**28.** With reference to food chains in ecosystems, consider the following statements: **(2013)**

1. A food chain illustrates the order in which a chain of organisms feed upon each other.
2. Food chains are found within the populations of a species.
3. A food chain illustrates the numbers of each organism which are eaten by others.

Which of the statements given above is/are correct?

(a) 1 only (b) 1 and 2 only
(c) 1, 2 and 3 (d) None

**29.** What would happen if phytoplankton of an ocean is completely destroyed for some reason? **(2012)**

1. The ocean as a carbon sink would be adversely affected.
2. The food chains in the ocean would be adversely affected.
3. The density of ocean water would drastically decrease.

Select the correct answer using the codes given below :

(a) 1 and 2 only (b) 2 only
(c) 3 only (d) 1, 2 and 3

**30.** The Millennium Ecosystem Assessment describes the following major categories of ecosystem services provisioning, supporting, regulating, preserving and cultural.

Which one of the following is supporting service? **(2012)**

(a) Production of food and water
(b) Control of climate and disease
(c) Nutrient cycling and crop pollination
(d) Maintenance of diversity

**31.** Consider the following : **(2011)**

1. Photosynthesis
2. Respiration
3. Decay of organic matter
4. Volcanic action.

Which of the above add carbon dioxide to the carbon cycle on Earth?

(a) 1 and 4 only
(b) 2 and 3 only
(c) 2, 3 and 4 only
(d) 1 and 4

**32.** In the context of ecosystem productivity, marine upwelling zones are important as they increase the marine productivity by bringing the **(2011)**

1. Decomposer microorganisms to the surface.
2. Nutrients to the surface.
3. Bottom-dwelling organisms to the surface.

Which of the statements given above is/are correct?

(a) 1 and 2
(b) 2 only
(c) 2 and 3
(d) 3 only

**33.** A pesticide which is a chlorinated hydrocarbon is sprayed on a food crop. The food chain is: Food crop – Rat – Snake – Hawk. In this food chain, the highest concentration of the pesticide would accumulate in which one of the following? **(2010)**

(a) Food crop
(b) Rat
(c) Snake
(d) Hawk

# Detailed Solutions

## Assessment Round

**1.** *(c)* Supporting service

**Ecosystem services** are the benefits that humans derive from natural ecosystems. They are typically categorised into **provisioning, regulating, supporting,** and **cultural services.** Let's analyse each type and determine which one matches the given characteristics:

- **Provisioning services** are the **products** obtained from ecosystems, such as **food, water, timber,** and **medicinal resources.** They do not include **nutrient cycling, soil formation,** or **biodiversity maintenance,** which are mentioned in the given characteristics.
- **Regulating services** include **processes** that regulate natural systems, such as climate **regulation, water purification, pollination,** and **pest control.** These services help regulate environmental conditions, but they do not include **soil formation** or **nutrient cycling** as described in the question.
- **Supporting services** are fundamental processes that are essential for the **functioning** of ecosystems and that **underpin** all other types of ecosystem services. Examples of supporting services include **nutrient cycling, soil formation,** and the **maintenance of biodiversity.** These services support **life** and other ecosystem services, making them essential for ecosystem health and productivity.
- **Cultural services** are the **non-material benefits** obtained from ecosystems, such as **recreational, aesthetic, spiritual,** and **educational** benefits. They do not include processes like **nutrient cycling** or **soil formation.**

**Thus, option (c) is the correct answer.**

**2.** *(b)* It refers to the concentration of inorganic nutrients that determine the ecosystem's productivity and varies seasonally.

**The term 'Standing State' in an ecosystem** refers to the concentration of inorganic nutrients that are available at a particular point in time. This is a key concept in understanding nutrient cycling and ecosystem productivity. It is the **quantity of inorganic nutrients like nitrogen, phosphorus, potassium, and other minerals that are present in the soil or water** at a particular time. The availability of these nutrients affects ecosystem productivity, and their concentration can vary seasonally due to factors such as nutrient uptake by plants, decomposition, and environmental changes.

**Thus, option (b) is the correct answer.**

**3.** *(b)* It denotes a gradual change in certain species traits across geographical regions in response to varying physiochemical factors like salinity and pH.

An ecocline is not a distinct boundary like an ecotone or a sudden shift in species composition or ecosystem appearance. Instead, it involves a **continuous gradient** where a species' traits, such as tolerance to factors like pH, humidity, or salinity, shift gradually across a geographic range. These shifts, driven by **natural selection and gene flow,** allow species to **adapt to subtle environmental changes** over extended regions, often influenced by factors such as rainfall or altitude.

**Thus, option (b) is the correct answer.**

**4.** *(c)* 1, 3 and 4 only

- **Statement 1 is correct:** In **humid tropical regions,** decomposition occurs at a high rate because the **warm temperatures and high moisture** provide an optimal environment for microbial and fungal activity. These conditions accelerate the breakdown of organic matter, making tropical regions some of the most active areas for decomposition.
- **Statement 2 is incorrect: Lignin** is a complex and resistant organic polymer commonly found in plant cell walls, especially in woody tissues. High lignin content in detritus **slows down the decomposition rate** because lignin is difficult for most decomposing organisms

to break down. Therefore, a high lignin content in detritus has a **negative correlation** with the rate of decomposition, as it resists microbial breakdown.

- **Statement 3 is correct:** Soil microbes, including bacteria and fungi, play a central role in the decomposition process, breaking down complex organic matter into simpler compounds. Their activity is influenced by both **environmental factors** (such as temperature and moisture) and **chemical factors** (such as pH, nutrient availability, and the composition of detritus). This combination of environmental and chemical factors determines the efficiency and speed of decomposition in any given ecosystem.
- **Statement 4 is correct :** In **colder climates,** even when adequate moisture is available, decomposition rates tend to be slower because **low temperatures inhibit microbial activity.** Decomposing organisms are less active in cold environments, and enzymes critical for breaking down organic matter operate less efficiently. As a result, organic matter can accumulate in colder regions, such as the Arctic tundra, where decomposition is significantly limited by low temperatures.

**Thus, option (c) is the correct answer.**

**5.** *(a)* 1 and 4 only

- **Statement 1 is correct:** An **organism** is indeed the most basic unit in ecology. It is the smallest level at which life processes occur and ecological interactions begin. Every organism interacts with other living beings **(biotic factors)** such as predators, prey, competitors, and symbionts.
- **Statement 2 is incorrect:** A **population** consists of individuals of the **same species** living in a particular area at a specific time. This allows for interbreeding and sharing of the gene pool.
- **Statement 3 is incorrect:** A **community** includes all the populations of different species living and interacting within a specific area. It focuses on biotic interactions such as predation, competition, and symbiosis. An **ecosystem** comprises the community (biotic factors) **plus** the abiotic environment (non-living factors) with which the organisms interact.
- **Statement 4 is correct:** A **biome** is a large geographical region characterised by specific climate conditions and dominant types of vegetation and animal life. Examples include deserts, grasslands, and tropical rainforests. Biomes consist of multiple **ecosystems** that share similar climatic and environmental conditions. These ecosystems collectively contribute to the overall characteristics of the biome.

**Thus, option (a) is the correct answer.**

**6.** *(b)* Ecosystem accounting is a framework that integrates measures of ecosystems and the flows of services from them with measures of economic and other human activity, building upon the System of Environmental-Economic Accounting (SEEA) Central Framework.

**Ecosystem accounting** is a method of integrating environmental, economic, and social data to provide a holistic view of the relationship between **natural ecosystems and human activities.** Let's examine each option to identify the correct one. It integrates ecosystem services, including biodiversity and environmental flows, with measures of **economic and human activities** to provide a comprehensive view of the value and sustainability of ecosystems. It aims to understand the economic contributions of ecosystems and how human activities affect them.

**Thus, option (b) is the correct answer.**

**7.** *(d)* Neither 1 and 2

- **Statement 1 is correct: Net Primary Productivity** (NPP) is the **amount of energy that remains** after respiration has been subtracted from Gross Primary Productivity (GPP). GPP represents the total amount of energy captured by photosynthesis, whereas NPP is the energy **available for the growth and reproduction of plants,** and subsequently for other organisms in the ecosystem. Therefore, NPP is always lower than GPP because respiration uses up some of the energy produced.

- **Statement 2 is correct: Primary productivity** is influenced by the **photosynthetic capacity of plants,** which depends on factors such as the availability of sunlight, carbon dioxide, water, nutrients, and temperature. The **efficiency and capacity of photosynthesis directly impact the rate of primary productivity in an ecosystem.**

**Thus, option (d) is the correct answer.**

**8.** *(d)* It is the initial phenotype an organism displays when it encounters a new environment, characterised by temporary and reversible changes.

Ecophenes are **temporary and reversible changes** in an organism's phenotype in response to environmental changes. These adaptations allow the organism to survive better in the new conditions but do not involve permanent genetic changes. Once the environmental conditions change back, the organism can return to its original phenotype.

**Thus, option (d) is the correct answer.**

**9.** *(b)* EFTs involve transferring public revenue from higher to lower levels of government based on ecological indicators, such as protected areas or watershed management areas.

Ecological Fiscal Transfers are indeed used to **transfer public revenue from higher levels** (national or state governments) **to lower levels** (local governments) based on their **ecological indicators.** Examples include areas designated as protected, watershed management, or forest conservation areas. The aim is to incentivise lower-level governments to prioritise and protect these ecological assets by providing financial compensation.

**Thus, option (b) is the correct answer.**

**10.** *(a)* 1, 2, and 4 only

- Ecotypes are characterised by **genetic distinctness,** which results from adaptations to specific environmental conditions. This genetic differentiation allows ecotypes to thrive in their particular habitats, making them different from other populations of the same species found in different environments.
- Ecotypes are defined by their **adaptation to specific environmental conditions** such as temperature, moisture, or soil type. These adaptations allow them to survive and reproduce more effectively in those conditions.
- Ecotypes are found in **specific geographic regions or habitats** that provide the environmental conditions they are adapted. Their distinct habitat preference plays a crucial role in their evolution and adaptation.

**Thus, option (a) is the correct answer.**

**11.** *(c)* A positive feedback loop amplifies changes in the population, leading to more births and a larger population

**A positive feedback loop** reinforces or **amplifies changes** in the system. If the population size increases, more individuals can reproduce, leading to **even more births** and a **larger population.** This positive reinforcement continues until the system encounters some limiting factor (e.g., limited resources). Therefore, a positive feedback loop leads to further amplification of the initial change.

**Thus, option (c) is the correct answer.**

**12.** *(a)* 1 only

- **Statement 1 is correct:** A food chain indeed **illustrates the flow of energy** in an ecosystem by showing which organisms eat which others, typically starting with a producer (such as plants) and moving through herbivores, carnivores, and decomposers.
- **Statement 2 is incorrect:** Food chains are **not found within the populations of a single species.** Instead, they **occur across different species,** with each level in the chain representing a different species or group of species within the ecosystem.
- **Statement 3 is incorrect:** A food chain **does not focus on illustrating the number of organisms eaten at each level;** instead, it represents the flow of energy through **different trophic levels,** showing which organisms are consumed but not the specific quantities involved.

**Thus, option (a) is the correct answer.**

**13.** *(d)* Food Web

- A **food web** is a complex network of interconnected food chains that show the energy and nutrient transfer among different organisms in an ecosystem. This description matches the given passage.
- **Trophic Cascade** refers to changes in population sizes and behavior across different trophic levels due to the addition or removal of a top predator, which is not what the passage describes.
- **Energy Flow Diagram** represents energy transfer through trophic levels but lacks the complexity of a food web.
- **Nutrient Cycle** refers to the recycling of nutrients in an ecosystem, not the complex trophic interactions described.

**Thus, option (d) is the correct answer.**

**14.** *(b)* 1 and 2 only

- **Statement 1 is correct:** The given food chain in a pond ecosystem typically follows this sequence: **Algae** (producers), **Water Fleas** (primary consumers), **Stickleback** (secondary consumers), and **Pike** (top predator). This is a plausible and common example of a simple aquatic food chain.
- **Statement 2 is correct:** Removing the Pike, the top predator, would likely **lead to an increase in Stickleback populations** (as predation pressure is reduced). However, this might later cause a decline in the Stickleback population due to resource depletion (overconsumption of their prey, such as Water Fleas).
- **Statement 3 is incorrect:** A food web with **more links is generally considered more resilient to species removal** because it **offers multiple pathways for energy flow.** In a complex food web, if one species is removed, others can often compensate, whereas in simpler food webs, the loss of a species might cause greater disruption.

**Thus, option (b) is the correct answer.**

**15.** *(a)* Only one

- **Statement 1 is incorrect:** A habitat is the natural environment in which a **particular species lives,** and it is not always defined by the presence of multiple species. It can be specific to just one species, meaning a habitat does not inherently require multiple species to be considered a habitat.
- **Statement 2 is incorrect:** The terms 'habitat' and 'environment' **are not interchangeable.** A habitat refers specifically to the place where an organism or species lives, while the environment is a broader term that includes all physical, chemical, and biological factors that affect organisms. The environment encompasses more than just a habitat.
- **Statement 3 is correct:** A habitat can exist based on its **physical characteristics** (e.g., soil, temperature, water availability) and does not need organisms to exist. For example, a desert or a forest can exist as a habitat even if no organisms are currently occupying it.

**Thus, option (a) is the correct answer.**

**16.** *(c)* It is a negative interaction where one organism produces harmful secretions that adversely affect another.

- **Antibiosis** is a type of negative ecological interaction where one organism produces substances that are harmful to another organism. Here, one organism produces **chemical secretions** (such as antibiotics or other toxins) that **inhibit or kill** another organism.
- This is common in microbes like **bacteria or fungi,** where the secretions may prevent the growth of competing species. This negative interaction plays a role in resource competition.

**Thus, option (c) is the correct answer.**

**17.** *(d)* 1, 2 and 3

- **Statement 1 is correct:** Grazing food chains begin with green plants (producers), and the primary consumers are typically herbivores that feed on these plants. This is the most common pathway of energy flow in ecosystems, especially in grasslands and aquatic systems.
- **Statement 2 is correct:** Detritus food chains start with detritus, which includes dead organic matter like fallen leaves or animal remains. These food chains are typically

found in the soil or sediments of aquatic ecosystems and involve decomposers such as bacteria and fungi.

- **Statement 3 is correct:** Supplementary food chains in ecosystems include parasites and scavengers. These organisms contribute to the overall complexity of the food web, but they are not primary pathways like grazing or detritus food chains.

**Thus, option (d) is the correct answer.**

***18.*** *(a)* 1, 3, 4 and 5 only

- **Statement 1 is correct: Habitat destruction** and **fragmentation** can lead to **a loss of available resources,** such as food, shelter, and breeding grounds, for many species. These changes can **alter predator-prey dynamics,** as fragmented habitats may make it difficult for predators to find prey or for prey to escape predators, thereby affecting the stability of the food chain.
- **Statement 2 is incorrect: Pollution** and **contamination** can have **far-reaching effects** on food chains and ecosystems. For example, pollutants like heavy metals or pesticides can enter the food chain and **bioaccumulate** as they move up trophic levels, affecting **multiple species** and ultimately **disrupting the entire food chain.** Thus, pollution does not only affect individual species but can destabilise the entire chain.
- **Statement 3 is correct: Overharvesting** can lead to the **depletion of key species,** which in turn disrupts the balance of food chains. For example, if a predator species is overharvested, the prey population may grow unchecked, leading to overgrazing or competition for resources. Conversely, if prey is overharvested, predators may face food shortages, affecting their populations as well.
- **Statement 4 is correct: Climate change** can lead to changes in **temperature, rainfall, and other environmental conditions,** which can shift species distributions to new habitats. This may disrupt predator-prey interactions as species migrate in search of suitable conditions. Some species may move to new locations where their predators or prey are absent, leading to an imbalance in the food chain.
- **Statement 5 is correct: Diseases and parasites** can spread through **food chains,** affecting the health of species at multiple trophic levels. For example, a disease that impacts prey species can also affect the **predators** that rely on them. **Parasites** can also move between hosts at different levels of the food chain, reducing **reproductive success** and survival rates.

**Thus, option (a) is the correct answer.**

***19.*** *(a)* Desert Willow → Desert Hare → Snake → Falcon → Coyote

- **Desert Willow** is the primary producer (plant) that provides energy through photosynthesis.
- **The Desert Hare** is a primary consumer (herbivore) that feeds on plants like the Desert Willow.
- **The Snake** is a secondary consumer (carnivore) that preys on small herbivores like the Desert Hare.
- **The Falcon** is a tertiary consumer (predatory bird) that feeds on snakes and other smaller animals.
- **The Coyote** is the apex predator at the top of the food chain, capable of preying on many animals, including the Falcon and Snake.

**Thus, option (a) is the correct answer.**

***20.*** *(b)* 3 only

- **Statement 1 is correct:** The **pyramid of energy** is **always upright** because as energy flows from one trophic level to the next, a significant portion is **lost as heat** (approximately 90%). Therefore, the energy available at each higher trophic level is always less than the level below it.
- **Statement 2 is correct:** The **pyramid** of **numbers** can sometimes be **inverted.** For example, in ecosystems where **a large number of small producers** (e.g., grasses) support **a smaller number of larger herbivores** (e.g., deer), the pyramid of numbers appears inverted.
- **Statement 3 is incorrect:** The **pyramid of biomass** in **aquatic ecosystems** is generally **inverted,** not upright. This is because the **biomass of phytoplankton** (primary producers) is usually much lower than the

**biomass of consumers** (such as fish). Phytoplankton reproduces rapidly and have a short lifespan, supporting larger consumers despite their lower standing biomass.

**Thus, option (b) is the correct answer.**

**21.** *(a)* Only one

- Among the three types of ecological pyramids, only the **pyramid of energy can never be inverted.** This is because energy flow in an ecosystem is always unidirectional — from producers to consumers, with **a loss of energy at each trophic level** due to metabolism and heat dissipation. Hence, the pyramid of energy always has a broad base and narrows at the top.
- **The pyramid of numbers and the pyramid of biomass** can be inverted. For example, in some ecosystems, a few large producers (such as trees) can support a large number of herbivores, inverting the pyramid of numbers. Similarly, in **aquatic ecosystems, phytoplankton** (small in biomass) can support a larger biomass of zooplankton, inverting the pyramid of biomass.

**Thus, option (a) is the correct answer.**

**22.** *(d)* Neither 1 nor 2

- **Statement 1 is incorrect:** Anaerobic decomposition does occur in the **absence of oxygen,** but it does not produce as much **energy as aerobic decomposition.** Anaerobic processes typically produce less energy and create biogas (methane, carbon dioxide) as byproducts, but not a significant amount of energy in the conventional sense.
- **Statement 2 is incorrect:** Anaerobic decomposition typically occurs at lower temperatures than aerobic composting. As a result, it may not reach the temperatures **necessary to effectively kill weed seeds and pathogens.**

**Thus, option (d) is the correct answer.**

**23.** *(c)* All three pairs

- **Pair 1 is correctly matched:** Ecotype represents a **permanent adaptation** to a specific environment, involving genetic changes, and is distinct yet interbreeds with geographically adjacent ecotypes.
- **Pair 2 is correctly matched:** Ecophene reflects **temporary adaptations** to environmental changes, with no genetic alteration, and these changes are reversible when conditions revert.
- **Pair 3 is correctly matched:** Ecospecies result from **environmentally induced genetic divergence** due to long-term separation of ecotones, leading to genetically distinct groups that cannot produce viable offspring together.

**Thus, option (c) is the correct answer.**

**24.** *(b)* Only two

- **Statement 1 is correct: Ecological succession** is the gradual process by which ecosystems change and develop over time. The **pioneer stage** is the initial stage of **ecological succession,** where the first species (often hardy species like lichens and mosses) colonise a barren or disturbed environment.
- **Statement 2 is incorrect:** The **climax stage** is characterised by **relative stability** in species composition and ecosystem structure. It is a more or less stable endpoint in succession, where species have adapted to the environment, and no further significant changes occur unless there is another disturbance.
- **Statement 3 is correct:** The **seral stage** refers to the transitional stages between the pioneer and climax stages. During this phase, **species diversity increases** as more species are established, and **interactions** such as competition, predation, and mutualism become more complex, leading the ecosystem toward the climax stage.

**Thus, option (b) is the correct answer.**

**25.** *(c)* In commensalism, one species benefits without affecting the other, while in predation, one species benefits by directly harming or consuming the other.

- In **commensalism,** one species benefits (e.g., cattle egrets eating insects stirred up by cattle), while the other species (cattle) is unaffected. In **predation,** one species benefits by directly harming or consuming the other, as seen in predator-prey relationships essential to biological control in agriculture.

**Thus, option (c) is the correct answer.**

***26.*** *(b)* 1 and 2 only

- **Statement 1 is correct:** Oceans cover about 70% of the Earth's surface, but their **net primary productivity** (about 55 billion tonnes annually) is relatively modest due to limited nutrient availability, despite their vast area.
- **Statement 2 is correct: Secondary productivity** refers to the rate at which **consumers** (herbivores, carnivores, and decomposers) convert the organic matter they consume into their biomass.
- **Statement 3 is incorrect:** The **primary productivity** of oceans is not high throughout the water column. While sunlight is abundant at the surface, it does not penetrate deeply into the water. Nutrients are often limited in the open ocean, which constrains productivity in many areas.

**Thus, option (b) is the correct answer.**

***27.*** *(d)* Neither 1 and 2

- **Statement 1 is correct: Net Primary Productivity (NPP)** is the amount of energy that remains after respiration has been subtracted from Gross Primary Productivity (GPP). GPP represents the **total amount of energy captured by photosynthesis,** whereas NPP is the energy **available for the growth and reproduction of plants,** and subsequently for other organisms in the ecosystem. Therefore, NPP is always lower than GPP because respiration uses up some of the energy produced.
- **Statement 2 is correct: Primary productivity** is influenced by the **photosynthetic capacity of plants,** which depends on factors such as the availability of sunlight, carbon dioxide, water, nutrients, and temperature. The **efficiency and capacity of photosynthesis directly impact the rate of primary productivity in an ecosystem.**

**Thus, option (d) is the correct answer.**

***28.*** *(a)* 1 and 2 only

- **Statement 1 is correct: Trophic cascades** refer to the ecological phenomenon where changes at the top of the food chain (e.g., removal of predators) can cause cascading effects that ripple through lower trophic levels, impacting the entire ecosystem.
- **Statement 2 is correct:** The **removal of a top predator** can cause an **increase in prey populations,** which can over-consume plant communities, leading to a decline in plant populations. This is a well-known effect of trophic cascades, such as the removal of wolves leading to overgrazing by deer.
- **Statement 3 is incorrect:** Trophic cascades can have **long-term effects** on ecosystems, and in many cases, the impact is significant and persistent, not necessarily short-lived.

**Thus, option (a) is the correct answer.**

***29.*** *(b)* In competition, the fitness of both species is reduced due to resource sharing, whereas in commensalism, one species benefits without affecting the other.

**Competition** occurs when two species vie for the same resources, reducing the fitness of both due to the struggle (e.g., the Abingdon tortoise and goats on the Galapagos Islands). **Commensalism** involves one species benefiting (e.g., cattle egrets feeding on insects around cattle) without impacting the other species.

**Thus, option (b) is the correct answer.**

***30.*** *(c)* Competition among individuals within a population intensifies as population density increases.

**Density-dependent** limiting factors are factors that influence population growth and regulation based on population density. These factors become more intense as the population density increases and can limit the size of the population. Competition for limited resources, such as food, space, and mates, is a **density-dependent limiting factor.** As population density increases, competition also increases, which can limit population growth and affect overall stability. This makes competition a classic example of a density-dependent factor.

**Thus, option (c) is the correct answer.**

**31.** *(a)* Only one

- **Ecosystem services** are generally classified into four categories: **Supporting Services, Provisioning Services, Regulating Services, and Cultural Services.** Supporting services are the fundamental ecological processes that sustain the functioning of ecosystems and enable other services.
- **Recreation and Tourism:** This is classified as a Cultural Service. It refers to **the non-material benefits people** obtain from ecosystems through **recreation, aesthetic experiences, and tourism.** It is not a supporting service.
- **Production of Food:** This is classified as a Provisioning Service. It refers to products like crops, livestock, fish, and other resources that ecosystems provide directly for human consumption. Again, this is not a supporting service.
- **Carbon Sequestration:** This is classified as a Regulating Service. It involves the **process by which ecosystems regulate the atmosphere** by absorbing carbon dioxide, thus mitigating climate change. It is not a supporting service.
- **Maintenance of Genetic Diversity:** This is a Supporting Service. Supporting services underpin the **ability of ecosystems to maintain other services,** and genetic diversity is crucial for ecosystem resilience, adaptation and evolution. It allows ecosystems to function and provides the foundation for the production of food, regulation of climate, etc.

**Thus, option (a) is the correct answer.**

**32.** *(d)* 1, 2 and 3

- **Statement 1 is correct:** Speciation is the process by which **new species form from existing ones due to evolutionary changes over time.** This can be driven by natural selection, genetic drift, mutations, and changes in environmental conditions that lead to the development of distinct species.
- **Statement 2 is correct: Geographic isolation separates populations** by physical barriers, such as mountains or rivers, leading to independent evolution whereas, behavioural isolation involves **differences in mating behaviours** that prevent interbreeding, and genetic isolation refers to the inability of populations to exchange genetic material, which can lead to reproductive barriers over time.
- **Statement 3 is correct:** Once reproductive isolation is established, the isolated populations can **no longer interbreed** and produce fertile offspring, which is a key step in the formation of new species.

**Thus, option (d) is the correct answer.**

**33.** *(a)* 1, 2 and 4 only

- **Pair 1 is correctly matched:** Hibernation is a **survival strategy used by some animals to escape cold temperatures** by entering a state of reduced metabolic activity. It allows them to conserve energy during winter when food resources are scarce.
- **Pair 2 is correctly matched:** Aestivation is a **state of suspended development or dormancy** that some organisms enter to avoid extreme heat and desiccation (dry conditions). It is commonly observed in hot and dry climates.
- **Pair 3 is incorrectly matched:** Diapause is a **state of suspended development,** usually observed in insects, that is not specific to avoiding cold temperatures. Instead, diapause can be triggered by adverse environmental conditions, including unfavorable photoperiods or food scarcity. It is distinct from hibernation and is not specifically linked to cold temperatures.
- **Pair 4 is correctly matched:** Migration is a behavioural adaptation where animals move to different environments to escape unfavourable conditions, such as extreme cold or heat, and find better feeding or breeding opportunities.

**Thus, option (a) is the correct answer.**

**34.** *(a)* 1 and 2 only

- **Statement 1 is correct:** A sere refers to the **entire sequence of communities** that change during **ecological succession** in a given area, starting from the pioneer community and ending with the climax community.
- **Statement 2 is correct: Secondary succession** occurs more rapidly than **primary succession**

because the soil is already present, and some organisms or organic matter may remain, allowing faster recovery and re-establishment of communities.

- **Statement 3 is incorrect: Xerarch succession** does not occur in wet environments; rather, it occurs in **dry environments. Hydrarch succession** is the type that occurs in **wet environments.**

**Thus, option (a) is the correct answer.**

***35.*** *(b)* In primary succession, pioneer species such as lichens and mosses colonise initially barren areas, whereas secondary succession happens more quickly in previously disturbed areas with existing soil.

**Ecological succession** is the gradual process by which ecosystems change and develop over time, involving a series of stages from pioneer species to a climax community. Primary succession starts in an area **without soil or organic matter, where pioneer species** like lichens and mosses play an important role in soil formation. Secondary succession occurs in areas where the community has been disturbed, but soil remains, making it faster since the foundation for plant growth is already present.

**Thus, option (b) is the correct answer.**

***36.*** *(d)* 1, 3 and 4 only

- **Statement 1 is correct: Ecotones** are **transition areas** between two distinct ecosystems or biomes. An example is **mangrove forests,** which are found between **marine** and **terrestrial** ecosystems. Ecotones exhibit characteristics of both adjoining ecosystems and often support diverse species from both environments.
- **Statement 2 is incorrect: Ecotones** can have **higher productivity** compared to adjacent ecosystems, especially due to the overlapping presence of species from both neighbouring areas and favourable conditions for growth. The statement that ecotones 'always have lower productivity' is incorrect.
- **Statement 3 is correct:** The **edge effect** refers to the phenomenon where **species richness** and **population density** are often higher at the boundary between two different habitats (in the ecotone) due to the availability of resources from both ecosystems and more varied habitats.
- **Statement 4 is correct: Edge species** are those that **thrive specifically in ecotones,** benefiting from the diverse conditions available in these transitional areas rather than being restricted to one of the adjoining ecosystems.

**Thus, option (d) is the correct answer.**

***37.*** *(c)* 1 and 3 only

- **Statement 1 is correct:** The **pyramid of numbers in a parasitic food chain** is inverted. In this case, a single host organism may support a large number of parasites, which in turn may host an even larger number of hyperparasites. Hence, the number of organisms increases as we move up the trophic levels, resulting in an inverted pyramid.
- **Statement 2 is incorrect:** The **pyramid of biomass in grassland** is typically **upright.** In grasslands, the producers (grasses) have the largest biomass, and the biomass decreases as we move up the trophic levels to herbivores and then to carnivores.
- **Statement 3 is correct:** The **pyramid of biomass in a pond** is often **inverted.** In aquatic ecosystems like ponds, the biomass of producers (such as phytoplankton) is smaller compared to the biomass of primary consumers (such as zooplankton), as phytoplankton reproduce and are consumed rapidly.

**Thus, option (c) is the correct answer.**

***38.*** *(b)* 1 and 3 only

- **Statement 1 is correct: Edge effects** refer to the **ecological changes and variations that occur at the boundaries between two distinct ecosystems or habitat types.** These boundaries are called ecotones, which represent transition zones that can include species from both adjacent ecosystems.
- **Statement 2 is incorrect:** Edge effects often create environmental conditions that are **different from those found in the interior of**

**either of the adjacent ecosystems.** The conditions at the edge can include factors like increased light, wind, temperature fluctuations, and exposure to predators.

- **Statement 3 is correct:** Species composition in ecotones often includes a unique mixture of species that are **adapted to both of the adjacent ecosystems.** This mixing of species can lead to increased biodiversity at the edge compared to the interior of either ecosystem. This phenomenon, known as the edge effect, can make ecotones particularly rich in species diversity.

**Thus, option (b) is the correct answer.**

***39.*** *(c)* Both 1 and 2

- **Statement 1 is correct: Species evenness** refers to how abundance is distributed across species within a community. Species evenness measures how equal the populations of different species are in a given community. High evenness means that the individuals are distributed relatively equally across all species, whereas low evenness indicates that a few species dominate in numbers over others.
- **Statement 2 is correct: Species richness** indicates the total number of species present in a given area. Species richness is a count of the number of different species found in a given area or community. It is a fundamental aspect of biodiversity, representing the variety of life.

**Thus, option (c) is the correct answer.**

***40.*** *(d)* 1, 2 and 3

- During ecological succession, **the total biomass of an ecosystem typically increases.** As succession progresses, more plants and other organisms establish and grow, leading to a greater accumulation of organic matter and an increase in biomass.
- The **number of organisms tends to increase during succession as more niches become available** and different species colonise the area. The community structure becomes more complex with an increasing number of organisms occupying different trophic levels.
- The **number of species (i.e., biodiversity) also generally increases during succession.** In the early stages, only a few hardy species (pioneer species) can survive, but as conditions improve, a greater variety of **species, including plants, animals, and microorganisms,** establish themselves, leading to higher species richness.

**Thus, option (d) is the correct answer.**

***41.*** *(c)* 2 and 3 only

- **Statement 1 is incorrect: Deep-sea hydrothermal ecosystems** rely on **chemosynthesis,** where bacteria use chemical energy instead of sunlight.
- **Statement 2 is correct:** On average, plants capture about 1% of sunlight that reaches their leaves and convert it into chemical energy through photosynthesis.
- **Statement 3 is correct:** The **10% rule** refers to the efficiency of energy transfer from one trophic level to the next, with the majority of energy being lost as heat.
- **Statement 4 is incorrect:** While energy pyramids are generally upright due to energy loss, it is not because of the continuous availability of energy at each level. Instead, the pyramid reflects the **laws of thermodynamics,** which result in energy loss at each step.

**Thus, option (c) is the correct answer.**

***42.*** *(a)* 1 and 2 only

**Primary consumers are organisms that feed directly on producers (e.g., plants and algae).** They are typically herbivores, meaning they consume plant material to obtain energy. Let's examine each of the given organisms to determine if they are primary consumers:

- Some ants are primary consumers when they feed on plant material, such as leaves, seeds, or nectar. These ants feed directly on producers, making them primary consumers.
- Deer are herbivores and feed on grass, leaves, and other plant materials. Since they feed directly on producers, they are primary consumers in an ecosystem.

- Foxes are omnivores or carnivores, meaning they primarily feed on small animals (such as rodents) and occasionally on plant materials. They are generally classified as secondary consumers because they feed on primary consumers or other organisms.
- Tigers are carnivores that feed on other animals, primarily herbivores. This makes them tertiary consumers or top-level predators, rather than primary consumers.

**Thus, option (a) is the correct answer.**

**43.** *(d)* 1, 2 and 3

- **Statement 1 is correct: Pioneer species** are the first organisms to colonise a disturbed or newly created area. They initiate the recovery of the ecosystem by creating favourable conditions for other species.
- **Statement 2 is correct:** A **seral community** is an intermediate stage in the process of ecological succession, where different communities succeed one another in a predictable order, ultimately leading to a climax community.
- **Statement 3 is correct:** A **climax community** represents the final, stable stage of ecological succession, where species composition remains relatively constant and is in equilibrium with the environment.

**Thus, option (d) is the correct answer.**

**44.** *(d)* 1, 2 and 3

- **Statement 1 is correct: Bioaccumulation** refers to the process by which toxic substances, such as heavy metals or pesticides, accumulate in an organism over time. These substances are taken up from the environment or food and are stored in the organism's tissues because they cannot be easily broken down or excreted.
- **Statement 2 is correct: Biomagnification** is the process by which the concentration of toxic substances increases at each successive trophic level in a food chain. As predators consume prey, the level of toxins becomes more concentrated, with apex predators (top of the food chain) being the most affected.
- **Statement 3 is correct:** Pollutants must **meet certain criteria** (long-lived, mobile, soluble in fats, biologically active) for biomagnification to occur effectively.

**Thus, option (d) is the correct answer.**

**45.** *(a)* Biomagnification refers to the tendency of pollutants to increase in concentration as they move from one trophic level to the next in a food chain.

Biomagnification is the process by **which certain toxic substances (e.g., heavy metals, persistent organic pollutants) become more concentrated at each successive trophic level.** As organisms at lower trophic levels accumulate pollutants, predators consuming multiple contaminated prey ingest higher pollutant quantities, leading to increased concentrations in their tissues. **Example:** Mercury accumulates in small fish; larger predatory fish (like tuna) eat many small fish, leading to higher mercury levels in their bodies.

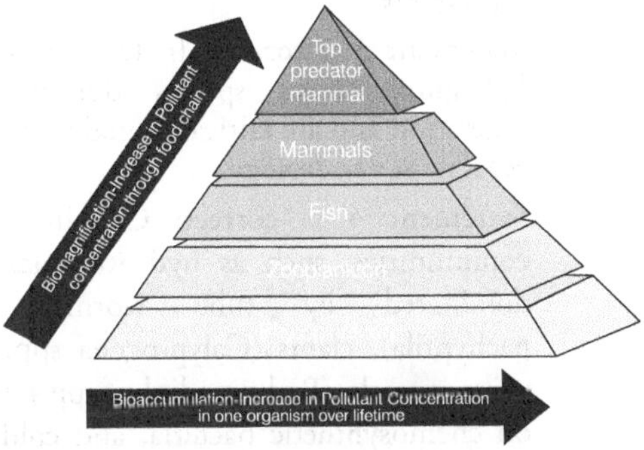


**Thus, option (a) is the correct answer.**

**46.** *(c)* In a food chain, a disturbance at any trophic level disrupts the entire system, whereas in a food web, such disturbances have minimal impact due to interconnected pathways.

- A **food chain** is a **linear sequence** that shows how each organism in an ecosystem depends on the next for food, usually consisting of **4-6 trophic levels**. Energy flows in a single, unidirectional path, from **producers** (plants) to **primary consumers** (herbivores) to **secondary** and **tertiary consumers** (carnivores).
- A **food web**, on the other hand, represents a **complex network of interconnected food chains** within an ecosystem, showing

multiple pathways through which energy flows. Organisms in a food web may have various food sources and may themselves be consumed by multiple predators, creating a more robust and interconnected system.

- Due to this interconnectivity, a disturbance at one trophic level in a food web does not significantly impact the entire system.

**Thus, option (c) is the correct answer**

**47.** *(d)* All four

- **Statement 1 is correct: Ecological dominance** refers to the control that certain species exert over others in an ecosystem due to factors such as population size, physical size, or the resources they consume.
- **Statement 2 is correct: Mangroves** are the dominant species in tropical tidal swamps and play a key role in stabilising these ecosystems.
- **Statement 3 is correct:** In **temperate bogs, Sphagnum moss** species dominate the vegetation and are critical to maintaining the ecosystem's hydrology.
- **Statement 4 is correct:** Certain seafloor communities, such as **hydrothermal vents** dominated by tube worms (Riftia pachyptila), **clams** (Calyptogena spp.), and **vent mussels** (Bathymodiolus spp.) relying on chemosynthetic bacteria, and cold seeps characterised by shipworms (Teredo spp.), are sometimes **dominated by brittle stars,** which significantly influence the composition of other species in these ecosystems.

**Thus, option (d) is the correct answer.**

**48.** *(a)* A biome refers to a specific region classified by its plants and animals, while an ecological niche describes the role and function of a species within its community.

- **A biome** is a **large geographical area characterised by specific climatic conditions and types of vegetation and animals.** Examples of biomes include forests, deserts, tundra, and grasslands. The temperature, soil, light, and water availability in a biome determine the types of life forms that can thrive there.
- **Ecological niche** refers to the **functional role of a species within its ecosystem.** It includes where the **species lives, what it eats, how it interacts** with other species, and **how it contributes to the energy flow** in its environment. Joseph Grinnell first introduced the concept of niche, highlighting that no two species can occupy the same niche in the same habitat for an extended time.

**Thus, option (a) is the correct answer.**

**49.** *(a)* 1-2-3-4-5

- **According to Clements' theory of ecological succession, the process follows this sequence:**
- **Nudation** : The development of a **bare area due to disturbances** or environmental factors.
- **Invasion** : The **migration and successful** establishment (ecesis) of a new species in the area.
- **Competition:** Interaction among species for resources.
- **Reaction:** Changes brought about in the environment by **the colonising species.**
- **Climax:** The establishment of **a stable community in equilibrium with the environment.**

**Thus, option (a) is the correct answer.**

**50.** *(c)* Only four pairs

- **Pair 1 is correctly matched:** In amensalism, one species is inhibited or harmed (e.g., a small plant shaded by a large tree), while the other species is unaffected.
- **Pair 2 is correctly matched:** In predation, one species (predator) benefits by hunting and consuming the other species (prey), which is harmed.
- **Pair 3 is correctly matched:** In parasitism, the parasite benefits by obtaining nourishment from the host, which is harmed (e.g., tapeworms in humans).
- **Pair 4 is correctly matched:** In competition, both species are adversely affected as they compete for a limited resource.
- **Pair 5 is incorrectly matched:** In commensalism, one species benefits (e.g., suckerfish attaching to sharks), while the other species is unaffected.

- **Pair 6 incorrectly matched:** In mutualism, both species benefit from the interaction (e.g., sea anemone and hermit crab).

**Thus, option (c) is the correct answer.**

**51.** *(c)* Only three

- **The nitrogen cycle** is a **gaseous cycle.** Nitrogen is primarily found in the atmosphere as $N_2$ gas, and the cycle involves processes like **nitrogen fixation, nitrification, denitrification, and assimilation.** It is largely controlled by the atmosphere, making it a gaseous nutrient cycle.
- **The sulfur cycle** is both **gaseous and sedimentary.** It involves the movement of sulfur between the atmosphere, biosphere, and lithosphere. Sulfur gases like sulfur dioxide ($SO_2$) can be released into the atmosphere, making it **partly gaseous.**
- **The carbon cycle** is a **gaseous cycle** carbon dioxide ($CO_2$) is present in the atmosphere, and the cycle involves **photosynthesis, respiration, and decomposition.** Carbon moves between the atmosphere, oceans, soil, and living organisms, and a major component involves **atmospheric carbon, making it a gaseous cycle.**
- **Phosphorus cycle** is a sedimentary cycle, not a gaseous one. Phosphorus does not have a significant gaseous phase under normal conditions. It mainly moves through **rocks, soil, water, and living organisms.**

**Thus, option (c) is the correct answer.**

**52.** *(b)* Only two

- **Pair 1 is correct: Nitrogen fixation** refers to the conversion of atmospheric **nitrogen** ($N_2$) into **ammonia** ($NH_3$) or related compounds. This process is carried out by nitrogen-fixing bacteria in the soil, in root nodules of legumes, or by lightning.
- **Pair 2 is incorrect: Nitrification** is the process of converting **ammonia** ($NH_3$) to **nitrites** ($NO_{2-}$) and then to **nitrates** ($NO_{3-}$). This is carried out by nitrifying bacteria, specifically **nitrosomonas (for ammonia to nitrite) and nitrobacter (for nitrite to nitrate).** The given statement confuses nitrification with ammonification.
- **Pair 3 is incorrect: Ammonification** refers to the process of converting organic nitrogen from dead organisms or waste products into **ammonia** ($NH_3$) or **ammonium ions** ($NH_{4-}$). **The conversion of ammonia to nitrates or nitrites is part of nitrification, not ammonification.**
- **Pair 4 is correct: Denitrification** is the process by which **nitrates** ($NO_{3-}$) are converted back into gaseous **nitrogen** ($N_2$) or **nitrous oxide** ($N_2O$) by denitrifying bacteria, releasing nitrogen back into the atmosphere and completing the nitrogen cycle.

**Thus, option (b) is the correct answer.**

**53.** *(b)* 1 and 3 only

- **Statement 1 is correct: Eutrophication is caused by the excessive leaching of nitrates and phosphates (from fertilisers used in agriculture) into aquatic ecosystems.** These nutrients stimulate excessive algae growth.
- **Statement 2 is incorrect:** The **growth of algae during eutrophication does not improve oxygen levels.** While algae produce oxygen during photosynthesis, the problem arises when they die and decompose, which leads to a significant reduction in oxygen levels due to bacterial decomposition.
- **Statement 3 is correct: Algal blooms can lead to the suffocation of aquatic organisms by reducing oxygen availability.** When algae die and decompose, the process consumes large amounts of oxygen, creating hypoxic conditions (low oxygen) that can suffocate fish and other aquatic life.

**Thus, option (b) is the correct answer.**

**54.** *(b)* Atmospheric deposition

- The **phosphorus cycle** differs from cycles like the nitrogen or carbon cycles in that it does not involve the atmosphere. **Phosphorus** is primarily cycled through the **lithosphere, biosphere, and hydrosphere,** not the atmosphere. Key processes in the phosphorus cycle include:
- **Weathering of rocks** (releases phosphorus into soil and water).

- **Plant uptake** (plants absorb phosphorus from the soil).
- **Decomposition** (organic matter breaks down, returning phosphorus to the soil).
- **Atmospheric deposition,** common in other cycles like the nitrogen cycle, is not part of the phosphorus cycle, as phosphorus does not exist in a gaseous form under normal conditions.

**Thus, option (b) is the correct answer.**

**55.** *(b)* The reservoir for sedimentary nutrient cycles primarily includes the Earth's crust, while the atmosphere and hydrosphere are less significant.

**Sedimentary nutrient cycles involve nutrients that are cycled primarily through rock and soil rather than the atmosphere.** The sedimentary nutrient cycle relies mainly on reservoirs in the Earth's crust, which store nutrients in the form of rocks and minerals. For example, phosphorus is stored in rocks and released through weathering. The atmosphere and hydrosphere are less significant in the sedimentary cycle compared to the Earth's crust.

**Thus, option (b) is the correct answer.**

**56.** *(c)* 1, 3, 4 and 5

- **Statement 1 is correct:** Atmospheric precipitation contributes **nitrogen primarily in the form of nitrates ($NO_3^-$)**, which can be deposited through rain or snow, adding nitrogen to ecosystems.
- **Statement 2 is incorrect: Geological sources do not significantly contribute** nitrogen to the atmosphere. Nitrogen is not commonly released from rocks through weathering, as it is not a primary component of most rocks.
- **Statement 3 is correct:** Agricultural land contributes significantly to atmospheric nitrogen **through the runoff of nitrogen-based fertilisers,** which can lead to nitrogen entering water bodies and being released into the atmosphere.
- **Statement 4 is correct:** Livestock, especially ruminants like cows, release nitrogen compounds such as ammonia **through manure and enteric fermentation.**
- **Statement 5 is correct:** Urban waste, particularly the breakdown of organic materials, contributes nitrogen to the ecosystem through processes such as the decomposition of food waste and sewage.

**Thus, option (c) is the correct answer.**

**57.** *(a)* 1 only

- **The sedimentary nutrient cycle** involves the movement of nutrients like phosphorus, sulfur, and calcium from the Earth's crust to living organisms and back. Nutrients are released from rocks through weathering, absorbed by plants, and passed through the food chain. Decomposition returns nutrients to the soil or water, eventually settling back into sediments or rocks.
- **Statement 1 is incorrect.** Sedimentary cycles are not considered **perfect cycles** because there can be significant losses of nutrients, particularly due to human activities such as agriculture and mining.
- **Statement 2 is correct.** The **phosphorus cycle** is **sedimentary** because its primary reservoir is in rocks and minerals.
- **Statement 3 is correct.** The reservoir of nutrients in sedimentary cycles (such as phosphorus) is located in the **Earth's crust,** from which nutrients are released through weathering.

**Thus, option (a) is the correct answer.**

**58.** *(c)* Phosphorus cycle

**The phosphorus cycle** is unique among the biogeochemical cycles because the weathering of rocks is the primary source of phosphorus entering the cycle. Unlike other cycles that have a significant gaseous phase, the phosphorus cycle is predominantly sedimentary, meaning that phosphorus is not found in significant quantities in the atmosphere. The phosphorus cycle is sedimentary, with the **weathering of rocks** being the main source of phosphorus released into the soil and water. Phosphorus is found in rocks **as phosphate minerals,** and it is released through **weathering and erosion.** Phosphorus is then taken up by plants and moves through the food chain. Unlike other cycles, phosphorus does not have a significant gaseous phase.

**Thus, option (c) is the correct answer.**

***59.*** *(b)* Only two

- **Statement 1 is correct:** The term 'Social Forestry' was indeed introduced by the **National Commission on Agriculture in 1976.** The aim was to **encourage local communities to actively participate in tree plantation** to meet their needs for fuelwood, fodder, timber and other products, and thereby reduce pressure on natural forests.
- **Statement 2 is correct:** Social Forestry focuses on planting trees in areas that are not part of the natural forest, such as **agricultural fields, roadsides, canals, village common lands** and **community spaces.** The **goal** is to **reduce the pressure on natural forests** by providing alternative resources for firewood, timber and other forest products, thus protecting natural ecosystems.
- **Statement 3 is incorrect: The main goal of Social Forestry** is not to clear forest land for agriculture but rather to **increase tree cover outside of natural forests.** It aims to **meet the community's needs** for forest products, reduce the dependency on natural forests and **contribute to environmental sustainability** by planting trees in non-forest areas.

**Thus, option (b) is the correct answer.**

***60.*** *(b)* 1 and 3 only

- **Sacred Groves** are the **tracts of virgin forests that are left untouched by the local inhabitants** and are protected by the local people due to their culture and religious beliefs. Sacred groves are relic vegetation of once-dominant flora. They are repositories of our rich biodiversity; they are also the last bastion where the rich culture and the customs of the indigenous people are still preserved.
- **Pair 1 is correctly matched: Sarna** is the name used for sacred groves in **Bihar.**
- **Pair 2 is incorrectly matched: Kavu** refers to sacred groves in **Kerala,** not Himachal Pradesh.
- **Pair 3 is correctly matched: Devarakadu** refers to sacred groves in **Karnataka.**

**Thus, option (b) is the correct answer.**

***61.*** *(a)* 1 and 2 only

- **Statement 1 is correct:** Atmospheric Rivers are elongated, narrow corridors in the atmosphere responsible for transporting vast amounts of water vapour from tropical regions toward higher latitudes. These moisture-laden air streams play a crucial role in the global hydrological cycle, contributing significantly to precipitation patterns, especially in coastal areas.
- **Statement 2 is correct:** Atmospheric Rivers often form in conjunction with extratropical cyclones. These cyclonic systems provide the necessary dynamics that facilitate the formation and maintenance of ARs. ARs are typically situated within **low-level jet streams,** which are fast-moving air currents in the lower troposphere. These jet streams act as highways, guiding the flow of moisture-rich air from the tropics towards the poles.
- **Statement 3 is incorrect:** Scientific research indicates that Atmospheric Rivers are responsible for transferring approximately **90%** of the moisture from the tropics to the poles, not just 50%. This substantial contribution underscores their significance in global moisture transport and weather systems.

**Thus, option (a) is the correct answer.**

***62.*** *(d)* 1, 2 and 3

- **Statement 1 is correct:** The GEPI **aims to assess the ecological impact of human interventions on the environment,** providing a measure of the state of ecosystems and the effect of development activities. It helps in determining the value of natural resources and the impact of economic activities on ecological health.
- **Statement 2 is correct:** The **four pillars of the Gross Environment Product Index** generally focus on aspects like **air quality, water resources, forests, biodiversity and other natural assets.** While air, water, and trees (forests) are important components, **soil is not specifically highlighted as one of the**

four main pillars of the GEPI. Instead, other factors like biodiversity and the overall natural environment are typically included.

- **Statement 3 is correct: The GEPI aims to quantify the contribution of natural ecosystems to the economy and human welfare by evaluating the value of ecosystem services,** such as water purification, carbon sequestration, biodiversity conservation, and recreational value. This helps policymakers integrate environmental considerations into economic planning. **The Gross Environment Product Index** (GEPI), launched by Uttarakhand, is a pioneering effort to quantify the value of ecosystem services and assess the ecological impact of human activities.

**Thus, option (d) is the correct answer.**

**63.** *(b)* Allelopathy refers to one organism producing chemicals that influence other organisms, while amensalism occurs when one organism is harmed and the other is unaffected.

- **Allelopathy** is a biological phenomenon where an **organism produces chemicals** (known as allelochemicals) that affect the growth, germination, or survival of other organisms in its environment. For example, plants like black walnuts release chemicals that inhibit the growth of other plants nearby.
- **Amensalism** is an **interaction between two different species where one species is harmed, while the other species is neither helped nor harmed.** An example of amensalism is when large trees block sunlight to smaller plants, preventing their growth, while the large trees remain unaffected.

**Thus, option (b) is the correct answer.**

**64.** *(c)* Epiphytes grow on the surface of other plants but obtain nutrients from the air and rain, not from the host.

**Epiphytes** are a type of plant that grows **on the surface of other plants,** usually on the branches or trunks of trees. They do this without causing harm to their host plant. Epiphytes are plants like **orchids, ferns, and bromeliads** that grow on other plants without extracting nutrients from them. They absorb nutrients and moisture from the **air, rain, and organic** matter, making them non-parasitic. They use the host only as a physical support to reach better light and air conditions.

**Thus, option (c) is the correct answer.**

**65.** *(b)* The Himalayas serve as a confluence of various bio-geographical zones, resulting in diverse habitats.

The Himalayan range is one of the world's most biodiverse regions, known for its extraordinary species diversity. The Himalayas are situated at the junction of several bio-geographical zones, including the **Indo-Malayan, Palaearctic, and Tibetan regions.** This results in a wide range of habitats and microclimates, which support an **immense diversity** of plant and animal species. The altitudinal variation from tropical to alpine regions further contributes to a wide array of ecosystems, making the Himalayas incredibly rich in biodiversity.

**Thus, option (b) is the correct answer.**

**66.** *(c)* It refers to the observation that both tropical areas and mountainous regions have high biodiversity, despite the general trend of biodiversity decreasing with latitude.

**Humboldt's Enigma** stems from Alexander von Humboldt's observation that biodiversity is typically higher in **tropical** areas due to factors like solar energy and primary productivity. However, he also noticed that certain mountainous regions defy this trend and are highly biodiverse despite being outside the tropics. These mountains serve as both cradles and museums of biodiversity, hosting species that either evolve in new habitats (cradles) or persist over time (museums).

**Thus, option (c) is the correct answer.**

**67.** *(c)* 1, 2 and 4 only

- **Statement 1 is correct: Composting** is a quintessential example of **waste valourisation,** where organic waste is transformed back into valuable soil amendments. This process not only **eliminates waste** but also **recycles nutrients,** thereby **closing the loop** in the nutrient cycle.
- **Statement 2 is correct: Recycling of non-biodegradable materials** like plastics and

metals is fundamental to the circular economy. It ensures that these materials **re-enter the production cycle,** thereby reducing the demand for virgin resources and **mitigating** environmental pollution. Recycling minimises **resource extraction, energy consumption,** and **greenhouse gas emissions** associated with the production of new materials.

- **Statement 3 is incorrect: Single-use products** epitomise the **linear economy model,** which follows a take-make-dispose trajectory. This approach **maximises waste generation and exhausts natural resources,** directly contravening the principles of **waste elimination** and **resource efficiency** central to the circular economy.
- **Statement 4 is correct:** The integration of **renewable energy** sources, such as **solar, wind,** and **hydroelectric power,** into production processes embodies the **sustainability** aspect of the circular economy. It **reduces carbon footprints, curtails greenhouse gas emissions, and promotes energy efficiency.** Shift towards to renewable energy diminishes dependence on **finite fossil fuels,** ensuring a **sustainable energy supply** and **enhancing the resilience** of production systems.

**Thus, option (c) is the correct answer**

***68.*** *(a)* Only one

- **Statement 1 is correct: Red Snow** is caused by the algae species **Chlamydomonas nivalis,** which contains **astaxanthin,** a red carotenoid pigment, in addition to chlorophyll. **Red snow,** also known as **watermelon snow,** is a phenomenon caused by the **growth of algae, specifically Chlamydomonas nivalis,** in snow. These algae contain red pigments (carotenoids) that give the snow a reddish or pinkish tint.
- **Statement 2 is correct: Chlamydomonas nivalis** is indeed a **cryophilic** species that thrives in freezing water, primarily in **polar and glacial regions.**
- **Statement 3 is incorrect: Chlamydomonas nivalis** exists in **polar and glacial regions,** not in tropical or temperate regions, and the red pigment helps in **absorbing heat** rather than protecting it from predators.

**Thus, option (a) is the correct answer.**

***69.*** *(a)* 1 only

- **Statement 1 is correct:** 'Red Tide' is **caused by the blooming of certain phytoplankton species (e.g., dinoflagellates) that contain pigments.** These blooms can sometimes discolour the water, giving it a reddish or brownish tint.
- **Statement 2 is incorrect:** Not all Red Tide events are harmful to marine life. While **some harmful algal blooms (HABs) can produce toxins that negatively affect marine ecosystems,** many red tides do not have significant harmful effects.
- **Statement 3 is incorrect:** The term 'Red Tide' is somewhat misleading because the water is not always red during these blooms. **The colour can range from brown, yellow, green, or even no visible discolouration** depending on the species of phytoplankton involved.

**Thus, option (a) is the correct answer.**

***70.*** *(c)* Only two

- **Pair 1 is incorrectly matched:** Allen's Rule does not primarily focus on larger or smaller animals in colder climates but rather on **body shape and limb length variations** about climate. According to Allen's Rule, endothermic animals in colder climates tend to have **shorter limbs and a more compact body shape** to minimise heat loss.
- **Pair 2 is incorrectly matched:** It addresses **variations in body size,** stating that larger animals are typically found in colder climates because a larger body size has a **lower surface area-to-volume ratio,** which aids in heat retention. However, the description incorrectly attributes body shape variation to Bergmann's Rule. **Body size** and not shape is the focus of Bergmann's Rule.
- **Pair 3 is correctly matched:** It refers to **darker pigmentation** found in animals from humid climates and **lighter colouration** in animals from colder and drier environments, as an adaptation to different environmental

conditions. Thus, this pair is **correctly matched.**

- **Pair 4 is correctly matched:** It describes the **range of environmental conditions** that influence a species' survival and distribution. It specifies that species thrive within a certain range for factors such as temperature, salinity, or humidity.

**Thus, option (c) is the correct answer.**

**71.** *(b)* Only two

- **Statement 1 is correct:** Gloger's Rule, states that animals in warmer and more humid environments tend to have **darker pigmentation,** while those in colder and drier regions exhibit **lighter pigmentation.** The adaptation helps with camouflage, thermoregulation, or UV protection based on the environmental context.
- **Statement 2 is incorrect:** This statement is overly absolute and does not account for the nuances and exceptions observed in nature. While Gloger's Rule generally applies across various species and environments, there are notable exceptions due to evolutionary history, local adaptations and migration patterns, which may lead certain species to deviate from the rule.
- **Statement 3 is correct:** The rule is often used to explain pigmentation variation within a species that lives in **geographically diverse climates** (e.g., a species of bird with darker plumage in tropical rainforests and lighter plumage in desert areas). This variation is a clear manifestation of Gloger's Rule, showing how environmental factors influence pigmentation within species.

**Thus, option (b) is the correct answer.**

**72.** *(d)* All four

- **Statement 1 is correct :** Freshwater ecosystems are classified into two main types: **Static (lentic) water,** which includes ponds, lakes and wetlands where water remains still. **Running (lotic) water,** which includes rivers and streams where water flows continuously.
- **Statement 2 is correct:** Freshwater ecosystems have **low salt content (typically less than 1% salinity),** which distinguishes them from marine ecosystems that have higher salt concentrations.
- **Statement 3 is correct:** Temperature variations in freshwater ecosystems can range from **tropical to polar regions.** This variation affects biodiversity and biological processes, as different species are adapted to specific temperature ranges.
- **Statement 4 is correct:** The availability of light is crucial for **aquatic plant growth through photosynthesis and significantly influences the overall ecosystem productivity.** Light penetration affects the growth of primary producers such as algae and submerged plants, which are the foundation of the aquatic food chain.

**Thus, option (d) is the correct answer.**

**73.** *(d)* None

- **Statement 1 is correct:** The **tundra biome** is known for its **harsh environmental conditions like low temperatures,** and it is classified into two types: Arctic tundra (found near the North Pole) and Alpine tundra (found in high mountain regions).
- **Statement 2 is correct:** The Arctic tundra **supports a limited range of plant life due to extreme cold.** Typical vegetation includes cotton grass, sedges, and lichens, which are well adapted to the short growing seasons and poor soils of the tundra.
- **Statement 3 is correct:** Animals in the tundra have special adaptations, **including large body size and thick fur, to retain heat and provide insulation against the cold.** Examples include polar bears, arctic foxes, and musk oxen.

**Thus, option (d) is the correct answer.**

**74.** *(b)* Tropical Semi-evergreen Forest.

- Tropical semi-evergreen forests receive annual rainfall exceeding 250 cm, creating moisture-rich soils that support thick vegetation. These forests lie between tropical evergreen and dry deciduous forests in terms of rainfall, with trees remaining predominantly evergreen, shedding leaves sporadically.

- Key species include **mahogany, white cedar** and **bamboo,** which thrive in the humid tropical climate. These forests are primarily found along the Western slopes of the **Western Ghats** and the **Andaman and Nicobar Islands**. The region's consistent temperature, between 25°-27°C, allows for both evergreen and deciduous species to coexist, fostering biodiversity. The forests play an important ecological role in supporting wildlife, regulating water cycles, and maintaining diverse ecosystems in these tropical areas.

**Thus, option (b) is the correct answer.**

**75.** *(c)* Tropical Wet Evergreen Forest

- **Tropical wet evergreen forests** are known for their tall, straight trees that remain green throughout the year. These forests are dense and often have multiple layers of vegetation, creating a closed canopy that allows little sunlight to penetrate the forest floor. This forest type is predominantly found in **India's Western Ghats, North-eastern states** (like Assam and Arunachal Pradesh), and parts of the Andaman and Nicobar Islands. These regions receive heavy rainfall, providing ideal conditions for wet evergreen forests to thrive. The presence of **jackfruit, betel nut palm and mango** indicates a **Tropical Wet Evergreen Forest,** as these species are typically found in moist, tropical environments with consistent rainfall.

**Thus, option (c) is the correct answer.**

**76.** *(b)* Tropical Semi-evergreen Forest

- **Tropical semi-evergreen forests** are a unique blend of wet evergreen and moist deciduous tree species. While evergreen trees are present, allowing the forest to remain green throughout much of the year, the forest also includes deciduous trees that shed leaves seasonally, making it a mixed type. These forests have a **dense canopy** due to the combination of evergreen and deciduous species, providing rich biodiversity.
- **Semi-evergreen forests** often support a wide variety of flora, as the mixed canopy provides diverse habitats for plant and animal life. **Tropical semi-evergreen forests** are primarily found in the **Western Ghats** and **Eastern Himalayas** in India, where rainfall is sufficient to support a mix of evergreen and deciduous species, but not consistently high enough to support purely evergreen forests.

**Thus, option (b) is the correct answer.**

**77.** *(d)* Tropical Thorn Forest

- Tropical thorn forests thrive in regions with **annual rainfall below 75 cm, humidity under 50%,** and **mean temperatures between 25°-30°C.** These **semi-arid conditions** drive adaptations for **moisture conservation,** resulting **in low-lying, scattered trees** typically **6 to 10 meters** high. Dominant flora include **Acacias** and **Euphorbias** with **deep roots** and **water-storing tissues,** alongside the **Indian wild date** and grasses that flourish during brief rainy seasons, enhancing the ecosystem's **resilience and biodiversity.**
- Geographically, these forests are primarily found in **Western India,** encompassing **Rajasthan, South-Western Punjab, Western Haryana, Kutch,** and adjacent parts of **Saurashtra,** where they transition into the **Thar desert.**
- The vegetation is dominated by **hardy species** like **neem, babul,** and various **cacti,** which serve as **keystone species** supporting numerous animal populations by providing **food and habitat.** Their **wide canopies** and **deep roots** reduce water loss and enhance **soil stability,** preventing erosion.

**Thus, option (d) is the correct answer.**

**78.** *(c)* 1, 3 and 4 only

- **Statement 1 is correct:** Equatorial rainforests are renowned for their **abundant precipitation,** often receiving **annual rainfall of up to 2500 mm or more.** This consistent rainfall is a defining feature of these ecosystems. The high rainfall contributes to **elevated humidity levels,** typically exceeding 77 **percent,** which sustains the lush vegetation and diverse wildlife.
- **Statement 2 is incorrect:** Equatorial rainforest soils are generally poor in **nutrient.** The high rainfall leads to leaching, where nutrients are washed away from the soil, leaving behind a **thin, nutrient-deficient**

layer. Due to nutrient scarcity, plants in equatorial rainforests have developed **specialised adaptations** such as **shallow root systems** to maximise nutrient uptake from the thin fertile layer.

- **Statement 3 is correct:** Equatorial rainforests are characterised by **exceptional biodiversity,** housing **up to 3000 different tree species** within a few square kilometers. The dense canopy and consistent moisture facilitate the growth of **epiphytes** (plants that grow on other plants) and **lianas** (woody vines), which add layers of complexity and support a myriad of animal species.
- **Statement 4 is correct:** Equatorial rainforests are indeed **centrally located around the equator,** spanning **0 to 10 degrees latitude** in both the **Northern** and **Southern Hemispheres.** Prominent regions include the **Amazon basin** in South America, the **Congo basin** in Africa, and vast areas in **South-East Asia** (e.g., Sumatra, New Guinea).

**Thus, option (c) is the correct answer.**

**79.** *(a)* 4 - 3 - 1 - 2 - 5

According to the India State of Forest Report 2021, the states with the highest forest cover as a percentage of their total geographical area in descending order are Mizoram (84.53%), Arunachal Pradesh (79.33%), Meghalaya (76.00%), Manipur (74.34%) and Nagaland (73.90%).

**Thus, option (a) is the correct answer.**

**80.** *(c)* 4 - 2 - 3 - 5 - 1

- **Total forest and tree cover** : 24.62% of India's total geographical area. **Forest cover:** 7,13,789 sq km, which constitutes 21.71% of the geographical area. **Tree Cover:** 2.91% of the geographical area.
- **Top states with increased forest cover:** Andhra Pradesh, Telangana, Odisha, Karnataka, Jharkhand.
- Forest cover in **hill districts:** 40.17%, but a decrease of 902 sq km (0.32%) was noted.
- Forest cover in **tribal districts:** 37.53%, with a decrease of 655 sq km within RFA/GW and an increase of 600 sq km outside RFA/GW.
- **Largest forest cover** (by state): **Madhya Pradesh > Arunachal Pradesh > Chhattisgarh > Odisha > Maharashtra**
- **Highest percentage of forest cover** (relative to the geographical area): **Mizoram (84.53%) > Arunachal Pradesh (79.33%) > Meghalaya (76.00%) > Manipur (74.34%) > Nagaland (73.90%)**

**Thus, option (c) is the correct answer.**

**81.** *(c)* 4 only

In the **State of Forest Report 2023, scrubs** (with a canopy density of less than 10%) are surveyed but **not categorised as forests.** The other three categories—**Very Dense Forests, Moderately Dense Forests, and Open Forests**—are all considered forest types.

**Thus, option (c) is the correct answer.**

**82.** *(a)* 1 only

The **State of Forest Report 2023** introduced the assessment of **forest cover in tiger reserves, tiger corridors, and Gir forest (home to the Asiatic lion). Forest carbon stock and scrub area assessments** were already part of previous reports.

**Thus, option (a) is the correct answer.**

**83.** *(c)* World Heritage Forests Report

- **The World Heritage Forests Report,** published by **UNESCO,** the **World Resources Institute, and IUCN,** provides the first global assessment of greenhouse gas emissions and sequestration by forests in UNESCO World Heritage Sites. The network of **257 World Heritage forests** (69 million hectares) absorbs **190 million tonnes of $CO_2$ annually,** equivalent to half of the UK's fossil fuel emissions. They store **13 billion tonnes of carbon,** with most of it concentrated in tropical regions.
- Over the past 20 years, **3.5 million hectares** of forest were lost, with **10 sites** emitting more carbon than they absorbed due to human activity and climate change. These sites include the **Sumatra Rainforest** (Indonesia), **Yosemite** (US), and **Kinabalu Park** (Malaysia).
- **India's Sundarbans** is among the top five global sites with the highest blue carbon

stocks, alongside the **Great Barrier Reef** and **Everglades.** Key drivers include **land clearance for agriculture, wildfires** and **extreme weather events.** Climate-related events and landscape fragmentation are expected to further impact these forests.

**Thus, option (c) is the correct answer.**

***84.*** *(d)* 1, 2, and 4 only

- **Statement 1 is correct:** The cold desert regions of India, such as Ladakh and Spiti valley, receive very low annual rainfall, typically less than 400 mm.
- **Statement 2 is correct:** In cold desert regions, temperatures can drop to extreme lows during winter, often as low as –50°C, especially in the higher altitudes.
- **Statement 3 is incorrect:** The **soil in cold deserts is generally poor in organic content** due to the lack of vegetation and limited decomposition, making it unsuitable for rich organic soil accumulation.
- **Statement 4 is correct:** The cold desert regions of India are home to unique wildlife, including the **Asiatic Ibex and Snow Leopard,** both of which are well adapted to the harsh, cold environment.

**Thus, option (d) is the correct answer.**

***85.*** *(a)* 1 and 3 only

- **Cold desert regions of India,** such as Ladakh and Spiti, are characterised by extreme temperatures and limited rainfall. The vegetation found in these regions is adapted to such harsh conditions and typically includes species that can survive low temperatures, poor soil, and dry conditions.
- **Juniperus (Juniper):** Juniper is commonly found in cold desert regions of India. It is well-adapted to the harsh, arid conditions of these regions.
- **Birch:** Birch trees are also found in the cold desert regions of India. They can grow in cold climates and are found at higher altitudes.
- **Oak:** Oak trees are typically found in temperate forests, not in cold desert regions. They are more common in the Himalayan region at lower altitudes where the conditions are not as harsh as those in cold deserts.
- **Pine:** Pine trees are also found in temperate regions, such as the lower Himalayas. They prefer well-drained soils and are not typically adapted to the extreme cold and arid conditions of the cold deserts.

**Thus, option (a) is the correct answer.**

***86.*** *(d)* 2 and 3 only

- **Statement 1 is incorrect:** While climatic changes and droughts do contribute to desertification, it is primarily driven by human activities such as overgrazing, deforestation, and unsustainable agricultural practices rather than natural climatic changes alone.
- **Statement 2 is correct:** Increased agricultural activities, such as over-cultivation, improper irrigation practices, and excessive use of chemical fertilisers, are significant contributors to desertification by degrading soil quality and leading to erosion and loss of productive land.
- **Statement 3 is correct:** According to reports, the total area undergoing land degradation in India is approximately 105.48 million hectares, highlighting the scale of desertification and land degradation across the country.

**Thus, option (d) is the correct answer.**

***87.*** *(a)* 2-4-1-3

- **Neustons** are organisms that float on the **surface** of the water, such as water striders and certain types of plankton.
- **Plankton** are organisms that drift with water currents, found primarily in the **upper layers** of water bodies.
- **Nekton** are free-swimming organisms like fish and marine mammals that can move **throughout the water column.**
- **Benthos** are organisms that live on the **bottom** of water bodies, such as crabs and starfish.

**Thus, option (a) is the correct answer.**

***88.*** *(b)* 1 and 3 only

- **Statement 1 is correct:** Eutrophication is **caused by the excessive leaching of nitrates and phosphates (from fertilisers used in** agriculture) into aquatic ecosystems. These nutrients stimulate excessive algae growth.

- **Statement 2 is incorrect:** The **growth of algae during eutrophication does not improve oxygen levels.** While algae produce oxygen during photosynthesis, the problem arises when they die and decompose, which leads to a significant reduction in oxygen levels due to bacterial decomposition.
- **Statement 3 is correct: Algal blooms can lead to the suffocation of aquatic organisms by reducing oxygen availability.** When algae die and decompose, the process consumes large amounts of oxygen, creating hypoxic conditions (low oxygen) that can suffocate fish and other aquatic life.

**Thus, option (b) is the correct answer.**

***89.*** *(d)* 1, 2, 3 and 4

- **Statement 1 is correct:** Phosphorus is primarily derived from the weathering and erosion of **phosphate rocks and minerals.** Unlike nitrogen and carbon, phosphorus does not have a significant atmospheric component and thus enters ecosystems mainly through geological and terrestrial processes.
- **Statement 2 is correct:** The **nitrogen cycle** involves significant atmospheric processes, including **nitrogen fixation, denitrification** and the presence of atmospheric nitrogen gas ($N_2$). In contrast, phosphorus does not cycle through the atmosphere in any substantial form. Phosphorus primarily cycles through **sedimentary processes,** involving the formation of phosphate rocks and their eventual weathering.
- **Statement 3 is correct:** The **sulfur cycle** encompasses both **sedimentary** and **gaseous phases.** Sulfur exists in various forms, including **sulfates** ($SO_{4^{2-}}$) in the soil and **gaseous compounds** like **sulfur dioxide** ($SO_2$) and **hydrogen sulfide** ($H_2S$) in the atmosphere. Sulfur enters the atmosphere primarily through **volcanic eruptions, combustion of fossil fuels.**
- **Statement 4 is correct:** In **terrestrial and aquatic ecosystems,** sulfur is commonly found as **sulfates** ($SO_{4^{2-}}$), which are readily absorbed by plants and microorganisms. Sulfur is an essential element in **sulfur-bearing amino** acids such as **cysteine** and **methionine,** which are fundamental building blocks of proteins. These amino acids are incorporated into the tissues of organisms, allowing sulfur to pass through the **food chain** from producers to consumers.

**Thus, option (d) is the correct answer.**

***90.*** *(a)* 1 and 2 only

- **Statement 1 is correct: Tropical moist deciduous forests** are predominantly located in **Central and Eastern India.** They extend across states such as **Madhya Pradesh, Chhattisgarh, Jharkhand, Odisha** and parts of **Karnataka, and Tamil Nadu.**
- **Statement 2 is correct: Tropical dry deciduous forests** are primarily situated in the **Northern and Central parts** of India. They are prevalent in states such as **Uttar Pradesh, Madhya Pradesh, Chhattisgarh, Bihar** and parts of **West Bengal.**
  - These forests are **absent** in the **North-Eastern** region of India, where **tropical rainforests** dominate due to higher precipitation and humidity.
- **Statement 3 is incorrect:** The statement suggests that **trees in tropical moist deciduous forests do not shed their leaves.** While they **shed leaves,** it is done **gradually** rather than all at once, maintaining canopy density.

**Thus, option (a) is the correct answer.**

***91.*** *(b)* Only two

- **Statement 1 is correct:** The Thar desert is characterised by **low and irregular rainfall,** typically ranging between **100 to 500 mm annually.** This limited precipitation contributes to its classification as an **arid** and **semi-arid** region. The region frequently experiences **droughts** due to the scarcity of consistent rainfall, exacerbating the desert's harsh climatic conditions.

- **Statement 2 is incorrect:** Western **disturbances** and **North-West monsoon** can bring some **winter rainfall** to the Thar desert. However, the term **'often penetrate'** is somewhat misleading. While winter rains do reach parts of the Thar desert, their **frequency and volume** are **limited** and **insufficient** to significantly alter the desert's arid conditions.
- **Statement 3 is incorrect:** The Thar desert does experience **extreme temperature fluctuations,** with **hot days** and **cold nights.** However, **temperatures rarely drop below freezing** (0°C). Nighttime temperatures during winter can become quite chilly, potentially approaching **0°C,** but **frequent sub-freezing temperatures are not typical.**
- **Statement 4 is correct:** The Thar desert generally maintains **low relative humidity,** especially during the **summer months,** contributing to its arid climate. The harsh climatic conditions make the environment **hostile to most vegetation,** limiting plant and animal life to **species with specialised adaptations** such as deep root systems, water storage capabilities, and nocturnal behaviours.

**Thus, option (b) is the correct answer.**

**92.** *(b)* 2 only

- **Statement 1 is incorrect:** Kelp forests are not confined to the Southern Hemisphere or tundra regions. Instead, they are found in **coastal waters of temperate regions** in both hemispheres. They thrive in nutrient-rich, shallow waters, particularly along the Pacific coast of North America, Southern Africa, and other temperate coastal regions.
- **Statement 2 is correct:** Kelp is indeed harvested for various industrial uses, including the production of **soda ash** (sodium carbonate), which is used in the manufacture of glass, paper, and other products.

**Thus, option (b) is the correct answer.**

**93.** *(c)* All three

- **Statement 1 is correct:** Mangroves are primarily found in **tropical and subtropical regions,** where they can thrive in coastal environments. Polar regions do not support mangrove growth due to the cold climate.
- **Statement 2 is correct:** Pneumatophores (breathing roots) and stilt roots are **adaptations** that help **mangroves survive in waterlogged and oxygen-deficient soils.** These roots provide stability and allow for gas exchange in harsh conditions.
- **Statement 3 is correct: Tamil Nadu has significant mangrove forests,** one of the famous locations being Pichavaram, which is one of the largest mangrove areas in South India.

**Thus, option (c) is the correct answer.**

**94.** *(b)* The neritic zone extends from the coast to the continental shelf, where the ocean is about 200 m deep.

- **The neritic zone** is the area from the coast to the continental shelf, reaching a depth of about 200 m. The littoral zone refers to the shallow shoreline, while the hadal zone represents the deepest ocean areas, and the bathypelagic zone extends between 1,000 m and 4,000 m.
- **Littoral Zone:** The shallow shoreline is influenced by the rise and fall of tides.
- **Neritic Zone:** Extends from the coast to the margin of the continental shelf, where the ocean reaches a depth of about 200 m.
- **Oceanic Zone:** Located beyond the continental shelf, encompassing deeper areas.
- **Epipelagic Zone:** The surface layer, extending from the surface to 200 m.
- **Mesopelagic Zone:** Ranges from 200 m to 1,000 m.
- **Bathypelagic Zone:** Extends from 1,000 m to 4,000 m.
- **Abyssal Zone:** From 4,000 m to 6,000 m.
- **Hadal Zone:** The deepest part, beyond 6,000 m.

**Thus, option (b) is the correct answer.**

**95.** *(a)* 1, 2 and 4 only

- **Statement 1 is correct: Zooxanthellae** are symbiotic algae that live within coral tissues, providing them with energy through photosynthesis. **Coral bleaching** occurs when corals expel their zooxanthellae or when there is a reduction in the **photosynthetic pigments** of the algae, causing the coral to lose its colour. This decline can be due to **stressful environmental conditions,** such as elevated sea temperatures, pollution, or changes in water salinity.

- **Statement 2 is correct:** Coral bleaching is a **reversible process** if the **stress conditions** (e.g., high temperature) subside quickly enough. The corals can **regain their zooxanthellae,** enabling them to recover. The ability to recover depends on the **severity of bleaching, duration of stress, and overall health of the coral ecosystem.**
- **Statement 3 is incorrect:** Coral bleaching is not **always irreversible.** Corals have the potential to recover and regain their **zooxanthellae** if environmental conditions improve quickly enough. Although prolonged bleaching can lead to coral death, recovery is possible if stressors like **temperature** or **pollution** return to normal levels within a relatively short time frame.
- **Statement 4 is correct: High temperatures,** particularly those **above 30°C,** can impair the photosynthetic efficiency of zooxanthellae by causing the production of **reactive oxygen species (ROS),** which damages the cellular components of the algae. This stress leads to the expulsion of zooxanthellae or the **breakdown of photosynthetic pigments,** resulting in the loss of symbiosis and, consequently, coral bleaching.

**Thus, option (a) is the correct answer.**

***96.*** *(c)* 1 and 3 only

- **Statement 1 is correct: Xenobiotics** are chemical substances that are **foreign to a biological system. Xenobiotics** like **copper (Cu)**, herbicides, and oil can indeed lead to the loss of **zooxanthellae** in corals when present in **elevated concentrations.** Zooxanthellae are crucial for the health of corals, providing them with essential nutrients through photosynthesis.
- **Statement 2 is incorrect:** The **bleaching** caused by xenobiotics is **not typically widespread and long-lasting.** This is because **high concentrations** of these contaminants are required to induce zooxanthellae loss, making such bleaching events **localised** and often **transitory** rather than extensive and persistent.
- **Statement 3 is correct:** Due to the necessity of **high concentrations** of xenobiotics to cause zooxanthellae loss, bleaching resulting from these sources is generally **extremely localised** and/or **transitory.** This means that while certain areas may experience bleaching due to contamination, it does not usually affect large regions or last for extended periods unless the pollutant levels remain high.

**Thus, option (c) is the correct answer.**

## Past Learning (Answers)

| | | | | | | | | | |
|---|---|---|---|---|---|---|---|---|---|
| 1 (b) | 2 (c) | 3 (a) | 4 (d) | 5 (a) | 6 (d) | 7 (c) | 8 (c) | 9 (c) | 10 (a) |
| 11 (d) | 12 (b) | 13 (a) | 14 (d) | 15 (c) | 16 (a) | 17 (a) | 18 (b) | 19 (a) | 20 (c) |
| 21 (a) | 22 (b) | 23 (c) | 24 (b) | 25 (c) | 26 (d) | 27 (b) | 28 (a) | 29 (a) | 30 (c) |
| 31 (c) | 32 (b) | 33 (d) | | | | | | | |

CHAPTER 02

# Environmental Pollution

## Assessment Round

**1.** Which of the following correctly describes a norm for fly ash usage and disposal issued by the Ministry of Environment, Forest and Climate Change (MoEFCC)?

(a) Power plants are required to sell fly ash at market rates to industries within a 300 kilometer radius.

(b) Cement industries within a 300 kilometer radius of a coal or lignite-based thermal power plant are required to use fly ash for cement manufacturing and the cost of transportation is shared by the thermal power plant and the industry.

(c) Construction agencies are required to purchase fly ash bricks from thermal power plants regardless of the distance from the power plant.

(d) Construction agencies must use fly ash only within 100 kilometers of thermal power plants.

**2.** With reference to particulate matter, consider the following statements:

1. PM2.5 is considered more harmful than PM10 because it can penetrate deeper into the lungs and enter the bloodstream.
2. Fugitive particulate matter primarily comes from volcanic eruptions and is released through chimneys or pipes.
3. Sulfur dioxide and nitrogen oxides contribute to the formation of particulate matter in the atmosphere.

How many of the statements given above is/are incorrect?

(a) Only one (b) Only two
(c) All three (d) None

**3.** Consider the following statements about particulate matter:

1. PM2.5 and PM10 are both primary pollutants that are directly emitted from sources such as vehicles and power plants.
2. Fugitive particulate matter is released into the atmosphere through industrial stacks and chimneys.
3. Natural sources of particulate matter include volcanic ash, sea salt and pollen.
4. PM2.5 is more harmful to health than PM10 as it can penetrate deeper into the lungs and potentially enter the bloodstream.

How many of the above statements is/are correct?

(a) Only one (b) Only two
(c) Only three (d) All four

**4.** With reference to Ammonia pollution, consider the following statements:

1. Ammonia production contributes significantly to the formation of PM2.5 particles, which pose severe health risks like respiratory and cardiovascular diseases.
2. The deposition of excess ammonia in aquatic ecosystems leads to oxygen depletion and disrupts the natural balance, contributing to eutrophication.
3. The production of ammonia releases nitrous oxide ($N_2O$), a greenhouse gas that has a global warming potential higher than carbon dioxide.

How many of the statements given above is/are incorrect?

(a) Only one (b) Only two
(c) All three (d) None

**5.** Consider the following statements about the environmental and health impacts of ammonia and sulfur dioxide ($SO_2$):

1. Ammonia pollution primarily affects soil quality, leading to acidification and reduced biodiversity in terrestrial ecosystems.
2. Sulfur dioxide ($SO_2$), when released in large quantities, contributes to global cooling by reflecting solar radiation away from the Earth.
3. PM2.5 formation is largely driven by sulfur dioxide emissions interacting with atmospheric chemicals.

How many of the statements given above is/are correct?

(a) Only one (b) Only two
(c) All three (d) None

**6.** Arrange the following gases in terms of their Global Warming Potential (GWP) (from highest to lowest):

1. Carbon Dioxide ($CO_2$)
2. Nitrous Oxide ($N_2O$)
3. Methane ($CH_4$)

Select the correct sequence from the codes given below :

(a) 2-3-1 (b) 3-2-1
(c) 1-2-3 (d) 3-1-2

**7.** Sulfur dioxide ($SO_2$) pollution is a serious environmental issue due to its harmful effects. Which of the following correctly describes $SO_2$'s role in both pollution and climate regulation?

(a) $SO_2$ causes acid rain, but its indirect effect is reducing global temperatures by forming brighter clouds.
(b) $SO_2$ causes respiratory diseases but has no impact on global temperatures.
(c) $SO_2$ causes discolouration of marble structures, but it doesn't affect climate patterns.
(d) $SO_2$ helps in cloud formation, which reduces pollution in urban areas.

**8.** With reference to the National Clean Air Programme (NCAP), consider the following features:

1. The base year for monitoring PM2.5 and PM10 concentration levels is set as 2015.
2. The programme aims for a 20% to 30% reduction of PM10 and PM2.5 levels by 2024.
3. The programme is implemented across 131 cities, including non-attainment cities and million-plus cities.

Which of the above statements are correct?

(a) 1 and 2 only (b) 2 and 3 only
(c) 1 and 3 only (d) 1, 2 and 3

**9.** Identify the pollutant(s) based on the following characteristics:

1. It is a powerful climate forcer but has a shorter atmospheric lifespan compared to carbon dioxide.
2. It contributes significantly to global warming, responsible for about 45% of current global warming.
3. It includes pollutants such as Black Carbon, Methane, Hydrofluorocarbons and Tropospheric Ozone.
4. These pollutants are targeted by the Climate and Clean Air Coalition (CCAC) to reduce both climate impact and air pollution.

Choose the correct term from the options below :

(a) Long-Lived Greenhouse Gases (LLGHGs)
(b) Short-Lived Climate Pollutants (SLCPs)
(c) Persistent Organic Pollutants (POPs)
(d) Volatile Organic Compounds (VOCs)

**10.** With reference to Biochemical Oxygen Demand (BOD), consider the following statements:

1. BOD is the amount of dissolved oxygen needed by aerobic organisms to break down organic material.
2. BOD can be used as an indicator to assess the efficiency of wastewater treatment plants.
3. A high BOD value indicates that the water is clean and has high levels of dissolved oxygen for aquatic life.

How many of the statements given above is/are correct?

(a) Only one (b) Only two
(c) All three (d) None

**11.** Which of the following best describes the 'SHESHA Technology'?

(a) It is a large-scale industrial waste management system.

(b) It is a compact, helical-shaped biodegradable waste converter aimed at decentralised waste processing.

(c) It is an advanced water filtration technology used in industries.

(d) It is a method for composting agricultural waste using chemicals.

**12.** With reference to 'Oil Zapping,' consider the following statements:

1. Oil Zapping is a bio-remediation technique that uses bacteria to break down oil spills.
2. OiliVorous is an enhanced version of Oil Zapper, capable of degrading oily wastes more efficiently due to an additional bacterial strain.
3. Oil Zapping involves the use of chemical agents to disperse the oil in the water.

Which of the given above statements are correct?

(a) 1 and 2 only (b) 1 and 3 only
(c) 2 and 3 only (d) 1, 2 and 3

**13.** In the context of oil spills and their management, which of the following techniques are associated with biological methods of oil spill clean-up?

1. Oil Zapping
2. Dispersants
3. Bioremediation
4. Skimmers

Select the correct answer using the codes given below :

(a) 1 and 3 only (b) 1, 2 and 3 only
(c) 2 and 4 only (d) 1, 3 and 4 only

**14.** Arrange the following in the correct sequence based on their contribution to nitrogen pollution in India, as per the Indian Nitrogen Assessment:

1. Chemical fertilisers
2. Sewage and biological waste
3. Fossil fuel combustion

Select the correct order using the codes given below :

(a) 1-2-3 (b) 2-1-3
(c) 1-3-2 (d) 3-1-2

**15.** Some nitrogen compounds play significant roles in air pollution. What is the main difference between nitrate radicals ($NO_3$) and nitrogen oxides (NOx)?

(a) Nitrate radicals are stable compounds, while nitrogen oxides are reactive.

(b) Nitrate radicals form primarily during the day, while nitrogen oxides form at night.

(c) Nitrate radicals are involved in the night time atmospheric chemistry, while nitrogen oxides contribute to daytime ozone formation.

(d) Nitrogen oxides are harmless in their natural form, while nitrate radicals are the primary cause of ozone depletion.

**16.** Which of the following correctly describes the role of nitrogen trioxide ($NO_3$) in the atmosphere?

(a) It forms during the daytime and aids in the removal of pollutants.

(b) It is a stable compound that plays no significant role in air pollution.

(c) It is a naturally occurring compound that helps in the decomposition of pollutants in the atmosphere.

(d) It oxidises volatile organic compounds at night, contributing to the formation of secondary organic aerosols and deteriorating air quality.

**17.** Which of the following best describes the effects of aerosols on Earth's energy budget?

(a) Aerosols that mainly scatter solar radiation contribute to warming by reducing reflected solar radiation.

(b) Black carbon (BC) aerosols, which absorb solar radiation, have a cooling effect on the Earth's energy budget.

(c) Aerosols that scatter solar radiation have a cooling effect by increasing the total reflected solar radiation from Earth.

(d) Absorbing aerosols like black carbon have no significant impact on the Earth's energy balance.

**18.** Which of the following correctly describes a provision under the Water (Prevention and Control of Pollution) Cess Act?

(a) The cess is levied on water consumed by industries, to raise funds for the Central and State Pollution Control Boards to prevent and control water pollution.

(b) The act imposes a cess on water used by individuals in residential areas to augment water resources.

(c) The act was last amended in 2021 to regulate water purification systems and ensure compliance with environmental standards.

(d) The cess is imposed on water used only for agricultural purposes to ensure the sustainability of water resources.

**19.** Which of the following statements best describes the term 'carbon fertilisation'?

(a) Increased plant growth due to increased concentration of carbon dioxide in the atmosphere

(b) Increased temperature of Earth due to increased concentration of carbon dioxide in the atmosphere

(c) Increased acidity of oceans as a result of increased concentration of carbon dioxide in the atmosphere

(d) Adaptation of all living beings on Earth to the climate change brought about by the increased concentration of carbon dioxide in the atmosphere

**20.** Consider the following statements regarding mercury pollution:

1. Gold mining activity is a source of mercury pollution in the world.
2. Coal-based thermal power plants cause mercury pollution.
3. There is no known safe level of mercury exposure.

How many of the above statements is/are incorrect?

(a) Only one (b) Only two
(c) All three (d) None

**21.** Consider the following statements regarding Persistent Organic Pollutants (POPs).

1. POPs are highly toxic to humans and wildlife and persist in the environment for long periods.
2. They are easily biodegradable and have limited transport across regions.
3. POPs bio-accumulate in the food chain and can lead to serious health effects such as cancer and immune system disruption.

How many of the statements given above is/are correct?

(a) Only one (b) Only two
(c) All three (d) None

**22.** With reference to arsenic, consider the following statements:

1. Inorganic arsenic, commonly found in contaminated water, is highly toxic and a confirmed carcinogen.
2. Long-term exposure to arsenic from drinking water can lead to cancer, skin lesions and cardiovascular diseases.
3. Organic arsenic compounds found in seafood are as toxic as inorganic arsenic compounds.

Which of the statements given above is/are correct?

(a) 1 and 2 only (b) 2 and 3 only
(c) 1 only (d) 1, 2 and 3

**23.** Consider the following statements regarding thermal stratification in temperate lakes:

1. Thermal stratification occurs when lakes separate into three thermal layers during late spring through early fall.
2. The epilimnion is the coldest and densest layer, settling at the bottom of the lake.
3. Thermal stratification is strongest in summer and can resist mixing by wind.

Which of the above statements is/are correct?

(a) 1 and 3 only
(b) 2 and 3 only
(c) 1 only
(d) 1, 2 and 3

**24.** Consider the following statements regarding ozone depletion and UV radiation:

1. UV rays are harmful to living organisms as they can damage DNA and proteins by breaking chemical bonds.
2. Ozone depletion is primarily caused by chlorofluorocarbons (CFCs) that accelerate the breakdown of ozone molecules in the stratosphere.
3. The thickness of the ozone layer is measured in Dobson Units (DU), indicating the concentration of ozone from the ground to the top of the atmosphere.
4. Ozone depletion is particularly severe over the Antarctic region, leading to the formation of the ozone hole.

Which of the statements given above are correct?

(a) 1 and 2 only (b) 2 and 3 only
(c) 1, 2 and 3 only (d) 1, 2, 3 and 4

**25.** Consider the following statements regarding acid rain:

1. Acid rain is caused by the reaction of sulfur dioxide ($SO_2$) and nitrogen oxides (NOx) with water, oxygen, and other chemicals in the atmosphere, leading to the formation of sulfuric and nitric acids.
2. Acid rain can fall to the ground in various forms, including rain, snow, fog, hail or even dust.
3. Natural sources like volcanic eruptions contribute the majority of $SO_2$ and NOx emissions leading to acid rain.
4. Acid rain typically has a pH between 4.2 and 4.4.

How many of the above statements is/are correct?

(a) Only one
(b) Only two
(c) Only three
(d) All four

**26.** What is Blue Baby Syndrome, and how is it related to groundwater contamination in India?

(a) It is caused by excessive fluoride levels in drinking water, leading to skeletal deformities.
(b) It results from high nitrate levels in drinking water, reducing the blood's ability to carry oxygen.
(c) It is caused by arsenic contamination, affecting skin pigmentation in babies.
(d) It is caused by lead contamination, leading to developmental delays in babies.

**27.** Which of the following statements regarding fluoride contamination in India are correct?

1. Excessive fluoride intake can lead to skeletal fluorosis, characterised by painful and stiff joints.
2. Knock-knee syndrome is commonly associated with prolonged exposure to high levels of fluoride in groundwater.
3. Fluoride contamination is prevalent in over 469 districts across 27 states of India.

Choose the correct answer from the options given below :

(a) 1 and 2 only (b) 2 and 3 only
(c) 1 and 3 only (d) 1, 2 and 3

**28.** In which of the following regions is uranium contamination in groundwater primarily associated with crystalline rocks such as granite?

(a) North-Western India
(b) Southern India, particularly Telangana
(c) Eastern India, especially West Bengal
(d) Central India, particularly Madhya Pradesh

**29.** Consider the following statements regarding lead poisoning:

1. Lead is naturally found in the Earth's crust, is highly malleable, and has good corrosion resistance, especially in non-acidic environments.
2. Lead exposure primarily results from the informal recycling of lead-acid batteries, leaded pipes and lead-based consumer products.
3. Long-term lead exposure can cause anemia, kidney damage, nervous system disruption, and behavioural problems in children.

How many of the above statements is/are correct?

(a) Only one (b) Only two
(c) All three (d) None

**30.** Which of the following are considered Qualitative pollutants?

1. Carbon dioxide
2. Pesticides (e.g., DDT)
3. Nitrogen oxides
4. Chemical fertilisers

Select the correct answer from the codes given below:

(a) 1 and 3 only
(b) 2 and 4 only
(c) 1, 2 and 3 only
(d) 1, 2, 3 and 4

**31.** Snow blindness, a disease, is primarily caused by:

(a) Thinning of the ozone layer.
(b) Global warming and glacial melt.
(c) Mercury contamination in drinking water.
(d) Sudden drop in temperatures in polar regions.

**32.** Which of the following are major contributors to nitrogen pollution in the environment?

1. Excess fertiliser applied to crops and fields
2. Runoff from hard surfaces such as rooftops and sidewalks
3. Emissions from fossil fuel use in electric power generation and transportation
4. Improperly treated waste from sewer and septic systems

Select the correct answer using the codes given below:

(a) 1 and 3 only
(b) 2 and 4 only
(c) 1, 3 and 4 only
(d) 1, 2, 3 and 4

**33.** Which one of the following statements is correct about the Keeling Curve?

(a) The Keeling Curve tracks the record of carbon dioxide ($CO_2$) concentrations measured at the Mauna Loa Observatory in Hawaii since 1958.
(b) The Keeling Curve represents the relationship between rising sea levels and global warming.
(c) The Keeling Curve monitors methane emissions from the Earth's oceans.
(d) The Keeling Curve represents the amount of $CO_2$ emissions from industrial sources in the United States.

**34.** Which of the following best describes Ozone and Ozone-Depleting Substances (ODS)?

(a) Ozone-Depleting Substances (ODS) are naturally occurring chemicals that do not affect the ozone layer.
(b) Stratospheric ozone is harmful to life on Earth, while tropospheric ozone protects the planet from harmful UV radiation.
(c) Ozone-Depleting Substances (ODS) are human-made chemicals containing chlorine and bromine that destroy ozone in the stratosphere.
(d) Tropospheric ozone is beneficial as it protects the Earth from ultraviolet (UV) radiation.

**35.** Which one of the following instruments is used to measure ozone levels?

(a) Seismograph
(b) Dobson Spectrophotometer
(c) Anemometer
(d) Hygrometer

**36.** Consider the following statements regarding Persistent Organic Pollutants (POPs):

1. Methoxychlor is used as a replacement for DDT and is toxic to invertebrates and fish.
2. UV-328 is the first non-halogenated chemical proposed to be added under the Stockholm Convention.
3. Dechlorane Plus is used as a flame retardant in electronic devices.
4. Perfluorohexane Sulphonic Acid (PFHxS) is used in non-stick cookware due to its resistance to friction, heat and chemicals.

How many of the above statements is/are correct?

(a) Only one
(b) Only two
(c) Only three
(d) All four

**37.** With reference to nanoparticle pollution, consider the following statements:

1. Nanoparticles can be transported over thousands of kilometers and remain suspended in the air for several days.
2. Nanoparticles have low reactivity and do not interact with other particles in the atmosphere.
3. Nanoparticles can be released due to natural processes such as forest fires and volcanic eruptions.

How many of the statements given above is/are correct?

(a) Only one
(b) Only two
(c) All three
(d) None

**38.** With reference to Radioactive Pollution, consider the following statements:

1. Radiation exposure causes mutations in the DNA of marine organisms, potentially leading to cancer.
2. Cosmic rays are natural sources of radioactive contamination in the Earth's crust.
3. Nuclear accidents, such as Fukushima, lead to the release of radioactive substances that can cause long-term environmental damage.

Which of the statements given above are correct?

(a) 1 and 2 only
(b) 2 and 3 only
(c) 1 and 3 only
(d) 1, 2 and 3

**39.** With reference to Non-Ionising Radiation, consider the following statements:

1. Non-ionising radiation has enough energy to ionise molecules, causing direct harm to biological tissues.
2. Long-wavelength UV radiation is a form of non-ionising radiation.
3. Non-ionising radiation includes electromagnetic waves from microwaves to radio waves.

How many of the statements given above is/are incorrect?

(a) Only one (b) Only two
(c) All three (d) None

**40.** With reference to Bharat Stage norms, which of the following statements are correct?

1. BS VI norms were introduced to reduce the emission of air pollutants from motor vehicles.
2. BS VI norms make onboard diagnostics mandatory for all vehicles.
3. The adoption of BS VI norms was delayed to 2024 due to technical challenges.

Select the correct answer using the codes given below:

(a) 1 and 2 only (b) 1 and 3 only
(c) 2 and 3 only (d) 1, 2 and 3

**41.** With reference to GRAP (Graded Response Action Plan), consider the following statements:

1. GRAP is a long-term action plan aimed at controlling vehicular emissions year-round.
2. GRAP creates a step-by-step plan for addressing air pollution in the Delhi-NCR region.
3. GRAP includes measures like stopping truck entry and closing brick kilns when air quality reaches emergency levels.

How many of the statements given above is/are correct?

(a) Only one (b) Only two
(c) All three (d) None

**42.** Which of the following statements correctly describes thermal pollution?

(a) Thermal pollution is caused by the discharge of hot water from power plants, raising the water temperature.
(b) Thermal pollution increases dissolved oxygen levels in water.
(c) Thermal pollution has no effect on aquatic organisms.
(d) Thermal pollution does not result from the cooling processes in power plants.

**43.** With reference to Marine Pollution, consider the following statements:

1. Marine pollution can result from oil spills, which release large quantities of petroleum into the ocean.
2. Oil spills can disrupt food chains by affecting plankton and benthos.
3. Plastic pollution has been documented only in shallow ocean waters.

Which of the statements given above are correct?

(a) 1 and 2 only (b) 2 and 3 only
(c) 1 and 3 only (d) 1, 2 and 3

**44.** With reference to Marine Plastic Pollution, consider the following statements:

1. Plastic waste is mistaken for prey by marine wildlife, leading to ingestion and suffocation.
2. Invisible plastic has been identified even in the Arctic region.
3. The economic damage caused by marine plastic pollution is projected to be insignificant by 2050.

Select the correct answer using the codes given below:

(a) 1 and 2 only
(b) 1 and 3 only
(c) 2 and 3 only
(d) 1, 2 and 3

**45.** With reference to Phytoremediation, consider the following statements:

1. Phytoremediation involves the use of plants to remove contaminants from soil and water.
2. Water hyacinth, an invasive species, can purify water by absorbing heavy metals.
3. Phytoremediation is ineffective for removing toxic materials from aquatic systems.

How many of the statements given above is/are correct?

(a) Only one (b) Only two
(c) All three (d) None

# OMR SHEET

**Assessment Round**

| | | | | | | | |
|---|---|---|---|---|---|---|---|
| 1 | (a) (b) (c) (d) | 31 | (a) (b) (c) (d) | 61 | (a) (b) (c) (d) | 91 | (a) (b) (c) (d) |
| 2 | (a) (b) (c) (d) | 32 | (a) (b) (c) (d) | 62 | (a) (b) (c) (d) | 92 | (a) (b) (c) (d) |
| 3 | (a) (b) (c) (d) | 33 | (a) (b) (c) (d) | 63 | (a) (b) (c) (d) | 93 | (a) (b) (c) (d) |
| 4 | (a) (b) (c) (d) | 34 | (a) (b) (c) (d) | 64 | (a) (b) (c) (d) | 94 | (a) (b) (c) (d) |
| 5 | (a) (b) (c) (d) | 35 | (a) (b) (c) (d) | 65 | (a) (b) (c) (d) | 95 | (a) (b) (c) (d) |
| 6 | (a) (b) (c) (d) | 36 | (a) (b) (c) (d) | 66 | (a) (b) (c) (d) | 96 | (a) (b) (c) (d) |
| 7 | (a) (b) (c) (d) | 37 | (a) (b) (c) (d) | 67 | (a) (b) (c) (d) | 97 | (a) (b) (c) (d) |
| 8 | (a) (b) (c) (d) | 38 | (a) (b) (c) (d) | 68 | (a) (b) (c) (d) | 98 | (a) (b) (c) (d) |
| 9 | (a) (b) (c) (d) | 39 | (a) (b) (c) (d) | 69 | (a) (b) (c) (d) | 99 | (a) (b) (c) (d) |
| 10 | (a) (b) (c) (d) | 40 | (a) (b) (c) (d) | 70 | (a) (b) (c) (d) | 100 | (a) (b) (c) (d) |
| 11 | (a) (b) (c) (d) | 41 | (a) (b) (c) (d) | 71 | (a) (b) (c) (d) | 101 | (a) (b) (c) (d) |
| 12 | (a) (b) (c) (d) | 42 | (a) (b) (c) (d) | 72 | (a) (b) (c) (d) | 102 | (a) (b) (c) (d) |
| 13 | (a) (b) (c) (d) | 43 | (a) (b) (c) (d) | 73 | (a) (b) (c) (d) | 103 | (a) (b) (c) (d) |
| 14 | (a) (b) (c) (d) | 44 | (a) (b) (c) (d) | 74 | (a) (b) (c) (d) | 104 | (a) (b) (c) (d) |
| 15 | (a) (b) (c) (d) | 45 | (a) (b) (c) (d) | 75 | (a) (b) (c) (d) | 105 | (a) (b) (c) (d) |
| 16 | (a) (b) (c) (d) | 46 | (a) (b) (c) (d) | 76 | (a) (b) (c) (d) | 106 | (a) (b) (c) (d) |
| 17 | (a) (b) (c) (d) | 47 | (a) (b) (c) (d) | 77 | (a) (b) (c) (d) | 107 | (a) (b) (c) (d) |
| 18 | (a) (b) (c) (d) | 48 | (a) (b) (c) (d) | 78 | (a) (b) (c) (d) | 108 | (a) (b) (c) (d) |
| 19 | (a) (b) (c) (d) | 49 | (a) (b) (c) (d) | 79 | (a) (b) (c) (d) | 109 | (a) (b) (c) (d) |
| 20 | (a) (b) (c) (d) | 50 | (a) (b) (c) (d) | 80 | (a) (b) (c) (d) | 110 | (a) (b) (c) (d) |
| 21 | (a) (b) (c) (d) | 51 | (a) (b) (c) (d) | 81 | (a) (b) (c) (d) | 111 | (a) (b) (c) (d) |
| 22 | (a) (b) (c) (d) | 52 | (a) (b) (c) (d) | 82 | (a) (b) (c) (d) | 112 | (a) (b) (c) (d) |
| 23 | (a) (b) (c) (d) | 53 | (a) (b) (c) (d) | 83 | (a) (b) (c) (d) | 113 | (a) (b) (c) (d) |
| 24 | (a) (b) (c) (d) | 54 | (a) (b) (c) (d) | 84 | (a) (b) (c) (d) | 114 | (a) (b) (c) (d) |
| 25 | (a) (b) (c) (d) | 55 | (a) (b) (c) (d) | 85 | (a) (b) (c) (d) | 115 | (a) (b) (c) (d) |
| 26 | (a) (b) (c) (d) | 56 | (a) (b) (c) (d) | 86 | (a) (b) (c) (d) | 116 | (a) (b) (c) (d) |
| 27 | (a) (b) (c) (d) | 57 | (a) (b) (c) (d) | 87 | (a) (b) (c) (d) | 117 | (a) (b) (c) (d) |
| 28 | (a) (b) (c) (d) | 58 | (a) (b) (c) (d) | 88 | (a) (b) (c) (d) | 118 | (a) (b) (c) (d) |
| 29 | (a) (b) (c) (d) | 59 | (a) (b) (c) (d) | 89 | (a) (b) (c) (d) | 119 | (a) (b) (c) (d) |
| 30 | (a) (b) (c) (d) | 60 | (a) (b) (c) (d) | 90 | (a) (b) (c) (d) | 120 | (a) (b) (c) (d) |

## Calculate Your Score

| | |
|---|---|
| **Correct (✓)** | |
| **Incorrect (✓)** | |
| **Unattempted** | |
| **Total Score** | |
| **Accuracy (%)** | |

## Reasons for Incorrect Answers?

| | |
|---|---|
| 1. Lack of Knowledge/Existing Source Insufficient | |
| 2. Lack of Multiple Revision | |
| 3. Common Sense Mistakes | |

**Note :**

1. Calculate total score as correct answers carry 2 marks each 1/3rd marks will deducted for **Incorrect** Answers.
2. Calculate Accuracy (%) by dividing the number of correct answers to the total number of attempted questions.

## Past Learning

**1.** According to the Environmental Protection Agency (EPA), which one of the following is the largest source of sulfur dioxide emissions? **(2024)**

(a) Locomotives using fossil fuels

(b) Ships using fossil fuels

(c) Extraction of metals from ores

(d) Power plants using fossil fuels

**2.** Consider the following statements : **(2024)**

**Statement I:** Many chewing gums found in the market are considered a source of environmental pollution.

**Statement II:** Many chewing gums contain plastic as gum base.

Which one of the following is correct in respect of the above statements?

(a) Both Statement I and Statement II are correct and Statement II explains Statement I.

(b) Both Statement I and Statement II are correct, but Statement II does not explain Statement I.

(c) Statement I is correct, but Statement II is incorrect.

(d) Statement I is incorrect, but Statement II is correct.

**3.** With reference to perfluoroalkyl and polyfluoroalkyl substances (PFAS) that are used in making many consumer products, consider the following statements : **(2024)**

1. PFAS are found to be widespread in drinking water, food and food packaging materials.
2. PFAS are not easily degraded in the environment.
3. Persistent exposure to PFAS can lead to bioaccumulation in animal bodies.

Which of the statements given above are correct?

(a) 1 and 2 only (b) 2 and 3 only

(c) 1 and 3 only (d) 1, 2 and 3

**4.** Consider the following: **(2023)**

1. Aerosols 2. Foam agents

3. Fire retardants 4. Lubricants

In the making of how many of the above are hydrofluorocarbons used?

(a) Only one (b) Only two

(c) Only three (d) All four

**5.** Consider the following statements regarding mercury pollution : **(2023)**

1. Gold mining activity is a source of mercury pollution in the world.
2. Coal-based thermal power plants cause mercury pollution.
3. There is no known safe level of exposure to mercury.

How many of the above statements is/are correct?

(a) Only one

(b) Only two

(c) All three

(d) None

**6.** Among the following crops, which one is the most important anthropogenic source of both methane and nitrous oxide? **(2022)**

(a) Cotton (b) Rice

(c) Sugarcane (d) Wheat

**7.** With reference to polyethylene terephthalate, the use of which is so widespread in our daily lives, consider the following statements : **(2022)**

1. Its fibers can be blended with wool and cotton fibres to reinforce their properties.
2. Containers made of it can be used to store any alcoholic beverage.
3. Bottles made of it can be recycled into other products.
4. Articles made of it can be easily disposed of by incineration without causing greenhouse gas emissions.

Which of the statements given above are correct?

(a) 1 and 3

(b) 2 and 4

(c) 1 and 4

(d) 2 and 3

**8.** Consider the following: **(2022)**

1. Carbon monoxide
2. Nitrogen oxide
3. Ozone
4. Sulfur dioxide

Excess of which of the above in the environment is/are cause(s) of acid rain?

(a) 1, 2 and 3 (b) 2 and 4 only
(c) 4 only (d) 1, 3 and 4

**9.** Which one of the following best describes the term 'greenwashing'? **(2022)**

(a) Conveying a false impression that a company's products are eco-friendly and environmentally sound
(b) Non-inclusion of ecological/ environmental costs in the Annual Financial Statements of a country
(c) Ignoring the disastrous ecological consequences while infrastructure development undertaking
(d) Making mandatory provisions for environmental costs in a government project/programme

**10.** In the context of WHO Air Quality Guidelines, consider the following statements: **(2022)**

1. The 24-hour mean of PM2.5 should not exceed 15 $\mu g/m^3$ and annual mean of PM2.5 should not exceed 5 $\mu g/m^3$.
2. In a year, the highest levels of ozone pollution occur during the periods of inclement weather.
3. PM10 can penetrate the lung barrier and enter the bloodstream.
4. Excessive ozone in the air can trigger asthma.

Which of the statements given above are correct?

(a) 1, 3 and 4 (b) 1 and 4 only
(c) 2, 3 and 4 (d) 1 and 2 only

**11.** With reference to furnace oil, consider the following statements: **(2021)**

1. It is a product of oil refineries.
2. Some industries use it to generate power.
3. Its use causes sulphur emissions into environment.

Which of the statements given above are correct?

(a) 1 and 2 only
(b) 2 and 3 only
(c) 1 and 3 only
(d) 1, 2 and 3

**12.** 'Triclosan', considered harmful when exposed to high levels for a long time, is most likely present in which of the following? **(2021)**

(a) Food preservatives
(b) Fruit-ripening substances
(c) Reused plastic containers
(d) Toiletries

**13.** Why is there a concern about copper smelting plants? **(2021)**

1. They may release lethal quantities of carbon monoxide into environment.
2. The copper slag can cause the leaching of some heavy metals into environment.
3. They may release sulphur dioxide as a pollutant.

Select the correct answer using the codes given below:

(a) 1 and 2 only
(b) 2 and 3 only
(c) 1 and 3 only
(d) 1, 2 and 3

**14.** Magnetite particles, suspected to cause neurodegenerative problems, are generated as environmental pollutants from which of the following? **(2021)**

1. Brakes of motor vehicles
2. Engines of motor vehicles
3. Microwave stoves within homes
4. Power plants
5. Telephone line

Select the correct answer using the codes given below:

(a) 1, 2, 3 and 5 only
(b) 1, 2 and 4 only
(c) 3, 4 and 5 only
(d) 1, 2, 3, 4 and 5

**15.** Consider the following statements: **(2020)**

1. Coal ash contains arsenic, lead and mercury.
2. Coal-fired power plants release sulphur dioxide and oxides of nitrogen into the environment.
3. High ash content is observed in Indian coal.

Which of the statements given above is/are correct?

(a) 1 only (b) 2 and 3 only
(c) 3 only (d) 1, 2 and 3

**16.** Which of the following are the reasons/factors for exposure to benzene pollution? **(2020)**

1. Automobile exhaust
2. Tobacco smoke
3. Wood burning
4. Using varnished wooden furniture
5. Using products made of polyurethane

Select the correct answer using the codes given below:

(a) 1, 2 and 3 only (b) 2 and 4 only
(c) 1, 3 and 4 only (d) 1, 2, 3, 4 and 5

**17.** Steel slag can be the material for which of the following? **(2019)**

1. Construction of base road
2. Improvement of agricultural soil
3. Production of cement

Select the correct answer using the codes given below:

(a) 1 and 2 only (b) 2 and 3 only
(c) 1 and 3 only (d) 1, 2 and 3

**18.** Consider the following statements: **(2019)**

1. Agricultural soils release nitrogen oxides into the environment.
2. Cattle release ammonia into the environment.
3. Poultry industry releases reactive nitrogen compounds into the environment.

Which of the statements given above is/are correct?

(a) 1 and 3 only (b) 2 and 3 only
(c) 2 only (d) 1, 2 and 3

**19.** Consider the following: **(2019)**

1. Carbon monoxide
2. Methane
3. Ozone
4. Sulfur dioxide

Which of the above are released into the atmosphere due to the burning of crop/biomass residue?

(a) 1 and 2 only
(b) 2, 3, and 4 only
(c) 1 and 4 only
(d) 1,2, 3 and 4

**20.** In India, the use of carbofuran, methyl parathion, phorate, and triazophos is viewed with apprehension. These chemicals are used as **(2019)**

(a) pesticides in agriculture
(b) preservatives in processed foods
(c) fruit-ripening agents
(d) moisturising agents in cosmetics

**21.** Biological Oxygen Demand (BOD) is a standard criterion for: **(2017)**

(a) Measuring oxygen levels in blood
(b) Computing oxygen levels in forest ecosystems
(c) Pollution assay in aquatic ecosystems
(d) Assessing oxygen levels in high altitude regions

**22.** Consider the following pairs : **(2017)**

| | Commonly used/consumed materials | Unwanted or controversial chemicals likely to be found in them |
|---|---|---|
| 1. | Lipstick | Lead |
| 2. | Soft drinks | Brominated vegetable oils |
| 3. | Chinese fast food | Monosodium glutamate |

Which of the pairs given above is/are correctly matched?

(a) 1 only
(b) 2 and 3 only
(c) 1 and 3 only
(d) 1, 2 and 3

**23.** In the context of solving pollution problems, what is/are the advantage/advantages of bioremediation technique? **(2017)**

1. It is a technique for cleaning up pollution by enhancing the same biodegradation process that occurs in nature.
2. Any contaminant with heavy metals such as cadmium and lead can be readily and completely treated by bioremediation using micro-organisms.
3. Genetic engineering can be used to create micro-organisms specifically designed for bioremediation.

Select the correct answer using the codes given below:

(a) 1 only
(b) 2 and 3 only
(c) 1 and 3 only
(d) 1, 2 and 3

**24.** In the cities of our country, which among the following atmospheric gases are normally considered in calculating the value of Air Quality Index? **(2016)**

1. Carbon dioxide
2. Carbon monoxide
3. Nitrogen dioxide
4. Sulfur dioxide
5. Methane

Select the correct answer using the codes given below:

(a) 1, 2 and 3 only
(b) 2, 3 and 4 only
(c) 1, 4 and 5 only
(d) 1, 2, 3, 4 and 5

**25.** What can be the impact of excessive/ inappropriate use of fertilisers in agriculture? Nitrogenous **(2015)**

1. Proliferation of nitrogen-fixing micro-organisms in soil can occur.
2. Increase in the acidity of soil can take place.
3. Leaching of nitrate to the ground- water can occur.

Select the correct answer using the codes given below:

(a) 1 and 3 only (b) 2 only
(c) 2 and 3 only (d) 1, 2 and 3

**26.** Which of the following are some important pollutants released by steel industry in India? **(2014)**

1. Oxides of sulfur 2. Oxides of nitrogen
3. Carbon monoxide 4. Carbon dioxide

Select the correct answer using the codes given below:

(a) 1, 3 and 4 only (b) 1 and 3 only
(c) 1 and 4 only (d) 1, 2, 3 and 4

**27.** Brominated flame retardants are used in many household products like mattresses and upholstery. Why is there some concern about their use? **(2014)**

1. They are highly resistant to degradation in the environment.
2. They are able to accumulate in humans and animals.

Select the correct answer using the codes given below:

(a) 1 only (b) 2 only
(c) Both 1 and 2 (d) Neither 1 nor 2

**28.** Which of the following can be found as pollutants in the drinking water in some parts of India? **(2013)**

1. Arsenic 2. Sorbitol
3. Fluoride 4. Formaldehyde
5. Uranium

Select the correct answer using the codes given below:

(a) 1 and 3 only (b) 2, 4 and 5 only
(c) 1, 3 and 5 only (d) 1, 2, 3, 4 and 5

**29.** Due to improper/ indiscriminate disposal of old and used computers or their parts, which of the following are released into the environment as e-waste? **(2013)**

1. Beryllium 2. Cadmium
3. Chromium 4. Heptachlor
5. Mercury 6. Lead
7. Plutonium

Select the correct answer using the codes given below:

(a) 1, 3, 4, 6 and 7 only
(b) 1, 2, 3, 5 and 6 only
(c) 2, 4, 5 and 7 only
(d) 1, 2, 3, 4, 5, 6 and 7

# Detailed Solutions

## Assessment Round

**1.** *(b)* Cement industries within a 300 kilometer radius of a coal or lignite-based thermal power plant are required to use fly ash for cement manufacturing, and the cost of transportation is shared by the thermal power plant, and the industry.

- **The Ministry of Environment, Forest and Climate Change (MoEFCC)** has issued norms for the usage and disposal of fly ash generated by coal or lignite-based thermal power plants to promote environmental sustainability and reduce the environmental impact of fly ash disposal.
- As per the MoEFCC norms, **cement industries located within a 300 kilometer radius of a thermal power plant** are required to utilise fly ash for cement manufacturing. The cost of transportation is shared between the thermal power plant and the industry to incentivise its use and reduce fly ash disposal in landfills.

**Thus, option (b) is the correct answer.**

**2.** *(a)* Only one

- **Statement 1 is correct:** PM2.5 refers to fine inhalable particles that are 2.5 micrometers in diameter or smaller. Due to their small sise, they can travel deeply into the lungs and even enter the bloodstream, making them more harmful to health than PM10.
- **Statement 2 is incorrect:** Fugitive particulate matter is particulate matter that has not passed through a stack, pipe, or vent before being released into the air. It primarily originates from soil dust, not volcanic eruptions and is often dispersed by wind or similar forces. Volcanic eruptions release ash, but this is not categorised as fugitive particulate matter.
- **Statement 3 is correct:** Sulfur dioxide ($SO_2$) and nitrogen oxides (NOx) are pollutants that can react in the atmosphere to form secondary particulate matter, contributing to PM2.5 and PM10 concentrations.

**Thus, option (a) is the correct answer.**

**3.** *(b)* Only two

- **Statement 1 is incorrect:** While both PM2.5 and PM10 can be emitted directly from sources like vehicles and power plants (primary sources), they can also form through secondary processes in the atmosphere due to chemical reactions, making them secondary pollutants as well.
- **Statement 2 is incorrect:** Fugitive particulate matter is not released through industrial stacks or chimneys, rather, it is released into the air by natural forces like wind or other forces, often from sources such as unpaved roads, construction sites, and soil erosion.
- **Statement 3 is correct:** Natural sources of particulate matter include volcanic ash, sea salt, and pollen. These particles contribute to PM10 and sometimes PM2.5 in the atmosphere.
- **Statement 4 is correct:** PM2.5 is finer and more harmful than PM10 because its smaller sise allows it to penetrate deeper into the lungs and enter the bloodstream, causing more serious health effects.

**Thus, option (b) is the correct answer.**

**4.** *(a)* Only one

- **Statement 1 is correct:** Ammonia emissions contribute to the formation of **PM2.5** particles by reacting with other compounds like sulfur dioxide and nitrogen oxides in the atmosphere. PM2.5 particles pose significant health risks such as respiratory and cardiovascular diseases.
- **Statement 2 is correct:** The deposition of excess ammonia in aquatic ecosystems contributes to eutrophication by increasing nutrient levels, leading to excessive growth of algae and subsequent oxygen depletion, which disrupts the natural balance of the ecosystem.
- **Statement 3 is incorrect:** The production of ammonia itself does not directly release nitrous oxide ($N_2O$). Nitrous oxide is primarily released from agricultural soils and

the use of nitrogen fertilisers, but not directly from ammonia production processes.

**Thus, option (a) is the correct answer.**

**5.** *(b)* Only two

- **Statement 1 is correct: Ammonia pollution** primarily stems from agricultural activities, such as the use of synthetic fertilisers and livestock farming. When these compounds settle on land, they can acidify the soil and water bodies, resulting in a **loss of biodiversity** in both terrestrial and aquatic ecosystems.
- **Statement 2 is correct: Sulfur dioxide ($SO_2$)**, when released into the atmosphere, forms sulfate aerosols that reflect sunlight, leading to a **global cooling** effect. This process is associated with **aerosol scattering** and **global dimming,** where less solar radiation reaches the Earth's surface, temporarily cooling the atmosphere.
- **Statement 3 is incorrect:** Although sulfur dioxide ($SO_2$) contributes to the formation of **PM2.5** through the production of sulfates, it is not the primary driver of PM2.5 formation. **PM2.5** is generated from a wide range of sources, including **vehicle emissions, biomass burning, industrial processes** and natural sources.

**Thus, option (b) is the correct answer.**

**6.** *(a)* 2-3-1

- **Global Warming Potential** (GWP) is a measure that compares the ability of different greenhouse gases to trap heat in the atmosphere relative to **carbon dioxide ($CO_2$)**, which is assigned a GWP of 1. It indicates how much heat a given gas will absorb over a specific period, usually **20, 100, or 500 years,** compared to the same amount of $CO_2$.
- **Nitrous Oxide ($N_2O$)** has the highest global warming potential (approximately 298 times that of $CO_2$). **Methane ($CH_4$)** has a global warming potential of roughly 25 times that of $CO_2$. **Carbon Dioxide ($CO_2$)** has the lowest global warming potential among these gases.

**Thus, option (a) is the correct answer.**

**7.** *(a)* $SO_2$ causes acid rain, but its indirect effect is reducing global temperatures by forming brighter clouds.

**Sulfur Dioxide ($SO_2$) is a significant contributor to acid rain,** which is caused when $SO_2$ in the atmosphere mixes with water vapor to form sulfuric acid, leading to harmful effects on plants, aquatic animals, and infrastructure.

**Thus, option (a) is the correct answer.**

**8.** *(b)* 2 and 3 only

- **Statement 1 is incorrect: The National Clean Air Programme** (NCAP) was launched by the Ministry of Environment, Forest and Climate Change (MoEFCC) in 2019 to tackle air pollution across India. However, the **base year for monitoring PM2.5 and PM10** concentration levels is set as 2017, not 2015.
- **Statement 2 is correct:** NCAP aims to achieve a **20% to 30% reduction** in concentrations of **PM2.5** and **PM10** by the year **2024**, relative to the levels of 2017. It is to be achieved through a range of measures, including stricter pollution control regulations for industries, vehicular emissions and waste management.
- **Statement 3 is correct:** The **NCAP** is being implemented across **131 cities,** which include both **non-attainment cities** (those that have not consistently met the National Ambient Air Quality Standards) and **million-plus cities** (cities with a population of more than 1 million).

**Thus, option (b) is the correct answer.**

**9.** *(b)* Short-Lived Climate Pollutants (SLCPs)

- **Short-Lived Climate Pollutants (SLCPs)** are climate forcers that remain in the atmosphere for a shorter duration compared to long-lived greenhouse gases like $CO_2$, but they have a significant impact on global warming.
- SLCPs have a much **shorter lifespan** in the atmosphere than $CO_2$, which remains for centuries. SLCPs contribute to nearly 45% of current global warming. Their reduction is crucial for mitigating climate change in the short term.

- **Black Carbon** (produced from incomplete combustion), **Methane** (from agriculture and landfills), **Hydrofluorocarbons** (used as refrigerants), and **Tropospheric Ozone** (secondary pollutant formed by precursor emissions) are the key SLCPs.

**Thus, option (b) is the correct answer.**

**10.** *(b)* Only two

- **Statement 1 is correct: Biochemical Oxygen Demand (BOD)** is a measure of the amount of dissolved oxygen required by aerobic micro-organisms (such as bacteria) to break down organic matter present in water. The higher the amount of organic matter, the more oxygen is consumed by these micro-organisms during the decomposition process.
- **Statement 2 is correct: BOD** is widely used as an important parameter to assess the **efficiency of wastewater treatment plants.** By measuring the **BOD levels** of water before and after treatment, it is possible to assess how effectively the wastewater treatment process is at removing organic pollutants.
- **Statement 3 is incorrect:** A **high BOD value** indicates that there is a large amount of organic matter in the water, which in turn demands a lot of dissolved oxygen to be broken down by aerobic organisms. **High BOD** often correlates with **polluted or contaminated water,** which could lead to oxygen depletion and harm aquatic ecosystems.

**Thus, option (b) is the correct answer.**

**11.** *(b)* It is a compact, helical-shaped biodegradable waste converter aimed at decentralised waste processing.

- **SHESHA is an innovative waste management system** designed for small-scale applications such as housing societies and restaurants. It is a compact, helical-shaped waste converter that processes biodegradable waste on-site, reducing reliance on centralised systems. These byproducts serve as renewable energy and soil enhancers.
- Inspired by the serpentine shape of the mythological snake Shesha, the system's design is both functional and symbolic, efficiently processing waste through a blend of mechanical and biological methods.

**Thus, option (b) is the correct answer.**

**12.** *(a)* 1 and 2 only

- **Statement 1 is correct: Oil Zapping** is indeed a **bio-remediation** method, primarily developed by the Tata Energy Research Institute (TERI). This technique employs **oil-degrading bacteria** that naturally break down hydrocarbons present in oil spills. These bacteria are capable of converting complex hydrocarbons into simpler, less harmful substances.
- **Statement 2 is correct: OiliVorous** is indeed an enhanced bio-remediation product that builds upon the principles of **Oil Zapper.** While Oil Zapper utilises a blend of five specific bacterial strains to break down hydrocarbons in oil spills, **OiliVorous** goes a step further by introducing an additional bacterial strain that improves the efficiency of degradation, especially for **oily sludge** and other complex oily wastes.
- **Statement 3 is incorrect: Oil Zapping** does not involve the use of **chemical dispersants.** Instead, it is a **biological process** that relies solely on naturally occurring or enhanced bacterial strains to break down the hydrocarbons present in oil spills.

**Thus, option (a) is the correct answer.**

**13.** *(a)* 1 and 3 only

- **Oil zapping** is a biological method that involves the use of **oil-degrading bacteria** to break down hydrocarbons in oil spills. These bacteria feed on the oil, **converting harmful substances** into less toxic products such as **carbon dioxide and water. Bioremediation** is another biological method where micro-organisms, including **bacteria and fungi,** are used to break down or remove hazardous substances, such as **oil, from contaminated environments.** This process accelerates the natural biodegradation of oil, making it a sustainable and effective way to deal with oil spills. Bioremediation can be applied both on land and in marine environments to clean up oil spills.

- **Dispersants** are chemical agents (not a biological method) used to break oil into smaller droplets, allowing it to disperse more easily in the water. This method does not remove the oil but helps reduce the impact on the shoreline and marine animals. **Skimmers are mechanical devices** used to remove oil from the surface of the water by collecting or skimming the oil. Skimmers are effective in calm water but less useful in rough seas or when oil is dispersed.

**Thus, option (a) is the correct answer.**

**14.** *(c)* 1-3-2

- **Chemical fertilisers:** The primary contributor, as the agricultural sector in India extensively uses nitrogen-based chemical fertilisers, which release large quantities of reactive nitrogen into the environment.
- **Fossil fuel combustion:** This is the second-largest contributor, as burning fossil fuels releases nitrogen oxides into the atmosphere, contributing to pollution.
- **Sewage and biological waste:** This is also a significant source of nitrogen pollution but contributes less compared to fertilisers and fossil fuel combustion. The sewage and organic waste contain nitrogenous compounds that can eventually enter water bodies and cause pollution.

**Thus, option (c) is the correct answer.**

**15.** *(c)* Nitrate radicals are involved in the nighttime atmospheric chemistry, while nitrogen oxides contribute to daytime ozone formation.

- Nitrogen Oxides (NOx) refers to a group of gases that include nitrogen oxide (NO) and nitrogen dioxide ($NO_2$). NOx is primarily produced by combustion processes, such as those occurring in vehicles and industrial processes. Nitrogen oxides are **highly reactive gases.**
- NOx plays a crucial role in the formation of **ground-level ozone** during the daytime through a series of photochemical reactions involving sunlight. NOx interacts with volatile organic compounds (VOCs) to create tropospheric ozone, a major component of **smog.**
- **Nitrate Radicals** ($NO_3$) are formed during nighttime as nitrogen dioxide ($NO_2$) reacts with ozone ($O_3$) in the absence of sunlight. $NO_3$ is a **highly reactive** radical that plays a role in nighttime atmospheric chemistry.
- Unlike NOx, which plays a significant role in daytime ozone formation, $NO_3$ is active at and can react with VOCs and other pollutants to form secondary organic aerosols, contributing to **particulate matter.**

**Thus, option (c) is the correct answer.**

**16.** *(d)* It oxidises volatile organic compounds at night, contributing to the formation of secondary organic aerosols and deteriorating air quality.

**Nitrogen trioxide** ($NO_3$) is formed in the atmosphere primarily at night. It acts as an oxidising agent, reacting with volatile organic compounds (VOCs). This process leads to the formation of secondary organic aerosols (SOAs), which contribute to air pollution and degrade air quality. Unlike other nitrogen oxides, $NO_3$ is more active at night because it rapidly decomposes in sunlight, making its effects significant during nighttime oxidation processes.

**Thus, option (d) is the correct answer.**

**17.** *(c)* Aerosols that scatter solar radiation have a cooling effect by increasing the total reflected solar radiation from Earth.

- **Aerosols** are tiny particles or droplets suspended in the atmosphere that can affect the **Earth's energy budget** by interacting with **solar radiation. Scattering aerosols** (like sulfate aerosols) primarily reflect **solar radiation** into space, which **increases the total reflected solar radiation** and reduces the amount of energy absorbed by the Earth, resulting in a **cooling effect.**
- **Black carbon (BC) aerosols,** on the other hand, **absorb solar radiation,** contributing to **warming,** not cooling, as they reduce the amount of radiation reflected into space.

**Thus, option (c) is the correct answer.**

**18.** *(a)* The cess is levied on water consumed by industries, to raise funds for the Central and State Pollution Control Boards to prevent and control water pollution.

The **Water (Prevention and Control of Pollution) Cess Act**, enacted in 1977, imposes a cess on water consumed by specific industries. The collected funds are used to support the activities of **the Central Pollution Control Board (CPCB)** and **State Pollution Control Boards (SPCBs)** in their efforts to prevent and control water pollution.

**Thus, option (a) is the correct answer**

**19.** *(a)* Increased plant growth due to increased concentration of carbon dioxide in the atmosphere

- **Carbon fertilisation** refers to the phenomenon where higher concentrations of **carbon dioxide** ($CO_2$) in the atmosphere stimulate plant growth. $CO_2$ is a critical component of **photosynthesis,** the process by which plants produce food. When $CO_2$ levels rise, plants can grow more efficiently because they have more of the raw material needed for photosynthesis.
- While increased $CO_2$ can promote plant growth, the benefits are limited by other factors such as water, nutrient availability, and temperature. Moreover, the positive effects of carbon **fertilisation** do not necessarily offset the negative impacts of climate change.

**Thus, option (a) is the correct answer.**

**20.** *(d)* None

- **Statement 1 is correct:** In **artisanal and small-scale gold mining,** mercury is used to extract gold from ore. This process releases mercury into the environment, contributing to significant mercury pollution globally.
- **Statement 2 is correct** : Coal naturally contains trace amounts of mercury, and when coal is burned in thermal power plants, mercury is released into the atmosphere, contributing to air and water pollution.
- **Statement 3 is correct.** According to health organisations such as the **World Health Organisation** (**WHO**), there is no known safe level of mercury exposure. Even small amounts can be toxic, leading to serious health issues, particularly affecting the nervous system.

**Thus, option (d) is the correct answer.**

**21.** *(b)* Only two

- **Statement 1 is correct: Persistent Organic Pollutants (POPs)** are chemical substances that are highly toxic to **both humans and wildlife.** Once released into the environment, they can remain there for years or even decades, continuing to cause harm. Eg– **polychlorinated biphenyls (PCBs)**, pesticides like **DDT**, and by-products of industrial processes like **dioxins.**
- **Statement 2 is incorrect: POPs are not** easily biodegradable. These pollutants are resistant to environmental degradation processes such as **chemical, biological and photolytic breakdown,** allowing them to remain intact in the environment for extended periods. Moreover, POPs can travel long distances through atmospheric and water currents.
- **Statement 3 is correct: POPs** tend to **bio-accumulation** and **bio-magnification** in the food chain. This accumulation of POPs in the food chain poses significant risks to **human health** and wildlife. **Health effects associated** with exposure to POPs include **cancer, immune system disruption, reproductive disorders, neurological damage, and hormonal imbalances.** Due to their **lipophilic (fat-loving) nature,** POPs accumulate in fatty tissues and remain in the bodies of organisms, causing long-term harm.

**Thus, option (b) is the correct answer.**

**22.** *(a)* 1 and 2 only

- **Statement 1 is correct: Inorganic arsenic is** highly toxic and is commonly found in **contaminated groundwater** in various parts of the world.The World Health Organisation (WHO) and various health agencies classify **inorganic arsenic** as a **Group 1 carcinogen.**The danger of inorganic arsenic lies in its ability to disrupt cellular functions and DNA, leading to **mutations and carcinogenesis.**
- **Statement 2 is correct:** Chronic arsenic exposure can result into- **Arsenicosis,** a

condition that manifests through **skin lesions,** such as hyperpigmentation and keratosis. **High risk of cancer,** particularly in **the skin, lungs, bladder, liver and kidneys. Cardiovascular diseases, including hypertension, atherosclerosis and heart disease.**

- **Statement 3 is incorrect: Organic arsenic compounds,** often found in seafood such as fish and shellfish, are **less toxic** than **inorganic arsenic** compounds. Organic arsenic compounds are typically excreted by the human body relatively quickly and do not accumulate or cause the same degree of harm as inorganic arsenic.

**Thus, option (a) is the correct answer.**

**23.** *(a)* 1 and 3 only

- **Statement 1 is correct: Thermal stratification** in temperate lakes occurs as the water temperature increases during **late spring** through **early fall.** This process causes the lake to separate into three distinct thermal layers due to differences in water temperature and density. These three layers are:
- **Epilimnion:** The upper, warm, and well-mixed layer that is exposed to sunlight.
- **Metalimnion (Thermocline):** The middle layer, where temperature decreases rapidly with depth.
- **Hypolimnion:** The deepest and coldest layer, which is denser and relatively isolated from surface mixing.
- **Statement 2 is incorrect:** The **epilimnion** is the **warmest** and **least dense** layer in the lake. It is the topmost layer, exposed to the sun's energy, where the water temperature is the highest. The **hypolimnion** is the **coldest and densest layer,** located at the bottom of the lake.
- **Statement 3 is correct: Thermal stratification** is strongest in the **summer** when the temperature difference between the surface and the bottom is the most pronounced. This creates a stable layering of water that **resists mixing** by wind due to the density differences between the layers.

**Thus, option (a) is the correct answer.**

**24.** *(d)* 1, 2, 3 and 4

- **Statement 1 is correct: UV radiation** has enough energy to break **chemical bonds in DNA** and **proteins,** causing damage at the cellular level. DNA mutations caused by UV exposure can lead to **cancer,** while damage to proteins can impair cellular functions. In humans, this can result in **skin cancer, eye cataracts and immune system suppression.**
- **Statement 2 is correct: Chlorofluorocarbons (CFCs)** are synthetic chemicals used in refrigerants, aerosol propellants, and solvents. These chemicals release **chlorine atoms** when they are broken down by UV radiation in the **stratosphere,** leading to the destruction of **ozone molecules** and reducing the protective ozone layer.
- **Statement 3 is correct: The thickness of the ozone layer** is measured in **Dobson Units (DU),** which represent the total amount of ozone in a column of the atmosphere from the Earth's surface to the top of the atmosphere. **1 DU** is defined as the amount of ozone that would form a layer 0.01 millimeters thick under standard temperature and pressure.
- **Statement 4 is correct: Ozone depletion** is particularly severe over the **Antarctic region,** leading to the formation of the **ozone hole.** This seasonal depletion is caused by the chemical reactions on **polar stratospheric clouds (PSCs),** which lead to the breakdown of ozone during the Antarctic spring.

**Thus, option (d) is the correct answer.**

**25.** *(c)* Only three

- **Statement 1 is correct: Acid rain occurs** when emissions of **sulfur dioxide ($SO_2$)** and **nitrogen oxides (NOx),** mainly from human activities such as **burning fossil fuels** (coal, oil, and gas), react in the atmosphere with **water, oxygen** and other chemicals to form **sulfuric acid** and **nitric acid.** Once these acids are formed, they mix with cloud water droplets and fall to the ground in the form of **acid rain.**
- **Statement 2 is correct: Acid deposition** occurs in two forms: **wet deposition** and **dry deposition.** Wet deposition refers to acid

rain, snow, fog, or hail, where acids are carried to the ground through precipitation. Dry deposition refers to acidic gases and particles (such as dust) that settle from the atmosphere in the absence of precipitation.

- **Statement 3 is incorrect:** While **natural sources like volcanic eruptions** do emit **sulfur dioxide** ($SO_2$) and **nitrogen oxides** (NOx), the majority of $SO_2$ and NOx emissions that cause acid rain come from **human activities.** These activities include **burning fossil fuels** in power plants, industrial processes, and vehicle emissions.
- **Statement 4 is correct: Acid rain** is significantly more acidic, with a pH typically ranging between 4.2 and 4.4. The pH of acid rain is lower because of the additional acids—**sulfuric acid and nitric acid**—formed from $SO_2$ and NOx emissions.

**Thus, option (c) is the correct answer.**

***26.*** *(b)* It results from high nitrate levels in drinking water, reducing the blood's ability to carry oxygen.

**Blue Baby Syndrome,** also known as **methemoglobinemia,** occurs when **nitrate** levels in drinking water react with hemoglobin to form methemoglobin, which cannot carry oxygen efficiently. This leads to oxygen deficiency in babies, causing a bluish discoloration of the skin.

**Thus, option (b) is the correct answer.**

***27.*** *(d)* 1, 2 and 3

- **Statement 1 is correct: Excessive fluoride intake** can indeed lead to **skeletal fluorosis,** a condition characterised by **painful and stiff joints.** Long-term exposure to high levels of fluoride, especially through drinking water, can result in the hardening and brittleness of bones, causing joint pain and mobility issues.
- **Statement 2 is correct: Knock-knee syndrome (genu valgum)**, a condition where the knees angle in and touch each other, is commonly associated with **prolonged exposure to high fluoride levels** in groundwater. This condition often manifests as a result of **skeletal fluorosis,** especially in children exposed to high fluoride concentrations during their developmental years.
- **Statement 3 is correct: Fluoride contamination** in groundwater is a widespread issue in India, affecting more than **469 districts across 27 states.** The presence of high fluoride levels in drinking water sources is a major public health concern in many parts of the country, leading to both dental and skeletal fluorosis.

**Thus, option (d) is the correct answer.**

***28.*** *(b)* Southern India, particularly Telangana

Uranium contamination in groundwater is primarily associated with **crystalline rocks** such as **granite.** These types of rocks are found in parts of Southern India, particularly in Telangana and **Andhra Pradesh.** Uranium leaches into groundwater from the weathering of granitic rocks, which are rich in uranium-bearing minerals. **Southern India,** especially **Telangana** and **Andhra Pradesh,** are known for having granite formations that contribute to **uranium contamination** in groundwater.

**Thus, option (b) is the correct answer.**

***29.*** *(c)* All three

- **Statement 1 is correct: Lead** is a naturally occurring heavy metal found in the Earth's crust. One of lead's most notable properties is its **resistance to corrosion,** particularly in non-acidic environments. This resistance has led to its historical use in water pipes, paints and other materials exposed to the elements.
- **Statement 2 is correct: Lead exposure** often results from improper or **informal recycling** practices, especially concerning **lead-acid batteries,** which are widely used in vehicles. Other major sources of lead exposure include **leaded pipes,** which can leach lead into drinking water, and **lead-based consumer products,** such as **paints, cosmetics,** and toys.
- **Statement 3 is correct: Long-term lead exposure** can lead to serious health issues, including **anemia, kidney damage, nervous system disruption,** and **behavioural** problems in children. Children are particularly vulnerable to lead poisoning due to their developing systems, and lead can

cause permanent neurological damage if not addressed early.

**Thus, option (c) is the correct answer.**

***30.*** *(b)* 2 and 4 only

- **Qualitative pollutants** are those that **do not naturally exist** in the environment and are introduced through human activities. Examples include **pesticides** (like DDT) and **chemical fertilisers.**
- **Quantitative pollutants,** on the other hand, naturally exist in the environment but become pollutants when their concentration increases beyond a certain level.
  **Examples** include **carbon dioxide** and **nitrogen oxides.**

**Thus, option (b) is the correct answer.**

***31.*** *(a)* Thinning of the ozone layer.

- **Snow Blindness,** also known as **arc eye** or **photokeratitis,** is a painful eye condition caused by overexposure to **ultraviolet (UV) light,** often due to **ozone depletion.** When too much UV light strikes the cornea, it causes a sunburn-like effect on its outermost layer, the **epithelium,** which is highly sensitive due to its many nerve endings.
- **Symptoms include** eye pain, headache, blurred vision, temporary vision loss, a sensation of something in the eye, swollen, red eyelids and watery eyes, and exaggerated glare around indoor lights.
- **Treatment and Recovery:** Resting the eyes by avoiding further UV exposure is essential, using cold compresses and artificial tears.

**Thus, option (a) is the correct answer.**

***32.*** *(d)* 1, 2, 3 and 4

**Nitrogen pollution** in the environment can be caused by a variety of sources, including **Excess fertiliser** runoff from agricultural fields, **Runoff from hard surfaces** (such as rooftops, sidewalks, and roads) that carry nitrogen into waterways during precipitation, **Emissions from fossil fuel use** in electric power generation, industry, and transportation, which increase nitrogen in the air, **Improper treatment of waste** in sewer and septic systems, which leads to nitrogen being discharged into waterways.

**Thus, option (d) is the correct answer.**

***33.*** *(a)* The Keeling Curve tracks the record of carbon dioxide (CO2) concentrations measured at the Mauna Loa Observatory in Hawaii since 1958.

**The Keeling Curve is a long-term record of atmospheric $CO_2$ concentrations,** first measured at the **Mauna Loa Observatory** in Hawaii starting in **1958.** It is a critical tool for understanding the increase in $CO_2$ levels and their contribution to global climate change. The curve recently recorded its largest-ever leap, reaching **425.22 ppm** in March 2024.

**Thus, option (a) is the correct answer.**

***34.*** *(c)* Ozone-Depleting Substances (ODS) are human-made chemicals containing chlorine and bromine that destroy ozone in the stratosphere.

- **Ozone-depleting substances** (ODS), such as **Chlorofluorocarbons** (CFCs) and **HCFCs,** are human-made chemicals that contain **chlorine and bromine.** These substances reach the stratosphere and undergo catalytic reactions, leading to the depletion of the **stratospheric ozone** layer, which protects Earth from harmful **UV radiation.**
- **Stratospheric ozone** (good ozone) is essential for absorbing UV radiation, while **tropospheric ozone** (bad ozone) is harmful as it contributes to air pollution and can cause respiratory issues.

**Thus, option (c) is the correct answer.**

***35.*** *(b)* Dobson Spectrophotometer

**Dobson Spectrophotometer** is an instrument used to measure **ozone** levels in the atmosphere. It measures the intensity of ultraviolet (UV) light absorbed by ozone, providing accurate readings of ozone concentration. Other methods for measuring ozone include the **Total Ozone Mapping Spectrometer** (TOMS) used on satellites, but the Dobson Spectrophotometer is one of the most widely used ground-based instruments for this purpose.

**Thus, option (b) is the correct answer..**

***36.*** *(d)* All four

- **Statement 1 is correct: Methoxychlor** was used as a **replacement for DDT,** but it has proven to be **toxic to invertebrates and fish,** leading to its inclusion under the **Stockholm Convention** as a POP.

- **Statement 2 is correct:** UV-328 is an **ultraviolet (UV) light stabiliser that is** commonly used in **plastics, coatings** and **other materials** to prevent damage from UV radiation. It is first **non-halogenated** (does not contain halogens like chlorine or bromine) compound **proposed for listing** under the **Stockholm Convention.**
- **Statement 3 is correct: Dechlorane Plus** is a highly chlorinated chemical compound used as a **flame retardant** in a variety of industrial and consumer products, including **electronic devices, wire coatings and plastics.**
- **Statement 4 is correct:** **Perfluorohexane Sulphonic Acid (PFHxS)** belongs to the class of **perfluorinated compounds (PFCs)**, which are known for their **resistance to heat, water, friction and chemicals.** PFHxS is used in various industrial applications, including **non-stick cookware, waterproof fabrics** and **firefighting foams.**

**Thus, option (d) is the correct answer.**

***37.*** *(b)* Only two

- **Statement 1 is correct:** Nanoparticles, due to their extremely small sise (typically between 1 to 100 nanometers), can travel long distances by remaining suspended in the atmosphere for extended periods. They are often transported by wind currents and can move across continents before settling out of the air.
- **Statement 2 is incorrect:** Nanoparticles have a high surface area to volume ratio, which makes them highly reactive. This reactivity allows them to interact with other particles, including pollutants and biological molecules, which can result in chemical transformations in the atmosphere.
- **Statement 3 is correct:** Natural processes such as volcanic eruptions, forest fires and weathering of rocks release large quantities of nanoparticles into the atmosphere. For instance, volcanic ash contains fine particles that can stay in the atmosphere for long periods and forest fires release soot, and black carbon nanoparticles. E-global burden of nanoparticles.

**Thus, option (b) is the correct answer.**

***38.*** *(d)* 1, 2 and 3

- **Statement 1 is correct: Radiation exposure, particularly ionising** radiation from radioactive materials, can cause damage to the DNA of living organisms. This damage can result in mutations, some of which may lead to cancer.
- **Statement 2 is correct:** Cosmic rays, which are **high-energy particles** from outer space, are a source of natural background radiation. When these rays interact with the Earth's atmosphere and crust, they generate radioactive isotopes such as carbon-14. This natural form of radiation contributes to the overall radiation exposure of organisms living on Earth.
- **Statement 3 is correct: Nuclear accidents,** such as the **Fukushima Daiichi disaster** in 2011, release large amounts of radioactive isotopes, including cesium-137, iodine-131, and strontium-90, into the environment. These radioactive materials can persist for decades and have far-reaching effects on ecosystems, human health, and food safety.

**Thus, option (d) is the correct answer.**

***39.*** *(a)* Only one

- **Statement 1 is incorrect: Non-ionising radiation,** by definition, does not have enough energy to remove tightly bound electrons from atoms or molecules (a process known as ionisation). Instead, it causes atoms and molecules to vibrate or heat up, which can still lead to biological effects, but not through ionisation.
- **Statement 2 is correct:** Long-wavelength UV radiation (specifically UV-A) is a form of non-ionising radiation. UV-A radiation does not ionise molecules but can still cause damage to living tissues by inducing chemical reactions, such as DNA damage in skin cells, leading to sunburns or long-term effects like skin cancer.
- **Statement 3 is correct:** Non-ionising radiation includes a wide range of electromagnetic waves, from radio waves to microwaves, infrared and visible light. These waves have lower energy compared to ionising radiation and are commonly used in various technologies such as telecommunications (radio waves) and cooking (microwaves).

**Thus, option (a) is the correct answer.**

**40.** *(a)* 1 and 2 only

- **Statement 1 is correct:** Bharat Stage (BS) VI emission norms were introduced by the Government of India to regulate and significantly reduce the emission of harmful air pollutants, such as nitrogen oxides (NOx), sulfur oxides (SOx), and particulate matter (PM), from motor vehicles. The BS VI norms are stricter than the previous BS IV.
- **Statement 2 is correct:** BS VI norms require onboard diagnostics (OBD) to be mandatory for all vehicles. This helps in ensuring that vehicles comply with emission standards and facilitates early detection of engine or emission-related issues.
- **Statement 3 is incorrect:** The implementation of BS VI norms was not delayed to 2024. In fact, India skipped the BS V stage and directly adopted BS VI norms in 2020, ahead of the originally planned schedule. This leapfrogging was done to address urgent concerns related to rising air pollution, particularly in urban areas.

**Thus, option (a) is the correct answer.**

**41.** *(b)* Only two

- **Statement 1 is incorrect: GRAP (Graded Response Action Plan)** is not a long-term action plan but rather an **emergency response** measure designed to tackle severe air pollution episodes in the Delhi-NCR region. It provides a graded approach to deal with pollution based on air quality levels, ranging from 'moderate' to 'severe' and 'emergency' situations.
- **Statement 2 is correct:** GRAP indeed creates a step-by-step plan for addressing air pollution. It outlines actions to be taken when air quality falls into different categories, including measures to be implemented when air pollution reaches alarming levels (e.g., 'Very Poor' or 'severe').
- **Statement 3 is correct:** GRAP includes stringent measures like halting the entry of trucks (except essential commodity trucks) and closing down brick kilns and other polluting industries when air quality reaches emergency levels. These measures are meant to reduce pollution sources during periods of extreme air pollution.

**Thus, option (b) is the correct answer.**

**42.** *(a)* Thermal pollution is caused by the discharge of hot water from power plants, raising the water temperature.

Thermal pollution occurs when power plants and industrial facilities **discharge heated water** or other effluents into nearby water bodies. This **raises the water temperature** by 5-15°C, affecting the aquatic ecosystem. The sudden increase in temperature can drastically lower the dissolved oxygen levels in the water, as warm water holds less oxygen than cold water. This oxygen depletion can suffocate fish and other aquatic organisms.

**Thus, option (a) is the correct answer.**

**43.** *(a)* 1 and 2 only

- **Statement 1 is correct:** Marine pollution often results from oil spills, which are major environmental disasters. Large quantities of petroleum released into the ocean can coat marine organisms, smothering marine life, destroying coral reefs and leading to the death of marine mammals, and birds, and the contamination of coastal areas.
- **Statement 2 is correct:** Oil spills disrupt marine food chains by affecting plankton and benthos, the primary producers, and bottom-dwellers in the food web. Plankton, absorbs oil, causing toxins to accumulate as they are consumed by higher trophic levels. Benthos can also be covered by oil, suffocating them and disrupting sediment-based ecosystems.
- **Statement 3 is incorrect:** Plastic pollution has been documented not only in shallow ocean waters but also in the deepest parts of the ocean, such as the Challenger Deep in the Mariana trench. Plastic debris, including microplastics, has been found in virtually every part of the world's oceans, from the surface to the seabed.

**Thus, option (a) is the correct answer.**

**44.** *(a)* 1 and 2 only

- **Statement 1 is correct:** Marine wildlife, such as **seabirds, fish, turtles and whales,** often mistake plastic debris for prey. The ingestion of plastic waste can lead to **suffocation, starvation and death,** as plastic clogs the digestive systems of these animals.

- **Statement 2 is correct:** Invisible plastic, also known as microplastics, has been identified even in **remote and pristine environments** such as the Arctic. These small plastic particles, often less than **5mm in size,** are pervasive and have been found in ice cores, water samples, and marine organisms far from human activity.
- **Statement 3 is incorrect:** The economic damage caused by marine plastic pollution is far from insignificant. In fact, it is projected to cause **over $13 billion in economic damage to marine ecosystems annually by 2050.** The costs arise from the impacts on fisheries, tourism and the loss of marine biodiversity.

**Thus, option (a) is the correct answer.**

***45.*** *(b)* Only two

- **Statement 1 is correct:** Phytoremediation is an environmentally friendly technique that uses plants to **remove, transfer, or stabilise contaminants from soil and water.** Plants can absorb heavy metals, pesticides, solvents, and other pollutants, either storing them in their tissues or transforming them into less harmful substances.
- **Statement 2 is correct: Water hyacinth,** an aquatic invasive species, is highly effective in phytoremediation due to its rapid growth and ability to absorb and accumulate heavy metals such as **lead, mercury and cadmium** from contaminated water. Despite its invasive nature.
- **Statement 3 is incorrect:** Phytoremediation is highly effective in removing toxic materials from both **soil and aquatic systems.** In water bodies, plants like water **hyacinth and mangroves** absorb heavy metals, nutrients, and other pollutants. This method is widely used in wetlands, ponds and sewage treatment plants.

**Thus, option (b) is the correct answer.**

## Past Learning (Answers)

| | | | | | | | | | |
|---|---|---|---|---|---|---|---|---|---|
| 1 (d) | 2 (a) | 3 (d) | 4 (c) | 5 (b) | 6 (b) | 7 (a) | 8 (b) | 9 (a) | 10 (b) |
| 11 (d) | 12 (d) | 13 (d) | 14 (b) | 15 (d) | 16 (d) | 17 (d) | 18 (d) | 19 (c,d) | 20 (a) |
| 21 (c) | 22 (d) | 23 (c) | 24 (b) | 25 (c) | 26 (d) | 27 (c) | 28 (a) | 29 (b) | |

CHAPTER 03

# Biodiversity

## Assessment Round

**1.** Consider the following statements regarding the measurement of biodiversity:

1. Species richness refers to the total number of different species found in a specific area or ecosystem.
2. Beta diversity measures the overall diversity across different ecosystems within a region.

Which of the above statements is/are incorrect?

(a) 1 only (b) 2 only
(c) Both 1 and 2 (d) Neither 1 nor 2

**2.** How does 'Species Diversity' differ from 'Genetic Diversity'?

(a) Species diversity focuses on genetic makeup.
(b) Species diversity includes the variety of living organisms, while genetic diversity is about variations within a species.
(c) Species diversity measures the total number of genes
(d) Species diversity is only relevant in aquatic ecosystems

**3.** Consider the following pairs about the different types of diversity:

| | Diversity Type | Description |
|---|---|---|
| 1. | Alpha Diversity | Measures the diversity within a particular habitat or local area. |
| 2. | Beta Diversity | Quantifies the change in species composition between habitats. |
| 3. | Gamma Diversity | Represents overall diversity at the regional or landscape scale. |

How many pairs given above is/are correctly matched?

(a) Only one
(b) Only two
(c) All three
(d) None

**4.** Consider the following statements regarding biodiversity patterns:

1. Biodiversity is typically higher in the lower latitudes (near the equator) compared to the higher latitudes (near the poles).
2. Along mountain gradients, biodiversity tends to be greater at lower altitudes than at higher altitudes.

Which of the statements given above is/are incorrect?

(a) 1 only (b) 2 only
(c) Both 1 and 2 (d) Neither 1 nor 2

**5.** Consider the following statements regarding patterns of biodiversity distribution:

1. Species diversity generally increases as we move away from the equator toward the poles.
2. The tropics harbour more species than temperate or polar areas.
3. Colombia has fewer bird species compared to Greenland.

Which of the statements given above is/are correct.

(a) 1 and 2 only
(b) 2 only
(c) 1 and 3 only
(d) 2 and 3

**6.** Which of the following criteria are used to identify biodiversity hotspots?

1. Species richness
2. Presence of invasive species
3. High endemism
4. Threat perception

Select the correct answer using the codes given below:

(a) 1 and 2 only (b) 2 and 4 only
(c) 1, 3 and 4 only (d) 1, 2, 3 and 4

**7.** Which of the following pairs of biodiversity hotspots in India and their corresponding geographical extents are not correctly matched?

1. **Himalaya**: Entire Indian Himalayan region including parts of Pakistan and China.
2. **Indo-Burma**: Entire North-Eastern India, including Assam and the Andaman group of Islands.
3. **Sundaland**: Nicobar Islands and parts of South-East Asia.
4. **Western Ghats and Sri Lanka**: Entire Western Ghats and Sri Lanka.

Choose the correct answer from the options given below:

(a) 1 and 2 only (b) 1 and 4 only
(c) 2 and 3 only (d) 2 and 4 only

**8.** With reference to biodiversity hotspots, consider the following statements:

1. A region must have at least 1,500 endemic vascular plant species to qualify as a biodiversity hotspot.
2. A biodiversity hotspot must have more than 30% of its original natural vegetation remaining.

Which of the statements given above is/are correct?

(a) 1 only
(b) 2 only
(c) Both 1 and 2
(d) Neither 1 nor 2

**9.** Consider the following statements about biodiversity hotspots:

1. Biodiversity hotspots are found only in tropical regions.
2. India has four biodiversity hotspots: Eastern Himalayas, Western Himalayas, Western Ghats, and Andaman and Nicobar Islands.

Which of the given above statements is/are incorrect?

(a) 1 only (b) 2 only
(c) Both 1 and 2 (d) Neither 1 nor 2

**10.** Consider the following groups of organisms and their biodiversity:

1. Insects are the most species-rich taxonomic group among animals.
2. Fungi have the highest species biodiversity among plants.
3. Fish have the highest species biodiversity among vertebrates.

How many of the above statements is/are correct?

(a) Only one (b) Only two
(c) All three (d) None

**11.** Consider the following causes of species extinction:

1. Habitat loss and fragmentation
2. Over-exploitation
3. Alien species invasions
4. Co-extinctions

Which of the above causes comes under 'The Evil Quartet'?

(a) 1 and 2 only
(b) 1, 2 and 3 only
(c) 1, 2, 3 and 4
(d) 2 and 3 only

**12.** Which of the following statements most correctly describes 'endemic species'?

(a) Species that are confined to a specific geographic area for their distribution.
(b) A group of organisms that are very uncommon, scarce, or infrequently encountered.
(c) Species were chosen to represent a particular habitat, issue, campaign, or environmental cause.
(d) Species that are the first to colonise a newly created environment and contribute to building an initial biological community through their interactions.

**13.** Which of the following statements is not true regarding Allen's rule and Bergmann's rule?

(a) Allen's rule suggests that mammals in colder climates have longer ears and limbs to retain heat.

(b) Bergmann's rule indicates that larger organisms are found at higher latitudes to conserve heat.

(c) Allen's rule is associated with the body surface area of mammals in cold environments.

(d) Both rules relate to how animals adapt to temperature variations in their habitats.

**14.** Which one of the following is not an example of an in-situ method of conservation of flora?

(a) Biosphere Reserve (b) Botanical Garden
(c) National Park (d) Wildlife Sanctuary

**15.** Which of the following statements correctly describes Ex-situ conservation?

(a) It focuses on conserving wildlife in their natural habitats.

(b) It is an example of a traditional conservation method without human intervention.

(c) It primarily aims to enhance biodiversity in a specific ecosystem.

(d) It involves the collection and maintenance of species outside their natural habitats under human care.

**16.** Which of the following threats are commonly faced by Biosphere Reserves in India?

1. Habitat destruction due to deforestation
2. Invasive species
3. Climate change

Select the correct answer using the codes given below:

(a) 1 and 2 only (b) 2 and 3 only
(c) 1 and 3 only (d) 1, 2 and 3

**17.** Which of the following locations have coral reefs?

1. Andaman and Nicobar Islands
2. Gulf of Kutch
3. Gulf of Mannar
4. Sunderbans

Select the correct answer using the codes given below:

(a) 1, 2 and 3 only (b) 2 and 4 only
(c) 1 and 3 only (d) 1, 2, 3 and 4

**18.** Consider the following statements regarding soil erosion in India:

1. The Brahmaputra valley in Assam is identified as the biggest hotspot for soil erosion in the country.
2. Soil Organic Carbon (SOC) content in Indian soils has increased significantly over the last 70 years.
3. The Soil Health Card Scheme aims to reduce reliance on chemical fertilisers through the promotion of organic farming.
4. Biochar application and regenerative agricultural practices are among the recommended measures to prevent soil erosion and improve soil health.

How many of the above statements is/are correct?

(a) Only one (b) Only two
(c) Only three (d) All four

**19.** Consider the following pairs:

| | Term | Definition |
|---|---|---|
| 1. | Alien Species | A species is introduced outside its natural past or present distribution, including parts like gametes, seeds, eggs, or propagules. |
| 2. | Invasive Alien Species | An alien species whose introduction or spread threatens the biological diversity of the region. |
| 3. | Naturalised Species | Alien species establish self-sustaining populations over several life cycles without direct human intervention. |

How many of the given above pairs is/are correctly matched?

(a) Only one pair (b) Only two pairs
(c) All three pairs (d) None

**20.** Which of the following best describes the impact of water hyacinths on freshwater ecosystems?

(a) It improves oxygen levels in the water, benefiting fish and aquatic plants.

(b) It enhances water quality by directly reducing the presence of pollutants and toxic substances without disrupting native ecosystems.

(c) It depletes oxygen levels in water, blocks sunlight, and makes waterbodies unsuitable for commercial fisheries and other activities.

(d) It serves as a native plant beneficial to waterbodies in India, supporting commercial fisheries and transportation.

**21.** Consider the following pairs regarding the regions of the Himalayan mountain system and their dominant flora:

| | Region | Dominant Flora |
|---|---|---|
| 1. | Himalayan Foothills | Deciduous forests |
| 2. | Western Himalayas | Coniferous forests and alpine meadows |
| 3. | Eastern Himalayas | Rhododendrons and bamboo |

Which of the above pairs are correctly matched?

(a) 1 and 2 only (b) 2 and 3 only
(c) 1 and 3 only (d) 1, 2 and 3

**22.** Which of the following statements is incorrect regarding the climatic conditions of the Himalayan mountain system?

1. The Western Himalayas experience heavy rainfall and temperate conditions.
2. The Eastern Himalayas receive heavy rainfall at lower altitudes.
3. The snow in the Eastern Himalayas is primarily at very high altitudes.

Select the correct answer using the codes given below:

(a) 1 only (b) 2 only
(c) 3 only (d) 1 and 3 only

**23.** With reference to the Indian Tiger (Royal Bengal Tiger), consider the following statements:

1. The Indian Tiger is the National Animal of India and is primarily found in high mountain habitats.
2. As a keystone species, the Indian Tiger plays a critical role in maintaining the balance of its ecosystem.
3. Each tiger has a unique pattern of stripes, which can be used to identify individuals.

Which of the given above statements is/are correct?

(a) 1 and 2 only
(b) 2 and 3 only
(c) 1 and 3 only
(d) 1, 2 and 3

**24.** Consider the following statements about 'Sundarbans Tiger Reserve':

**Assertion** (A) : The Sundarbans Tiger Reserve is known for its unique aquatic hunting techniques by tigers.

**Reason** (R) : The mangrove habitat in the Sundarbans has forced tigers to adapt to a semi-aquatic lifestyle, including swimming long distances between islands.

Which of the below option are correct in context of above statments :

(a) Both A and R are correct, and R is the correct explation of A.

(b) Both A and R are correct, but R is not the correct explanation of A.

(c) A is correct, but R is incorrect.

(d) A is incorrect, but R is correct.

**25.** In biological communities, certain species play a crucial role in maintaining the structure and function of the ecosystem by influencing the survival of many other species. What are these species called?

(a) Keystone species
(b) Allopatric species
(c) Sympatric species
(d) Threatened species

**26.** Three of the following criteria have contributed to the recognition of Western Ghats-Sri Lanka and Indo-Burma regions as hotspots of biodiversity:

1. Species richness
2. Vegetation density
3. Endemism
4. Ethno-botanical importance
5. Threat perception
6. Adaptation of flora and fauna to warm and humid conditions

Which of the above are correct criteria in this context?

(a) 1, 2 and 6 only (b) 2, 4 and 6 only
(c) 1, 3 and 5 only (d) 3, 4 and 6 only

**27.** Wetlands play a crucial role in biodiversity conservation and climate change mitigation. In this context, which of the following are types of wetlands found in India?

1. Myristica swamps
2. Oxbow lakes
3. Salt marshes
4. Coral reefs

Choose the correct answer from the options given below:

(a) 1 and 3 only
(b) 1, 2 and 3 only
(c) 2, 3 and 4 only
(d) 1, 2, 3 and 4

**28.** With reference to Amur Falcons, consider the following statements:

1. Amur Falcons breed in South-East Russia and Northern China.
2. They migrate to Southern Africa through India, covering a distance of 22,000 km.
3. They are classified as Critically Endangered by the IUCN.

How many of the statements given above is/are correct?

(a) Only one (b) Only two
(c) All three (d) None

**29.** Which of the following statements correctly describes the criteria for a region to qualify as a Biodiversity Hotspot?

(a) A region must have at least 1,500 endemic species of vascular plants and retain more than 30% of its original natural vegetation.
(b) A region must have at least 1,500 endemic species of vascular plants and retain 30% or less of its original natural vegetation.
(c) A region must be located in a tropical zone with a high percentage of endangered species.
(d) A region must have significant traditional knowledge and be recognised as a mega-diverse country.

**30.** Consider the following statements about India's biodiversity:

1. India is home to 4 out of the 36 globally recognised Biodiversity Hotspots.
2. India ranks fifth in the world in terms of reptile endemism.
3. India is recognised as one of the eight Vavilovian centers of origin and diversity of crop plants.

How many of the above statements is/are correct?

(a) Only one
(b) Only two
(c) All three
(d) None

**31.** Which of the following can pose threats to the biodiversity of a geographical area?

1. Global warming
2. Fragmentation of habitat
3. Invasion of alien species
4. Promotion of vegetarianism

Select the correct answer from the codes given below:

(a) 1, 2 and 3 only
(b) 2 and 3 only
(c) 1 and 4 only
(d) 1, 2, 3 and 4

**32.** Which of the following best describes 'Extended Producer Responsibility (EPR)'?

(a) It is an environmental policy where the producer is only responsible for the product during its manufacturing phase.

(b) It is an environmental policy where the producer's responsibility extends to the post-consumer stage of a product's life cycle.

(c) It is a policy that transfers all waste management responsibilities to consumers after the product is sold.

(d) It is a corporate social responsibility initiative that encourages producers to donate unused products.

**33.** What does the 30×30 Target in global biodiversity conservation aim to achieve by the year 2030?

(a) Protecting 30% of the world's land and sea areas through the establishment of protected areas and other conservation measures.

(b) Reducing carbon emissions by 30% to mitigate climate change impacts on biodiversity.

(c) Ensuring that 30% of all endangered species are conserved through captive breeding programmes.

(d) Allocating 30% of global biodiversity funding to developing countries for conservation efforts.

**34.** Consider the following statements about 'Biodiversity Credit':

1. A biodiversity credit is similar to a carbon offset in that it compensates for environmental damage by financing conservation activities.
2. Biodiversity credits are designed to fund long-term conservation and restoration of nature, providing a higher-order contribution than simply offsetting negative impacts.
3. Unlike biodiversity offsets, biodiversity credits require location-specific compensation, ensuring that conservation efforts occur in the same location as the environmental damage.

How many of the above statements is/are correct?

(a) Only one

(b) Only two

(c) All three

(d) None

**35.** Which of the following best describes 'Krill'?

(a) Large marine mammals that primarily feed on plankton.

(b) Small crustaceans are found in all the world's oceans, feeding on phytoplankton and zooplankton, and serving as a main food source for many larger animals.

(c) Marine reptiles are known for their migratory patterns.

(d) Sea birds consume large quantities of fish.

**36.** The 'Red Data Books' published by the International Union for Conservation of Nature and Natural Resources (IUCN) contain lists of:

1. Endemic plant and animal species present in the biodiversity hotspots.
2. Threatened plant and animal species.
3. Protected sites for the conservation of nature and natural resources in various countries.

Select the correct answer using the codes given below.

(a) 1 and 3 only

(b) 2 only

(c) 2 and 3 only

(d) 3 only

**37.** With reference to TRAFFIC, consider the following statements:

1. It was established by the World Wildlife Fund (WWF) and IUCN in 1976.
2. TRAFFIC monitors wildlife trade and provides recommendations on sustainable trade practices.
3. TRAFFIC functions independently but remains under the direct control of WWF.

Which of the statements given above are correct?

(a) 1 and 2 only (b) 2 and 3 only

(c) 1 and 3 only (d) 1, 2 and 3

**38.** Which of the following statements about the Bengal florican (Houbaropsis bengalensis) is/are correct?

1. The Bengal florican is classified as a Critically Endangered species.
2. It has a wide distribution across South Asia, including Bangladesh.
3. The Bengal florican is an indicator of a healthy grassland ecosystem.

Select the correct answer from the codes given below:

(a) 1 only (b) 1 and 3 only
(c) 2 and 3 only (d) 1, 2 and 3

**39.** Which of the following statements about the Pygmy Hog (Porcula salvania) is/are correct?

1. The Pygmy Hog is the smallest wild pig in the world, weighing about 8 kgs.
2. It is an indicator species for the management status of grassland habitats.
3. The Pygmy Hog is currently found in multiple regions across the Southern Himalayan foothills.

Select the correct answer using the codes given below:

(a) 1 and 2 only (b) 2 and 3 only
(c) 1, 2 and 3 (d) 1 and 3 only

**40.** With reference to the conservation of forests in India, consider the following statements:

1. Reserved forests are typically upgraded to wildlife sanctuaries, which may then be upgraded to national parks, with each category receiving increasing levels of protection and funding.
2. In protected forests, all activities, including hunting and grazing, are strictly prohibited.
3. Reserved forests are declared through a notification by the Central Government, while protected forests are designated by State Governments.

How many of the statements given above is/are correct?

(a) Only one (b) Only two
(c) All three (d) None

**41.** Which of the following statements correctly describes the objectives and initiatives of Project Tiger in India?

1. Project Tiger was launched in 1973 to ensure the maintenance of a viable tiger population.
2. The National Tiger Conservation Authority (NTCA) is responsible for implementing the project and approving conservation plans.
3. Project Tiger provides financial assistance to all states at a uniform rate without special provisions for any region.
4. A new division named 'Project Tiger and Elephant Division' has been created under the Ministry of Environment, Forest and Climate Change.

Select the correct answer using the codes given below:

(a) 1, 2 and 4 only
(b) 1, 3 and 4 only
(c) 2 and 3 only
(d) 1, 2 and 3 only

**42.** With reference to the Convention on Conservation of Migratory Species of Wild Animals (CMS), consider the following statements:

1. CMS provides a global platform for the conservation and sustainable use of migratory animals and their habitats.
2. The Great Indian bustard, mainland Asian elephant, and Bengal florican are migratory species from India listed in the Appendix of the convention.
3. Appendix I of the CMS lists migratory species that need or would benefit from international cooperation, while Appendix II lists species threatened with extinction.

Which of the statements given above are correct?

(a) 1 and 2 only
(b) 2 and 3 only
(c) 1 and 3 only
(d) 1, 2 and 3

**43.** In the context of the Convention on Conservation of Migratory Species of Wild Animals (CMS), which of the following migratory species from India have been listed in Appendix I of the convention?

1. Great Indian bustard
2. Bengal florican
3. Asian elephant
4. Snow leopard

Select the correct answer from the options given below:

(a) 1, 2 and 3 only
(b) 1 and 2 only
(c) 2 and 4 only
(d) 1, 2, 3 and 4

**44.** In the context of the IUCN Red List, which of the following categories indicates that a species is threatened with global extinction?

1. Critically Endangered (CR)
2. Endangered (EN)
3. Vulnerable (VU)
4. Near Threatened (NT)

Select the correct answer using the codes given below:

(a) 1, 2 and 3 only
(b) 1 and 2 only
(c) 2, 3 and 4 only
(d) 1, 2, 3 and 4

**45.** Which of the following correctly describes the ergosterol found in mushrooms?

(a) A protein found in mushrooms, responsible for their high water content.
(b) A carbohydrate present in fungi that helps in photosynthesis.
(c) A cholesterol-like compound in mushrooms that can be converted into Vitamin D when exposed to ultraviolet light.
(d) A fat-soluble vitamin found exclusively in mushrooms.

**46.** Consider the following statements about Salim Ali's Fruit Bat and the Indian Flying Fox:

1. Salim Ali's Fruit Bat is endemic to the Western Ghats and classified as Critically Endangered by the IUCN Red List.
2. The Indian Flying Fox is found in several countries across the Indian subcontinent and is listed as Least Concern due to its broader range and population.
3. Both species are critical for the ecosystem, contributing significantly to pollination and seed dispersal of several commercially valuable plants.
4. The decline of bat populations worldwide is primarily due to habitat destruction and poaching, which also severely impacts both these species.

How many of the above statements is/are correct?

(a) Only one
(b) Only two
(c) Only three
(d) All four

**47.** With reference to the Namdapha Flying Squirrel, consider the following statements:

1. The Namdapha Flying Squirrel is classified as Endangered on the IUCN Red List of Threatened Species.
2. The Namdapha Flying Squirrel is endemic to the Patkai range in Arunachal Pradesh, India.
3. It was rediscovered after 42 years of being considered possibly extinct.
4. The Namdapha Flying Squirrel was the only member of the Biswamoyopterus genus until the discovery of other flying squirrels in South-East Asia.

Which of the given statements are correct?

(a) 1, 2 and 4 only (b) 2, 3 and 4 only
(c) 1, 2, 3 and 4 (d) 1, 3 and 4 only

**48.** Consider the following statements about vultures in India:

1. The White-rumped Vulture, Indian Vulture, and Slender-billed Vulture are all classified as Critically Endangered by the IUCN due to population decline caused primarily by diclofenac use.
2. The Egyptian Vulture and Red-headed Vulture are listed as Endangered, with both species facing threats from habitat loss and poisoning.
3. Himalayan Griffon Vulture and Cinerous Vulture are wintering species in India and are categorised as Near Threatened by the IUCN.
4. The Vulture Breeding Centre in Pinjore, Haryana focuses on the Ex-situ breeding of Gyps species to replenish their populations in the wild.

How many of the above statements is/are correct?

(a) Only one
(b) Only two
(c) Only three
(d) All four

**49.** With reference to an organisation known as 'BirdLife International,' which of the following statements is/are correct?

1. It is a global partnership of conservation organisations.
2. The concept of 'biodiversity hotspots' originated from this organisation.
3. It identifies the sites known/referred to as 'Important Bird and Biodiversity Areas'.

Select the correct answer using the codes given below:

(a) 1 only
(b) 2 and 3 only
(c) 1 and 3 only
(d) 1, 2 and 3

**50.** In India, in which one of the following types of forests is teak a dominant tree species?

(a) Tropical moist deciduous forest
(b) Tropical rain forest
(c) Tropical thorn scrub forest
(d) Temperate forest with grasslands

**51.** With reference to the International Union for Conservation of Nature (IUCN) and the Convention on International Trade in Endangered Species of Wild Fauna and Flora (CITES), which of the following statements is/are correct?

1. IUCN is an organ of the United Nations, and CITES is an international agreement between governments.
2. IUCN runs thousands of field projects around the world to better manage natural environments.
3. CITES is legally binding on the states that have joined it, but this Convention does not take the place of national laws.

Select the correct answer from the options given below:

(a) 1 only (b) 2 and 3 only
(c) 1 and 3 only (d) 1, 2 and 3

**52.** Consider the following statements regarding biodiversity hotspots:

1. Biodiversity hotspots are located only in tropical regions.
2. India has four biodiversity hotspots, i.e., Eastern Himalayas, Western Himalayas, Western Ghats, and Andaman and Nicobar Islands.
3. Eastern Himalayas was originally part of the Indo-Burma biodiversity hotspot but was reclassified in 2004.

Select the incorrect answer using the codes given below:

(a) 1 and 2 only (b) 2 and 3 only
(c) 1, 2 and 3 (d) 1 and 3 only

**53.** In the context of Eco-Sensitive Areas (ESAs) in the Western Ghats, consider the following statements:

1. Eco-Sensitive Areas (ESAs) are notified under the Environment Protection Act of 1986 by the Ministry of Environment, Forest and Climate Change (MoEFCC).
2. The Kasturirangan Committee recommended declaring 60,000 square kilometers of the Western Ghats as ESA, covering parts of Karnataka.
3. Eco-Sensitive Areas are located within 10 kilometers of Protected Areas, National Parks and Wildlife Sanctuaries.

Which of the above statements are correct?

(a) 1 and 2 only
(b) 2 and 3 only
(c) 1, 2 and 3
(d) 1 and 3 only

**54.** With reference to the Red Sanders (Pterocarpus santalinus), consider the following statements:

1. Red Sanders is a species of Pterocarpus endemic to the Southern-Eastern Ghats of South India.
2. Red Sanders grows primarily in tropical rainforests of South India.
3. Red Sanders thrives in dry, rocky soils and lateritic conditions in areas like Andhra Pradesh.

How many of the statements given above is/are correct?

(a) Only one
(b) Only two
(c) All three
(d) None

**55.** If there is a significant decline in the population of butterflies, what could be the possible consequences?

1. Pollination of certain plants may be negatively impacted.
2. There could be an increase in fungal infections of some cultivated plants.
3. A decline in butterfly populations may lead to a reduction in the populations of some species of wasps, spiders and birds.

Select the correct answer using the codes given below:

(a) 1 only
(b) 2 and 3 only
(c) 1 and 3 only
(d) 1, 2 and 3

**56.** The term 'sixth mass extinction' or 'sixth extinction' is often mentioned in discussions regarding:

(a) Widespread monoculture practices in agriculture and large-scale commercial farming with indiscriminate use of chemicals may lead to the loss of native ecosystems.
(b) Fears of a possible meteorite collision with the Earth shortly, similar to the one that caused the extinction of dinosaurs 65 million years ago.
(c) Large-scale cultivation of genetically modified crops, potentially leading to the disappearance of native crop plants and loss of food biodiversity.
(d) Mankind's over-exploitation of natural resources, habitat fragmentation, ecosystem destruction, pollution and global climate change.

**57.** With reference to animal behaviour, consider the following statements:

1. Orangutans are known to use sticks as tools to extract insects from holes in trees or logs.
2. Otters use sticks to scrape insects out of crevices.
3. Sloth bears use their long, flexible lips to suck insects out of crevices rather than using tools.

How many of the above statements is/are correct?

(a) Only one
(b) Only two
(c) All three
(d) None

**58.** Consider the following statements regarding Biodiversity Management Committees (BMCs) in India:

1. In India, the BMCs play a crucial role in realising the objectives of the Nagoya Protocol.
2. BMCs have key responsibilities in determining access and benefit sharing, including the authority to levy collection fees on access to biological resources within their jurisdiction.

Which of the statements given above is/are correct?

(a) 1 only
(b) 2 only
(c) Both 1 and 2
(d) Neither 1 nor 2

**59.** Consider the following pairs of wetlands/lakes and their locations:

| | | |
|---|---|---|
| 1. | Hokera Wetland | Punjab |
| 2. | Renuka Wetland | Himachal Pradesh |
| 3. | Rudrasagar Lake | Tripura |
| 4. | Sasthamkotta Lake | Tamil Nadu |

How many of the above pairs is/are correctly matched?

(a) Only one pair
(b) Only two pairs
(c) Only three pairs
(d) All four pairs

**60.** Consider the following statements regarding Biodiversity Heritage Sites (BHS) in India:

1. Biodiversity Heritage Sites are areas with unique, ecologically fragile ecosystems that host a high diversity of wild and domesticated species, including rare and keystone species.
2. As per the Biological Diversity Act, of 2002, State Governments are empowered to notify areas as Biodiversity Heritage Sites in consultation with local bodies.
3. The creation of Biodiversity Heritage Sites imposes strict restrictions on the local community's practices and usages.
4. The first Biodiversity Heritage Site in India was the Nallur Tamarind Grove in Karnataka, declared in 2007.

Choose the correct answer from the options given below:

(a) 1 and 2 only (b) 1, 2 and 4 only
(c) 2 and 3 only (d) 1, 2, 3 and 4

**61.** What is the main objective of the Convention on the Conservation of Migratory Species of Wild Animals (CMS) COP 14, and what are its key highlights?

(a) To discuss climate change mitigation efforts and provide solutions for renewable energy in a range of states.
(b) To enhance protection and conservation efforts for migratory species by adopting listing proposals and addressing various threats such as habitat degradation, illegal trade and bycatch.
(c) To promote the expansion of human settlements into migratory species habitats to boost economic development in range states.
(d) To implement policies that encourage the hunting of migratory species for population control in range states.

**62.** In the context of migratory bird flyways in India, consider the following statements:

1. The Central Asian Flyway (CAF) passes through the Indian subcontinent and is crucial for migratory birds from Central Asia.
2. The East Asian-Australasian Flyway (EAAF) primarily covers East Asia and South-East Asia but also includes parts of Eastern and North-Eastern India.
3. The Asian East African Flyway (AEAF) passes through India, primarily linking Asian regions to East Africa.

Which of the above statements are correct?

(a) 1 and 3 only
(b) 2 and 3 only
(c) 1, 2 and 3
(d) 1 and 2 only

**63.** Which of the following statements regarding Permafrost and Environmental Sensitive Zones (ESZs) is/are correct?

1. Permafrost refers to ground that remains frozen for at least two consecutive years and is found in Arctic regions.
2. ESZs help in in-situ conservation and minimise man-animal conflicts and forest depletion.
3. Permafrost regions are always covered with snow, whereas ESZs strictly prohibit all forms of human activities.

Select the correct answer using the codes given below:

(a) 1 and 2 only
(b) 1 and 3 only
(c) 2 and 3 only
(d) 1,2,3 and 4

**64.** Which of the following statements is correct about baseflow and its impact on rivers in peninsular India?

(a) Baseflow refers to the portion of stream flow that originates from groundwater discharge and contributes to flooding by reducing the time lag between rainfall and runoff in rivers.
(b) Baseflow is the surface water runoff from rainfall and has no impact on the flooding of rivers in peninsular India.
(c) Baseflow refers to water flowing over the surface, which contributes to the quick drainage of excess rainfall into rivers.
(d) Baseflow is an artificial method of increasing water levels in rivers and does not occur naturally.

**65.** Which of the following best describes the Global Geoparks Network (GGN)?

(a) A profit-making organisation that promotes tourism in UNESCO World Heritage Sites.
(b) A non-profit international association established in 2014 to foster networking and collaboration among global geoparks under the auspices of UNESCO.
(c) An organisation that focuses on the conservation of wildlife sanctuaries and national parks worldwide.
(d) A UNESCO initiative to provide financial aid to underdeveloped regions.

**66.** With reference to the Fourth Global Mass Coral Bleaching Event, consider the following statements:

1. Coral bleaching occurs when corals expel the symbiotic algae, known as zooxanthellae, due to stressful conditions such as changes in temperature or light.
2. The Fourth Global Mass Coral Bleaching Event was the first event in the last 10 years.
3. Coral reefs are formed by hard corals, which establish a symbiotic relationship with microscopic algae that give them their colours.

How many of the above statements is/are correct?

(a) Only one
(b) Only two
(c) All three
(d) None

**67.** Consider the following statements about the 'Baobab Tree (Genus: Adansonia)':

1. Baobab trees are long-lived deciduous trees, found in Africa, Madagascar, and Australia.
2. The tree is known as the 'upside-down tree' because, during the dry season, its leafless branches resemble roots.
3. Fiber from the bark of the Baobab tree is used to make products like rope and cloth.

How many of the above statements is/are included in the description of the Baobab Tree?

(a) Only one
(b) Only two
(c) All three
(d) None

**68.** In the context of Jerdon's Courser, which of the following statements regarding its conservation and habitat are correct?

1. Jerdon's Courser is a nocturnal bird found only in the Eastern Ghats.
2. It is exclusively endemic to Andhra Pradesh, specifically within the Sri Lankamalleswara Wildlife Sanctuary in Kadapa, Andhra Pradesh.
3. Jerdon's Courser is listed under Schedule II of the Wildlife (Protection) Act, 1972.

Select the correct answer using the codes given below:

(a) 1 and 2 only (b) 2 and 3 only
(c) 1 and 3 only (d) 1, 2 and 3

**69.** Consider the following statements about 'Agarwood (Aquilaria malaccensis)':

1. Agarwood is an evergreen tree native to North-East India, Bangladesh, Bhutan, and parts of South-East Asia.
2. It is highly valued for its aromatic oil and chips in the market.
3. Agarwood is listed as 'Endangered' by the IUCN.

How many of the above statements is/are correct?

(a) Only one (b) Only two
(c) All three (d) None

**70.** Which of the following statements best describes 'Eurythermal' organisms?

(a) They are organisms that thrive in a narrow range of temperatures.
(b) They are organisms whose internal temperature varies considerably.
(c) They are organisms that can tolerate and thrive in a wide range of temperatures.
(d) They are organisms that cannot tolerate changes in water salinity.

**71.** Which of the following statements best describes 'Poikilotherms'?

(a) They are organisms whose internal temperature remains constant.
(b) They are adapted to thrive in a wide range of natural terrain.
(c) They are restricted to a narrow range of latitudes.
(d) They are organisms whose internal temperature varies considerably.

**72.** Match the following organisations with their roles in the Global River Cities Alliance (GRCA):

| | Organisations | | Roles |
|---|---|---|---|
| A. | National Mission for Clean Ganga (NMCG) | 1. | Pledged financial and technical support for the GRCA |
| B. | National Institute for Urban Affairs (NIUA) | 2. | Role of the Secretariat for the GRCA |
| C. | World Bank | 3. | Inspired the formation of the GRCA through the establishment of India's River Cities Alliance |

Choose the correct answer from the codes given below:

(a) A-3, B-2, C-1 (b) A-2, B-1, C-3
(c) A-1, B-3, C-2 (d) A-3, B-1, C-2

**73.** With reference to the 'Global River Cities Alliance (GRCA)', consider the following statements:

1. The GRCA was launched at COP28 to foster global collaboration for the advancement of sustainable river management practices in urban settings.
2. The National Mission for Clean Ganga (NMCG) and the Ministry of Jal Shakti will serve as the Secretariat for the GRCA.
3. Multilateral funding agencies, including the World Bank and Asian Development Bank, are providing financial and technical support to the GRCA initiative.

Which of the statements given above are correct?

(a) 1 and 2 only
(b) 2 and 3 only
(c) 1 and 3 only
(d) 1, 2 and 3

# OMR SHEET

**Assessment Round**

| | | | | | | | |
|---|---|---|---|---|---|---|---|
| 1 | ⓐ ⓑ ⓒ ⓓ | 31 | ⓐ ⓑ ⓒ ⓓ | 61 | ⓐ ⓑ ⓒ ⓓ | 91 | ⓐ ⓑ ⓒ ⓓ |
| 2 | ⓐ ⓑ ⓒ ⓓ | 32 | ⓐ ⓑ ⓒ ⓓ | 62 | ⓐ ⓑ ⓒ ⓓ | 92 | ⓐ ⓑ ⓒ ⓓ |
| 3 | ⓐ ⓑ ⓒ ⓓ | 33 | ⓐ ⓑ ⓒ ⓓ | 63 | ⓐ ⓑ ⓒ ⓓ | 93 | ⓐ ⓑ ⓒ ⓓ |
| 4 | ⓐ ⓑ ⓒ ⓓ | 34 | ⓐ ⓑ ⓒ ⓓ | 64 | ⓐ ⓑ ⓒ ⓓ | 94 | ⓐ ⓑ ⓒ ⓓ |
| 5 | ⓐ ⓑ ⓒ ⓓ | 35 | ⓐ ⓑ ⓒ ⓓ | 65 | ⓐ ⓑ ⓒ ⓓ | 95 | ⓐ ⓑ ⓒ ⓓ |
| 6 | ⓐ ⓑ ⓒ ⓓ | 36 | ⓐ ⓑ ⓒ ⓓ | 66 | ⓐ ⓑ ⓒ ⓓ | 96 | ⓐ ⓑ ⓒ ⓓ |
| 7 | ⓐ ⓑ ⓒ ⓓ | 37 | ⓐ ⓑ ⓒ ⓓ | 67 | ⓐ ⓑ ⓒ ⓓ | 97 | ⓐ ⓑ ⓒ ⓓ |
| 8 | ⓐ ⓑ ⓒ ⓓ | 38 | ⓐ ⓑ ⓒ ⓓ | 68 | ⓐ ⓑ ⓒ ⓓ | 98 | ⓐ ⓑ ⓒ ⓓ |
| 9 | ⓐ ⓑ ⓒ ⓓ | 39 | ⓐ ⓑ ⓒ ⓓ | 69 | ⓐ ⓑ ⓒ ⓓ | 99 | ⓐ ⓑ ⓒ ⓓ |
| 10 | ⓐ ⓑ ⓒ ⓓ | 40 | ⓐ ⓑ ⓒ ⓓ | 70 | ⓐ ⓑ ⓒ ⓓ | 100 | ⓐ ⓑ ⓒ ⓓ |
| 11 | ⓐ ⓑ ⓒ ⓓ | 41 | ⓐ ⓑ ⓒ ⓓ | 71 | ⓐ ⓑ ⓒ ⓓ | 101 | ⓐ ⓑ ⓒ ⓓ |
| 12 | ⓐ ⓑ ⓒ ⓓ | 42 | ⓐ ⓑ ⓒ ⓓ | 72 | ⓐ ⓑ ⓒ ⓓ | 102 | ⓐ ⓑ ⓒ ⓓ |
| 13 | ⓐ ⓑ ⓒ ⓓ | 43 | ⓐ ⓑ ⓒ ⓓ | 73 | ⓐ ⓑ ⓒ ⓓ | 103 | ⓐ ⓑ ⓒ ⓓ |
| 14 | ⓐ ⓑ ⓒ ⓓ | 44 | ⓐ ⓑ ⓒ ⓓ | 74 | ⓐ ⓑ ⓒ ⓓ | 104 | ⓐ ⓑ ⓒ ⓓ |
| 15 | ⓐ ⓑ ⓒ ⓓ | 45 | ⓐ ⓑ ⓒ ⓓ | 75 | ⓐ ⓑ ⓒ ⓓ | 105 | ⓐ ⓑ ⓒ ⓓ |
| 16 | ⓐ ⓑ ⓒ ⓓ | 46 | ⓐ ⓑ ⓒ ⓓ | 76 | ⓐ ⓑ ⓒ ⓓ | 106 | ⓐ ⓑ ⓒ ⓓ |
| 17 | ⓐ ⓑ ⓒ ⓓ | 47 | ⓐ ⓑ ⓒ ⓓ | 77 | ⓐ ⓑ ⓒ ⓓ | 107 | ⓐ ⓑ ⓒ ⓓ |
| 18 | ⓐ ⓑ ⓒ ⓓ | 48 | ⓐ ⓑ ⓒ ⓓ | 78 | ⓐ ⓑ ⓒ ⓓ | 108 | ⓐ ⓑ ⓒ ⓓ |
| 19 | ⓐ ⓑ ⓒ ⓓ | 49 | ⓐ ⓑ ⓒ ⓓ | 79 | ⓐ ⓑ ⓒ ⓓ | 109 | ⓐ ⓑ ⓒ ⓓ |
| 20 | ⓐ ⓑ ⓒ ⓓ | 50 | ⓐ ⓑ ⓒ ⓓ | 80 | ⓐ ⓑ ⓒ ⓓ | 110 | ⓐ ⓑ ⓒ ⓓ |
| 21 | ⓐ ⓑ ⓒ ⓓ | 51 | ⓐ ⓑ ⓒ ⓓ | 81 | ⓐ ⓑ ⓒ ⓓ | 111 | ⓐ ⓑ ⓒ ⓓ |
| 22 | ⓐ ⓑ ⓒ ⓓ | 52 | ⓐ ⓑ ⓒ ⓓ | 82 | ⓐ ⓑ ⓒ ⓓ | 112 | ⓐ ⓑ ⓒ ⓓ |
| 23 | ⓐ ⓑ ⓒ ⓓ | 53 | ⓐ ⓑ ⓒ ⓓ | 83 | ⓐ ⓑ ⓒ ⓓ | 113 | ⓐ ⓑ ⓒ ⓓ |
| 24 | ⓐ ⓑ ⓒ ⓓ | 54 | ⓐ ⓑ ⓒ ⓓ | 84 | ⓐ ⓑ ⓒ ⓓ | 114 | ⓐ ⓑ ⓒ ⓓ |
| 25 | ⓐ ⓑ ⓒ ⓓ | 55 | ⓐ ⓑ ⓒ ⓓ | 85 | ⓐ ⓑ ⓒ ⓓ | 115 | ⓐ ⓑ ⓒ ⓓ |
| 26 | ⓐ ⓑ ⓒ ⓓ | 56 | ⓐ ⓑ ⓒ ⓓ | 86 | ⓐ ⓑ ⓒ ⓓ | 116 | ⓐ ⓑ ⓒ ⓓ |
| 27 | ⓐ ⓑ ⓒ ⓓ | 57 | ⓐ ⓑ ⓒ ⓓ | 87 | ⓐ ⓑ ⓒ ⓓ | 117 | ⓐ ⓑ ⓒ ⓓ |
| 28 | ⓐ ⓑ ⓒ ⓓ | 58 | ⓐ ⓑ ⓒ ⓓ | 88 | ⓐ ⓑ ⓒ ⓓ | 118 | ⓐ ⓑ ⓒ ⓓ |
| 29 | ⓐ ⓑ ⓒ ⓓ | 59 | ⓐ ⓑ ⓒ ⓓ | 89 | ⓐ ⓑ ⓒ ⓓ | 119 | ⓐ ⓑ ⓒ ⓓ |
| 30 | ⓐ ⓑ ⓒ ⓓ | 60 | ⓐ ⓑ ⓒ ⓓ | 90 | ⓐ ⓑ ⓒ ⓓ | 120 | ⓐ ⓑ ⓒ ⓓ |

## Calculate Your Score

| | |
|---|---|
| **Correct (✓)** | |
| **Incorrect (✓)** | |
| **Unattempted** | |
| **Total Score** | |
| **Accuracy (%)** | |

## Reasons for Incorrect Answers?

| | |
|---|---|
| 1. Lack of Knowledge/Existing Source Insufficient | |
| 2. Lack of Multiple Revision | |
| 3. Common Sense Mistakes | |

**Note :**

1. Calculate total score as correct answers carry 2 marks each 1/3rd marks will deducted for **Incorrect** Answers.
2. Calculate Accuracy (%) by dividing the number of correct answers to the total number of attempted questions.

## Past Learning

**1.** Consider the following: **(2024)**

1. Carabid beetles 2. Centipedes
3. Flies 4. Termites
5. Wasps

Parasitoid species are found in how many of the above kinds of organisms?

(a) Only two (b) Only three
(c) Only four (d) All five

**2.** Which one of the following is the correct description of '100 Million Farmers'? **(2024)**

(a) It is a platform for accelerating the transition towards food and water systems that are net-zero (carbon), nature-positive and that aims to increase farmer resilience.

(b) It is an international alliance and a network of individuals and farming organisations interested in supporting and strengthening the development of the organic animal husbandry.

(c) It is a digital platform fully integrated with service providers and built on blockchain that lets buyers, sellers, and third parties trade fertilisers quickly and securely.

(d) It is a platform with the mission of encouraging the farmers to form Farmer Product Organisations or Agribusiness Consortiums, thus facilitating the access to global open markets to sell their products.

**3.** Consider the following statements: **(2024)**

**Statement I:** India does not import apples from the United States of America.

**Statement II:** In India, the law prohibits the import of Genetically Modified food without the approval of the competent authority.

Which one of the following is correct in respect of the above statements?

(a) Both Statement I and Statement II are correct and Statement II explains Statement I.

(b) Both Statement I and Statement II are correct, but Statement II does not explain Statement I.

(c) Statement I is correct, but Statement II is incorrect.

(d) Statement I is incorrect, but Statement II is correct.

**4.** The organisms 'Cicada, Froghopper, and Pond skater' are : **(2024)**

(a) Birds (b) Fish
(c) Insects (d) Reptiles

**5.** Consider the following statements: **(2024)**

1. Lions do not have a particular breeding season.
2. Unlike most other big cats, cheetahs do not roar.
3. Unlike male lions, male leopards do not proclaim their territory by scent marking.

Which of the statements given above are correct?

(a) 1 and 2 only (b) 2 and 3 only
(c) 1 and 3 only (d) 1, 2 and 3

**6.** Which one of the following shows a unique relationship with an insect that has coevolved with it and that is the only insect that can pollinate this tree? **(2024)**

(a) Fig (b) Mahua
(c) Sandalwood (d) Silk cotton

**7.** Consider the following: **(2024)**

1. Butterflies 2. Fish
3. Frogs

How many of the above has/have poisonous species among them?

(a) Only one (b) Only two
(c) All three (d) None

**8.** 'Invasive Species Specialist Group' (that develops Global Invasive Species Database) belongs to which one of the following organisations? **(2023)**

(a) The International Union for Conservation of Nature

(b) The United Nations Environment Programme

(c) The United Nations World Commission for Environment and Development

(d) The World Wide Fund for Nature

**9.** Consider the following fauna: **(2023)**

1. Lion-tailed Macaque
2. Malabar Civet
3. Sambar Deer

How many of the above is/are generally nocturnal or most active after sunset?

(a) Only one (b) Only two
(c) All three (d) None

**10.** Which of the following organisms perform a waggle dance for others of their kin to indicate the direction and the distance to a source of their food? **(2023)**

(a) Butterflies (b) Dragonflies
(c) Honey Bees (d) Wasps

**11.** Consider the following statements: **(2023)**

1. Some mushrooms have medicinal properties.
2. Some mushrooms have psychoactive properties.
3. Some mushrooms have insecticidal properties.
4. Some mushrooms have bioluminescent properties.

How many of the above statements is/are correct?

(a) Only one (b) Only two
(c) Only three (d) All four

**12.** Consider the following statements regarding the Indian squirrels: **(2023)**

1. They build nests by making burrows in the ground.
2. They store their food materials like nuts and seeds in the ground.
3. They are omnivorous.

How many of the above statements is/are correct?

(a) Only one (b) Only two
(c) All three (d) None

**13.** Which one of the following makes a tool with a stick to scrape insects from a hole in a tree or a log of wood? **(2023)**

(a) Fishing cat (b) Orangutan
(c) Otter (d) Sloth bear

**14.** Consider the following statements : **(2023)**

1. Some microorganisms can grow in environments with temperature above the boiling point of water.
2. Some microorganisms can grow in environments with temperature below the freezing point of water.
3. Some microorganisms can grow in highly acidic environment with a pH below 3.

How many of the above statements is/are correct?

(a) Only one (b) Only two
(c) All three (d) None

**15.** Consider the following statements: **(2023)**

Once the Central Government notifies an area as a 'Community Reserve' :

1. The Chief Wildlife Warden of the state becomes the governing authority of such forest
2. Hunting is not allowed in such area
3. People of such area are allowed to collect non-timber forest produce
4. People of such area are allowed traditional agricultural practices

How many of the above statements is/are correct?

(a) Only one (b) Only two
(c) Only three (d) All four

**16.** With reference to Gucchi sometimes mentioned in the news, consider the following statements: **(2022)**

1. It is a fungus.
2. It grows in some Himalayan forest areas.
3. It is commercially cultivated in the Himalayan foothills of North-Eastern India.

Which of the statements given above is/are correct?

(a) 1 only (b) 3 only
(c) 1 and 2 only (d) 2 and 3 only

**17.** Certain species of which one of the following organisms are well known as cultivators of fungi? **(2022)**

(a) Ant (b) Cockroach
(c) Crab (d) Spider

**18.** Which of the following is not a bird? **(2022)**
(a) Golden Mahseer
(b) Indian Nightjar
(c) Spoonbill
(d) White Ibis

**19.** Consider the following statements: **(2022)**

**Statement I:** Marsupials are not naturally found in India.

**Statement II:** Marsupials can thrive only in montane grasslands with no predators.

Which one of the following is correct in respect of the above statements?
(a) Both Statement I and Statement II are correct, and Statement II is the correct explanation for Statement I.
(b) Both Statement I and Statement II are correct, and Statement II is not the correct explanation for Statement I.
(c) Statement I is correct, but Statement II is incorrect.
(d) Statement I is incorrect, but Statement II is correct.

**20.** Consider the following animals: **(2021)**
1. Hedgehog
2. Marmot
3. Pangolin

To reduce the chance of being captured by predators, which of the above organisms rolls up/roll up and protects/protect its/their vulnerable parts?
(a) 1 and 2 only (b) 2 only
(c) 3 only (d) 1 and 3 only

**21.** Which one of the following is used in preparing a natural mosquito repellent? **(2021)**
(a) Congress grass (b) Elephant grass
(c) Lemongrass (d) Nutgrass

**22.** Which one of the following is a filter feeder? **(2021)**
(a) Catfish (b) Octopus
(c) Oyster (d) Pelican

**23.** With reference to Indian elephants, consider the following statements : **(2020)**
1. The leader of an elephant group is a female.
2. The maximum gestation period can be 22 months.
3. An elephant can normally go on calving till the age of 40 years only.
4. Among the states in India, the highest elephant population is in Kerala.

Which of the statements given above is/are correct?
(a) 1 and 2 only (b) 2 and 4 only
(c) 3 only (d) 1, 3 and 4 only

**24.** With reference to India's biodiversity, Ceylon frogmouth, Coppersmith barbet, Gray-chinned minivet and White-throated redstart are **(2020)**
(a) Birds (b) Primates
(c) Reptiles (d) Amphibians

**25.** Recently, there was a growing awareness in our country about the importance of Himalayan nettle (Girardinia diversifolia) because it is found to be a sustainable source of **(2019)**
(a) anti-malarial drug
(b) biodiesel
(c) pulp for paper industry
(d) textile fibre

**26.** Consider the following statements: **(2019)**
1. Asiatic lion naturally found in India only
2. Double-humped camel is naturally found in India only
3. One-horned rhinoceros is naturally found in India only

Which one of the statement given above is/are correct?
(a) 1 only (b) 2 only
(c) 1 and 3 only (d) 1, 2 and 3

**27.** Consider the following pairs : **(2019)**

Wildlife: Naturally found in
1. Blue finned mahseer: Cauvery river
2. Irrawaddy dolphin: Chambal river
3. Rusty-spotted cats: Eastern ghats

Which one of the pairs given above are correctly matched?
(a) 1 and 2 only (b) 2 and 3 only
(c) 1 and 3 only (d) 1, 2 and 3

**28.** If you want to see gharials in their natural habitat, which one of the following is the best place to visit? **(2017)**

(a) Bhitarkanika Mangroves
(b) Chambal River
(c) Pulicat Lake
(d) Deepor Beel

**29.** The term M-STRIPES' is sometimes seen in the news in the context of **(2017)**

(a) Captive breeding of Wild Fauna
(b) Maintenance of Tiger Reserves
(c) Indigenous Satellite Navigation System
(d) Security of National Highways

**30.** Due to some reasons, if there is a huge fall in the population of species of butterflies, what could be its likely consequence/consequences? **(2017)**

1. Pollination of some plants could be adversely affected.
2. There could be a drastic increase in the fungal infections of some cultivated plants.
3. It could lead to a fall in the population of some species of wasps, spiders and birds.

Select the correct answer using the codes given below:

(a) 1 only (b) 2 and 3 only
(c) 1 and 3 only (d) 1, 2 and 3

**31.** What is/are unique about 'Kharai camel', a breed found in India? **(2016)**

1. It is capable of swimming up to three kilometers in seawater.
2. It survives by grazing on mangroves.
3. It lives in the wild and cannot be domesticated.

Select the correct answer using the codes given below.

(a) 1 and 2 only
(b) 3 only
(c) 1 and 3 only
(d) 1, 2 and 3

**32.** In which of the following regions of India are you most likely to come across the 'Great Indian Hornbill' in its natural habitat? **(2016)**

(a) Sand deserts of North-West India
(b) Higher Himalayas of Jammu and Kashmir
(c) Salt marshes of Western Gujarat
(d) Western Ghats

**33.** Recently, for the first time in our country, which of the following States has declared a particular butterfly as 'state Butterfly'? **(2016)**

(a) Arunachal Pradesh
(b) Himachal Pradesh
(c) Karnataka
(d) Maharashtra

**34.** With reference to 'Red Sanders', sometimes seen in the news, consider the following statements: **(2016)**

1. It is a tree species found in a part of South India.
2. It is one of the most important trees in the tropical rain forest areas of South India.

Which of the statements given above is/are correct?

(a) 1 only
(b) 2 only
(c) Both 1 and 2
(d) Neither 1 nor 2

**35.** With reference to 'dugong', a mammal found in India, which of the following statements is/are correct? **(2015)**

1. It is a herbivorous marine animal.
2. It is found along the entire coast of India.
3. It is given legal protection under Schedule I of the Wildlife (Protection) Act, 1972.

Select the correct answer using the codes given below.

(a) 1 and 2 only
(b) 2 only
(c) 1 and 3 only
(d) 3 only

**36.** Which one of the following is the national aquatic animal of India? **(2015)**
(a) Saltwater crocodile (b) Olive ridley turtle
(c) Gangetic dolphin (d) Gharial

**37.** Other than poaching, what are the possible reasons for the decline in the population of Ganges River Dolphins? **(2014)**
1. Construction of dams and barrages on rivers
2. Increase in the population of crocodiles in rivers
3. Getting trapped in fishing nets accidentally
4. Use of synthetic fertilisers and other agricultural chemicals in crop fields in the vicinity of rivers.

Select the correct answer using the codes given below.
(a) 1 and 2 only (b) 2 and 3 only
(c) 1, 3 and 4 only (d) 1, 2, 3 and 4

**38.** If you walk through countryside, you are likely to see some birds stalking alongside the cattle to seise the insects disturbed by their movement through grasses. **(2014)**

Which of the following is/are such bird/birds?
1. Painted Stork
2. Common Myna
3. Black-necked Crane

Select the correct answer using the codes given below.
(a) 1 and 2 only (b) 2 only
(c) 2 and 3 only (d) 3 only

**39.** With reference to Neem tree, consider the following statements: **(2014)**
1. Neem oil can be used as a pesticide to control the proliferation of some species of insects and mites.
2. Neem seeds are used in the manufacture of biofuels and hospital detergents.
3. Neem oil has applications in pharmaceutical industry.

Which of the statements given above is/are correct?
(a) 1 and 2 only (b) 3 only
(c) 1 and 3 only (d) 1, 2 and 3

**40.** In which of the following States is lion-tailed macaque found in its natural habitat? **(2013)**
1. Tamil Nadu
2. Kerala
3. Karnataka
4. Andhra Pradesh

Select the correct answer using the codes given below.
(a) 1, 2 and 3 only
(b) 2 only
(c) 1, 3 and 4 only
(d) 1, 2, 3 and 4

**41.** Consider the following: **(2013)**
1. Star tortoise
2. Monitor lizard
3. Pygmy hog
4. Spider monkey

Which of the above are naturally found in India?
(a) 1, 2 and 3 only
(b) 2 and 3 only
(c) 1 and 4 only
(d) 1, 2, 3 and 4

**42.** Consider the following fauna of India: **(2013)**
1. Gharial
2. Leatherback turtle
3. Swamp deer

Which of the above is/are endangered?
(a) 1 and 2 only
(b) 3 only
(c) 1, 2 and 3
(d) None

**43.** Vultures which used to be very common in Indian countryside some years ago are rarely seen nowadays. This is attributed to **(2012)**
(a) The destruction of their nesting sites by new invasive species
(b) A drug used by cattle owners for treating their diseased cattle
(c) Scarcity of food available to them
(d) A widespread, persistent, and fatal disease among them

# Detailed Solutions

## Assessment Round

1. *(d)* Neither 1 nor 2
   - **Statement 1 is correct: Species richness** refers to the total number of different species present in a particular area or ecosystem. It is a simple count of species and an important component of biodiversity measurement.
   - **Statement 2 is correct: Beta diversity** measures the diversity between different ecosystems within a region. It helps assess the change in species composition from one ecosystem to another.

   **Thus, option (d) is the correct answer.**

2. *(b)* Species diversity includes the variety of living organisms, while genetic diversity is about variations within a species.
   - **Species diversity** refers to the variety of **different species** within an ecosystem, encompassing all types of plants, animals, fungi, bacteria, etc. It measures **how many species are present** and **how evenly distributed** they are. On the other hand, **genetic diversity** refers to the variation of genes within a particular species, which ensures adaptability and resilience to environmental changes. Genetic diversity allows populations to adapt and survive in changing environments.
   - **Species diversity** is relevant in all types of ecosystems, not just aquatic ones. It can be found in **terrestrial, marine, freshwater**, and other ecosystems. It is crucial for the **stability, productivity,** and **resilience** of all ecosystems, whether they are forest ecosystems, grasslands, or aquatic environments.

   **Thus, option (b) is the correct answer.**

3. *(c)* All three pairs
   - **Pair 1 is correctly matched: Alpha diversity** refers to the **diversity within a specific habitat or local area.** It measures the **number of species** or taxa present within a single ecosystem. It provides insights into the **species richness** (the number of species) and **evenness** (how evenly individuals are distributed among the species) within a single habitat.
   - **Pair 2 is correctly matched: Beta diversity** represents the **change in species composition** or **turnover** between different habitats or sites within a region. It measures the **variation in species composition** among multiple locations and helps identify **unique species assemblages. Beta diversity** helps to compare how different two habitats are in terms of their species content.
   - **Statement 3 is correctly matched: Gamma diversity** refers to the **overall diversity at a regional or landscape scale.** It measures the **total number of species** across multiple habitats or sites within a larger geographic area. **Gamma diversity** provides a comprehensive view of the **total species pool** and reflects the **cumulative diversity** of all the habitats within a given region.

   **Thus, option (c) is the correct answer.**

4. *(d)* Neither 1 nor 2
   - **Statement 1 is correct:** Biodiversity is **generally greater in tropical regions near the equator (lower latitudes)** than in temperate and polar regions (higher latitudes). This is due to the stable climate, higher temperature and greater primary productivity in the tropics, which support a wide variety of species.
   - **Statement 2 is correct:** As elevation increases along mountain slopes, environmental conditions become harsher (colder temperatures, reduced oxygen levels, and limited vegetation). As a result, **species diversity tends to decrease at higher altitudes.** The lower altitudes, with more moderate temperatures and richer vegetation, support greater biodiversity.

   **Thus, option (d) is the correct answer.**

5. *(b)* 2 only
   - **Statement 1 is incorrect: Species diversity** is typically **highest near the equator** and

decreases as one moves toward the poles. This pattern is known as the **latitudinal diversity gradient**. Tropical regions, close to the equator, provide favourable conditions such as stable temperatures, abundant rainfall and diverse habitats, which support a higher number of species.

- **Statement 2 is correct: Tropical regions** are renowned for their **exceptionally high biodiversity**. Factors contributing to this include
  - **Climate Stability:** Consistently warm temperatures and high rainfall support diverse ecosystems,
  - **Habitat Diversity:** From rainforests to coral reefs, the variety of habitats in the tropics provides niches for numerous species,
  - Evolutionary Processes: High rates of speciation and endemism are common in tropical areas.
- **Statement 3 is incorrect: Colombia** is one of the **world's most biodiverse countries,** especially renowned for its **avian diversity**. It boasts over **1,900 bird species,** making it one of the top countries globally for bird diversity. **Greenland,** on the other hand, has a much colder climate and limited habitats, supporting only **a small number of bird species** (approximately 100-150 species).

**Thus, option (b) is the correct answer.**

**6.** *(c)* 1, 3 and 4 only

- **Biodiversity hotspots** are identified based on species richness, high endemism (species found nowhere else), and threat perception (areas under significant threat from human activities or habitat loss). These are critical factors for designating a region as a hotspot. **Species richness** is one of the key criteria for identifying biodiversity hotspots. Regions with a large number of species are prioritised for conservation.
- **The presence of invasive species is not a criterion** used to define biodiversity hotspots. Instead, hotspots focus on native biodiversity and the threat to these species.
- **High endemism** is a critical factor, as hotspots are characterised by a significant number of species that are found only in that particular region. **Threat perception** (i.e., high levels of habitat loss and other threats) is also an important factor.

**Thus, option (c) is the correct answer.**

**7.** *(c)* 2 and 3 only

- **Statement 1 is correct:** The Himalaya biodiversity hotspot includes the **Indian Himalayan region,** extending to parts of **Pakistan and China.**
- **Statement 2 is incorrect:** The Indo-Burma hotspot includes parts of North-Eastern India but does not include **Assam or the Andaman Islands.**
- **Statement 3 is incorrect:** The Sundaland hotspot includes the Nicobar Islands, but it is distinct from **South-East Asia,** which is not entirely part of this hotspot.
- **Statement 4 is correct:** The Western Ghats and Sri Lanka form a continuous hotspot, covering both the **Western Ghats and Sri Lanka.**

**Thus, option (c) is the correct answer.**

**8.** *(a)* 1 only

- **Statement 1 is correct:** To qualify as a **biodiversity hotspot,** a region must have **at least 1,500 endemic vascular plant species.** This high level of endemism indicates a rich and unique biodiversity that is a key criterion for hotspot designation. Key hotspots in India include the **Western Ghats, Eastern Himalayas, Indo-Burma** and **Sundaland.**
- **Statement 2 is incorrect:** The actual criterion for a biodiversity hotspot requires that a region has lost **at least 70% of its original natural vegetation,** meaning **no more than** 30% of its original habitat remains.

**Thus, option (a) is the correct answer.**

**9.** *(d)* Both 1 and 2

- **Statement 1 is incorrect:** Biodiversity hotspots are not limited to tropical regions. While many of them are located in tropical areas, such as the **Amazon** and the **Western Ghats,** they are also found in temperate regions. For example, the **Mediterranean basin** and parts of **New Zealand, Polynesia and Micronesian** are biodiversity hotspots located in temperate regions.

- **Statement 2 is incorrect:** India has four **recognised biodiversity hotspots,** but the list does not include the **Western Himalayas** or the **Andaman and Nicobar Islands.** The four biodiversity hotspots in India are the Himalayas, Western Ghats, Indo-Burma (which includes parts of North-East India and Myanmar), and Sundaland (which includes the Andaman and Nicobar Islands as part of a broader region).

**Thus, option (d) is the correct answer.**

***10.*** *(b)* Only two

- **Statement 1 is correct:** Insects are the most species-rich group among animals, with over one **million identified species,** which accounts for more than half of all known animal species. This makes insects the most diverse group, contributing significantly to overall animal biodiversity. Examples include **beetles, butterflies, ants** and many others.
- **Statement 2 is incorrect: Fungi** are not classified as **plants.** Fungi belong to a separate kingdom called **Fungi.** The group with the highest biodiversity among plants is typically considered to be the **flowering plants** (angiosperms), which have the greatest number of species.
- **Statement 3 is correct:** Fish are the most species-rich group among vertebrates. There are over **33,000 species** of fish, making them the most diverse group of vertebrates. They are found in a wide range of habitats, including freshwater and marine ecosystems, which contributes to their high diversity.

**Thus, option (b) is the correct answer.**

***11.*** *(c)* 1, 2, 3 and 4

The **Evil Quartet** refers to the major causes of species extinction, which include

- **Habitat loss and fragmentation:** Destruction of natural habitats leads to loss of biodiversity.
- **Over-exploitation:** Excessive hunting, fishing, or harvesting reduces species populations.
- **Alien species invasions:** Invasive species outcompete native species, leading to declines in biodiversity.
- **Co-extinctions:** When one species goes extinct, it can lead to the extinction of species that depend on it.

**Thus, option (c) is the correct answer.**

***12.*** *(a)* Species that are confined to a specific geographic area for their distribution.

An **endemic species is native to and restricted within a particular geographic region.** This means that the species naturally occurs only in that specific area and nowhere else in the world. Endemism can result from various factors such as geographical isolation (e.g., islands), unique environmental conditions, or evolutionary history that prevent the species from spreading to other regions.

**Thus, option (a) is the correct answer.**

***13.*** *(a)* Allen's rule suggests that mammals in colder climates have longer ears and limbs to retain heat.

- **Allen's rule** states that endothermic animals (like mammals) in colder climates tend to have **shorter ears and limbs.** Shorter appendages minimise surface area relative to body volume, reducing heat loss and helping the animal retain heat. **Allen's Rule** is associated with the **body surface area** of mammals in different environments.
- **Bergmann's rule** posits that **larger-bodied organisms are typically found in higher latitudes** (colder climates) because a larger body size reduces the surface area-to-volume ratio, thereby conserving heat more effectively.

**Thus, option (a) is the correct answer.**

***14.*** *(b)* Botanical Garden

- **In-situ conservation** refers to the **conservation of species in their natural habitat.** It involves protecting and preserving species in the ecosystems where they naturally occur. It includes National Parks, Wildlife Sanctuaries, Biosphere Reserve, Marine Protected Areas and Sacred Groves.
- **Ex-situ conservation,** on the other hand, involves **protecting species by removing part of the population from a threatened habitat** and placing them in a controlled environment, such as zoos, botanical gardens, or seed banks.

**Thus, option (b) is the correct answer.**

**15.** *(d)* It involves the collection and maintenance of species outside their natural habitats under human care.

**Ex-situ conservation** refers to the practice of **conserving species** by removing them from their natural habitat and maintaining them in **artificial environments** such as zoos, botanical gardens, or seed banks. This method is often used when the species is endangered and cannot survive in its natural habitat due to threats like habitat destruction or overexploitation.

**Thus, option (d) is the correct answer.**

**16.** *(d)* 1, 2 and 3

- **Deforestation** is a major threat to Biosphere Reserves in India. **Habitat destruction,** driven by activities such as agriculture, logging, and infrastructure development, leads to the loss of biodiversity and ecosystem degradation, posing a significant threat to these protected areas.
- **Invasive species** can disrupt ecosystems by outcompeting native species, altering habitats, and causing ecological imbalances. Many Biosphere Reserves in India face challenges from invasive plant and animal species that threaten the survival of native flora and fauna.
- **Climate change** is another significant threat to Biosphere Reserves. Changes in temperature, rainfall patterns and the frequency of extreme weather events affect ecosystems and biodiversity, leading to habitat loss, altered species distributions, and increased vulnerability for species already under threat.

**Thus, option (d) is the correct answer.**

**17.** *(a)* 1, 2 and 3 only

- **Coral reefs** are underwater ecosystems formed by the accumulation of **calcium carbonate skeletons** secreted by coral polyps. They thrive in warm, shallow, tropical waters and provide habitat for a diverse range of marine species.
- **Andaman and Nicobar Islands:** These islands host extensive **fringing coral reefs** due to their **warm tropical waters** and low human disturbance, creating ideal conditions for coral growth.
- **Gulf of Kutch, Gujarat:** This area known for its coral reefs, especially around the **Marine National Park,** despite **harsh environmental conditions** like high salinity and turbidity.
- **Gulf of Mannar:** This area is rich in coral reefs and is recognised as a **marine biosphere reserve,** located between **India** and **Sri Lanka.**
- **Sundarbans:** Due to its **brackish waters** and high sedimentation, this **mangrove region** does not support coral reefs, as the conditions are unsuitable for coral growth.

**Thus, option (a) is the correct answer.**

**18.** *(b)* Only two

- **Statement 1 is correct:** The **Brahmaputra valley** in Assam has been highlighted as a major hotspot for soil erosion in India. This region is highly susceptible to erosion due to heavy rainfall, steep slopes, and human activities, making it one of the areas with the most significant soil loss in the country.
- **Statement 2 is incorrect: Soil organic carbon** (SOC) content in Indian soils has **declined** over the past 70 years, primarily due to overuse of chemical fertilisers, intensive agriculture, and lack of organic inputs. The SOC content has decreased from about **1% to 0.3%.** This reduction in
- **Statement 3 is incorrect:** The **Soil Health Card Scheme** is an initiative aimed at promoting the balanced use of fertilisers by providing farmers with information on the nutrient status of their soil. However, it **does not specifically promote organic farming** or aim to reduce reliance on chemical fertilisers entirely. Instead, it focuses on optimal nutrient management based on soil testing to ensure balanced fertiliser use. SOC affects soil fertility and water retention capacity.
- **Statement 4 is correct: Biochar application** and **regenerative agricultural practices** are indeed recommended for improving soil health and preventing soil erosion. Biochar helps retain nutrients and moisture, while regenerative agriculture practices such as no-till farming, cover cropping, and composting enhance soil structure and reduce erosion.

**Thus, option (b) is the correct answer.**

**19.** *(c)* All three pairs

- **Pair 1 is correctly matched:** Alien species are those introduced outside their natural range. This can include any reproductive part like seeds or gametes, which may grow or spread in a new habitat.
- **Pair 2 is correctly matched:** Invasive alien species are a subset of alien species that pose a threat to local biodiversity by outcompeting, predating, or otherwise harming native species.
- **Pair 3 is correctly matched:** Naturalised species are alien species that establish self-replicating populations in a new area and can persist without ongoing human intervention.

**Thus, option (c) is the correct answer.**

**20.** *(c)* It depletes oxygen levels in water, blocks sunlight, and makes waterbodies unsuitable for commercial fisheries and other activities.

- Water hyacinth, though aesthetically pleasing, is an **invasive aquatic weed** that spreads quickly and negatively impacts **freshwater ecosystems.** It blocks sunlight and reduces oxygen levels in the water, creating unsuitable conditions for commercial fisheries, transportation, and recreational activities. Despite some beneficial uses, like phytoremediation, it generally poses serious challenges to waterbody health and ecosystem balance.

**Thus, option (c) is the correct answer.**

**21.** *(d)* 1, 2 and 3

- **Pair 1 is correct: The Himalayan foothills,** also known as the Shivalik, are characterised by **deciduous forests.** These forests consist of trees like **sal (Shorea robusta), chestnut, maple, etc** and various other species typical of deciduous vegetation, which shed their leaves during specific seasons.
- **Pair 2 is correct:** The **Western Himalayas** are characterised by **coniferous forests** at mid to higher elevations, with species such as **pine, deodar and spruce.** At higher altitudes, there are also **alpine meadows,** which are areas of grassland found above the tree line.
- **Pair 3 is correct:** The **Eastern Himalayas** are known for their **rich biodiversity** due to higher rainfall, and they are dominated by **rhododendron forests** and various species of **bamboo.** These plants thrive in the humid conditions of the Eastern Himalayas.

**Thus, option (d) is the correct answer.**

**22.** *(d)* 1 and 3 only

- **Statement 1 is incorrect:** The **Western Himalayas** do not experience **heavy rainfall,** instead, they receive relatively **low precipitation,** especially in comparison to the Eastern Himalayas. The Western Himalayas are influenced by the **Western Disturbances** during the winter, leading to snowfall rather than heavy rainfall. The climatic conditions are **temperate to cold,** but the rainfall is not significant.
- **Statement 2 is correct:** The **Eastern Himalayas** are known for their **heavy rainfall,** particularly at **lower altitudes.** This is due to their proximity to the **Bay of Bengal,** which brings **moist monsoon** winds that lead to significant rainfall in the region. This makes the Eastern Himalayas much wetter than the Western Himalayas.
- **Statement 3 is incorrect:** While it is true that **snowfall** occurs at **high altitudes** in the **Eastern Himalayas,** it is not limited to very high altitudes. Snow can occur at varying elevations, especially during the colder months, depending on local topography and weather patterns.

**Thus, option (d) is the correct answer.**

**23.** *(b)* 2 and 3 only

- **Statement 1 is incorrect:** While it is true that the **Indian Tiger** is the **National Animal of India,** it is **not primarily found in high mountain habitats.** The **Royal Bengal Tiger** inhabits a wide range of habitats including tropical and subtropical forests, grasslands, mangroves, and even swampy areas. It is more commonly found in regions like **Ranthambore, Sundarbans,** and other lowland areas, not in **high mountain habitats.**
- **Statement 2 is correct:** The **Indian Tiger** is indeed considered a **keystone species.** Its presence helps maintain the ecological balance by regulating the populations of prey

species, thereby ensuring the health of the entire ecosystem. The tiger's role in the food chain makes it crucial for ecosystem stability.

- **Statement 3 is correct:** The **stripe patterns** of tigers are unique to each individual, much like human fingerprints. This unique pattern allows researchers and wildlife officials to identify and track individual tigers for conservation purposes.

**Thus, option (b) is the correct answer.**

***24.*** *(a)* Both A and R are correct, and R is the correct explanation for A.

- **Statement 1 is correct:** The **Sundarbans Tiger Reserve** is known for its tigers exhibiting unique **aquatic hunting techniques.** The tigers here are often observed **swimming** in the tidal channels of the **mangrove forests,** which is a behaviour rarely seen in tigers from other habitats. Their ability to hunt in water sets them apart from other tiger populations.
- **Statement 2 is correct:** The **mangrove habitat** of the Sundarbans consists of numerous **islands** and **water channels.** The tigers have adapted to this environment by developing a **semi-aquatic lifestyle,** enabling them to **swim long distances** between islands. This adaptation has made them proficient at navigating and hunting in water, which is a survival strategy unique to this ecosystem.

**Thus, option (a) is the correct answer.**

***25.*** *(a)* Keystone species

**A keystone species** is a species that has a disproportionately large effect on its environment relative to its abundance. These species play a critical role in maintaining the structure of an ecological community, influencing which other species can survive and thrive. For example, a predator that controls the population of herbivores, preventing overgrazing and preserving the ecosystem's balance, would be considered a keystone species. The removal of a keystone species can lead to significant changes in the community structure, often resulting in a loss of biodiversity.

**Thus, option (a) is the correct answer.**

***26.*** *(c)* 1, 3 and 5

- Biodiversity hotspots are regions that are extremely rich in species and exhibit high levels of **endemism** (species that are found only in a particular region and nowhere else). However, they are also under significant threat, primarily from human activities.
- **Correct Criteria: Species richness** refers to the high diversity of species found in an area. Biodiversity hotspots like the **Western Ghats-Sri Lanka** and **Indo-Burma** regions are recognised for having a high number of different species, contributing to their designation as hotspots.
- **Endemism** is a key criterion for recognising biodiversity hotspots. The **Western Ghats-Sri Lanka** and **Indo-Burma** regions have many species that are found nowhere else in the world, making them areas of significant conservation importance.
- A key criterion for identifying biodiversity hotspots is that they face significant threats from human activities, such as deforestation, habitat destruction, and climate change. The **Western Ghats-Sri Lanka** and **Indo-Burma** regions face high levels of threat, contributing to their recognition as biodiversity hotspots.

**Thus, option (c) is the correct answer.**

***27.*** *(d)* 1, 2, 3 and 4

- **Myristica swamps** are rare freshwater swamp forests primarily found in the **Western Ghats.** They are important for water retention and biodiversity, especially due to the unique species of **Myristica trees** that thrive in waterlogged conditions.
- **Oxbow lakes** are formed by the meandering of rivers and are commonly found in the **Gangetic plains** and other river systems in India. They provide important wetland habitats for aquatic species and play a role in flood regulation.
- **Salt marshes Coastal** wetlands, like the **salt marshes** found in areas such as the **Rann of Kutch** and **Sundarbans,** are important for providing habitats for a wide range of species and their role in coastal protection and carbon sequestration.

- **Coral reefs** Although coral reefs are marine ecosystems, they are included under the **Ramsar Convention** definition of wetlands. Coral reefs in India, such as those in the **Gulf of Mannar, Lakshadweep** and the **Andaman and Nicobar Islands,** play a crucial role in marine biodiversity conservation, and coastal protection.

**Thus, option (d) is the correct answer.**

***28.*** *(b)* Only two

- **Statement 1 is correct: Amur Falcons** breed in the forests of **South-East Russia** and **Northern China** before embarking on their long migration journey. These regions are their primary breeding grounds.
- **Statement 2 is correct:** Amur Falcons undertake one of the longest migration journeys of any bird, travelling from their breeding grounds to **Southern Africa** *via* **India,** covering around **22,000 kilometers** annually.
- **Statement 3 is incorrect:** Amur Falcons are not classified as **Critically Endangered.** They are listed as **Least Concern (LC)** by the IUCN due to their large range and stable population, although they do face threats during migration, especially from hunting.

**Thus, option (b) is the correct answer.**

***29.*** *(b)* A region must have at least 1,500 endemic species of vascular plants and retain 30% or less of its original natural vegetation.

- The concept of a **Biodiversity Hotspot** was introduced by **Norman Myers** to identify regions that are both biologically rich and under severe threat. A region qualifies as a **Biodiversity Hotspot** based on two specific criteria:
- The region must contain at least **1,500 species of vascular plants** that are **endemic,** meaning they are not found anywhere else in the world. This highlights the importance of the region in conserving unique plant species.
- The region must have experienced significant habitat loss, retaining **30% or less of its original natural vegetation.** This indicates that the region is under threat and requires urgent conservation efforts to protect the remaining biodiversity.

**Thus, option (b) is the correct answer.**

***30.*** *(b)* Only two

- **Statement 1 is correct:** India is home to **4 of the 36** globally recognised biodiversity hotspots: the **Himalayas, the Western Ghats, Indo-Burma,** and **Sundaland** (which **includes the Nicobar Islands).**
- **Statement 2 is incorrect:** India ranks **high in reptile endemism,** but **not specifically** fifth in the world.
- **Statement 3 is correct:** India is **recognised as one of the eight Vavilovian centers of origin and diversity of crop plants.** These centers are important as they are the origin points for many of the world's major crop species.

**Thus, option (b) is the correct answer.**

***31.*** *(a)* 1, 2 and 3 only

- **Statement 1 is correct: Global warming** is a significant threat to biodiversity. **Global warming** leads to climate change, which can alter habitats, shift climate zones, and increase the frequency of extreme weather events. Species that cannot adapt quickly to these changes may face extinction.
- **Statement 2 is correct: Habitat fragmentation** occurs when large habitats are divided into smaller, isolated sections due to human activities like deforestation, urbanisation, and the construction of roads. This fragmentation limits the movement of species, reduces genetic diversity, and makes populations more vulnerable to external threats.
- **Statement 3 is correct: Invasive alien species** are non-native organisms introduced to an ecosystem, either intentionally or accidentally. They can outcompete native species for resources, introduce new diseases, and disrupt existing food chains, leading to a decline in native biodiversity.
- **Statement 4 is incorrect:** Promoting vegetarianism is generally **not a threat to biodiversity.** It can have a positive impact. Vegetarian diets typically require fewer resources and less land compared to meat-based diets. Reducing meat consumption can lead to decreased deforestation and habitat destruction caused by livestock farming.

**Thus, option (a) is the correct answer.**

**32.** *(b)* It is an environmental policy where the producer's responsibility extends to the post-consumer stage of a product's life cycle.

**Extended Producer Responsibility** (EPR) is an environmental policy approach where a producer's responsibility for a product is extended beyond the production and sale stages to include the post-consumer phase, meaning the producer is responsible for managing the product's disposal, recycling, or reuse. This policy encourages producers to take environmental responsibility for the entire lifecycle of their products, reducing waste and promoting sustainable practices.

**Thus, option (b) is the correct answer.**

**33.** *(a)* Protecting 30% of the world's land and sea areas through the establishment of protected areas and other conservation measures.

- The **30×30 Target** is a significant global biodiversity conservation goal that aims to protect 30% of the Earth's land and sea areas by the year 2030. This protection is to be achieved through the establishment of **Protected Areas** (PAs) and other **Area-Based Conservation Measures** (OECMs). Additionally, the target includes a related commitment to **restore** at least 30% of degraded land or marine ecosystems by 2030.
- **Protected Areas (PAs):** These are regions designated for the conservation of nature, biodiversity, and ecosystem services. **Other Area-Based Conservation Measures (OECMs):** These include areas that are not officially designated as PAs but still contribute significantly to biodiversity conservation.
- **Restoration Activities:** The target also emphasises starting restoration efforts on degraded lands and marine ecosystems to enhance biodiversity and ecosystem health.

**Thus, option (a) is the correct answer.**

**34.** *(a)* Only one

- **Statement 1 is incorrect:** While both **biodiversity credits** and carbon offsets involve financing environmental projects, **biodiversity credits differ significantly** from carbon offsets. Biodiversity credits focus on **nature-positive actions** and long-term conservation, rather than merely compensating for specific environmental damages.
- **Statement 2 is correct:** This statement correctly captures the essence of biodiversity credits. They aim to **fund ongoing conservation and restoration efforts,** contributing positively to biodiversity rather than just offsetting negative impacts. This represents a **higher-order contribution** compared to traditional offset mechanisms.
- **Statement 3 is incorrect:** This statement **misrepresents the key difference** between biodiversity credits and biodiversity offsets. In reality, **biodiversity offsets** are typically **location-specific,** requiring that conservation efforts occur in the same area as the environmental damage. In contrast, **biodiversity credits** offer more flexibility, allowing companies to support conservation projects **regardless of their location,** thereby promoting broader environmental benefits.

**Thus, option (a) is the correct answer.**

**35.** *(b)* Small crustaceans found in all the world's oceans, feeding on phytoplankton and zooplankton and serving as a main food source for many larger animals.

- **Krill** are small crustaceans that inhabit all the world's oceans. They play a crucial role in marine ecosystems by feeding on **phytoplankton and zooplankton,** which are primary producers in the aquatic food web. Due to their abundance and high biomass, especially in the Southern Ocean where the **Antarctic krill species** is one of the animals with the largest total biomass, krill serve as a vital food source for a variety of larger marine animals, including **baleen whales, seals, penguins, and fish.**

**Key Characteristics of Krill**

| Size and Habitat | Diet |
|---|---|
| **Small Crustaceans:** Typically ranging from 1 to 6 centimeters in length.<br>**Global Distribution:** Found in all major oceans, with significant populations in the Antarctic region. | **Phytoplankton and Zooplankton:** Krill primarily consume these microscopic organisms, converting them into a form that larger predators can utilise. |

| Ecological Role | Behaviour |
|---|---|
| **Main Prey for Larger Animals:** Their role as a foundational species makes them essential for the survival of numerous marine predators.<br>**Biomass:** In the Southern Ocean, Antarctic krill constitute one of the largest biomass groups, underscoring their importance in that ecosystem. | **Vertical Migration:** Krill exhibit vertical migration patterns, ascending to the ocean surface at night to feed and descending to deeper waters during the day to avoid predators. |

**Thus, option (b) is the correct answer.**

***36.*** *(b)* 2 only

- **Statement 1 is incorrect:** The **'Red Data Books'** primarily focus on threatened species rather than specifically listing **endemic species** in biodiversity hotspots. While some endemic species may be included if they are threatened, the primary criterion for inclusion is the **conservation status** (e.g., Vulnerable, Endangered, Critically Endangered) rather than endemism alone.
- **Statement 2 is correct:** The **'Red Data Books'** are comprehensive inventories that **list plant and animal species** assessed as **threatened** with extinction. These assessments are based on criteria such as population size, rate of decline, and geographic distribution. **'Red Data Books'** published by the **International Union for Conservation of Nature and Natural Resources (IUCN).**
- **Statement 3 is incorrect:** While the IUCN does play a role in identifying and designating protected areas through initiatives like the **World Database on Protected Areas** (WDPA), the 'Red Data Books' themselves do not list protected sites. Instead, they focus on the status of species. Information about protected areas is maintained separately from the **'Red Data Books'**.

**Thus, option (b) is the correct answer.**

***37.*** *(a)* 1 and 2 only

- **Statement 1 is correct: TRAFFIC** was indeed **founded in 1976** as a joint initiative of the **World Wildlife Fund (WWF)** and the **International Union for Conservation of Nature (IUCN)** to monitor and report on wildlife trade and promote sustainable trade practices.
- **Statement 2 is correct: TRAFFIC** monitors illegal wildlife trade, provides analysis and recommendations for improving trade regulation, and promotes **sustainable trade practices** to protect endangered species.
- **Statement 3 is incorrect:** While **TRAFFIC** works closely with WWF and IUCN, it functions as an **independent organisation.** It is **not under the direct control** of WWF, though it collaborates with WWF on many projects.

**Thus, option (a) is the correct answer.**

***38.*** *(b)* 1 and 3 only

- **Statement 1 is incorrect:** According to the **IUCN Red List of Threatened Species,** the **Bengal florican** is currently classified as **Critically Endangered.** The classification is based on factors such as population size, rate of decline, and geographic range. While the species faces significant threats from habitat loss and degradation.
- **Statement 2 is incorrect:** The **Bengal florican** has a **limited and patchy distribution** across South Asia. Its primary habitats are found in the grasslands of Northern India, Nepal, and parts of Pakistan. While it does occur in **Bangladesh,** its presence there is not extensive enough to be considered a **wide distribution.**
- **Statement 3 is correct:** The **Bengal florican** relies on **unexploited tall** grasslands with sparse tree cover for breeding and foraging. Its presence indicates the **health and quality of grassland ecosystems.** A thriving Bengal florican population suggests that the grasslands are well-managed, with minimal disturbances and sufficient habitat heterogeneity to support its ecological needs.

**Thus, option (b) is the correct answer.**

***39.*** *(a)* 1 and 2 only

- **Statement 1 is correct:** The **Pygmy Hog** holds the distinction of being the **smallest wild pig** globally. Adult pygmy hogs typically weigh around **8 kilograms,** making them significantly smaller than other wild pig species.
- **Statement 2 is correct:** The **Pygmy Hog** primarily inhabits **tall grasslands** and **semi-evergreen grasslands** in regions like the **Southern Himalayan foothills** and parts of **Assam.** As an **indicator species,** the presence and health of pygmy hog populations reflect the **quality and management status** of these grassland ecosystems.
- **Statement 3 is incorrect:** The **current distribution** of the **Pygmy Hog** is **highly restricted.** They are primarily found in specific **protected areas** such as **Manas National Park, Dibru-Saikhowa National Park,** and a few other localised regions in **Assam,** India. Their habitat is limited to these **small, fragmented grassland pockets,** making their presence confined rather than widespread across multiple regions.

**Thus, option (a) is the correct answer.**

***40.*** *(a)* Only one

- **Statement 1 is correct: Hierarchy of Protected Areas:** In India, the classification and protection levels of forest areas follow a hierarchical structure. **Reserved forests** are areas with stringent protection where activities like logging, hunting, and grazing are heavily regulated or prohibited. They can be upgraded to **Wildlife Sanctuaries,** which offer a higher level of protection, primarily focusing on conserving wildlife and their habitats. Further upgrading can lead to the designation of **National Parks,** which provide the highest level of protection, strictly prohibiting all forms of exploitation and ensuring the conservation of biodiversity.
- **Statement 2 is incorrect:** These areas are designated under the **Indian Forest Act, of 1927,** and while they receive more protection than unprotected areas, they are **less restrictive** than **Reserved Forests or Wildlife Sanctuaries.** In Protected Forests, certain activities like **controlled grazing, agricultural practices,** and **limited hunting** may be **allowed under specific regulations.** The prohibition is not absolute, and these areas often serve as buffer zones around more strictly protected regions.
- **Statement 3 is incorrect:** Both **Reserved Forests** and **Protected Forests** in India are **declared by the State Governments** under the **Indian Forest Act, of 1927.** While the **Central Government** oversees national forest policies and provides guidelines, the **actual designation and management** of these forests are **primarily the responsibility of the respective State Governments.**

**Thus, option (a) is the correct answer.**

***41.*** *(a)* 1, 2 and 4 only

- **Statement 1 is correct: Project Tiger** was indeed **launched in 1973** with the primary objective of **conserving the Bengal tiger** and ensuring a **viable population** across various habitats in India. This initiative marked India's commitment to preserving its iconic and endangered species.
- **Statement 2 is correct:** The **National Tiger Conservation Authority (NTCA)** was established in **2005** under the **Wildlife (Protection) Act of 1972.** It serves as the **executive body** responsible for the **implementation of Project Tiger, approving conservation plans,** and ensuring that tiger reserves adhere to the prescribed conservation measures. The NTCA plays a pivotal role in the strategic planning and execution of tiger conservation efforts across India.
- **Statement 3 is incorrect: Project Tiger** does not provide **uniform financial assistance** to all states. Instead, **funding allocations** are **based on specific criteria,** including the **size of the tiger reserve, level of threat, habitat requirements** and **conservation needs** of each region. This targeted approach ensures that resources are allocated efficiently to areas with the **highest conservation priorities.**
- **Statement 4 is correct:** Recognising the **interconnectedness** of tiger and elephant conservation, the **Ministry of Environment, Forest and Climate Change** established the **'Project Tiger and Elephant Division'.** This **integrated approach** facilitates **coordinated**

conservation efforts for both species, addressing common challenges such as **habitat fragmentation**, **human-wildlife conflict** and **poaching**. By merging the administrative frameworks of Project Tiger and Project Elephant, the division aims to **enhance the effectiveness of** conservation strategies.

**Thus, option (a) is the correct answer.**

**42.** *(a)* 1 and 2 only

- **Statement 1 is correct:** The Convention on the Conservation of Migratory Species of Wild Animals (CMS), also known as the Bonn Convention, is an international treaty under the United Nations Environment Programme (UNEP). CMS aims to provide a global platform for the conservation and sustainable use of migratory animals and their habitats. It focuses on species that migrate across international borders, promoting cooperation among nations to ensure the conservation of migratory species throughout their migratory range.
- **Statement 2 is correct:** The Great Indian bustard, mainland Asian elephant, and Bengal florican are indeed migratory species from India listed in the CMS Appendix. These species are migratory within the ecological definition used by CMS, as they travel across different regions or habitats during certain periods of the year, often in search of food or breeding grounds. Their inclusion in the CMS Appendixes highlights the need for cooperative conservation efforts to protect these vulnerable species.
- **Statement 3 is incorrect:** CMS has two Appendixes with different designations:
- **Appendix** I lists migratory species that are threatened with extinction and require strict protection, including measures to conserve their habitats, remove obstacles to migration, and control other factors that endanger them.
- **Appendix** II includes species that would benefit from international cooperation but are not necessarily threatened with extinction. It aims to encourage collaborative efforts among countries to manage and conserve these species.

**Thus, option (a) is the correct answer.**

**43.** *(a)* 1, 2 and 3 only

- **Great Indian Bustard** – Listed in Appendix I
- **Bengal florican** – Listed in Appendix I
- **Asian elephant** – Listed in Appendix I during the 13th COP of CMS
- **Snow leopard** – Listed in other conservation frameworks, but not in CMS Appendix I.

**Thus, option (a) is the correct answer.**

**44.** *(a)* 1, 2 and 3 only

| | |
|---|---|
| **Critically Endangered (CR)**<br>**Species that face an extremely high risk of** extinction in the immediate future. These species have seen drastic population declines or face severe threats to their survival. **For example:** Great Indian Bustard, Gharial, etc | **Endangedred (EN)**<br>Species that are at a **very high risk** of extinction **shortly.** These species have significant population declines and face serious threats, but not as extreme as those categorised as Critically Endangered. **For example:** Asian Elephant, Bengal Tiger, etc. |
| **Vulnerable (VU)**<br>Species that are at a **high risk** of extinction in the **medium-term future.** These species are not immediately on the brink of extinction but are facing enough threats to be at risk. **Example:** Ganges River Dolphin, Snow Leopard, etc | **Near Threatened (NT)**<br>Species that do not currently qualify as threatened but are **close to qualifying** or are **likely to qualify shortly.** These species are under some pressure but are not yet at significant risk of extinction. **For example:** Blackbuck and Leopard, etc. |

**Thus, option (a) is the correct answer.**

**45.** *(c)* A cholesterol-like compound in mushrooms that can be converted into vitamin D when exposed to ultraviolet light.

- **Ergosterol** is a **cholesterol-like compound** found in **mushrooms** and other fungi. It is not a protein, carbohydrate, or fat-soluble vitamin. Ergosterol plays a significant role in the structure and function of fungal cell membranes, similar to how cholesterol functions in animal cells.

- When **mushrooms are exposed** to **ultraviolet (UV) light, ergosterol** is converted into **Vitamin D2** (a form of Vitamin D). This is particularly important because mushrooms are one of the few non-animal sources of Vitamin D, making them valuable for people following plant-based diets.

**Thus, option (c) is the correct answer.**

**46.** *(c)* Only three

- **Statement 1 is incorrect:** Salim Ali's Fruit Bat is endemic to the Southern-Western Ghats, but it is classified as **Endangered** on the IUCN Red List, not Critically Endangered.
- **Statement 2 is correct:** The Indian Flying Fox has a widespread distribution across the **Indian subcontinent,** including countries like India, Nepal, Pakistan, Sri Lanka, and Bangladesh, and it is **categorised as Least Concern** on the IUCN Red List due to its relatively stable population in its range.
- **Statement 3 is correct:** Both species play a crucial role in **ecosystem services, especially in pollination and seed dispersal,** which are vital for the survival of over 500 plant species, including several of commercial and ecological importance like mangoes, bananas, and cardamom.
- **Statement 4 is correct:** Anthropogenic factors such as habitat destruction, deforestation, and poaching are major threats to both bat species, contributing to their population decline. These factors are particularly dangerous for species like Salim Ali's Fruit Bat, which is restricted to a specific geographical range and for the Indian Flying Fox, which is hunted for meat.

**Thus, option (c) is the correct answer.**

**47.** *(b)* 2, 3 and 4 only

- **Statement 1 is incorrect:** The Namdapha Flying Squirrel is classified as Critically Endangered, not just Endangered. Its highly restricted range and lack of recent sightings prior to the rediscovery contributed to its Critically Endangered status.
- **Statement 2 is correct:** The Namdapha Flying Squirrel is endemic to the Mesua ferrea jungles on the Western slopes of the Patkai range in Arunachal Pradesh, where it was first discovered in Namdapha National Park in 1981.
- **Statement 3 is correct:** After a period of 42 years of no sightings or evidence, the Namdapha Flying Squirrel was recently rediscovered, raising hopes for its survival and conservation.
- **Statement 4 is correct:** The Namdapha Flying Squirrel was initially the sole member of the genus Biswamoyopterus. However, two other species were later discovered: the Laotian Giant Flying Squirrel in 2013 and the Mount Gaoligong Flying Squirrel in 2018, both of which belong to the same genus.

**Thus, option (b) is the correct answer.**

**48.** *(c)* Only three

- **Statement 1 is correct:** The White-rumped Vulture, Indian Vulture, and Slender-billed Vulture are all classified as **Critically Endangered** by the IUCN. The primary reason for their drastic population decline is the use of **diclofenac, a veterinary drug,** which causes kidney failure in these scavenging birds when they consume carcasses treated with it.
- **Statement 2 is incorrect:** The **Egyptian Vulture** is classified as Endangered, but the Red-headed Vulture is listed as **Critically Endangered,** not Endangered. Both species face threats from **habitat loss, poisoning, and food shortages,** but their IUCN classifications differ.
- **Statement 3 is correct:** Both the Himalayan Griffon Vulture and Cinerous Vulture are classified as Near Threatened by the IUCN. These vultures are largely wintering species in India, meaning they migrate to the region during certain seasons, but face threats from declining food availability and habitat changes.
- **Statement 4 is correct:** The Vulture Breeding Centre at Pinjore, Haryana, was established to **breed and conserve Gyps** species (such as **White-rumped Vulture** and **Slender-billed Vulture**) in captivity. This ex-situ conservation programme is a crucial part of efforts to restore declining populations by releasing bred vultures back into the wild.

**Thus, option (c) is the correct answer.**

**49.** *(c)* 1 and 3 only

- **Statement 1 is correct: BirdLife International** is a global partnership of conservation organisations that work together to conserve birds, their habitats, and global biodiversity.
- **Statement 2 is incorrect:** The concept of **'biodiversity hotspots'** was developed by **Norman Myers** and was popularised by **Conservation International**, not BirdLife International.
- **Statement 3 is correct: BirdLife International** identifies sites known as **'Important Bird and Biodiversity Areas'** (**IBAs**), which are crucial for the conservation of bird populations and overall biodiversity.

**Thus, option (c) is the correct answer.**

**50.** *(a)* Tropical moist deciduous forest

**Teak (Tectona grandis)** is a dominant tree species in **tropical moist deciduous forests** in India. These forests experience a distinct dry season and a wet monsoon season, which provides the ideal conditions for teak to thrive. These forests are commonly found in states like **Madhya Pradesh, Maharashtra, Odisha, Karnataka** and **Kerala.**

**Thus, option (a) is the correct answer.**

**51.** *(b)* 2 and 3 only

- **Statement 1 is incorrect: IUCN is an independent international organisation** and not an organ of the United Nations. It collaborates with governments and other international organisations, but it is not a part of the UN structure.
- **Statement 2 is correct:** IUCN works globally, running numerous field projects aimed at conserving biodiversity, managing natural resources, and promoting sustainable development.
- **Statement 3 is correct: CITES** is an international agreement that regulates trade in endangered species. While it is legally binding on member states, it does not supersede national laws, rather, it provides a framework that countries must implement through their own legal systems.

**Thus, option (b) is the correct answer.**

**52.** *(a)* 1 and 2 only

- **Statement 1 is incorrect:** Biodiversity hotspots are **not restricted to tropical regions;** they can also be found in temperate areas. While many hotspots are indeed found in the tropics, such as the Indo-Burma and Sundaland hotspots, others exist outside the tropics, such as the **California Floristic Province** and the **Mediterranean Basin.** These regions are known for their high levels of species richness and endemism, even though they are not located within the tropics.
- **Statement 2 is incorrect:** India has **four recognised biodiversity hotspots,** they are: **Himalaya:** Includes the entire Indian Himalayan region, covering both the Eastern and Western Himalayas. **Indo-Burma:** Covers North-Eastern India (except Assam), parts of **South-East** Asia, and includes the **Andaman Islands. Western Ghats and Sri Lanka:** Covers the Western Ghats region in India and Sri Lanka. **Sundaland:** Includes the **Nicobar Islands,** as well as parts of **Indonesia,** Malaysia, and other South-East Asian nations. The Western Himalayas are not considered a separate hotspot, and **Andaman and Nicobar Islands** are part of two different hotspots: the **Andaman Islands** are part of the **Indo-Burma hotspot,** while the Nicobar Islands are part of the **Sundaland hotspot.** Therefore, this statement is incorrect.
- **Statement 3 is correct:** The **Eastern Himalayas** were initially included in the **Indo-Burma** biodiversity hotspot. However, during a reappraisal conducted in **2004**, the **Eastern Himalayas** were classified as part of a separate **Himalaya hotspot,** which was distinguished from the rest of the Indo-Burma region due to its unique biogeographic and ecological characteristics.

**Thus, option (a) is the correct answer.**

**53.** *(a)* 1 and 2 only

- **Statement 1 is correct:** Eco-Sensitive Areas (ESAs) are notified by the **Ministry of Environment, Forest and Climate Change** (**MoEFCC**) under the **Environment Protection Act of 1986.** The primary purpose of notifying ESAs is to **create a buffer** zone around Protected Areas, National Parks, and Wildlife Sanctuaries to minimise the negative impacts of human activities on these ecologically fragile regions. The **Environment Protection Act gives MoEFCC the authority to declare regions as ESAs** to regulate activities in and around sensitive ecosystems.

- **Statement 2 is correct:** The **Kasturirangan Committee** was constituted to **re-evaluate the earlier recommendations of the Madhav Gadgil Committee** regarding the conservation of the Western Ghats. The Kasturirangan Committee recommended that **approximately 60,000 square kilometers** of the Western Ghats should be declared as Eco-Sensitive Areas (ESA), with a significant portion covering parts of Karnataka. Specifically, the report suggested that **20,668 square kilometers** of the area falls within Karnataka, covering **1,576 villages.** The recommendation aimed to balance development and conservation by protecting ecologically important areas while considering the livelihood concerns of local communities.
- Statement 3 is incorrect the **10 kilometer** radius around Protected Areas, National Parks and Wildlife Sanctuaries is a **general guideline** for declaring Eco-Sensitive Zones (SEZs), it is not an absolute rule. The **extent of ESAs may vary** based on ecological importance, human habitation, and other factors. In the case of the **Western Ghats,** the Eco-Sensitive Area designated by the Kasturirangan Committee goes well beyond the **10 kilometer buffer** to include entire ecologically fragile landscapes.

**Thus, option (a) is the correct answer.**

**54.** *(b)* Only two

- **Statement 1 is correct: Red Sanders,** also known as **Pterocarpus santalinus,** is **endemic** to the **Southern-Eastern Ghats** of India, specifically found in parts of **Andhra Pradesh** and **Tamil Nadu.** This means that the species naturally occurs only in this specific region, which includes dry deciduous forests.
- **Statement 2 is incorrect: Red Sanders** does not primarily grow in **tropical rainforests.** Instead, it is typically found in **dry deciduous forests** and prefers **dry, rocky soils** with relatively low rainfall. It does **not thrive** in the wet, humid conditions typical of tropical rainforests. The regions in which Red Sanders grows are known for their **dry climatic conditions,** rather than tropical rainforest characteristics.
- **Statement 3 is correct: Red Sanders** indeed thrives in **dry, rocky soils** and **lateritic conditions,** particularly in parts of **Andhra Pradesh.** These conditions are characteristic of the **Eastern Ghats** region where Red Sanders grows naturally. The species is well adapted to these challenging conditions, which also limits its geographical range.

**Thus, option (b) is the correct answer.**

**55.** *(c)* 1 and 3 only

- **Statement 1 is correct:** Butterflies are important **pollinators** for many flowering plants. A decline in their population could lead to reduced pollination, especially for plant species that depend on them, which may negatively affect the reproduction and health of these plants.
- **Statement 2 is incorrect:** Butterflies do not play a significant role in controlling fungal infections on cultivated plants. Fungal infections are usually influenced by environmental conditions (like moisture) and specific pest-control mechanisms, not by butterfly populations.
- **Statement 3 is correct:** Butterflies are part of the food chain, and many species of wasps, spiders and birds feed on them. A decline in butterfly populations could reduce the availability of food for these species, leading to a decline in their populations as well.

**Thus, option (c) is the correct answer.**

**56.** *(d)* Mankind's over-exploitation of natural resources, habitat fragmentation, ecosystem destruction, pollution, and global climate change

The term '**sixth mass extinction**' or '**sixth extinction**' refers to the ongoing extinction event caused by **human activities,** which is leading to an alarming loss of biodiversity. It is characterised by the accelerated rate at which species are becoming extinct, primarily due to factors such as habitat destruction, pollution, over-exploitation of resources, and climate change. This extinction event is considered the **sixth** because there have been five previous mass extinctions in Earth's history, with the most fam.

**Thus, option (d) is the correct answer.**

***57.*** *(b)* Only two

- **Statement 1 is correct : Orangutans** have demonstrated tool use in the wild, including using **sticks** to extract insects such as ants or termites from tree holes or logs. This behaviour shows their high intelligence and problem-solving skills.
- **Statement 2 is incorrect: Otters** are known for using stones as tools to crack open shellfish, but they do not typically use sticks to scrape insects from crevices.
- **Statement 3 is correct: Sloth bears** have specialised feeding techniques, using their **long, flexible** lips to suck out insects like termites and ants from crevices, rather than relying on tools.

**Thus, option (b) is the correct answer.**

***58.*** *(c)* Both 1 and 2

- **Statement 1 is correct: Biodiversity Management Committees (BMCs)** play an essential role in realising the objectives of the Nagoya Protocol, which is focused on **access to genetic resources and the fair and equitable sharing of benefits arising from their use.** BMCs help in preserving biodiversity, regulating its use, and ensuring benefits are shared with the local community.
- **Statement 2 is correct:** BMCs have key responsibilities, including **determining access and benefit-sharing (ABS) and levying fees for access to biological resources within their jurisdiction.** They prepare and maintain a People's Biodiversity Register (PBR), which contains information on the availability and knowledge of local biological resources.

**Thus, option (c) is the correct answer.**

***59.*** *(b)* Only two pairs

- **Pair 1 is incorrect: Hokera wetland** is located in **Jammu and Kashmir,** not Punjab. It is an important **Ramsar site** and provides a significant habitat for various species of migratory birds like mallard and gadwall, etc.
- **Pair 2 is correct: Renuka wetland** is located in **Himachal Pradesh.** It is a **natural lake** and has been designated as a Ramsar site. The wetland is of cultural and ecological significance and supports a variety of flora and fauna like **tun, harar, bahera, tor tor etc.**
- **Pair 3 is correct: Rudrasagar lake** is located in **Tripura.** It is a **Ramsar** site and an important wetland in the state, known for its role in supporting diverse species, including migratory birds **like the Asian palm swift, Indian pond heron, etc.** It also has cultural significance due to the nearby **Neermahal Palace.**
- **Pair 4 is incorrect: Sasthamkotta lake** is located in **Kerala,** not Tamil Nadu. It is the largest freshwater lake in Kerala and is also designated as a **Ramsar** site. It plays a crucial role in supplying drinking water to the surrounding areas and supports a unique ecosystem.

**Thus, option (b) is the correct answer.**

***60.*** *(b)* 1, 2 and 4 only

- **Statement 1 is correct: Biodiversity Heritage Sites (BHS)** are designated areas that hold unique and **ecologically fragile ecosystems.** These sites are characterised by a high diversity of wild and domesticated species, and they often include rare, endangered, or keystone species like freshwater black softshell turtles (critically endangered) found in Hajong Tortoise Lake, Assam.
- **Statement 2 is correct:** The **Biological Diversity Act, 2002** empowers **State Governments** to declare certain areas as **Biodiversity Heritage Sites** in consultation with **local bodies** such as Panchayats, Municipalities, or other community-level organisations. This is intended to foster community involvement in the **conservation and protection** of ecologically significant areas.
- **Statement 3 is incorrect:** The goal of designating an area as a **Biodiversity Heritage Site** is to encourage community-led

conservation and preserve unique ecosystems while respecting traditional knowledge and practices.

**BHS designation does not impose strict restrictions** on the local community's practices but rather seeks to involve the community in **sustainable management.**

- **Statement 4 is correct:** The **Nallur Tamarind Grove** in **Karnataka** was indeed the **first Biodiversity Heritage Site** declared in India. It was designated as a BHS in **2007** and is known for its **historical and ecological significance** with numerous tamarind trees that are estimated to be hundreds of years old.

**Thus, option (b) is the correct answer.**

**61.** *(b)* To enhance protection and conservation efforts for migratory species by adopting listing proposals and addressing various threats such as habitat degradation, illegal trade and bycatch.

- The **CMS COP 14** focused on **conservation** and **protection** of migratory species by adopting proposals to list 14 species for enhanced conservation efforts. The conference emphasised the importance of international cooperation among **range states** to address key threats like **habitat degradation, illegal trade, bycatch,** and other human activities. It also sought to improve the status of species recognised as vulnerable, endangered, or critically endangered in the **IUCN Red List.**

**Thus, option (b) is the correct answer.**

**62.** *(d)* 1 and 2 only

- **Statement 1 is correct: The Central Asian Flyway (CAF)** is a major migratory route that passes through India. It stretches from **Central Asia and Siberia** to the **Indian subcontinent,** and India provides essential habitats for these migratory birds, particularly during the winter season.
- **Statement 2 is correct:** The **East Asian-Australasian Flyway (EAAF)** primarily includes **East Asia, South-East Asia,** and **Australasia,** but it also **touches parts of India,** especially the **Eastern coast and North-Eastern regions.** However, the coverage is limited compared to other countries on this flyway, but India still serves as an important region for certain migratory birds.
- **Statement 3 is incorrect:** There is no recognised **Asian East African Flyway (AEAF).** Instead, the correct flyway is the **West Asian-East African Flyway (WAEAF),** which extends across **West Asia to East Africa.** This flyway does not significantly pass through India; instead, it involves regions like the **Middle East** and **East Africa.**

**Thus, option (d) is the correct answer.**

**63.** *(a)* 1 and 2 only

- **Statement 1 is correct:** Permafrost refers to ground that remains at or below 0°C for at least two consecutive years. It is commonly found in Arctic regions, as well as in high-altitude areas. Permafrost plays a crucial role in regulating the Earth's carbon cycle since it stores large amounts of organic carbon that, if thawed, could release greenhouse gases into the atmosphere.
- **Statement 2 is correct:** Environmental Sensitive Zones (ESZs), also known as Ecologically Fragile Areas (EFAs), are regions designated around protected areas, such as national parks and wildlife sanctuaries. They aim to protect biodiversity by minimising human interference, thereby supporting in-situ conservation of species and reducing conflicts between humans and wildlife. Additionally, ESZs help limit activities that may lead to forest depletion and environmental degradation.
- **Statement 3 is incorrect:** While permafrost regions often have snow cover in winter, they are not always covered with snow, as snow melts during the warmer months in many permafrost areas. Permafrost refers to the frozen condition of the ground below the surface, regardless of snow cover on top. Additionally, ESZs do not strictly prohibit all forms of human activities; instead, they regulate activities depending on the specific guidelines for each zone, allowing for sustainable use while protecting the ecological integrity of the area.

**Thus, option (a) is the correct answer.**

**64.** *(a)* Baseflow refers to the portion of stream flow that originates from groundwater discharge and contributes to flooding by reducing the time lag between rainfall and runoff in rivers.

- **Baseflow** is the portion of stream flow that comes from **groundwater discharge** into streams or rivers. This process occurs over an extended period and can significantly impact river flow.
- The recent study on the **river basins of peninsular India** (Narmada, Tapi, Mahanadi, Godavari, Krishna, Cauvery) found that **higher baseflow** contributes to flooding by reducing the time lag between rainfall events and river runoff.
- Catchments with higher baseflow are more prone to rapid flooding during rainfall due to the combination of groundwater discharge and incoming rainfall runoff.

**Thus, option (a) is the correct answer.**

**65.** *(b)* A non-profit international association established in 2014 to foster networking and collaboration among global geoparks under the auspices of UNESCO.

The **Global Geoparks Network (GGN)** is a non-profit international association founded in 2014. It operates under the **umbrella of UNESCO,** focusing on promoting networking and collaboration among **Global Geoparks.** The GGN facilitates knowledge sharing and supports sustainable development in geopark regions, promoting conservation, education, and responsible tourism.

**Thus, option (b) is the correct answer.**

**66.** *(b)* Only two

- The **Fourth Global Mass Coral Bleaching** Event (2014-2017) was the **longest** and most **intense** on record, affecting over **70% of coral reefs worldwide.** The primary cause was **ocean warming** due to climate change, further intensified by the **2015-2016 El Nino.** It led to **massive coral mortality,** with the **Great Barrier Reef** losing over **50% of its coral cover.** The event disrupted **marine biodiversity,** impacting **fisheries** and **tourism,** emphasising the need for **urgent climate** action and enhanced **coral protection.**
- **Statement 1 is correct: Coral bleaching** occurs when corals expel **zooxanthellae** (symbiotic algae), due to stressful conditions such as changes in temperature, light, or nutrients. This causes the corals to lose their color and turn white.
- **Statement 2 is incorrect:** The Fourth Global Mass Coral Bleaching Event was **the second such event** in the last 10 years, with the earlier event lasting from **2014 to 2017.** It is not the first in the last decade.
- **Statement 3 is correct:** Coral reefs are formed by **hard corals, which establish a symbiotic relationship** with microscopic algae **(zooxanthellae)** that provide them with nutrients and give them their characteristic colours.

**Thus, option (b) is the correct answer.**

**67.** *(c)* All three

- **Statement 1 is correct: Baobab trees are long-lived deciduous trees** that shed their leaves during the dry season. The **Adansonia genus** consists of several species, which are primarily found in Africa (particularly in the savannas), **Madagascar,** and **Australia.** They are known for their massive trunks, which can store significant amounts of water.
- **Statement 2 is correct:** The **Baobab** is often called the **'upside-down tree'** because, during the **dry season,** its branches become **leafless,** and the bare branches resemble the appearance of **roots sticking up into the sky,** giving the impression of an upside-down tree.
- **Statement 3 is correct:** The **bark** of the **Baobab tree** is known to provide a strong **fiber,** which is used by local communities to make products like **rope, cloth and baskets.** The bark regenerates after being harvested, making it a renewable resource for local populations.

**Thus, option (c) is the correct answer.**

**68.** *(a)* 1 and 2 only

- **Statement 1 is correct: Jerdon's Courser** (Rhinoptilus bitorquatus) is indeed a **nocturnal bird,** which means it is active primarily during the night. It is found exclusively in the **Eastern Ghats** of India, particularly in areas that have thorny scrub and open patches. Its activity during the night makes it particularly elusive and difficult to study.

- **Statement 2 is correct: Jerdon's Courser** is known to be **exclusively endemic** to **Andhra Pradesh** and is found primarily within the **Sri Lankamalleswara Wildlife Sanctuary** in **Kadapa district,** Andhra Pradesh. The sanctuary and the surrounding areas serve as the last known habitat for this **critically endangered species.** Habitat fragmentation, quarrying, and disturbance have threatened its very limited distribution, making it extremely vulnerable.
- **Statement 3 is incorrect: Jerdon's Courser** is listed under **Schedule I** of the **Wildlife (Protection) Act, 1972.** Schedule I provides the highest level of protection under Indian law, similar to other highly threatened species, which means it receives the strictest protection and conservation measures.

**Thus, option (a) is the correct answer.**

**69.** *(b)* Only two

- **Statement 1 is correct: Agarwood** (Aquilaria malaccensis) is an **evergreen tree** and is native to **North-East India,** including states like Assam and Arunachal Pradesh, as well as Bangladesh, Bhutan, and parts of **South-East Asia** (such as Myanmar, Thailand, Malaysia, and Indonesia). It grows in **tropical and subtropical forests** in these regions.
- **Statement 2 is correct: Agarwood** is highly prized for its **aromatic resin,** which produces a distinctive and **valuable fragrance** used in **perfumes, incense,** and **essential oils.** The resin is formed as a **response to fungal infection or injury,** and it is extracted and sold in the form of **oil** and **chips.**
- **Statement 3 is incorrect: Agarwood** (Aquilaria malaccensis) is listed as **'Vulnerable'** on the **IUCN Red List,** not as 'Endangered.' The species faces threats due to **illegal logging, overharvesting,** and **habitat destruction.**

**Thus, option (b) is the correct answer.**

**70.** *(c)* They are organisms that can tolerate and thrive in a wide range of temperatures.

**Eurythermal** organisms are those that can **tolerate and thrive in a wide range of temperatures.** They are adapted to withstand **fluctuations in temperature** without experiencing significant negative effects. The ability to survive in both low and high temperatures allows these organisms to inhabit diverse environments. **Eurythermal organisms can tolerate and thrive in a wide range** of temperatures. Examples of eurythermal organisms include certain types of **fish** (such as the common carp), **crustaceans,** and **birds.** Their adaptability allows them to survive in environments with fluctuating temperatures, such as estuaries, intertidal zones, and temperate regions.

**Thus, option (c) is the correct answer.**

**71.** *(d)* They are organisms whose internal temperature varies considerably.

- **Poikilotherms** are organisms whose **internal body temperature fluctuates** with the environmental temperature. Unlike **homeotherms** (such as mammals and birds), which maintain a constant internal temperature, poikilotherms do not regulate their body temperature internally and are highly dependent on external heat sources to function.
- **Examples** of poikilotherms include **reptiles, amphibians, fish, and invertebrates.** For instance, a lizard's body temperature will increase in the Sun and decrease in cooler surroundings. This means their activity levels are closely tied to external temperatures-active when warm and sluggish in cold conditions.

**Thus, option (d) is the correct answer.**

**72.** *(a)* A-3, B-2, C-1

- **National Mission for Clean Ganga (NMCG):** This is the leading organisation for the Ganges' conservation efforts and broader initiatives involving river management in India. It would typically handle extensive responsibilities beyond financial support, yet in the options provided, **it's listed explicitly with financial and technical support.**

- **National Institute for Urban Affairs (NIUA):** Known for its focus on urban development and policy, the NIUA would be suitable for administrative and coordination roles, such as acting as the Secretariat for initiatives like the GRCA.
- **World Bank:** This international financial institution typically supports sustainability projects around the world through inspiration, funding, and expertise. Its role in inspiring the formation of strategic alliances or enhancing existing frameworks through financial and technical assistance fits well with inspiring the formation of the GRCA.

**Thus, option (a) is the correct answer.**

**73.** *(d)* 1, 2 and 3

- **Statement 1 is correct:** The **Global River Cities Alliance (GRCA)** was launched during **COP28** in **Dubai.** The main aim of the GRCA is to promote **global collaboration** for sustainable river **management practices** in **urban settings.** The alliance brings together cities that are situated along rivers to share knowledge, strategies, and best practices for river conservation, restoration, and sustainable urban development. It encompasses a diverse array of nations and river cities, including countries such as **India, Egypt, Netherlands, Denmark, Ghana, Australia, Bhutan, Cambodia, and Japan,** among others. With a membership of over **275 river cities across 11 countries.**
- **Statement 2 is correct:** The **National Mission for Clean Ganga (NMCG)** and the **Ministry of Jal Shakti** is the **Secretariat** for the GRCA. The NMCG has been instrumental in leading the river conservation movement in India, particularly with the **Namami Gange Programme.**
- **Statement 3 is correct:** The **Global River Cities Alliance** is receiving **financial and technical support** from multilateral funding agencies like the **World Bank** and **Asian Development Bank (ADB).** These organisations are providing **both funding and expertise to support the alliance's objectives of sustainable urban river management, as well as capacity-building** for local bodies.

**Thus, option (d) is the correct answer.**

## Past Learning (Answers)

| | | | | | | | | | |
|---|---|---|---|---|---|---|---|---|---|
| 1 (b) | 2 (a) | 3 (d) | 4 (c) | 5 (d) | 6 (a) | 7 (c) | 8 (a) | 9 (b) | 10 (c) |
| 11 (d) | 12 (a) | 13 (b) | 14 (c) | 15 (c) | 16 (c) | 17 (a) | 18 (a) | 19 (c) | 20 (d) |
| 21 (c) | 22 (c) | 23 (a) | 24 (a) | 25 (d) | 26 (a) | 27 (c) | 28 (b) | 29 (b) | 30 (c) |
| 31 (a) | 32 (d) | 33 (d) | 34 (a) | 35 (c) | 36 (c) | 37 (c) | 38 (b) | 39 (c) | 40 (a) |
| 41 (a) | 42 (c) | 43 (b) | | | | | | | |

CHAPTER 04

# Conservation and Protected Areas

## Assessment Round

**1.** Consider the following statements regarding Conservation Reserves and Community Reserves in India:

**Statement I:** Conservation Reserves can only be declared in areas owned by the State Government that are adjacent to National Parks and Sanctuaries.

**Statement II:** Community Reserves can be declared on private or community land where individuals or communities voluntarily commit to conserve wildlife and its habitat.

Which one of the following is correct with respect to the above statements?

(a) Both Statements I and II are correct.

(b) Statement I is correct, but Statement II is not correct.

(c) Statement I is not correct, but Statement II is correct.

(d) Both Statements I and II are not correct.

**2.** Consider the following statements:

**Statement I:** The Bio-rock technology helps in coral restoration by providing coral fragments with an artificial structure where they can grow faster and stronger.

**Statement II:**In Bio-rock technology, steel structures are submerged into the ocean, and a low-voltage current is passed through them to stimulate the crystallisation of minerals such as calcium carbonate ($CaCO_3$).

Which one of the following is correct with respect to the above statements?

(a) Both Statement I and Statement II are correct, Statement II is the correct explanation for Statement I.

(b) Both Statement I and Statement II are correct, but Statement II is not the correct explanation for Statement I.

(c) Statement I is correct, but Statement II is incorrect.

(d) Statement I is incorrect, but Statement II is correct.

**3.** Consider the following conservation efforts:

1. Project Tiger
2. National Mission for Clean Ganga
3. MAB Programme (Man and Biosphere)

Which of the above are directly linked to the protection of Biosphere Reserves in India?

(a) 1 only (b) 3 only

(c) 1 and 3 only (d) 1, 2 and 3

**4.** Which of the following pairs regarding wildlife conservation initiatives are aimed at curbing illegal wildlife trade in India?

1. Operation Softgold – Launched to curb the illegal trade in shahtoosh wool from the endangered Tibetan antelope (chiru).
2. Biodiversity Conservation and Ganga Rejuvenation Programme – Focuses on the conservation of biodiversity along the Ganga river and the rejuvenation of its ecosystem.
3. Operation Wildnet – An initiative to curb online illegal wildlife trade in India by tracking and prosecuting offenders.

Select the correct pairs using the codes given below:

(a) 1 and 2 only (b) 1 and 3 only

(c) 2 and 3 only (d) 1, 2 and 3

**5.** With reference to the Wildlife Crime Control Bureau (WCCB), consider the following statements:

1. It is a statutory body established under the Wildlife Protection Act, of 1972.
2. The WCCB functions under the Ministry of Environment, Forest and Climate Change (MoEFCC).
3. The Bureau is primarily responsible for intelligence gathering, coordination with states and dissemination of wildlife crime information.

Which of the statements given above are correct?

(a) 1 and 2 only
(b) 1 and 3 only
(c) 2 and 3 only
(d) 1, 2 and 3

**6.** With reference to the 5th Water Bird Census conducted at Kaziranga National Park, consider the following statements:

1. The census recorded a 27% increase in the number of resident and migratory waterbirds.
2. The census revealed the presence of over 50,000 birds, including species like the Baer's pochard and Bengal florican.
3. Kaziranga recorded the highest concentration of Bengal floricans after Manas National Park and Orang National Park.

How many of the above statements is/are incorrect?

(a) Only one
(b) Only two
(c) All three
(d) None

**7.** Which of the following initiatives or tools related to forest fires are correctly described?

1. The Bambi Bucket is a specialised container used by helicopters to collect water from natural sources like rivers or ponds and discharge it over forest fires.
2. The National Action Plan for Forest Fires (NAPFF) was launched in 2018 to reduce forest fires by empowering forest fringe communities to collaborate with state forest departments.
3. The Forest Fire Prevention and Management Scheme (FPM) is a state-sponsored programme aimed at reducing the occurrence of forest fires in remote and inaccessible regions.

Select the correct answer from the options given below:

(a) 1 and 2 only
(b) 2 and 3 only
(c) 1 and 3 only
(d) 1, 2 and 3

**8.** Which of the following National Parks is unique for being a swamp with floating vegetation that supports a rich biodiversity?

(a) Bhitarkanika National Park
(b) Keibul Lamjao National Park
(c) Keoladeo Ghana National Park
(d) Sultanpur National Park

**9.** Consider the following statements regarding the Wildlife Institute of India (WII) and its roles:

1. The Wildlife Institute of India was established in 1982 and is an autonomous institution under the Ministry of Environment, Forest and Climate Change (MoEFCC).
2. The President of the WII Society is the Director of the Institute.
3. The State of India's Birds 2023 report highlighted that long-distance migratory birds have faced a sharp decline, particularly species that breed in the Antarctic region.
4. Bengal Florican, a Critically Endangered species, is primarily found in the Himalayan Terai and northeastern grasslands of India.

How many of the above statements is/are correct?

(a) Only one (b) Only two
(c) Only three (d) All four

**10.** Consider the following statements regarding the findings of the State of India's Birds 2023 report:

1. Long-distance migratory birds, especially shorebirds breeding in the Arctic, have shown a drastic decline of nearly 80% in their populations in India.
2. Some bird species, such as the Indian Peafowl, Rock Pigeon and Asian Koel, have shown increasing population trends.
3. The Bengal Florican, a critically endangered bird, is restricted to the Western Ghats and Eastern Coastal Plains of India.
4. The Indian Skimmer is listed as Critically Endangered and is found around river systems such as the Ganga, Chambal and Godavari.

How many of the above statements is/are correct?

(a) Only one (b) Only two
(c) Only three (d) All four

**11.** With reference to the Bombay Natural History Society (BNHS), consider the following statements:

1. BNHS is an autonomous organisation under the Ministry of Environment and Forests.
2. BNHS works to conserve nature through action-based research, education and public awareness.
3. BNHS organises and conducts nature trails and camps for the general public.

Which of the statements given above is/are correct?

(a) 1 and 3 only
(b) 2 only
(c) 2 and 3 only
(d) 1, 2 and 3

**12.** Consider the following statements:

1. The Animal Welfare Board of India was established under the Environment (Protection) Act, 1986.
2. The National Tiger Conservation Authority(NTCA) is a statutory body.
3. The National Ganga River Basin Authority is chaired by the Prime Minister.

Which of the above statements is/are correct?

(a) 1 only (b) 2 and 3 only
(c) 2 only (d) 1, 2 and 3

**13.** Consider the following statements regarding the Sundarbans Biosphere Reserve :

**Statement I:** The Sundarbans Biosphere Reserve supports a significant population of the endangered Royal Bengal Tiger.

**Statement II:** The reserve is primarily composed of tropical dry deciduous forests.

Which one of the following is correct with respect to the above statements?

(a) Both Statement I and Statement II are correct, Statement II is the correct explanation for Statement I.
(b) Both Statement I and Statement II are correct, but Statement II is not the correct explanation for Statement I.
(c) Statement I is correct, but Statement II is incorrect.
(d) Statement I is incorrect, but Statement II is correct.

**14.** Which Tiger Reserve is located in the Terai region along the border with Nepal and is the only Tiger Reserve in Bihar?

(a) Dudhwa Tiger Reserve
(b) Valmiki Tiger Reserve
(c) Simlipal Tiger Reserve
(d) Bandhavgarh Tiger Reserve

**15.** With reference to Project Elephant and Kaziranga National Park, consider the following statements:

1. Kaziranga National Park is a UNESCO World Heritage Site located between the Brahmaputra river and Karbi Anglong hills.
2. Project Elephant was launched in 1992 to provide financial and technical support to states with significant elephant populations.
3. The highest number of elephant population in India is found in Kerala.

How many of the statements given above is/are correct?

(a) Only one (b) Only two
(c) All three (d) None

**16.** Arrange the following Natural World Heritage Sites of India in the order of their recognition by UNESCO :

1. Kaziranga National Park
2. Sundarbans National Park
3. Nanda Devi and Valley of Flowers National Park
4. Great Himalayan National Park

Select the correct sequence using the codes given below:

(a) 1-2-3-4 (b) 1-3-2-4
(c) 1-2-4-3 (d) 3-1-2-4

**17.** Identify the national park based on the following characteristics:

1. It is located in the Golaghat and Nagaon districts of Assam.
2. It is a World Heritage Site and a Tiger Reserve.
3. It is home to the largest population of Indian one-horned rhinoceros in the world.

Which national park is the correct answer as per the above characteristics?

(a) Manas National Park
(b) Kaziranga National Park
(c) Orang National Park
(d) Dibru-Saikhowa National Park

**18.** Consider the following statements about Mudumalai Tiger Reserve:

1. It is part of the Nilgiri Biosphere Reserve, which is a UNESCO World Heritage Site.
2. Mudumalai shares a boundary with Bandipur Tiger Reserve in Karnataka and Wayanad Wildlife Sanctuary in Kerala.
3. It is known for large populations of Asian elephants and has rich biodiversity including Elephant Grass, Bamboo and valuable timber species like Teak and Rosewood.
4. Mudumalai Tiger Reserve is famous for being home to Sangai Deer.

How many of the above statements is/are correct?

(a) Only one
(b) Only two
(c) Only three
(d) All four

**19.** With reference to Keibul Lamjao National Park and Loktak lake, consider the following statements:

1. Keibul Lamjao National Park is the only floating national park in the world.
2. Loktak lake supports the largest population of the critically endangered Sangai deer.
3. The Loktak Hydroelectric Project has enhanced the conservation of phumdis by maintaining constant water levels.

Which of the above statements are correct?

(a) 1 and 2 only
(b) 1 and 3 only
(c) 2 and 3 only
(d) 1, 2 and 3

**20.** Consider the following pairs:

| | Protected Area | Well-known for |
|---|---|---|
| 1. | Bhitarkanika, Odisha | Saltwater Crocodile |
| 2. | Desert National Park, Rajasthan | Great Indian Bustard |
| 3. | Eravikulam, Kerala | Hoolock Gibbon |

How many of the pairs given above is/are correctly matched?

(a) Only one (b) Only two
(c) All three (d) None

**21.** Which one of the following National Parks has a climate that varies from tropical to subtropical, temperate and arctic?

(a) Khangchendzonga National Park
(b) Nandadevi National Park
(c) Neora Valley National Park
(d) Namdapha National Park

**22.** Which of the following protected areas are most likely to be the natural habitats of the musk deer?

1. Askot Wildlife Sanctuary
2. Gangotri National Park
3. Kishanpur Wildlife Sanctuary
4. Manas National Park

Select the correct answer using the codes given below:

(a) 1 and 2 only (b) 2 and 3 only
(c) 3 and 4 only (d) 1 and 4 only

**23.** With reference to Biosphere Reserves in India, consider the following statements:

1. Biosphere Reserves are recognised by UNESCO and are managed under the Intergovernmental Man and the Biosphere (MAB) Programme.
2. The designation of a site as a Biosphere Reserve alters the legal status of the land and resources within it.
3. The core area of a Biosphere Reserve must support viable populations representing all trophic levels in the ecosystem.

How many of the statements given above is/are correct?

(a) Only one (b) Only two
(c) All three (d) None

**24.** Identify the Biosphere Reserve based on the following statements:

1. It is located in the Satpura Hills of Madhya Pradesh.
2. It consists of three protected areas, including Pachmarhi Wildlife Sanctuary.
3. It is home to the endangered Barasingha.

Which Biosphere Reserve is described in the above statements?

(a) Nanda Devi
(b) Pachmarhi
(c) Dehang-Dibang
(d) Nilgiri

**25.** With reference to the Nanda Devi Biosphere Reserve consider the following statements:

1. It is located in the states of Uttarakhand and Himachal Pradesh.
2. It is part of the UNESCO Man and Biosphere (MAB) programme.
3. The reserve is home to endangered species such as the Snow Leopard and the Musk Deer.

How many of the statements given above is/ are correct?

(a) Only one
(b) Only two
(c) All three
(d) None

**26.** Consider the following Biosphere Reserves:

1. Simlipal 2. Gulf of Mannar
3. Cold Desert 4. Pachmarhi

How many of the above is/ are part of the UNESCO Man and Biosphere (MAB) programme?

(a) Only one (b) Only two
(c) Only three (d) All four

**27.** With reference to the Agasthyamalai Biosphere Reserve, consider the following statements:

1. It includes parts of Kerala and Tamil Nadu.
2. It supports a population of Lion-Tailed Macaque and Nilgiri Tahr.
3. It is the southernmost biosphere reserve in India.

Which of the given statements are correct?

(a) 1 and 2 only (b) 2 and 3 only
(c) 1 and 3 only (d) 1, 2 and 3

**28.** Which of the following Biosphere Reserves are known for hosting endemic species?

1. Great Nicobar
2. Gulf of Mannar
3. Kutch
4. Dehang-Dibang

Select the correct answer using the codes given below:

(a) 1 and 3 only (b) 1, 2 and 4 only
(c) 2 and 4 only (d) 1, 2, 3 and 4

**29.** Arrange the following Biosphere Reserves from South to North:

1. Nilgiri Biosphere Reserve
2. Gulf of Mannar Biosphere Reserve
3. Sundarbans Biosphere Reserve
4. Nanda Devi Biosphere Reserve
5. Achanakmar-Amarkantak Biosphere Reserve
6. Khangchendzonga National Park

Choose the correct order from South to North:

(a) 1-2-5-6-3-4
(b) 2-1-5-3-6-4
(c) 2-1-5-3-6-4
(d) 2-1-5-3-4-6

**30.** Which of the following Tiger Reserves are located in the Western Ghats region?
1. Mudumalai Tiger Reserve
2. Bandipur Tiger Reserve
3. Nagarjuna Sagar Tiger Reserve
4. Kalakad Mundanthurai Tiger Reserve

Select the correct answer from the codes given below:
(a) 1, 2 and 4 only
(b) 1, 2 and 3 only
(c) 2, 3 and 4 only
(d) 1, 2, 3 and 4

**31.** With reference to Kanha Tiger Reserve consider the following statements:
1. It is the only habitat of the endangered hard ground Barasingha.
2. It is part of the Nilgiris Biosphere Reserve.
3. It is located in the Satpura Range.

How many of the above statements is/ are correct?
(a) Only one (b) Only two
(c) All three (d) None

**32.** Identify the Tiger Reserve based on the following statements:
1. It is located in the Nallamala range and spans across three districts in Andhra Pradesh.
2. The Krishna river forms its southern boundary.
3. It has the largest core area among all tiger reserves in India.

Which Tiger Reserve is being described in the above statements?
(a) Nagarjuna Sagar Tiger Reserve
(b) Simlipal Tiger Reserve
(c) Tadoba Andhari Tiger Reserve
(d) Kalakad Mundanthurai Tiger Reserve

**33.** Consider the following pairs:

| | Place | Location |
|---|---|---|
| 1. | Dampa Tiger Reserve | Mizoram |
| 2. | Gumti Wildlife Sanctuary | Sikkim |
| 3. | Saramati Peak | Nagaland |

How many of the above pairs is/are incorrectly matched?
(a) Only one
(b) Only two
(c) All three
(d) None

**34.** With reference to the Cheetah Project in India, consider the following statements:
1. The Cheetah Project Steering Committee (CPSC) has been formed to oversee the introduction of African cheetahs in India.
2. The project aims to introduce a minimum of 100 cheetahs over five years.
3. The Cheetah Project is funded by the Compensatory Afforestation Fund Management and Planning Authority (CAMPA) and Project Tiger.

How many of the statements given above is/ are incorrect?
(a) Only one
(b) Only two
(c) All three
(d) None

**35.** Consider the following statements about the cheetah reintroduction project in Kuno National Park:

**Statement I:** Cheetahs were reintroduced in India from Namibia after being declared extinct in the country in 1952.

**Statement II:** Cheetahs are listed as Vulnerable on the IUCN Red List due to habitat loss and human-wildlife conflict.

Which one of the following is correct in respect of the above statements?
(a) Both Statement I and Statement II are correct and Statement II is the correct explanation for Statement I.
(b) Both Statement I and Statement II are correct, but Statement II is not the correct explanation for Statement I.
(c) Statement I is correct, but Statement II is incorrect.
(d) Statement I is incorrect, but Statement II is correct.

**36.** With reference to coral reefs, consider the following statements:

1. Coral polyps form a symbiotic relationship with zooxanthellae, a type of algae, which helps in the process of photosynthesis.
2. Coral reefs thrive in oceanic waters with high salinity and a high level of sedimentation.
3. Atolls are circular or oval-shaped coral reefs that form around volcanic islands that have subsided below sea level.

How many of the statements given above is/are correct?

(a) Only one
(b) Only two
(c) All three
(d) None

**37.** Which river delta is home to the Bhitarkanika National Park and the Gahirmatha Wildlife Sanctuary, both known for their rich biodiversity, including Olive Ridley turtles?

(a) Godavari Delta
(b) Brahmani-Baitarni Delta
(c) Mahanadi Delta
(d) Krishna Delta

**38.** In the context of Marine Protected Areas (MPAs), which of the following actions would directly support achieving Aichi Biodiversity Target 11?

1. Establishing MPAs in regions with high biodiversity and ecosystem services.
2. Allowing only sustainable fishing practices within all MPAs.
3. Expanding tourism and recreational activities in sensitive marine habitats.
4. Increasing the global marine protected area coverage to 10% of coastal and marine regions.

Select the correct answer using the codes given below:

(a) 1, 2, and 4 only
(b) 1, 3 and 4 only
(c) 1 and 4 only
(d) 2, 3 and 4 only

**39.** Which of the following Biosphere Reserves is known for the Dugong or Sea Cow?

(a) Simlipal (b) Gulf of Mannar
(c) Sundarbans (d) Great Nicobar

**40.** Consider the following statements regarding Biodiversity Heritage Sites (BHS) in India:

1. BHS can be declared by the State Governments without the involvement of local bodies.
2. BHS is meant to protect areas with high endemism and rare species, which also hold cultural significance.
3. State Biodiversity Boards are required to consult with the Central Government before notifying a BHS.

How many of the above statements is/are correct?

(a) Only one
(b) Only two
(c) All three
(d) None

**41.** Which of the following wetlands is known for hosting the largest population of Irrawaddy dolphins in India?

(a) Bhitarkanika Wetlands
(b) Sundarbans Wetland
(c) Chilika Lake
(d) Deepor Beel

**42.** With reference to Olive Ridley Turtles, consider the following statements:

1. Olive Ridley turtles are found primarily along the Indian coast and are not seen in other parts of the world.
2. The Arribada phenomenon, where thousands of turtles come together to nest, is a unique feature of Olive Ridley turtles.
3. The Odisha coast is the most significant nesting ground for Olive Ridley turtles in India.

Which of the statements given above are correct?

(a) 1 and 2 only (b) 2 and 3 only
(c) 1 and 3 only (d) 1, 2 and 3

**43.** With reference to Olive Ridley Turtle Conservation, consider the following statements:

1. The Turtle Excluder Device (TED) is mandatory for fishing trawlers in Odisha to prevent turtle entanglement.
2. Gahirmatha Beach in Odisha is the largest nesting ground for Olive Ridley turtles in the world.
3. Olive Ridley turtles are listed under Appendix I of CITES.

How many of the above statements is/are incorrect?

(a) Only one
(b) Only two
(c) All three
(d) None

**44.** Consider the following statements about vultures in India:

1. The White-rumped Vulture, Indian Vulture and Slender-billed Vulture are all classified as Critically Endangered by the IUCN due to population decline caused primarily by diclofenac use.
2. The Egyptian Vulture and Red-headed Vulture are listed as Endangered, with both species facing threats from habitat loss and poisoning.
3. Himalayan Griffon Vulture and Cinerous Vulture are wintering species in India and are categorised as Near Threatened by the IUCN.
4. The Vulture Breeding Centre in Pinjore, Haryana focuses on the ex situ breeding of Gyps species to replenish their populations in the wild.

How many of the above statements is/ are correct?

(a) Only one (b) Only two
(c) Only three (d) All four

**45.** Consider the following statements regarding Panna Biosphere Reserve:

1. The Panna Biosphere Reserve is located in Madhya Pradesh and it includes both the Panna National Park and parts of the Gangau Wildlife Sanctuary.
2. The area is known for its teak forests and dry mixed forests, with the River Narmada flowing through it.
3. The reserve has been added to UNESCO's World Network of Biosphere Reserves.
4. The Gond, Khairuas and Yadavas are among the major ethnic groups residing in the reserve area.

Which of the statements given above are correct?

(a) 1 and 3 only (b) 2 and 4 only
(c) 1, 3 and 4 only (d) 1, 2, 3 and 4

**46.** Consider the following statements regarding Biodiversity Management Committees (BMCs) in India:

1. In India, the BMCs play a crucial role in realising the objectives of the Nagoya Protocol.
2. BMCs have key responsibilities in determining access and benefit sharing, including the authority to levy collection fees on access to biological resources within their jurisdiction.

Which of the statements given above is/are correct?

(a) 1 only (b) 2 only
(c) Both 1 and 2 (d) Neither 1 nor 2

**47.** Which of the following statements is/are correct regarding various wildlife sanctuaries and national parks in India?

1. The Mahuadanr Wildlife Sanctuary in Jharkhand is the only wildlife sanctuary in India dedicated to wolves.
2. The Little Rann of Kutch is home to the endemic species of the Wild Asian Ass.
3. Velavadar Grasslands in Gujarat are famous for the last cheetahs in India and Blackbucks.
4. Dachigam National Park in Jammu and Kashmir is the only place where Hanguls are found.

Select the correct answer using the codes given below:

(a) 1 and 2 only
(b) 2, 3 and 4 only
(c) 1, 2 and 4 only
(d) All of the above

**48.** In which of the following regions has the largest decline in leopard population been observed according to the Status of Leopards in India 2022 report?

(a) Central India and Eastern Ghats
(b) Shivalik Hills and Gangetic Plains
(c) Madhya Pradesh
(d) Western Ghats

**49.** Consider the following pairs:

| | Aspect | Location and Description |
|---|---|---|
| 1. | Nanjarayan Bird Sanctuary, Tamil Nadu | Located on the banks of the Cauvery river, known for hosting endangered species of birds. |
| 2. | Kazhuveli Sanctuary, Tamil Nadu | Located on the Coromandel Coast, supports long-distance migratory birds, declared Tamil Nadu's 16th bird sanctuary in 2021. |
| 3. | Tawa Reservoir, Madhya Pradesh | Located at the confluence of the Tawa and Denwa rivers, plays a crucial role in irrigation and supports migratory bird species. |

How many above pairs is/are correctly matched?

(a) Only one (b) Only two
(c) All three (d) None

**50.** The Kanchenjunga National Park is known for its stunning natural and cultural features. In this context, which of the following features are associated with the park?

1. Zemu Glacier, one of the largest glaciers in Asia.
2. Mt. Kanchenjunga, the third-highest peak in the world.
3. Milam Glacier, located in the Kumaon Himalayas.
4. Sacred traditions involving Mayel Lyang and Beyul.

Select the correct answer from the codes given below:

(a) 1 and 3 only (b) 2 and 4 only
(c) 1, 2 and 4 only (d) 1, 2, 3 and 4

**51.** Consider the following statements about the Great Himalayan National Park (GHNP):

1. The Great Himalayan National Park was constituted in 1984 and is located in the Banjaar Sub-Division of Kullu district in Himachal Pradesh.
2. The park is home to 10% of the world's and 50% of India's endemic plant species.
3. The GHNP is the source of the rivers Jiwa Nal, Sainj, Tirthan and Parvati, all tributaries of the river Beas.
4. The GHNP was awarded the UNESCO World Heritage Site status in 2014 for its biodiversity conservation.

Which of the statements given above is/are correct?

(a) 1 and 3 only (b) 1, 2 and 4 only
(c) 2, 3 and 4 only (d) 1, 2, 3 and 4

**52.** Which of the following statements is/are correct about the Kaziranga National Park?

1. It is a UNESCO World Heritage Site.
2. It has been recognised as an 'Important Bird and Biodiversity Area (IBA)' by BirdLife International.
3. River Brahmaputra flows through it.

Select the correct answer using the codes given below:

(a) 1 only (b) 1 and 2 only
(c) 2 and 3 only (d) 1, 2 and 3

**53.** UNESCO's Man and the Biosphere (MAB) Programme aims to achieve which of the following objectives?

1. Establishing a scientific basis for improving relationships between people and their environments.
2. Focusing on natural sciences exclusively for the conservation of biosphere resources.
3. Promoting innovative approaches to economic development that are socially, culturally and environmentally sustainable.
4. Predicting the consequences of today's actions on the environment for better resource management.

Select the correct answer using the codes given below:

(a) 1, 2 and 3 only (b) 1, 3 and 4 only
(c) 2, 3 and 4 only (d) 1, 2, 3 and 4

**54.** Consider the following statements regarding Keoladeo National Park:

**Statement I:** Keoladeo National Park is a wetland of international importance and serves as a critical wintering ground for migratory waterfowl from the Central Asian Flyway.

**Statement II:** The park was placed on the Montreux Record in 1990 due to the successful restoration of the Siberian Crane population and improved water management practices.

Which one of the following is correct in respect of the above statements?

(a) Both Statement I and Statement II are correct and Statement II is the correct explanation for Statement I.

(b) Both Statement I and Statement II are correct, but Statement II is not the correct explanation for Statement I

(c) Statement I is correct, but Statement II is incorrect.

(d) Statement I is incorrect, but Statement II is correct.

**55.** Consider the following statements regarding the Kashmir Musk Deer (KMD):

1. The Kashmir Musk Deer is classified as an endangered species by the IUCN.
2. The species is highly sought after by poachers for its musk or scent glands.
3. It is the only species of musk deer found in the Himalayan region.

How many of the statements given above is/are correct?

(a) Only one
(b) Only two
(c) All three
(d) None

**56.** Consider the following statements regarding the Leatherback Turtle:

1. Leatherback Turtles are the largest sea turtles in the world and are considered a Vulnerable species by the IUCN.
2. The Andaman and Nicobar Islands constitute the only nesting population of Leatherback Turtles in India.
3. Leatherback Turtles primarily feed on jellyfish and play a significant role in controlling their populations.

How many of the above statements is/are incorrect?

(a) Only one
(b) Only two
(c) All three
(d) None

**57.** With reference to geo-heritage in India, consider the following statements:

1. Geo-heritage sites are geological features of cultural or scientific importance, providing insights into Earth's history and used for educational purposes.
2. The Geological Survey of India (GSI) is responsible for identifying and declaring Geological Heritage Sites and National Geological Monuments in the country.
3. India currently has 34 officially designated Geological Heritage Sites.

How many of the statements given above is/are correct?

(a) Only one (b) Only two
(c) All three (d) None

**58.** Consider the following statements regarding the Indian Wild Ass:

1. The Indian Wild Ass is found only in and around the Rann of Kutch.
2. It has been classified as Near Threatened by the International Union for Conservation of Nature (IUCN).
3. The primary threat to the Indian Wild Ass comes from the spread of Prosopis juliflora, a shrub species.

How many of the above statements is/are correct?

(a) Only one (b) Only two
(c) All three (d) None

**59.** Which of the following factors are responsible for the decline in leopard populations in regions like Odisha, Kerala and Uttarakhand, as per the Status of Leopards in India 2022 report?

1. Habitat loss due to mining and human activities
2. Targeted poaching for skins and body parts
3. Competition with tigers within protected areas
4. Road accidents

Select the correct answer from the given options:

(a) 1 and 2 only
(b) 1, 2 and 4 only
(c) 2 and 3 only
(d) 1, 2, 3 and 4

**60.** What is the primary goal of the International Big Cat Alliance (IBCA)?

(a) To focus solely on conserving the tiger population in a range of countries.
(b) To conserve all big cat species and their habitats through global cooperation and to align biodiversity conservation with local needs and sustainable development goals.
(c) To reintroduce big cat species into non-range countries that have lost these species.
(d) To promote tourism in areas where big cats reside to generate revenue for local governments.

**61.** A sandy and saline area is the natural habitat of an Indian animal species. The animal has no predators in that area but its existence is threatened due to the destruction of its habitat. Which one of the following could be that animal?

(a) Indian wild buffalo
(b) Indian wild ass
(c) Indian wild boar
(d) Indian gazelle

**62.** Consider the following :

1. Black-necked crane
2. Cheetah
3. Flying squirrel
4. Snow leopard

Which of the above are naturally found in India?

(a) 1, 2 and 3 only
(b) 1, 3 and 4 only
(c) 2 and 4 only
(d) 1, 2, 3 and 4

**63.** Melanochlamys droupadi is recently seen in the news. Which of the following options best describes it?

(a) It is a new species of tropical fish discovered in the Bay of Bengal, named after President Droupadi Murmu.
(b) It is a newly discovered marine species of head-shield sea slug found along the coasts of West Bengal and Odisha, named after President Droupadi Murmu.
(c) It is a species of coral found in the Indian Ocean, named to honor President Droupadi Murmu for her environmental contributions.
(d) It is a newly discovered species of crab found in Odisha and West Bengal, known for its unique red colour.

**64.** Consider the following statements regarding the Snow Leopard Population Assessment in India (SPAI) Program and its findings:

1. The SPAI is the first-ever comprehensive scientific exercise conducted to assess snow leopard populations across India's trans-Himalayan region.
2. The assessment recorded a population of 718 snow leopards in India, with the majority found in Ladakh.
3. Conservation efforts highlighted by the report include the establishment of a Snow Leopard Cell under the Wildlife Institute of India (WII) for long-term population monitoring.

Which of the above statement(s) are correct?

(a) 1 and 2 only
(b) 2 and 3 only
(c) 1 and 3 only
(d) 1, 2 and 3

**65.** Arrange the following protected areas in West Bengal from West to East:

1. Jaldapara National Park
2. Gorumara National Park
3. Buxa Tiger Reserve
4. Sundarbans National Park
5. Neora Valley National Park
6. Singalila National Park

Select the correct order from the codes given below:

(a) 6-1-2-5-3-4
(b) 1-6-5-3-2-4
(c) 6-1-5-2-3-4
(d) 6-1-2-5-3-4

**66.** What is the primary cause behind the golden coloration in Golden tigers?

(a) Golden tigers have a separate sub-species that exhibits their unique golden colour.
(b) The golden colouration in Golden tigers is caused by a recessive gene called 'wideband,' which reduces melanin production, leading to a golden or blond appearance with reduced orange stripes.
(c) Golden tigers are a result of a mutation in the Tabby gene that causes them to lack any orange coloration.
(d) The golden colour of Golden tigers is caused by environmental factors that alter the skin pigmentation of Bengal tigers in the wild.

**67.** Which of the following regions has the highest number of elephant corridors according to the Elephant Corridors of India, 2023 Report?

(a) Southern India
(b) West Bengal
(c) Northern India
(d) East Central region

**68.** How many of the following statements regarding the Global Declaration for River Dolphins are correct?

1. The Global Declaration for River Dolphins aims to halt the decline of all river dolphin species by implementing measures like eradicating unsustainable fishing practices and creating protected areas.
2. The declaration was signed by 11 countries from Asia and South America, including India, Bangladesh and Brazil.
3. The declaration aims to protect river dolphins by focusing exclusively on research and monitoring efforts.
4. World River Dolphin Day, celebrated on 24th October, is promoted to raise awareness about the conservation of river dolphins.

Choose the correct answer from the options given below:

(a) Only one
(b) Only two
(c) Only three
(d) All four

**69.** Arrange the following Biosphere Reserves from West to East:

1. Panna Biosphere Reserve
2. Khangchendzonga National Park
3. Simlipal Biosphere Reserve
4. Sundarbans Biosphere Reserve

Choose the correct order from the options given below :

(a) 1-4-2-3
(b) 1-3-4-2
(c) 1-3-2-4
(d) 1-2-3-4

**70.** Identify the tiger reserve based on the following statements:

1. It is located in the northern part of Goa, in Sanguem taluka, near Valpoi town.
2. The reserve encompasses picturesque waterfalls, including Vazra Sakla Falls and Virdi Falls.
3. It is known for the nesting grounds of critically endangered Long-billed vultures near Vazra Falls.

Choose the correct answer from the options given below:

(a) Mhadei Tiger Reserve
(b) Anshi Tiger Reserve
(c) Bandipur Tiger Reserve
(d) Dandeli Tiger Reserve

**71.** Identify the term based on the following description:

1. It is the totality of microorganisms, including bacteria, viruses, protozoa and fungi, along with their collective genetic material present in the gastrointestinal tract (GIT).
2. It plays a crucial role in nutrient absorption, synthesis of enzymes, vitamins, and amino acids and production of short-chain fatty acids (SCFAs).
3. It is distinct from "microbiota," which usually refers to the microorganisms found within a specific environment.

Choose the correct answer from the codes given below:

(a) Gut Microbiome
(b) Gut Flora
(c) Probiotics
(d) Gastric Microbiota

**72.** Consider the following statements regarding BirdLife International and Important Bird and Biodiversity Areas (IBAs):

1. BirdLife International is the world's largest nature conservation partnership, working to conserve birds, their habitats, and global biodiversity.
2. It is the official Red List Authority for birds under the IUCN.
3. Important Bird and Biodiversity Areas (IBAs) are classified into four categories, including sites with biome-restricted species and congregations of birds.
4. The Bombay Natural History Society (BNHS) is the partner organisation of BirdLife International in India.

How many of the above statements is/are correct?

(a) Only one
(b) Only two
(c) Only three
(d) All four

**73.** Some protected areas in India are designated as Wildlife Sanctuaries, while others are designated as National Parks. What is the difference between the two?

(a) Wildlife Sanctuaries are declared by the State Government, whereas National Parks are declared by the Central Government.
(b) In Wildlife Sanctuaries, certain human activities like grazing and collection of firewood are permitted, whereas in National Parks, human activities are strictly prohibited.
(c) Wildlife Sanctuaries focus solely on the conservation of wild animals, whereas National Parks focus on the conservation of both flora and fauna, as well as landscapes.
(d) There is no significant legal difference between Wildlife Sanctuaries and National Parks under the Wild Life (Protection) Amendment Act, 2022.

**74.** Identify the wildlife sanctuary based on the following characteristics:

1. It is part of the Western Ghats and is located in Karnataka's Uttara Kannada district.
2. The sanctuary is known for its rich biodiversity and diverse wildlife.
3. It is associated with the Kali Tiger Reserve, which includes another protected area called Anshi National Park.

Which wildlife sanctuary is being described?

(a) Bandipur Wildlife Sanctuary
(b) Nagarhole Wildlife Sanctuary
(c) Dandeli Wildlife Sanctuary
(d) Kudremukh Wildlife Sanctuary

**75.** What is the difference between tortoises and turtles?

(a) Tortoises have a high-domed, rounded, heavy shell and primarily live in water, while turtles have a streamlined shell and are primarily land-dwelling.
(b) Tortoises are adapted for terrestrial life with thick, columnar legs, while turtles have flipper-like legs adapted for aquatic environments.
(c) Both tortoises and turtles have similar shell shapes but different habitats and diets.
(d) There is no significant difference between tortoises and turtles in terms of their physical features or habitats.

**76.** With reference to protected areas in India, which of the following statements are correct?

1. The boundaries of a National Park can be altered by the State Government without any consultation or approval from the National Board of Wildlife.
2. Jim Corbett National Park, established in 1936, is India's first national park, located at the foothills of the Himalayas in Uttarakhand.
3. In Biosphere Reserves, the core zone allows no human activities, while the buffer zone and transition zone allow regulated human activities.

Select the correct answer using the codes given below:

(a) 2 only (b) 1 and 2 only
(c) 2 and 3 only (d) 1, 2 and 3

**77.** Other than poaching, what are the possible reasons for the decline in the population of Ganges River Dolphins?

1. Construction of dams and barrages on rivers.
2. Increase in the population of crocodiles in rivers.
3. Getting trapped in fishing nets accidentally.
4. Use of synthetic fertilizers and other agricultural chemicals in crop fields in the vicinity of rivers.

Select the correct answer using the codes given below.

(a) 1 and 2 only
(b) 2 and 3 only
(c) 1, 3 and 4 only
(d) 1, 2, 3 and 4

**78.** Consider the following statements regarding the Mangrove Alliance for Climate:

1. The Mangrove Alliance for Climate was launched at COP27 with the goal of promoting mangroves as a nature-based solution to climate change.
2. The initiative is led by India and Indonesia, with support from other nations like UAE, Sri Lanka and Japan.
3. It aims to encourage private sector philanthropy and support blue carbon solutions through mangrove restoration.

How many of the statements given above is/are incorrect?

(a) Only one
(b) Only two
(c) All three
(d) None

**79.** How does the National Biodiversity Authority (NBA) contribute to the protection of Indian agriculture?

1. The NBA prevents biopiracy and protects indigenous and traditional genetic resources.
2. The NBA directly monitors and supervises scientific research on the genetic modification of crop plants.
3. Applications for Intellectual Property Rights (IPR) related to genetic or biological resources cannot be filed without the NBA's approval.

Which of the statements given above is/are correct?

(a) 1 only
(b) 2 and 3 only
(c) 1 and 3 only
(d) 1, 2 and 3

**80.** Which of the following best describes a key focus of the New Delhi Declaration for Asian Rhino Range Countries?

(a) Encouraging controlled rhino horn trade among range countries to curb illegal poaching.
(b) Promoting transboundary collaboration for the conservation of the greater one-horned rhino and the expansion of rhino habitats.
(c) Establishing captive breeding programmes exclusively for Javan rhinos in protected enclosures.
(d) Limiting conservation efforts to the Sumatran rhino population in Indonesia and Malaysia.

**81.** With reference to the current status and conservation efforts for rhino species, consider the following statements:

1. The Greater one-horned rhino populations in India and Nepal are thriving due to enhanced protection efforts.
2. The creation of a linked rhino corridor in Assam connects all major protected areas where rhinos are found, such as Kaziranga National Park and Manas National Park.
3. The project to create DNA profiles for all rhinos in India was introduced to help monitor population health and track migration patterns.

How many of the above statements is/are correct?

(a) Only one (b) Only two
(c) All three (d) None

**82.** The New Delhi Declaration on Asian rhinos focuses primarily on which of the following?

(a) Encouraging international trade of rhino horns to fund conservation efforts.
(b) Limiting conservation efforts exclusively to the Javan and Sumatran rhino populations.
(c) Increasing captive breeding programs for all Asian rhino species.
(d) Promoting transboundary collaboration among Asian rhino range countries, particularly India, Nepal and Bhutan, for the conservation and protection of the Greater one-horned rhino.

**83.** With reference to Ex-Situ Conservation, which of the following methods focuses on preserving genetic diversity?

1. Seed banks and gene banks
2. Long-term captive breeding
3. Cryopreservation of gametes and embryos
4. Zoological gardens or zoos

Select the correct answer using the codes given below:

(a) 1 and 3 only
(b) 1, 2, and 3 only
(c) 1, 3, and 4 only
(d) 1, 2, 3 and 4

**84.** With reference to Seed Banks and Gene Banks, which of the following statements are correct?

1. Seed banks store genetic material to protect species from extinction due to natural catastrophes.
2. The Indian Seed Vault is located in the Svalbard Global Seed Vault in the Arctic Ocean.
3. The Indian Seed Vault is a joint venture of the National Bureau of Plant Genetic Resources and DRDO.

Select the correct answer using the codes given below:

(a) 1 only (b) 1 and 3 only
(c) 2 and 3 only (d) 1, 2 and 3

**85.** With reference to Cryopreservation, consider the following statements:

1. It involves preserving biological material by cooling cells to extremely low temperatures.
2. Cryopreservation can preserve biological samples indefinitely by suspending their metabolic activities.
3. Cryopreservation is used only for animal conservation and not for plants.

Which of the statements given above are correct?

(a) 1 and 2 only (b) 2 and 3 only
(c) 1 and 3 only (d) 1, 2 and 3

**86.** With reference to National Parks, consider the following statements:

1. National Parks can only be declared by the State Government.
2. Grazing and other human activities are permitted inside National Parks, as allowed by the Wildlife Protection Act of 1972.
3. National Parks are protected under Category II of IUCN.
4. The first national park in India was established as Hailey National Park in Uttarakhand in 1936.

How many of the statements given above is/are correct?

(a) Only one (b) Only two
(c) Only three (d) All four

**87.** With reference to Wildlife Sanctuaries, consider the following statements:

1. A wildlife sanctuary can be upgraded to a National Park.
2. Wildlife sanctuaries are declared by the Central Government alone.
3. Sanctuaries are protected under Category IV of IUCN.

Which of the statements given above are correct?

(a) 1 and 2 only
(b) 1 and 3 only
(c) 2 and 3 only
(d) 1, 2 and 3

**88.** Arrange the following areas in the correct order of protection, from highest to lowest:

1. Wildlife Sanctuary
2. National Park
3. Protected Forest
4. Reserved Forest

Choose the correct option from the codes given below:

(a) 4-2-3-1 (b) 1-2-4-3
(c) 2-4-1-3 (d) 2-1-4-3

**89.** With reference to Ecologically Sensitive Zones (ESZ), which of the following activities are permitted?

1. Ongoing agricultural or horticultural practices
2. Establishment of hotels and resorts
3. Organic farming
4. Erection of electrical cables

Select the correct answer using the codes given below:

(a) 1 and 2 only (b) 2 and 4 only
(c) 1 and 3 only (d) 1, 3 and 4 only

**90.** With reference to Sacred groves, consider the following statements:

1. Sacred groves are protected by local communities due to their religious and cultural significance.
2. Sacred groves in India are protected under the Wildlife (Protection) Amendment Act, 2002.
3. Sacred groves are only found in the Khasi Hills of Meghalaya.

Which of the statements given above are correct?

(a) 1 and 2 only
(b) 2 and 3 only
(c) 1 and 3 only
(d) 1, 2 and 3

**91.** With reference to the three species of crocodilians in India—Gharial, Mugger, and Saltwater Crocodile—consider the following statements:

1. The Gharial is critically endangered and can be found in clean river habitats like the National Chambal Sanctuary.
2. The Mugger Crocodile is an extinct species found only in Bhutan.
3. The Saltwater Crocodile is listed as Vulnerable by the IUCN and is found along the coastal regions of India, including the Andaman and Nicobar Islands.

Which of the statements given above are correct?

(a) 1 only (b) 1 and 3 only
(c) 2 and 3 only (d) 1, 2 and 3

**92.** With reference to Elephant Corridors in India, consider the following statements:

1. West Bengal has the highest number of elephant corridors, constituting 17% of the total.
2. The biggest threats to elephant corridors in central India are coal mining and iron ore mining.
3. Southern India has the fewest number of elephant corridors compared to other regions of India.

Which of the statements given above are correct?

(a) 2 and 3 only (b) 1 and 2 only
(c) 1 and 3 only (d) 1, 2 and 3

# OMR SHEET

**Assessment Round**

| | | | | | | | |
|---|---|---|---|---|---|---|---|
| 1 | (a) (b) (c) (d) | 31 | (a) (b) (c) (d) | 61 | (a) (b) (c) (d) | 91 | (a) (b) (c) (d) |
| 2 | (a) (b) (c) (d) | 32 | (a) (b) (c) (d) | 62 | (a) (b) (c) (d) | 92 | (a) (b) (c) (d) |
| 3 | (a) (b) (c) (d) | 33 | (a) (b) (c) (d) | 63 | (a) (b) (c) (d) | 93 | (a) (b) (c) (d) |
| 4 | (a) (b) (c) (d) | 34 | (a) (b) (c) (d) | 64 | (a) (b) (c) (d) | 94 | (a) (b) (c) (d) |
| 5 | (a) (b) (c) (d) | 35 | (a) (b) (c) (d) | 65 | (a) (b) (c) (d) | 95 | (a) (b) (c) (d) |
| 6 | (a) (b) (c) (d) | 36 | (a) (b) (c) (d) | 66 | (a) (b) (c) (d) | 96 | (a) (b) (c) (d) |
| 7 | (a) (b) (c) (d) | 37 | (a) (b) (c) (d) | 67 | (a) (b) (c) (d) | 97 | (a) (b) (c) (d) |
| 8 | (a) (b) (c) (d) | 38 | (a) (b) (c) (d) | 68 | (a) (b) (c) (d) | 98 | (a) (b) (c) (d) |
| 9 | (a) (b) (c) (d) | 39 | (a) (b) (c) (d) | 69 | (a) (b) (c) (d) | 99 | (a) (b) (c) (d) |
| 10 | (a) (b) (c) (d) | 40 | (a) (b) (c) (d) | 70 | (a) (b) (c) (d) | 100 | (a) (b) (c) (d) |
| 11 | (a) (b) (c) (d) | 41 | (a) (b) (c) (d) | 71 | (a) (b) (c) (d) | 101 | (a) (b) (c) (d) |
| 12 | (a) (b) (c) (d) | 42 | (a) (b) (c) (d) | 72 | (a) (b) (c) (d) | 102 | (a) (b) (c) (d) |
| 13 | (a) (b) (c) (d) | 43 | (a) (b) (c) (d) | 73 | (a) (b) (c) (d) | 103 | (a) (b) (c) (d) |
| 14 | (a) (b) (c) (d) | 44 | (a) (b) (c) (d) | 74 | (a) (b) (c) (d) | 104 | (a) (b) (c) (d) |
| 15 | (a) (b) (c) (d) | 45 | (a) (b) (c) (d) | 75 | (a) (b) (c) (d) | 105 | (a) (b) (c) (d) |
| 16 | (a) (b) (c) (d) | 46 | (a) (b) (c) (d) | 76 | (a) (b) (c) (d) | 106 | (a) (b) (c) (d) |
| 17 | (a) (b) (c) (d) | 47 | (a) (b) (c) (d) | 77 | (a) (b) (c) (d) | 107 | (a) (b) (c) (d) |
| 18 | (a) (b) (c) (d) | 48 | (a) (b) (c) (d) | 78 | (a) (b) (c) (d) | 108 | (a) (b) (c) (d) |
| 19 | (a) (b) (c) (d) | 49 | (a) (b) (c) (d) | 79 | (a) (b) (c) (d) | 109 | (a) (b) (c) (d) |
| 20 | (a) (b) (c) (d) | 50 | (a) (b) (c) (d) | 80 | (a) (b) (c) (d) | 110 | (a) (b) (c) (d) |
| 21 | (a) (b) (c) (d) | 51 | (a) (b) (c) (d) | 81 | (a) (b) (c) (d) | 111 | (a) (b) (c) (d) |
| 22 | (a) (b) (c) (d) | 52 | (a) (b) (c) (d) | 82 | (a) (b) (c) (d) | 112 | (a) (b) (c) (d) |
| 23 | (a) (b) (c) (d) | 53 | (a) (b) (c) (d) | 83 | (a) (b) (c) (d) | 113 | (a) (b) (c) (d) |
| 24 | (a) (b) (c) (d) | 54 | (a) (b) (c) (d) | 84 | (a) (b) (c) (d) | 114 | (a) (b) (c) (d) |
| 25 | (a) (b) (c) (d) | 55 | (a) (b) (c) (d) | 85 | (a) (b) (c) (d) | 115 | (a) (b) (c) (d) |
| 26 | (a) (b) (c) (d) | 56 | (a) (b) (c) (d) | 86 | (a) (b) (c) (d) | 116 | (a) (b) (c) (d) |
| 27 | (a) (b) (c) (d) | 57 | (a) (b) (c) (d) | 87 | (a) (b) (c) (d) | 117 | (a) (b) (c) (d) |
| 28 | (a) (b) (c) (d) | 58 | (a) (b) (c) (d) | 88 | (a) (b) (c) (d) | 118 | (a) (b) (c) (d) |
| 29 | (a) (b) (c) (d) | 59 | (a) (b) (c) (d) | 89 | (a) (b) (c) (d) | 119 | (a) (b) (c) (d) |
| 30 | (a) (b) (c) (d) | 60 | (a) (b) (c) (d) | 90 | (a) (b) (c) (d) | 120 | (a) (b) (c) (d) |

## Calculate Your Score

| | |
|---|---|
| **Correct (✓)** | |
| **Incorrect (✓)** | |
| **Unattempted** | |
| **Total Score** | |
| **Accuracy (%)** | |

## Reasons for Incorrect Answers?

| | |
|---|---|
| 1. Lack of Knowledge/Existing Source Insufficient | |
| 2. Lack of Multiple Revision | |
| 3. Common Sense Mistakes | |

**Note :**

1. Calculate total score as correct answers carry 2 marks each 1/3rd marks will deducted for **Incorrect** Answers.
2. Calculate Accuracy (%) by dividing the number of correct answers to the total number of attempted questions.

## Past Learning

**1.** Consider the following pairs: **(2024)**

| | Country | Animals found in its natural habitat |
|---|---|---|
| 1. | Brazil | Indri |
| 2. | Indonesia | Elk |
| 3. | Madagascar | Bonobo |

How many of the pairs given above is/are correctly matched?

(a) Only one (b) Only two
(c) All three (d) None

**2.** Which one of the following is the best example of repeated falls in sea level, giving rise to present-day extensive marshland?

(a) Bhitarkanika Mangroves
(b) Marakkanam Salt Pans
(c) Naupada Swamp
(d) Rann of Kutch

**3.** Consider the following pairs : **(2022)**

| | Wetland/Lake | Location |
|---|---|---|
| 1. | Hokera Wetland | Punjab |
| 2. | Renuka Wetland | Himachal Pradesh |
| 3. | Rudrasagar Lake | Tripura |
| 4. | Sasthamkotta Lake | Tamil Nadu |

How many pairs given above is/are correctly matched?

(a) Only one pair (b) Only two pairs
(c) Only three pairs (d) All four pairs

**4.** 'Biorock technology' is talked about in which one of the following situations? **(2022)**

(a) Restoration of damaged coral reefs
(b) Development of building materials using plant residue
(c) Identification of areas for exploration/extraction of shale gas
(d) Providing salt licks for wild animals in forests/protected areas

**5.** With reference to India's Desert National Park, which of the following statements are correct? **(2022)**

1. It is spread over two districts.
2. There is no human habitation inside the Park.
3. It is one of the natural habitats of the Great Indian Bustard.

Select the correct answer using the codes given below:

(a) 1 and 2 only
(b) 2 and 3 only
(c) 1 and 3 only
(d) 1, 2 and 3

**6.** Among the following Tiger Reserves, which one has the largest area under 'Critical Tiger Habitat'? **(2020)**

(a) Corbett
(b) Ranthambore
(c) Nagarjunsagar-Srisailam
(d) Sunderbans

**7.** Which of the following Protected Areas are located in Cauvery basin? **(2020)**

1. Nagarhole National park
2. Papikonda National park
3. Sathyamangalam Tiger Reserve
4. Wayanad Wildlife sanctuary

Select the correct answer using the codes given below :

(a) 1 and 2 only (b) 3 and 4 only
(c) 1, 3 and 4 only (d) 1,2, 3 and 4

**8.** Which one of the following protected areas is well-known for the conservation of a sub-species of the Indian swamp deer (Barasinga) that thrives well in hard ground and is exclusively graminivorous? **(2020)**

(a) Kanha National Park
(b) Manas National Park
(c) Mudumalai Wildlife Sanctuary
(d) Tal Chhapar Wildlife Sanctuary

**9.** Which of the following are the most likely places to find the musk deer in its natural habitat? **(2020)**

1. Askot Wildlife Sanctuary
2. Gangotri National Park
3. Kishanpur Wildlife Sanctuary
4. Manas National Park

Select the correct answer using the codes given below

(a) 1 and 2 only
(b) 2 and 3 only
(c) 3 and 4 only
(d) 1 and 4 only

**10.** Which one of the following national parks lies completely in the Temperate alpine zone? **(2019)**

(a) Manas national park
(b) Namdapha national park
(c) Neora Valley National Park
(d) Valley of Flower National Park

**11.** Consider the following States : **(2019)**

1. Chhattisgarh
2. Madhya Pradesh
3. Maharashtra
4. Odisha

With reference to the States mentioned above, in terms of percentage of forest cover to the total area of State, which one of the following is the correct ascending order?

(a) 2-3-1-4 (b) 2-3-4-1
(c) 3-2-4-1 (d) 3-2-1-4

**12.** Which one of the following are Agasthyamala biosphere reserve? **(2019)**

(a) Neyyar, Peppara and Shendurney wildlife sanctuaries and Kalakad Mundanthurai tiger reserve
(b) Mudumalai sathayamangalam and Wayanad wildlife sanctuaries and silent valley national park
(c) Kaundinya Gundla Bhrameshwaram and Papikonda Wildlife Sanctuaries and Mukurthi National park
(d) Kawal and Shree Venkateshwara wildlife sanctuaries; and Nagarjunasagar-Srisailam tiger reserve

**13.** In which one of the following States is Pakhui Wildlife Sanctuary located? **(2018)**

(a) Arunachal Pradesh
(b) Manipur
(c) Meghalaya
(d) Nagaland

**14.** Recently there was a proposal to translocate some of the lions from their natural habitat in Gujarat to which one of the following sites? **(2017)**

(a) Corbett National Park
(b) Kuno Palpur Wildlife Sanctuary
(c) Mudumalai Wildlife Sanctuary
(d) Sariska National Park

**15.** From the ecological point of view, which one of the following assumes importance in being a good link between the Eastern Ghats and the Western Ghats? **(2017)**

(a) Sathyamangalam Tiger Reserve
(b) Nallamala Forest
(c) Nagarhole National Park
(d) Seshachalam Biosphere Reserve

**16.** 'Gadgil Committee Report' and 'Kasturirangan Committee Report', sometimes seen in the news, are related to:

(a) constitutional reforms **(2016)**
(b) Ganga Action Plan
(c) linking of rivers
(d) protection of Western Ghats

**17.** Which one of the following National Parks has a climate that varies from tropical to subtropical, temperate and arctic? **(2015)**

(a) Khangchendzonga National Park
(b) Nandadevi National Park
(c) Neora Valley National Park
(d) Namdapha National Park

**18.** Which of the following National Parks is unique in being a swamp with floating vegetation that supports a rich biodiversity? **(2015)**

(a) Bhitarkanika National Park
(b) Keibul Lamjao National Park
(c) Keoladeo Ghana National Park
(d) Sultanpur National Park

**19.** Consider the following pairs : **(2014)**
1. Dampa Tiger Reserve : Mizoram
2. Gumti Wildlife Sanctuary: Sikkim
3. Saramati Peak : Nagaland

Which of the above pairs is/are correctly matched?
(a) 1 only
(b) 2 and 3 only
(c) 1 and 3 only
(d) 1, 2 and 3

**20.** Consider the following pairs : **(2014)**

| | Wetlands | Confluence of rivers |
|---|---|---|
| 1. | Harike Wetlands | Confluence of Beas and Satluj/Sutlej |
| 2. | Keoladeo Ghana National Park | Confluence of Banas and Chambal |
| 3. | Kolleru Lake | Confluence of Musi and Krishna |

Which of the above pairs is/are correctly matched?
(a) 1 only (b) 2 and 3 only
(c) 1 and 3 only (d) 1, 2 and 3

**21.** The most important strategy for the conservation of biodiversity together with traditional human life is the establishment of
(a) Biosphere reserves **(2014)**
(b) Botanical gardens
(c) National parks
(d) Wildlife sanctuaries

**22.** Consider the following pairs: **(2013)**
1. Nokrek Biosphere Reserve: Garo Hills
2. Loktak (Loktak) Lake : Barail Range
3. Namdapha National Park: Dafla Hills

Which of the above pairs is/are correctly matched?
(a) 1 only
(b) 2 and 3 only
(c) 1, 2 and 3
(d) None

**23.** Consider the following protected areas: **(2012)**
1. Bandipur 2. Bhitarkanika
3. Manas 4. Sunderbans

Which of the above are declared Tiger Reserves?
(a) 1 and 2 only (b) 1, 3 and 4 only
(c) 2, 3, and 4 only (d) 1, 2, 3 and 4

**24.** In which one among the following categories of protected areas in India are local people not allowed to collect and use biomass? **(2012)**
(a) Biosphere Reserves
(b) National Parks
(c) Wetlands declared under Ramsar Convention
(d) Wildlife Sanctuary

**25.** Consider the following pairs : **(2010)**

| | Protected area | Well-known for |
|---|---|---|
| 1. | Bhitarkanika, Orissa | Salt Water Crocodile |
| 2. | Desert National Park | Great Indian Bustard Rajasthan |
| 3. | Eravikulam, Kerala | Hoolock Gibbon |

Which of the pairs given above is/are correctly matched?
(a) 1 only (b) 1 and 2 only
(c) 2 only (d) 1, 2 and 3

**26.** Two important rivers–one with its source in Jharkhand (and known by a different name in Odisha), and another, with its source in Odisha–merge at a place only a short distance from the coast of the Bay of Bengal before flowing into the sea.
This is an important site of wildlife and biodiversity and a protected area. Which one of the following could be this? **(2011)**
(a) Bhitarkanika (b) Chandipur-on-sea
(c) Gopalpur-on-sea (d) Simlipal

**27.** Which of the following can be threats to the biodiversity of a geographical area? **(2012)**
1. Global warming
2. Fragmentation of habitat
3. Invasion of alien species
4. Promotion of vegetarianism

Select the correct answer using the codes given below :
(a) 1, 2 and 3 only (b) 2 and 3 only
(c) 1 and 4 only (d) 1, 2, 3 and 4

# Detailed Solutions

## Assessment Round

**1.** *(c)* Statement I is not correct, but Statement II is correct.

- **Statement I is incorrect:** While **State Government-owned lands** are commonly used for Conservation Reserves, they can also be declared on lands owned by other entities, including **private lands**, provided they are adjacent to National Parks or Sanctuaries and meet the necessary conservation criteria.
- **Statement II is correct: Community Reserves** are established on **private or community-owned lands,** where the landowners voluntarily commit to conserving wildlife and their habitats. It ensures the participation of local stakeholders in conservation efforts, fostering sustainable management practices.

**Thus, option (c) is the correct answer.**

**2.** *(a)* Both Statement I and Statement II are correct and Statement II is the correct explanation for Statement I.

- **Statement I is correct: Bio-rock technology** is an innovative method used for coral reef restoration and marine habitat enhancement. It is developed by marine scientists Wolf Hilbertz and Tom Goreau. Bio-rock technology provides a base structure that accelerates coral growth by reducing the energy corals typically expend in building their calcium carbonate skeletons.
- **Statement II is correct:** It involves steel structures that serve as a base for coral attachment. When a low-voltage current is applied, it stimulates the crystallization of minerals, especially calcium carbonate, which helps create an artificial reef that mimics natural coral reefs.

**Thus, option (a) is the correct answer.**

**3.** *(b)* 3 only

- **Option 1 is incorrect: Project Tiger** is specifically focused on the **conservation of tigers** and their habitats, primarily through the establishment and management of **tiger reserves.** It is not directly linked to the protection of **Biosphere Reserves,** which have a broader focus on ecosystem conservation.
- **Option 2 is incorrect:** The **National Mission for Clean Ganga** focuses on the **cleaning and rejuvenation of the Ganga river** and its tributaries. It is not directly linked to the protection of **Biosphere Reserves,** which encompass a range of ecosystems beyond river systems.
- **Option 3 is correct:** The **Man and Biosphere (MAB) Programme,** launched by **UNESCO,** is directly related to the **protection and sustainable management of Biosphere Reserves.** It promotes the **conservation of biodiversity** and the sustainable use of natural resources in these reserves.

**Thus, option (b) is the correct answer.**

**4.** *(b)* 1 and 3 only

- **Pair 1 is correct:** This initiative is aimed at curbing the **illegal trade of shahtoosh wool** from the endangered **Tibetan antelope (chiru).** The trade in shahtoosh products is illegal, as it contributes to the decline of the chiru population, making this initiative directly related to tackling illegal wildlife trade.
- **Pair 2 is incorrect:** This programme focuses on **ecosystem and biodiversity conservation** along the Ganga river, including species like the Ganges river Dolphin, but it is **not aimed at curbing illegal wildlife trade.**
- **Pair 3 is correct:** This initiative is focused on **curbing online illegal wildlife trade** in India. It involves tracking and prosecuting individuals involved in illegal wildlife trade through digital platforms, making it a key effort to combat illegal wildlife trafficking.

**Thus, option (b) is the correct answer.**

**5.** *(d)* 1, 2 and 3

- **Statement 1 is correct:** The **Wildlife Crime Control Bureau (WCCB)** was established as a **statutory body** under the provisions of the **Wildlife Protection Act, 1972.** Its role is to combat organised wildlife crime by enforcing the provisions of this law.
- **Statement 2 is correct:** The WCCB operates under the administrative control of the **Ministry of Environment, Forest and Climate Change (MoEFCC)**, which oversees wildlife protection and conservation efforts in India.
- **Statement 3 is correct:** The WCCB's primary responsibilities include gathering intelligence on wildlife crimes, coordinating with various State Governments and law enforcement agencies, and disseminating information related to wildlife crime to combat illegal activities.

**Thus, option (d) is the correct answer.**

**6.** *(a)* Only one

- **Statement 1 is correct:** Recent bird censuses, particularly in places like **Kaziranga National Park,** have recorded a **27% increase** in the population of **resident and migratory waterbirds.** This indicates a healthy ecosystem and improved conservation efforts in the region. The exact percentage of increase might vary slightly in different censuses, but the general trend of growth is correct.
- **Statement 2 is correct:** The census indeed recorded the presence of over **50,000 birds,** and **Baer's pochard** and **Bengal florican** were among the species identified. These species are notable for their conservation status, with **Baer's pochard** being critically endangered and **Bengal florican** also facing serious threats to its population.
- **Statement 3 is incorrect:** While **Kaziranga** is an important habitat for **Bengal floricans,** the highest concentration of this species is generally recorded in **Manas** and **Orang National Parks.** Kaziranga has populations of Bengal floricans but does not record the highest concentration after these two parks, making this statement incorrect.

**Thus, option (a) is the correct answer.**

**7.** *(a)* 1 and 2 only

- **Statement 1 is correct:** The **Bambi Bucket** is a **specialised firefighting tool** that is used by helicopters to collect and transport water. It is typically **lowered into natural water sources** like **rivers, ponds, lakes, or reservoirs** to collect water, which is then discharged over forest fires to extinguish them.
- **Statement 2 is correct:** The **National Action Plan for Forest Fires (NAPFF)** was launched **in 2018 to reduce the incidence of forest fires** and minimise the loss of forest cover and biodiversity. The plan emphasises involving **forest fringe communities by empowering** them through **training** and **collaboration** with state forest departments.
- **Statement 3 is incorrect:** The **Forest Fire Prevention and Management Scheme (FPM)** is **centrally sponsored.** It aims to reduce the occurrence and impact of forest fires, particularly in **remote and inaccessible regions.** It provides financial assistance to states for capacity building, equipment and infrastructure to manage forest fires effectively.

**Thus, option (a) is the correct answer.**

**8.** *(b)* Keibul Lamjao National Park

**Keibul Lamjao National Park,** located in **Manipur,** is unique for being the only **floating national park** in the world. It lies within **Loktak lake,** a large freshwater lake that has floating masses of decomposed plant material known as **phumdis.** These phumdis provide the park with its floating vegetation, creating a **swamp-like habitat** that supports a rich biodiversity, including the **endangered Sangai deer** (Manipur's state animal).

**Thus, option (b) is the correct answer.**

**9.** *(b)* Only two

- **Statement 1 is correct:** The **Wildlife Institute of India (WII),** established in **1982,** is an autonomous institution under the **Ministry of Environment, Forest and Climate Change (MoEFCC).** Located in **Dehradun,** it conducts wildlife research, training and education to support biodiversity conservation in India.

- **Statement 2 is incorrect:** The **President of the WII Society** is not the Director of the Institute. Instead, the **President** is usually the **Minister of Environment, Forest, and Climate Change** or a high-ranking government official from the **MoEFCC**. The **Director of the Institute** is the **head of the administration** and oversees the day-to-day activities and programmes, but does not hold the position of President of the WII Society.
- **Statement 3 is incorrect:** The **State of India's Birds 2023** report highlighted that **long-distance migratory birds** have faced a **sharp decline**, primarily those that **migrate long distances** and **breed in areas like Central Asia, Siberia,** or the **Arctic regions.** However, the report **did not specifically mention species** that breed in the **Antarctic region.**
- **Statement 4 is correct:** The **Bengal Florican** (Houbaropsis bengalensis) is a **Critically Endangered** bird species, primarily found in the **Himalayan Terai** grasslands of **Uttar Pradesh** and **Assam,** as well as in the **northeastern grasslands** of India. It inhabits areas such as **Kaziranga National Park** and other similar grassland ecosystems in the Terai region.

**Thus, option (b) is the correct answer.**

**10.** *(b)* Only two

- **Statement 1 is correct:** According to the **State of India's Birds 2023** report, **long-distance migratory birds,** particularly **shorebirds breeding in the Arctic,** have indeed shown a **drastic decline** in their populations, with some species experiencing **declines of up to 80%** in India.
- **Statement 2 is correct:** The **State of India's Birds 2023** report mentions that **generalist bird species** like the **Indian Peafowl, Rock Pigeon, and Asian Koel** have shown **increasing population trends.** These birds have **adapted well to urban and modified environments,** allowing them to thrive.
- **Statement 3 is incorrect:** The **Bengal Florican** (Houbaropsis bengalensis), a **Critically Endangered bird,** is primarily found in the **Terai grasslands** of the Himalayan foothills and **northeastern grasslands** of India, particularly in states like **Assam, Uttar Pradesh,** and other parts of the Terai region. It is **not restricted** to the **Western Ghats** or the **Eastern Coastal Plains** of India.
- **Statement 4 is incorrect:** The **Indian Skimmer** (Rynchops albicollis) is listed as **Endangered,** not **Critically Endangered.** It is found in and around **river systems** such as the **Ganga, Chambal, and Godavari.** The species is known for its distinctive skimming behaviour, where it flies over the water with its lower beak cutting the surface to catch fish.

**Thus, option (b) is the correct answer.**

**11.** *(c)* 2 and 3 only

- **Statement 1 is incorrect:** The **Bombay Natural History Society (BNHS)** is a non-governmental organisation (NGO) and not an autonomous organisation under the Ministry of Environment and Forests. It is an independent entity, although it works closely with governmental bodies and international organisations on conservation initiatives.
- **Statement 2 is correct:** The **BNHS** focuses on **nature conservation** through **action-based research, education, and public awareness.** The organisation researches various wildlife species, habitats, and ecosystems. It also runs **conservation projects** and **educational programmes** to raise public awareness about the importance of biodiversity conservation.
- **Statement 3 is correct: BNHS** organises and conducts **nature trails, birdwatching tours** and **camps** for the **general public** to promote awareness and understanding of wildlife and natural habitats.

**Thus, option (c) is the correct answer.**

**12.** *(b)* 2 and 3 only

- **Statement 1 is incorrect:** The **Animal Welfare Board of India (AWBI)** was **not established** under the **Environment (Protection) Act, 1986.** Instead, it was established in 1962 under the **Prevention of Cruelty to Animals Act, 1960.** The AWBI is responsible for promoting animal welfare, providing guidance and ensuring the implementation of the provisions of the **Prevention of Cruelty to Animals Act.**

- **Statement 2 is correct:** The **National Tiger Conservation Authority** (NTCA) is a **statutory body** that was established under the provisions of the **Wildlife (Protection) Act,** 1972, specifically through an amendment introduced in **2006.** NTCA's role is to ensure the **effective conservation of tigers** in India by overseeing the implementation of Project Tiger and various conservation measures.
- **Statement 3 is correct:** The **National Ganga River Basin Authority** (NGRBA), established in 2009 and chaired by the **Prime Minister of India,** aimed to ensure the comprehensive conservation and rejuvenation of the Ganga river. Its focus was on **inter-ministerial** and **interstate coordi-nation** for cleaning the river. In 2016, NGRBA was replaced by the **National Ganga Council,** which also remains chaired by the Prime Minister.

**Thus, option (b) is the correct answer.**

***13.*** *(c)* Statement I is correct, but Statement II is incorrect.

- **Statement I is correct:** The Sundarbans Biosphere Reserve indeed supports a significant population of the **endangered Royal Bengal Tiger.** The Sundarbans is the largest mangrove forest in the world and is famous for its unique population of tigers, which have adapted to the mangrove ecosystem.
- **Statement II is incorrect:** Sundarbans is primarily composed of mangrove forests, not tropical dry deciduous forests. The unique ecosystem of the Sundarbans includes tidal waterways, mudflats and small islands with dense mangrove vegetation, which is very different from dry deciduous forests.

**Thus, option (c) is the correct answer.**

***14.*** *(b)* Valmiki Tiger Reserve

Valmiki Tiger Reserve is the only tiger reserve located in the state of Bihar. It is situated in the **Terai region** along the border with Nepal, making it geographically unique. The reserve is part of the larger Valmiki National Park and is home to a rich variety of flora and fauna, including Bengal tigers.

**Thus, option (b) is the correct answer.**

***15.*** *(b)* Only two

- **Statement 1 is correct: Kaziranga National Park,** in Assam, is indeed a **UNESCO World Heritage Site.** It is situated between the **Brahmaputra river** to the North and the **Karbi Anglong hills** to the South. The park is famous for its large population of **one-horned rhinoceroses** and is home to many other species, including elephants and tigers.
- **Statement 2 is correct: Project Elephant** was launched in **1992** with the aim of providing **financial and technical support** to states that have significant elephant populations. Its objectives include the protection of elephants, their habitats, and migration corridors, as well as addressing issues like human-elephant conflict.
- **Statement 3 is incorrect: Karnataka,** not Kerala, holds the **highest population of elephants** in India. According to the last elephant census, Karnataka leads in terms of elephant numbers, followed by Assam and Kerala.

**Thus, option (b) is the correct answer.**

***16.*** *(a)* 1-2-3-4

- **Kaziranga National Park (1985):** It is located in **Assam,** was recognised by UNESCO in 1985. It is known for its large population of **one-horned rhinoceroses,** making it one of the most important protected areas in India. The park's floodplain ecosystem supports a rich variety of species, including elephants, tigers and water buffaloes.
- **Sundarbans National Park (1987):** It is located in the **Sundarbans delta** in **West Bengal,** was recognised by UNESCO in **1987.** It is the largest **mangrove forest** in the world and is home to the famous **Bengal tiger.** The unique ecosystem of the Sundarbans, with its tidal rivers, swamps and mangroves, makes it a globally significant site for biodiversity conservation.
- **Nanda Devi and Valley of Flowers National Parks (1988):** The **Nanda Devi National Park** and the **Valley of Flowers** in

**Uttarakhand** were together recognised by UNESCO in **1988** for their outstanding natural beauty and rich biodiversity. Nanda Devi is known for its rugged terrain and alpine flora, while the Valley of Flowers is famous for its stunning floral diversity, including numerous endemic species.

- **Great Himalayan National Park (2014):** The **Great Himalayan National Park,** located in **Himachal Pradesh,** was the last of these to be recognised by UNESCO in **2014.** This park is notable for its exceptional biodiversity and the presence of endangered species such as the **snow leopard** and **Himalayan brown bear.**

**Thus, option (a) is the correct answer.**

**17.** *(b)* Kaziranga National Park

- **Kaziranga National Park** is situated in the **Golaghat** and **Nagaon** districts of **Assam,** making it geographically aligned with the description.
- **Kaziranga** was designated a **UNESCO World Heritage Site** in 1985 due to its exceptional natural habitat and biodiversity. It is also a **Tiger Reserve,** with a significant population of tigers.
- **Kaziranga National Park** is world-famous for hosting the **largest population of Indian one-horned rhinoceroses.** The park is a critical conservation area for this species, which was once near extinction but now thrives due to successful protection efforts.

**Thus, option (b) is the correct answer.**

**18.** *(c)* Only three

- **Statement 1 is correct:** The **Mudumalai Tiger Reserve** is part of the **Nilgiri Biosphere Reserve,** which is recognised for its biodiversity. However, it is important to note that while the Nilgiri Biosphere Reserve is part of the **UNESCO Man and Biosphere Programme,** it is not a **World Heritage Site.** So, while this statement is partially correct, it should not be fully counted as correct for this question.
- **Statement 2 is correct:** Mudumalai Tiger Reserve is located in **Tamil Nadu** and shares boundaries with **Bandipur Tiger Reserve** in **Karnataka** and **Wayanad Wildlife Sanctuary** in **Kerala.** This creates a large contiguous wildlife habitat across the three states.
- **Statement 3 is correct:** Mudumalai is known for its large populations of **Asian elephants** and rich biodiversity, including flora such as **Elephant Grass and bamboo,** and valuable timber species like **Teak** and **Rosewood.**
- **Statement 4 is incorrect:** The **Sangai Deer** (also known as the **Brow-antlered Deer**) is native to **Manipur,** particularly in the **Keibul Lamjao National Park,** not Mudumalai Tiger Reserve. Mudumalai is not known for hosting Sangai Deer.

**Thus, option (c) is the correct answer.**

**19.** *(a)* 1 and 2 only

- **Statement 1 is correct: Keibul Lamjao National Park,** located in **Manipur,** is indeed the **only floating national park in the world.** It is unique because it is made up of **floating biomass** known as **phumdis**—mats of vegetation, soil, and organic matter that float on **Loktak lake.**
- **Statement 2 is correct: Loktak lake,** along with **Keibul Lamjao National Park,** is home to the largest population of the **critically endangered Sangai deer** (Rucervus eldii eldii), which is also known as the **Manipur brow-antlered deer.** The **Sangai is endemic to Manipur,** and its habitat is closely tied to the **phumdis** in Keibul Lamjao.
- **Statement 3 is incorrect:** The **Loktak Hydroelectric Project,** which was commissioned in the early 1980s, has had **adverse effects** on the conservation of **phumdis.** The project involved damming the lake, which resulted in **fluctuations in water levels** rather than maintaining a constant level. These fluctuations have caused the **phumdis to deteriorate,** affecting the habitat of the Sangai deer and threatening the stability of the national park's ecosystem.

**Thus, option (a) is the correct answer.**

**20.** *(b)* Only two

- **Pair 1 is correctly matched:** Bhitarkanika National Park in Odisha is famous for its large population of **saltwater crocodiles,** one of the largest populations in India. The park also has a rich biodiversity, including mangrove forests and various species of flora and fauna.

- **Pair 2 is correctly matched** :The **Great Indian Bustard**, a critically endangered bird species, is one of the primary attractions of the Desert National Park in Rajasthan. This park is crucial for the conservation of this rare species.
- **Pair 3 is incorrectly matched: Eravikulam National Park** is known for the **Nilgiri Tahr**, a rare mountain goat found in the Western Ghats. The **Hoolock Gibbon**, on the other hand, is native to Northeast India and not found in Kerala.

**Thus, option (b) is the correct answer.**

***21.*** *(d)* Namdapha National Park

**Namdapha National Park,** located in **Arunachal Pradesh,** is unique in having a **climate that varies from tropical to subtropical, temperate, and arctic.** This variation is due to its wide altitudinal range, which spans from lowland tropical forests to high-altitude snow-covered peaks. The park covers altitudes from about 200 meters to over 4,500 meters, resulting in diverse climatic zones and rich biodiversity.

**Thus, option (d) is the correct answer.**

***22.*** *(a)* 1 and 2 only

- **Option 1 is correct:** The **musk deer** is primarily found in **high-altitude regions** of the Himalayas. **Askot Wildlife Sanctuary,** located in the **Himalayan region** of **Uttarakhand** is known for housing **musk deer** in its natural alpine and sub-alpine habitats.
- **Option 2 is correct: Gangotri National Park** is also located in the **Himalayan region** of Uttarakhand, **Gangotri National Park** provides an ideal habitat for **musk deer** due to its high-altitude, cold environment.
- **Option 3 is incorrect: Kishanpur Wildlife Sanctuary** is located in the **Terai region** of **Uttar Pradesh** and is not known for housing musk deer. It primarily hosts species like swamp deer and tigers.
- **Option 4 is incorrect: Manas National Park** is located in **Assam,** known for its rich biodiversity, but it does not have a high-altitude habitat suitable for musk deer.

**Thus, option (a) is the correct answer.**

***23.*** *(b)* Only two

- **Statement 1 is correct: Biosphere Reserves** are indeed **recognised by UNESCO** as part of the **Man and the Biosphere (MAB) Programme.** This international initiative aims to promote sustainable development based on local community efforts and sound science.
- **Statement 2 is incorrect:** The **designation of a Biosphere Reserve** promotes **conservation, research and sustainable development** but **does not inherently change the legal ownership or status** of the land and resources. Legal protections and regulations depend on existing national and state laws governing protected areas in India.
- **Statement 3 is correct:** The **core area** of a **Biosphere Reserve** is designated for **strict conservation** of biodiversity and ecosystems. It aims to **maintain viable populations of species** across **all trophic levels** (producers, consumers, decomposers) to ensure **ecological integrity** and **functional stability** of the ecosystem.

**Thus, option (b) is the correct answer.**

***24.*** *(b)* Pachmarhi

- **Pachmarhi Biosphere Reserve** is located in the **Satpura Range** of **Madhya Pradesh,** India, and was established in 1999, covering **4,926.28 square kilometers.** It includes **Pachmarhi Wildlife Sanctuary, Satpura National Park, and Bori Sanctuary. Satpura National Park** serves as the core zone, while the other two areas form buffer zones. The eastern boundary of the biosphere reserve lies along a road with cultivation farms, close to the **Dudhi river,** while the **southern boundary borders the Tawa plateau.**
- The reserve's **flora** includes **moist deciduous, dry deciduous** and **subtropical hill forests,** with prominent species like **Teak, Sal, Indian Ebony** and several medicinal plants such as **Arjun tree** and **Indian snakeroot.** The **fauna** includes a rich diversity of **mammals** (e.g., **Bengal tiger, leopard, Indian giant squirrel),**

birds (over 300 species, including **peafowl** and **hornbill**), **reptiles and amphibians** (e.g., **cobras, pythons, frogs**) and various **insects**.

**Thus, option (b) is the correct answer.**

**25.** *(b)* Only two

- **Statement 1 is incorrect**: The **Nanda Devi Biosphere Reserve** is located **entirely within the state of Uttarakhand**, not Himachal Pradesh. It includes areas such as the **Nanda Devi National Park** and the **Valley of Flowers National Park**, both of which are in Uttarakhand.
- **Statement 2 is correct**: The **Nanda Devi Biosphere Reserve** is part of the **UNESCO Man and Biosphere (MAB) programme**, which promotes conservation and sustainable development. It was designated as a UNESCO biosphere reserve in **2004**, recognising its ecological importance and commitment to conservation.
- **Statement 3 is correct**: The **Nanda Devi Biosphere Reserve** is home to several **endangered species**, including the **Snow Leopard** and the **Musk Deer**. These species thrive in the high-altitude ecosystems of the reserve, which provides a critical habitat for their survival.

**Thus, option (b) is the correct answer.**

**26.** *(c)* Only three

It was initiated by UNESCO in 1971. It is an intergovernmental scientific programme that aims to establish a scientific basis for the improvement of relationships between people and their environments. MAB integrates natural and social sciences, economics and education to enhance human well-being, ensure fair distribution of benefits and preserve natural and managed ecosystems. This promotes creative and culturally suitable approaches to economic development that are environmentally sustainable.

**India's Biosphere as part of the MAB programme:**

| Biosphere Reserve | Description |
|---|---|
| Nilgiri Biosphere Reserve (Tamil Nadu, Kerala, Karnataka) | designated in 2000 |
| Gulf of Mannar Biosphere Reserve (Tamil Nadu) | designated in 2001 |
| Sundarbans Biosphere Reserve (West Bengal) | designated in 2001 |
| Nanda Devi Biosphere Reserve (Uttarakhand) | designated in 2004 |
| Nokrek Biosphere Reserve (Meghalaya) | designated in 2009 |
| Pachmarhi Biosphere Reserve (Madhya Pradesh) | designated in 2009 |
| Simlipal Biosphere Reserve (Odisha) | designated in 2009 |
| Achanakmar- Amarkantak Biosphere Reserve (Madhya Pradesh and Chhattisgarh) | designated in 2012 |
| Great Nicobar Biosphere Reserve (Andaman and Nicobar Islands) | designated in 2013 |
| Agasthyamala Biosphere Reserve (Tamil Nadu and Kerala) | designated in 2016 |
| Khangchendzonga Biosphere Reserve (Sikkim) | designated in 2018 |
| Panna Biosphere Reserve (Madhya Pradesh) | designated in 2020 |

**Thus, option (c) is the correct answer.**

**27.** *(d)* 1, 2 and 3

- **Statement 1 is correct**: It includes parts of Kerala and Tamil Nadu – This is correct. The Agasthyamalai Biosphere Reserve spans across the Western Ghats and includes parts of both Kerala and Tamil Nadu.
- **Statement 2 is correct**: It supports a population of Lion-Tailed Macaque and Nilgiri Tahr – This is correct. The reserve is home to several endangered species, including the Lion-Tailed Macaque and the Nilgiri Tahr, both of which are endemic to the Western Ghats region.
- **Statement 3 is correct**: It is the southernmost biosphere reserve in India – This is correct. The Agasthyamalai Biosphere Reserve is the southernmost biosphere reserve in India, located at the southern end of the Western Ghats.

**Thus, option (d) is the correct answer.**

**28.** *(b)* 1, 2 and 4 only

- **Option 1 is correct:** The **Great Nicobar Biosphere Reserve** is known for its **high endemism**, especially among its flora and fauna. Many species, including the **Nicobar Megapode, Nicobar Tree Shrew,** and unique plant species, are found only in this region.
- **Option 2 is correct:** The **Gulf of Mannar** is rich in marine biodiversity and is home to several **endemic species,** particularly in its coral reefs and seagrass ecosystems. Many species of fish, corals, and marine plants are found only in this region.
- **Option 3 is incorrect:** While **Kachchh** (or **Kutch**) is known for its unique ecosystem, especially the **Rann of Kutch,** it is **not particularly noted for endemism.** It is more famous for migratory species like the Greater Flamingo.
- **Option 4 is correct:** The **Dehang-Dibang Biosphere Reserve** in **Arunachal Pradesh** is part of the **Eastern Himalayas,** a global biodiversity hotspot, and hosts several **endemic species,** especially in its flora and fauna, including unique species of orchids and primates.

**Thus, option (b) is the correct answer.**

**29.** *(b)* 2-1-5-3-6-4

- The correct order of **biosphere reserves** from **South to North** is as follows: **Gulf of Mannar Biosphere Reserve → Nilgiri Biosphere Reserve → Achanakmar-Amarkantak Biosphere Reserve → Sundarbans Biosphere Reserve → Khangchendzonga National Park → Nanda Devi Biosphere Reserve.**
- **The Gulf of Mannar Biosphere Reserve (Tamil Nadu)** covers an area of **10,500 square kilometers,** including **21 islands** and their surrounding coral reefs.
- **Nilgiri Biosphere Reserve** was established in **1986,** and it spans **Tamil Nadu, Kerala** and **Karnataka.** It covers an area of **5,520 square kilometers.** The reserve encompasses the **Nilgiri Hills,** the **Western Ghats** and the **Eastern Ghats.**
- **Achanakmar-Amarkantak Biosphere Reserve** located in Chhattisgarh and Madhya Pradesh, covers 3,835 square kilometers. It is a part of the Maikal Hills in the Satpura Range. The reserve forms the origin of two important rivers—**Narmada and Son.**
- **Sundarbans Biosphere Reserve** (West Bengal) covers an area of 9,630 square kilometers and is part of the largest mangrove forest in the world.
- **Kangchenjunga National Park (Sikkim)** covers an area of **1,784 square kilometers.** It is dominated by **Mount Khangchendzonga,** the **third-highest peak in the world.**
- **Nanda Devi Biosphere Reserve** covers an area of **5,148 square kilometers.** It is situated in the **Garhwal Himalayas.**

**Thus, option (b) is the correct answer.**

**30.** *(a)* 1, 2 and 4 only

- **Option 1 is correct: Mudumalai Tiger Reserve** is located in the **Nilgiri Hills,** which are part of the **Western Ghats.** It lies at the junction of Karnataka, Kerala and Tamil Nadu and is known for its biodiversity and rich flora and fauna.
- **Option 2 is correct: Bandipur Tiger Reserve** is situated in the state of **Karnataka,** along the border with Tamil Nadu. It is part of the **Nilgiri Biosphere Reserve,** which is in the **Western Ghats.**
- **Option 3 is incorrect: Nagarjuna Sagar Tiger Reserve** is located in **Andhra Pradesh** and **Telangana,** and it is part of the **Eastern Ghats,** not the Western Ghats.
- **Option 4 is correct: Kalakad Mundanthurai Tiger Reserve** is situated in **Tamil Nadu** and forms part of the southern **Western Ghats.** It is known for its rich biodiversity and is one of the important tiger habitats in the region.

**Thus, option (a) is the correct answer.**

**31.** *(a)* Only one

- **Statement 1 is correct: Kanha Tiger Reserve in Madhya Pradesh** is renowned for being the **only habitat of the endangered hard-ground Barasingha,** also known as the swamp deer. The reserve has been successful in protecting and increasing the population of this species which was once on the brink of extinction.

- **Statement 2 is incorrect: Kanha Tiger Reserve** is located in **Madhya Pradesh,** and it is not part of the **Nilgiris Biosphere Reserve.** The Nilgiris Biosphere Reserve is located in the Western Ghats, spanning Tamil Nadu, Kerala, and Karnataka.
- **Statement 3 is incorrect: Kanha Tiger Reserve** is part of the **Maikal Range,** which is an extension of the **Satpura Range,** but the reserve itself is not directly within the **Satpura Range.**

**Thus, option (a) is the correct answer.**

**32.** *(a)* Nagarjuna Sagar Tiger Reserve

- The **Nagarjuna Sagar-Srisailam Tiger Reserve** is situated in the **Nallamala Hills,** which stretch across **Andhra Pradesh** and **Telangana.** The reserve spans across several districts, including **Prakasam, Kurnool and Guntur** in Andhra Pradesh, making it one of the largest tiger reserves in southern India.
- The **Krishna river** forms the **southern boundary** of the reserve, adding a crucial natural barrier and source of water for the wildlife within the reserve. This is a distinguishing geographic feature of the Nagarjuna Sagar-Srisailam Tiger Reserve.
- The **core area of Nagarjuna Sagar-Srisailam Tiger Reserve** is the largest among all tiger reserves in India. With a vast expanse of protected forest, it serves as a critical habitat for tigers and other species, enhancing conservation efforts in the region.

**Thus, option (a) is the correct answer.**

**33.** *(a)* Only one

- **Pair 1 is correct: Dampa Tiger Reserve** is indeed located in **Mizoram,** in northeastern India. It is the largest wildlife sanctuary in the state and is situated in the **Mamit district** near the border with Bangladesh. It is known for its rich biodiversity, including **tigers, leopards** and various species of birds and primates.
- **Pair 2 is incorrect: Gumti Wildlife Sanctuary** is not located in Sikkim. It is situated in the state of Tripura in northeastern India. Gumti Wildlife Sanctuary is known for its rich variety of wildlife, including **elephants, sambar, barking deer,** and several bird species.
- **Pair 3 is correct: Saramati Peak** is located in **Nagaland.** It is the **highest peak** in Nagaland, with an elevation of **3,826 meters,** and is situated near the border between Nagaland and Myanmar. The peak is part of the **Purvanchal Range** and offers panoramic views of the surrounding region.

**Thus, option (a) is the correct answer.**

**34.** *(b)* Only two

- **Statement 1 is correct:** The **Cheetah Project Steering Committee** (CPSC) was established to oversee the reintroduction of **African cheetahs** into India. This committee is responsible for planning, coordinating and ensuring the successful implementation of the project.
- **Statement 2 is incorrect:** The **initial phase** of the **Cheetah Project** in India does **not** aim to introduce **100 cheetahs.** Instead, the **Union Cabinet** approved the reintroduction of approximately **50 cheetahs** over several years, not necessarily confined to a five-year timeframe.
- **Statement 3 is incorrect:** The **Cheetah Project** is primarily funded through **Project Cheetah,** which is a dedicated initiative under the Ministry of Environment, Forest and Climate Change. There is **no direct funding linkage** between **CAMPA** or **Project Tiger** and the **Cheetah Project.**

**Thus, option (b) is the correct answer.**

**35.** *(b)* Both Statement I and Statement II are correct, but Statement II is not the correct explanation for Statement I.

- **Statement I is correct:** Cheetahs were officially declared extinct in **India in 1952.** The Government of India, in collaboration with **Namibia,** reintroduced cheetahs to **Kuno National Park** in Madhya Pradesh in 2022 as part of the **Cheetah Reintroduction Project.** This is the first reintroduction of cheetahs into the wild in India.
- **Statement II is correct:** Cheetahs are classified as **Vulnerable** on the **IUCN Red List,** primarily due to **habitat loss, human-wildlife conflict,** and a reduction in their prey base. These factors have caused a decline in their population globally.

- However, **Statement II** is not the direct reason for **Statement I** (the reintroduction of cheetahs in India). While both statements are correct, the cause of the cheetah extinction in India in 1952 was due to overhunting, not primarily habitat loss or human-wildlife conflict.

**Thus, option (b) is the correct answer.**

***36.*** *(b)* Only two

- **Statement 1 is correct:** Coral polyps have a symbiotic relationship with zooxanthellae, which photosynthesize and provide nutrients to the corals. This is crucial for the growth and energy supply of coral reefs.
- **Statement 2 is incorrect:** Coral reefs thrive in areas with relatively low salinity and waters free from sedimentation , not in high-salinity or sediment-heavy waters. This ensures the coral polyps are not smothered or stressed by excess salt and particles.
- **Statement 3 is correct:** Atolls form when volcanic islands subside completely below sea level, leaving coral reefs that continue to grow upwards. These coral formations are usually circular or oval-shaped, enclosing a central lagoon.

**Thus, option (b) is the correct answer.**

***37.*** *(b)* Brahmani-Baitarni Delta

- The **Bhitarkanika National Park** and **Gahirmatha Wildlife Sanctuary** are located in the **Brahmani-Baitarni Delta** in the state of **Odisha.** This region is known for its **rich biodiversity,** including its dense mangrove forests and a variety of wildlife such as **saltwater crocodiles,** migratory birds and notably, the **Olive Ridley turtles,** which come to nest in large numbers on the beaches of **Gahirmatha.**
- **Bhitarkanika National Park** is famous for its unique mangrove ecosystem and serves as a habitat for diverse species of flora and fauna.
- **Gahirmatha Wildlife Sanctuary** is world-renowned as the **largest nesting site** for **Olive Ridley turtles,** where the turtles engage in the mass nesting phenomenon known as **Arribada.**

**Thus, option (b) is the correct answer.**

***38.*** *(a)* 1, 2 and 4 only

- **Statement 1 is correct:** Establishing **Marine Protected Areas (MPAs)** in regions that have **high biodiversity** and **important ecosystem services** directly aligns with **Aichi Target 11.** This helps protect **critical habitats, endangered species** and **key ecosystem functions,** making it an essential action for meeting the target.
- **Statement 2 is correct:** Sustainable use of resources within MPAs is aligned with the **effective management** aspect of Aichi Target 11. **Sustainable fishing** practices ensure that marine resources are harvested responsibly, thus supporting the conservation goals of MPAs while balancing human needs.
- **Statement 3 is incorrect:** Expanding **tourism and recreational activities** in **sensitive marine habitats** can potentially lead to **habitat degradation** and **disturbance** of marine life. This is not in alignment with Aichi Target 11, which emphasises **effective management** and **conservation** of critical habitats. Increasing tourism, particularly in **sensitive areas,** can introduce pressures that contradict the objectives of maintaining ecosystem health and biodiversity.
- **Statement 4 is correct: Aichi Biodiversity Target 11** aims to protect **at least 17%** of terrestrial and inland water areas and **10%** of coastal and marine areas through **effectively managed, ecologically representative** and **well-connected systems** of protected areas.

**Thus, option (a) is the corrérct answer.**

***39.*** *(b)* Gulf of Mannar

The **Gulf of Mannar Biosphere Reserve,** located along the **southeast coast of India** in Tamil Nadu, is known for its rich marine biodiversity and is a significant habitat for the **Dugong,** also known as the **Sea Cow.** Dugongs are marine herbivores that rely on seagrass beds, which are abundant in the Gulf of Mannar.

**Thus, option (b) is the correct answer.**

***40.*** *(b)* Only two

- **Statement 1 is incorrect:** The **Biological Diversity Act, of 2002** emphasises the involvement of **local communities** and stakeholders in the designation process. Declaring BHS without consulting or involving local bodies would go against the principles outlined in the Act.

- **Statement 2 is correct: BHS** is designated to **protect regions that exhibit high levels of biodiversity,** including areas with **high endemism** (species unique to a specific geographic location) and **rare or threatened species.** Additionally, these sites often hold **cultural, historical, or traditional significance.**
- **Statement 3 is correct:** While the **State Government** has the authority to declare BHS based on State Biodiversity Boards (SBB) recommendations, the **Central Government,** primarily through the **National Biodiversity Authority** (NBA), oversees and reviews these designations to ensure they meet national standards and criteria.

**Thus, option (b) is the correct answer.**

**41.** *(c)* Chilika Lake

**Chilika Lake,** located in the state of **Odisha,** is the largest coastal lagoon in India and is renowned for hosting the **largest population of Irrawaddy dolphins** in the country. These dolphins are primarily found in the brackish waters of the lake and are a key attraction for conservationists and tourists alike. Chilika Lake is a **Ramsar Site,** recognised for its rich biodiversity and importance for migratory birds.

**Thus, option (c) is the correct answer.**

**42.** *(b)* 2 and 3 only

- **Statement 1 is incorrect:** Olive Ridley turtles are **not exclusive to the Indian coast;** they are found in **tropical and subtropical waters** of the Pacific, Atlantic, and Indian Oceans. They nest on various coastlines around the world, though the Indian coast, especially Odisha, is one of their key nesting sites.
- **Statement 2 is correct:** The **Arribada phenomenon** is a distinctive and remarkable feature of **Olive Ridley turtles.** During Arribada, **thousands of female turtles** come ashore at the same time to nest on specific beaches. This synchronised mass nesting is unique to Olive Ridley turtles and a few other species.
- **Statement 3 is correct:** The **Odisha coast,** particularly at **Gahirmatha Beach, Rushikulya,** and **Devi River Mouth,** is among the most significant **nesting sites** for **Olive Ridley turtles** in the world. These areas support massive nesting populations during the breeding season.

**Thus, option (b) is the correct answer.**

**43.** *(d)* None

- **Statement 1 is correct:** The **Turtle Excluder Device** (TED) is a tool used in fishing trawlers to prevent the accidental entanglement of sea turtles, including **Olive Ridley turtles,** in fishing nets. In **Odisha,** where large populations of Olive Ridley turtles nest, the use of TEDs is mandatory for **trawlers** to reduce turtle mortality during the nesting season.
- **Statement 2 is correct: Gahirmatha Beach,** located on the **Odisha coast,** is indeed the **largest nesting site** for **Olive Ridley turtles** globally. Every year, tens of thousands of Olive Ridleys come ashore at Gahirmatha for mass nesting, or **Arribada.**
- **Statement 3 is correct:** Olive Ridley turtles are listed under Appendix I of CITES, which provides the highest level of international protection.

**Thus, option (d) is the correct answer.**

**44.** *(c)* Only three

- **Statement 1 is correct:** The White-rumped Vulture, Indian Vulture, and Slender-billed Vulture are all classified as Critically Endangered by the IUCN. The primary reason for their drastic population decline is the use of diclofenac, a veterinary drug, which causes kidney failure in these scavenging birds when they consume carcasses treated with it.
- **Statement 2 is incorrect:** The Egyptian Vulture is classified as Endangered, but the Red-headed Vulture is listed as Critically Endangered, not Endangered. Both species face threats from habitat loss, poisoning, and food shortages, but their IUCN classifications differ.

- **Statement 3 is correct:** Both the Himalayan Griffon Vulture and Cinerous Vulture are classified as Near Threatened by the IUCN. These vultures are largely wintering species in India, meaning they migrate to the region during certain seasons, but face threats from declining food availability and habitat changes.
- **Statement 4 is correct:** Vulture Breeding Centre at Pinjore, Haryana, was established to breed and conserve Gyps species (eg- White-rumped Vulture and Slender-billed Vulture) in captivity. This ex situ conservation programme is a crucial part of efforts to restore declining populations by releasing bred vultures back into the wild.

**Thus, option (c) is the correct answer.**

***45.*** *(c)* 1, 3 and 4 only

- **Statement 1 is correct:** Panna Biosphere Reserve is located in **Madhya Pradesh** and includes **Panna National Park** and parts of the **Gangau Wildlife Sanctuary**. This reserve is recognised for its efforts in **tiger conservation** and its rich **biodiversity**.
- **Statement 2 is incorrect:** The **Panna Biosphere Reserve** is known for its **teak forests, dry mixed deciduous forests,** and diverse wildlife. However, the river that flows through the reserve is the **Ken river**, not the **Narmada river**. The **Ken river** is an important feature of the reserve and supports the **biodiversity** of the area.
- **Statement 3 is correct: Panna Biosphere Reserve** was designated as part of **UNESCO's World Network of Biosphere Reserves** in **2020**. This recognition highlights the significance of the reserve's biodiversity and conservation initiatives.
- **Statement 4 is correct:** The **Panna Biosphere Reserve** is home to various tribal communities, including the **Gond, Khairuas** and **Yadavas,** who rely on the forest for their livelihood and maintain a close cultural relationship with the natural environment.

**Thus, option (c) is the correct answer.**

***46.*** *(c)* Both 1 and 2

- **Statement 1 is correct: Biodiversity Management Committees (BMCs)** play an essential role in realising the objectives of the Nagoya Protocol, which is focused on **access to genetic resources and the fair and equitable sharing of benefits arising from their use.** BMCs help in preserving biodiversity, regulating its use, and ensuring benefits are shared with the local community.
- **Statement 2 is correct:** BMCs have key responsibilities, including **determining access and benefit-sharing (ABS) and levying fees for access to biological resources within their jurisdiction.** They prepare and maintain a People's Biodiversity Register (PBR), which contains information on the availability and knowledge of local biological resources.

**Thus, option (c) is the correct answer.**

***47.*** *(c)* 1, 2 and 4 only

- **Statement 1 is correct: Mahuadanr Wildlife Sanctuary** in the **Latehar district** of **Jharkhand** is notable for its focus on the conservation of **wolves.** It is the **only wildlife sanctuary in India** specifically dedicated to **wolf conservation,** providing an important habitat for the Indian wolf.
- **Statement 2 is correct:** The **Little Rann of Kutch** in **Gujarat** is known for being the habitat of the **Indian Wild Ass** (Equus hemionus khur), which is also called the **Wild Asian Ass.** It is an **endemic species** found only in this region of India.
- **Statement 3 is incorrect:** Velavadar **Grasslands** (also known as **Blackbuck National Park)** in **Gujarat** are famous for the **blackbuck** population. However, **cheetahs are no longer found naturally in India** since they went extinct in the 1950s. Velavadar does not have any remaining cheetah population, though there are recent efforts to reintroduce cheetahs in other areas of India, such as **Kuno National Park** in Madhya Pradesh.
- **Statement 4 is correct: Dachigam National Park,** located in **Jammu and Kashmir,** is the **only place** where the **Hangul** (Kashmir stag) is found in the wild. It is **critically endangered** and Dachigam serves as its primary habitat.

**Thus, option (c) is the correct answer.**

**48.** *(b)* Shivalik Hills and Gangetic Plains

According to the **Status of Leopards in India 2022** report, the **Shivalik Hills and Gangetic Plains** region has experienced the largest decline in leopard population, with a 3.4% decline per annum. The population in this region dropped from 1,253 in 2018 to 1,109 in 2022. In contrast, regions like Central India and Eastern Ghats saw a population growth of 1.5%.

**Thus, option (b) is the correct answer.**

**49.** *(b)* Only two

- **Pair 1 is incorrectly matched:** The **Nanjarayan Bird Sanctuary** is not located on the banks of the **Cauvery river.** It is situated near **Tiruppur** in Tamil Nadu and is known for its waterbird population, particularly during the migratory season. However, it is not specifically known for hosting **endangered species** or being located along the **Cauvery river.**
- **Pair 2 is correctly matched: Kazhuveli Bird Sanctuary** is located on the **Coromandel Coast** in Tamil Nadu. It supports a variety of **long-distance migratory birds** and was declared Tamil Nadu's **16th bird sanctuary in 2021.** The sanctuary is an important wetland for birds and is recognised for its ecological importance.
- **Pair 3 is correctly matched: Tawa Reservoir** is located at the **confluence of the Tawa and Denwa rivers** in Madhya Pradesh. It is significant for **irrigation** and also supports a range of **migratory bird species** during the winter months.

**Thus, option (b) is the correct answer.**

**50.** *(c)* 1, 2 and 4 only

- **Statement 1 is correct: Zemu Glacier** is one of the largest glaciers in the **eastern Himalayas** and is located in **Sikkim,** within **Khangchendzonga National Park.** It is a key feature of the park, contributing to its stunning natural beauty and providing an important source of water for the region.
- **Statement 2 is correct: Mt. Kanchenjunga,** also spelled **Kangchenjunga,** is the **third-highest peak in the world,** standing at an elevation of **8,586 meters.** The mountain is the centerpiece of **Khangchendzonga National Park** and is an iconic feature of the park, contributing to its recognition as a **UNESCO World Heritage Site.**
- **Statement 3 is incorrect: Milam Glacier** is not located within **Khangchendzonga National Park.** It is situated in the **Kumaon Himalayas** of **Uttarakhand,** India. Therefore, it is **not** a feature of **Khangchendzonga National Park.**
- **Statement 4 is correct: Khangchendzonga National Park** is culturally significant, as it is intertwined with the **sacred traditions** of the local **Lepcha** community. The concept of **Mayel Lyang** refers to the sacred land of the Lepchas and **Beyul** refers to hidden sacred valleys in Tibetan Buddhism, which are believed to be places of peace and refuge. These cultural elements are closely tied to the park's identity.

**Thus, option (c) is the correct answer.**

**51.** *(b)* 1, 2 and 4 only

- **Statement 1 is correct:** The **Great Himalayan National Park** is located in the **Banjaar Sub-Division** of **Kullu district** in **Himachal Pradesh,** in the **far Western Himalayas.** The park was constituted in **1984** and was formally notified as a national park in **1999.**
- **Statement 2 is correct:** The **Great Himalayan National Park** encompasses four distinct valleys, each rich in a diverse range of endemic and exotic flora and fauna. The **Himalayas** are renowned for harboring around **10% of the world's** and **50% of India's endemic plant species such as podophyllum hexandrum, Dactylorhiza categoria, etc.** The park offers numerous trekking opportunities, catering to both **amateurs** and **experienced trekkers,** allowing visitors to explore its stunning landscapes and unique biodiversity.
- **Statement 3 is incorrect:** GHNP is home to the **Tirthan, Sainj** and **Jiwa Nal** rivers, which are tributaries of the **Beas** river. However, the **Parvati river** does **not originate** within GHNP. The **Parvati river** originates from the **Parvati Valley** in the **Kullu district,** which is nearby but not part of GHNP.

- **Statement 4 is correct: In June 2014, the Great Himalayan National Park was added to the UNESCO list of World Heritage Sites** under the criterion of **"outstanding significance for biodiversity conservation".** This recognition highlights the unique ecosystems and the efforts for conservation in the park.

**Thus, option (b) is the correct answer.**

***52.*** *(d)* 1, 2 and 3

- **Statement 1 is correct: Kaziranga National Park,** located in the state of Assam, India, was designated as a **UNESCO World Heritage** Site in **1985.** This recognition was due to the park's outstanding value in preserving its unique and diverse wildlife, particularly the **Indian one-horned rhinoceros.** Kaziranga is also known for its high density of **tigers, elephants, wild water buffalo** and **swamp** deer.
- **Statement 2 is correct: Kaziranga National** Park has been recognised as an **Important Bird and Biodiversity Area (IBA)** by **BirdLife International.** This is due to its significant role in conserving various species of birds, including migratory birds and numerous endangered and endemic species. The park is home to over **480 species of birds,** making it an important region for bird conservation.
- **Statement 3 is correct:** The **Brahmaputra river,** one of the major rivers of India, flows along the **northern boundary of Kaziranga National Park.** The river plays a crucial role in the formation of Kaziranga's unique landscape, providing **water resources** and influencing the ecology of the area.

**Thus, option (d) is the correct answer.**

***53.*** *(b)* 1, 3 and 4 only

- **Statement 1 is correct:** The **UNESCO Man and the Biosphere (MAB) Programme,** launched in **1971,** is an intergovernmental scientific initiative that promotes **sustainable development** through the conservation of ecosystems, biodiversity and the sustainable use of natural resources. One of the main goals of the **MAB Programme** is to create a **scientific foundation** for enhancing the relationship between humans and nature.
- **Statement 2 is incorrect:** The MAB Programme does not focus exclusively on **natural sciences.** Instead, it adopts a **multidisciplinary approach** that includes **natural sciences, social sciences, economics** and **education** to address the challenges of sustainable development.
- **Statement 3 is correct:** The MAB Programme encourages **innovative and sustainable approaches** to economic development that consider **social, cultural** and **environmental** dimensions. It aims to develop models that balance the needs of human development with the need for environmental conservation.
- **Statement 4 is correct:** The **MAB Programme** aims to improve **predictive capabilities** to understand the environmental impacts of human actions. This enables better **resource management** by anticipating the potential future consequences of current environmental practices.

**Thus, option (b) is the correct answer.**

***54.*** *(c)* Statement I is correct, but Statement II is incorrect.

- **Statement I is correct: Keoladeo National Park,** also known as **Bharatpur Bird Sanctuary,** is a wetland of international importance (a Ramsar site). It serves as a critical wintering ground for migratory waterfowl from the Central Asian Flyway.
- **Statement II is incorrect:** Keoladeo National Park was placed on the **Montreux Record in 1990,** but it was not due to the successful restoration of the Siberian Crane population. It was placed on the Montreux Record due to deteriorating water conditions, habitat degradation and challenges related to water supply and management, which had adversely affected the habitat for migratory birds.

**Thus, option (c) is the correct answer.**

***55.*** *(b)* Only two

- **Statement 1 is correct:** The **Kashmir Musk Deer** (Moschus cupreus) is listed as **Endangered** on the **IUCN Red List.** The population of the species has been declining due to habitat loss and **poaching** for its musk gland, which is highly valuable in the illegal market.

- **Statement 2 is correct: Kashmir Musk Deer** are highly targeted by **poachers** for their **musk glands**, which produce a highly valuable substance used in traditional medicines and perfumes. The demand for **musk** is one of the primary reasons for the decline of the species, making it a significant threat to their survival.
- **Statement 3 is incorrect**: The **Kashmir Musk Deer** is not the only species of musk deer found in the **Himalayan region**. There are multiple species of **musk deer** in the Himalayas, including the **Himalayan Musk Deer** (Moschus leucogaster) and **Alpine Musk Deer** (Moschus chrysogaster).

**Thus, option (b) is the correct answer.**

**56.** *(d)* None

- **Statement 1 is correct**: Leatherback Turtles are the largest sea turtles globally and are classified as 'Vulnerable' by the IUCN. Some sub-populations are even classified as 'Critically Endangered'.
- **Statement 2 is correct**: The **Leatherback Turtle** (Dermochelys coriacea), the largest sea turtle in the world, nests exclusively in **India** on the **Andaman and Nicobar Islands.** Notable nesting sites include **Galathea Bay** in **Great Nicobar Island** and **Little Andaman Island**, which provide suitable, undisturbed beaches for egg-laying. Conservation organisations, alongside the **Forest Department**, monitor and protect these nesting areas to improve **hatching success.** Important sites include **Galathea National Park** and **South Bay** and **West Bay** beaches, with initiatives such as patrolling and **community engagement.**
- **Statement 3 is correct**: Leatherback Turtles primarily feed on jellyfish, playing a crucial ecological role in controlling jellyfish populations, which can cause damage to fishing equipment when present in large numbers.

**Thus, option (d) is the correct answer.**

**57.** *(c)* All three

- **Statement 1 is correct: Geo-heritage sites** are geological features that hold significant **cultural** or **scientific importance.** These sites provide valuable insights into **Earth's history,** including geological processes, paleontological records and geomorphologica features, and they are often used for **educational and research** purposes.
- **Statement 2 is correct**: The **Geological Survey of India** (GSI) is the authority responsible for **identifying** and **declaring Geological Heritage Sites** and **National Geological Monuments** in the country. GSI works to preserve significant geological features that help in understanding Earth's natural history and in educating the public.
- **Statement 3 is incorrect**: The **number of Geological Heritage Sites** in India has been changing as more sites are added or modified. As of recent records, **India has 34 Geological Heritage Sites** officially designated by the **Geological Survey of India (GSI) with the latest being the Ramgarh crater in Rajasthan.**

**Thus, option (c) is the correct answer.**

**58.** *(c)* All three

- **Statement 1 is correct**: The **Indian Wild Ass** (Equus hemionus khur), also known as the **Khur**, is primarily found in and around the **Rann of Kutch** in **Gujarat**, specifically in the **Little Rann of Kutch** and **Great Rann of Kutch**. Recently, its range has expanded to some parts of **southern Rajasthan** and **northern Maharashtra**, but the Rann of Kutch remains its core habitat.
- **Statement 2 is correct**: The **Indian Wild Ass** is classified as **Near Threatened** by the **International Union for Conservation of Nature** (IUCN). The population faces **pressures from habitat degradation, human activities and other factors.**
- **Statement 3 is correct**: **Prosopis juliflora** is an **invasive shrub species** that has spread widely in the **Rann of Kutch, and it is considered a significant threat to the Indian Wild Ass.** It has altered the **natural habitat by reducing the availability of open grazing areas and native grasses,** thereby affecting the food resources available to the Indian Wild Ass.

**Thus, option (c) is the correct answer.**

**59.** *(b)* 1, 2 and 4 only

- **Option 1 is correct:** One of the significant reasons for the decline of leopards is **habitat loss**, driven by **mining, deforestation** and increasing **human activities**. Leopards are losing their natural habitats and being forced into smaller and more fragmented areas.
- **Option 2 is correct: Leopards** are often poached for their **skins** and **body parts**, which are in high demand in the illegal wildlife trade. This is a direct threat to their population.
- **Option 3 is incorrect:** While **leopards** and **tigers** coexist in some areas, competition with tigers is not a primary cause of the leopard population decline. Leopards often adapt to different ecological niches and avoid direct competition with tigers.
- **Option 4 is correct: Leopards** frequently fall victim to **road accidents**, especially as infrastructure such as roads and highways fragment their natural habitats. This adds to the mortality rate, contributing to the population decline.

**Thus, option (b) is the correct answer.**

**60.** *(b)* To conserve all big cat species and their habitats through global cooperation and to align biodiversity conservation with local needs and sustainable development goals.

- The **International Big Cat Alliance (IBCA)** is a multi-country coalition aimed at conserving **big cat species** such as tigers, lions, leopards, snow leopards, pumas, jaguars, and cheetahs, along with the landscapes they inhabit.
- Its **primary goal** is to collaborate on conservation efforts and **mitigate the adverse effects of climate change** while advocating for policies that align with both **biodiversity conservation** and **local community needs.**

**Thus, option (b) is the correct answer.**

**61.** *(b)* Indian wild ass

**Indian wild ass (Equus hemionus khur)**, which is found primarily in the **saline and sandy desert** regions of the **Rann of Kutch** in **Gujarat.** The Indian wild ass has no natural predators in this region but is **threatened due to habitat destruction**, primarily caused by human activities such as industrial development, road construction and habitat fragmentation.

**Thus, option (b) is the correct answer.**

**62.** *(b)* 1, 3 and 4 only

- **Option 1 is correct:** The **black-necked crane** is naturally found in **India**, primarily in the **Ladakh** region of Jammu and Kashmir and in **Arunachal Pradesh** during the winter months. It is an important species in high-altitude wetlands and is revered in local cultures.
- **Option 2 is incorrect: Not naturally found in India (recently reintroduced)** The **cheetah** was declared extinct in India in 1952. However, it has been **recently reintroduced** in 2022 as part of a conservation effort. As per the question, cheetahs were not naturally found in India at the time of this examination (2012), but historically they were present.
- **Option 3 is correct:** Several species of **flying squirrels** are found in India, particularly in the **Northeastern forests** and the Western Ghats. The Indian giant flying squirrel is one of the prominent species.
- **Option 4 is correct:** The **snow leopard** is found in the high-altitude regions of India, especially in the Himalayan ranges in states like Jammu and Kashmir, Himachal Pradesh, Uttarakhand, Sikkim, and Arunachal Pradesh.

**Thus, option (b) is the correct answer.**

**63.** *(b)* It is a newly discovered marine species of head-shield sea slug found along the coasts of West Bengal and Odisha, named after President Droupadi Murmu.

- **Melanochlamys droupadi** is a marine species of **head-shield sea slug** that was discovered by the **Zoological Survey of India (ZSI)** along the coasts of **West Bengal** and **Odisha.** This species is notable for its **brownish-black body with a ruby-red spot** and its **hermaphroditic** nature.
- The species was named after **President Droupadi Murmu** and is part of a genus generally found in temperate regions, though some species, including Melanochlamys droupadi, are tropical.

**Thus, option (b) is the correct answer.**

***64.*** *(d)* 1, 2 and 3

- **Statement 1 is correct:** The **Snow Leopard Population Assessment in India** (**SPAI**) is indeed the first comprehensive and scientific effort to estimate the **snow leopard population** across India's **trans-Himalayan region**, which spans states like **Ladakh, Himachal Pradesh, Uttarakhand, Sikkim** and **Arunachal Pradesh**. The programme aimed to establish a baseline population number and distribution of snow leopards in these regions.
- **Statement 2 is correct:** The **SPAI assessment** recorded a population of **718 snow leopards in India**, which highlights the current status of the species in the **trans-Himalayan region**. The report indicates that the **majority of snow leopards** are indeed found in **Ladakh**, which serves as a **critical habitat due to its extensive high-altitude terrain**, which is suitable for snow leopards.
- **Statement 3 is correct:** As part of the SPAI programme and the broader **Global Snow Leopard and Ecosystem Protection Programme (GSLEP)**, the **Wildlife Institute of India (WII)** established a **Snow Leopard Cell**. This cell aims to facilitate **long-term monitoring**, conservation planning, and coordination among various stakeholders to protect and conserve snow leopard populations in India.

**Thus, option (d) is the correct answer.**

***65.*** *(a)* 6-1-2-5-3-4

The correct order of the protected areas in West Bengal from West to East is: **Singalila National Park → Jaldapara National Park → Gorumara National Park → Neora Valley National Park → Buxa Tiger Reserve → Sundarbans National Park** (located in the extreme East, near the Bay of Bengal)

**Thus, option (a) is the correct answer.**

***66.*** *(b)* The golden colouration in Golden tigers is caused by a recessive gene called 'wideband', which reduces melanin production, leading to a golden or blond appearance with reduced orange stripes.

Golden tigers, or golden tabby tigers, are **not a separate sub-species** but a **colour variation** of Bengal tigers. Their colouration is due to a **recessive wideband gene**, which reduces **melanin production**, leading to their distinctive golden or blond fur. The **tabby mutation** is responsible for the orange stripes. This genetic condition is rare and results from the inheritance of two recessive genes.

**Thus, option (b) is the correct answer.**

***67.*** *(d)* East Central region

According to the **Elephant Corridors of India, 2023 Report**, the **East Central region** contributes the highest number of elephant corridors, accounting for 35% (52 corridors) of the total. **West Bengal** follows closely with the highest number in any single state, totaling **26 corridors** (17%). Southern India registered **32 corridors** (21%), while **Northern India** has the lowest count with **18 corridors** (12%).

**Thus, option (d) is the correct answer.**

***68.*** *(c)* Only three

- **Statement 1 is correct:** The **Global Declaration for River Dolphins** aims to halt the decline of river dolphin species through actions like **eradicating unsustainable fishing practices**, improving water quality and creating **protected areas.**
- **Statement 2 is correct:** The **Global Declaration for River Dolphins** was signed by **11 countries** from **Asia and South America**, including key range countries like **India, Bangladesh, Brazil,** and others. **These countries are home to river dolphins such as the Ganges River Dolphin, Indus River Dolphin** and **Amazon River Dolphin**, which makes their participation crucial in river dolphin conservation.
- **Statement 3 is incorrect:** While **research and monitoring** are part of the efforts, the declaration includes broader initiatives, such as **engaging local communities**, improving river management and addressing water pollution.
- **Statement 4 is correct: World River Dolphin Day** is celebrated on **24th October** each year to raise **awareness** about the **conservation of river dolphins.** The day serves as a **reminder of the importance of**

**protecting these endangered species** and highlights the efforts being made globally to improve their populations.

**Thus, option (c) is the correct answer.**

***69.*** *(c)* 1-3-2-4

- The correct order from the West to East: Panna Biosphere Reserve → Simlipal Biosphere Reserve → Khangchendzonga National Park → Sundarbans Biosphere Reserve.
- **Panna Biosphere Reserve (Madhya Pradesh):** Encompasses **Panna National Park** and parts of **Gangau Wildlife Sanctuary.** Known for **tiger reintroduction, Ken river,** and **dry deciduous forests.** Recognised as a **UNESCO Biosphere Reserve in 2020.**
- **Simlipal Biosphere Reserve (Odisha):** Includes **Simlipal National Park and Tiger Reserve.** Rich in **moist and dry deciduous forests, Bengal tigers** and **Asian elephants.** Known for **Barehipani** and **Joranda** waterfalls. Part of the **UNESCO MAB Programme** since 2009.
- **Khangchendzonga National Park (Sikkim):** Named after **Mount Khangchendzonga,** featuring **glaciers, forests,** and **alpine meadows.** Home to **snow leopards** and **red pandas,** and has **cultural significance.** A **UNESCO World Heritage Site since 2016.**
- **Sundarbans Biosphere Reserve (West Bengal):** The largest **mangrove forest** in the world, located near the **Bay of Bengal.** Known for the **Royal Bengal Tiger, mangrove flora,** and **unique tidal ecosystem.** Declared a **UNESCO World Heritage Site** in 1987.

**Thus, option (c) is the correct answer.**

***70.*** *(a)* Mhadei Tiger Reserve

- **Mhadei Tiger Reserve** is located in the **northern part of Goa,** specifically in the **Sanguem taluka,** close to **Valpoi town.** This region is rich in biodiversity and is part of the larger Western Ghats ecosystem, which is a global biodiversity hotspot.
- The reserve is renowned for its **picturesque waterfalls,** including **Vazra Sakla Falls** and **Virdi Falls,** which add to the scenic beauty of the area. These waterfalls are key tourist attractions within the reserve and are surrounded by dense forest landscapes.
- One of the most significant aspects of Mhadei Tiger Reserve is that it serves as an important nesting ground for the **critically endangered Long-billed vultures.** These birds, which are facing severe threats from habitat loss and poisoning, find a haven near **Vazra Falls,** making this reserve crucial for their conservation.

**Thus, option (a) is the correct answer.**

***71.*** *(a)* Gut Microbiome

- **Gut Microbiome** refers to the **totality of microorganisms** (including bacteria, viruses, protozoa, and fungi) and their **collective genetic material** present in the gastrointestinal tract (GIT).
- It plays a critical role in processes such as **nutrient absorption, synthesis of enzymes, vitamins, and amino acids** and the production of **short-chain fatty acids** (SCFAs) that are vital for gut health.
- The term **'microbiome'** encompasses both the microorganisms and their genetic material, whereas **"microbiota"** generally refers to just the microorganisms themselves. This distinction makes "gut microbiome" the correct term for the concept described.

**Thus, option (a) is the correct answer.**

***72.*** *(d)* All four

- **Statement 1 is correct: BirdLife International** is the world's largest nature conservation partnership, comprising a global network of **non-governmental organisations** (NGOs) working in over **100 countries.** Their primary mission is to **conserve birds,** their **habitats,** and **biodiversity** globally while promoting the sustainable use of natural resources.
- **Statement 2 is correct: BirdLife International** serves as the **Red List Authority** for birds under the **International Union for Conservation of Nature (IUCN).** It is responsible for **assessing the conservation status of all bird species worldwide** and providing data that contributes to the **IUCN Red List** of Threatened Species.

- **Statement 3 is correct: Important Bird and Biodiversity Areas (IBAs)** are designated based on specific criteria that reflect their importance for bird conservation. They are classified as **sites with globally threatened species, species with restricted ranges, biome-restricted species** and **sites with significant congregations of birds**. These categories help identify areas critical for bird conservation globally.
- **Statement 4 is correct:** The **Bombay Natural History Society (BNHS)** is indeed the **partner organisation** of **BirdLife International** in **India**. BNHS works on various conservation initiatives in India, including the identification and conservation of **IBAs** and promoting research on birds and their habitats.

**Thus, option (d) is the correct answer.**

**73.** *(b)* In Wildlife Sanctuaries, certain human activities like grazing and collection of firewood are permitted, whereas in National Parks, human activities are strictly prohibited.

| Wildlife Sanctuaries | National Parks |
|---|---|
| **Human Activities Permitted:** In Wildlife Sanctuaries, certain regulated human activities are allowed. Local communities may have traditional rights, such as grazing livestock, collecting firewood, and minor forest produce, subject to management regulations and permissions. | **Human Activities Prohibited:** National Parks have stricter protection measures compared to Wildlife Sanctuaries. Human activities such as grazing, hunting, and extraction of resources are strictly prohibited. The rights of people are minimal or entirely restricted to ensure higher levels of conservation. |
| **Management Authority:** The **Chief Wildlife Warden** controls, manages, and maintains all sanctuaries. The State Government appoints a Collector to determine the rights of persons within the sanctuary. | **Management Authority:** The **Chief Wildlife Warden** ensures that destruction, damage, or diversion of wildlife does not take place in National Parks. The State Government appoints a Collector to determine the rights of persons within the National Park. |

**Thus, option (b) is the correct answer.**

**74.** *(c)* Dandeli Wildlife Sanctuary

The **Dandeli Wildlife Sanctuary** is located in the **Uttara Kannada district** of Karnataka and forms an integral part of the **Western Ghats**. It is known for its **rich biodiversity** and is also associated with the **Kali Tiger Reserve**, which includes both the Dandeli Wildlife Sanctuary and **Anshi National Park**.

**Thus, option (c) is the correct answer.**

**75.** *(b)* Tortoises are adapted for terrestrial life with thick, columnar legs, while turtles have flipper-like legs adapted for aquatic environments.

- **Tortoises** are **primarily terrestrial** and **have high-domed, heavy shells**, with **thick, columnar legs** and **claw-like toes**, making them well-suited for life on land. The key differences between tortoises and turtles are **habitat, shell shape and limb structure.**
- **Turtles** are **adapted for aquatic environments** and have **thinner, more streamlined shells** along with **flipper-like legs** or **webbed feet**, enabling them to navigate water efficiently.

**Thus, option (b) is the correct answer.**

**76.** *(c)* 2 and 3 only

- **Statement 1 is incorrect:** The boundaries of a **National Park** cannot be altered by the State Government alone. According to the **Wildlife (Protection) Act, of 1972**, any alteration to the boundaries of a national park requires prior consultation and approval from the **National Board for Wildlife** (NBWL). This ensures that decisions regarding protected areas are in line with national conservation policies and priorities.
- **Statement 2 is correct: Jim Corbett National Park,** originally established in **1936** as **Hailey National Park**, is indeed the **first national park** of India. It is located in the **foothills of the Himalayas** in **Uttarakhand.** The park was later renamed after the renowned hunter-turned-conservationist **Jim Corbett**, who played a key role in its establishment. The park is famous for its **Bengal tigers, diverse flora**, and **fauna**.
- **Statement 3 is correct: Biosphere Reserves** are divided into three zones: The **core zone** is

a strictly protected area where **no human activities** are allowed. This area is meant to protect the **ecosystem** and conserve biodiversity in its pristine form. **Buffer Zone:** The **buffer zone** surrounds the core zone and allows for **limited human activities** such as **ecotourism, research,** and **education.** These activities are regulated and must be sustainable to ensure minimal impact on the core zone. The **transition zone** is the outermost part of the biosphere reserve, where **regulated human activities** such as **agriculture, settlements** and **resource extraction** are permitted. These activities are aimed at supporting local communities while promoting sustainable development.

**Thus, option (c) is the correct answer.**

**77.** *(c)* 1, 3 and 4 only

- **Statement 1 is correct:** Construction of dams and barrages on rivers is a major threat to Ganges River Dolphins. These structures fragment their habitat, block their migratory routes and alter water flow, making it difficult for dolphins to survive.
- **Statement 2 is incorrect:** While crocodiles are predators, an **increase in their population** is not a significant factor in the decline of dolphin populations. Crocodiles and dolphins have coexisted for a long time, and there is no substantial evidence linking crocodile population increases to dolphin decline.
- **Statement 3 is correct: Getting trapped in fishing nets accidentally** is a major reason for dolphin mortality. Dolphins often get entangled in fishing gear, which can lead to injury or death.
- **Statement 4 is correct: The use of synthetic fertilizers and agricultural chemicals** can lead to river pollution, affecting water quality and food availability for the dolphins. Eutrophication and contamination from these chemicals harm the entire aquatic ecosystem.

**Thus, option (c) is the correct answer.**

**78.** *(a)* Only one

- **Statement 1 is correct:** The **Mangrove Alliance for Climate** (MAC) was indeed launched during **COP27** in **Sharm El-Sheikh, Egypt,** to promote **mangroves** as a **nature-based solution** to combat **climate change.** Mangroves are highly effective in **carbon sequestration** and play a crucial role in mitigating the impacts of climate change while also providing **ecosystem services** like coastal protection and supporting marine biodiversity.
- **Statement 2 is incorrect:** The **Mangrove Alliance for Climate** was initiated by the **United Arab Emirates (UAE)** and **Indonesia,** not by **India.** It also has the support of several other countries, including **India, Sri Lanka** and **Japan,** but India is not a leading country in the alliance. The focus is on increasing **mangrove cover** globally and encouraging cooperation for the **restoration** and **protection** of mangrove ecosystems.
- **Statement 3 is correct:** One of the key objectives of the **Mangrove Alliance for Climate** is to promote **blue carbon solutions** by encouraging **mangrove restoration.** It also seeks **private sector involvement** and **philanthropy** to fund and support these initiatives, recognising the role of mangroves in **blue carbon sequestration** and climate mitigation.

**Thus, option (a) is the correct answer.**

**79.** *(c)* 1 and 3 only

- **Statement 1 is correct:** The National Biodiversity Authority (NBA) plays a critical role in protecting India's biodiversity by preventing **biopiracy** (unauthorised use of biological resources) and ensuring the protection of **indigenous genetic resources.** This helps safeguard traditional knowledge and the genetic material crucial for Indian agriculture.
- **Statement 2 is incorrect:** While the NBA regulates access to biological resources, it does not **directly monitor or supervise** scientific research on genetic modification. Such research falls under the purview of other regulatory bodies like the Genetic Engineering Appraisal Committee (GEAC).
- **Statement 3 is correct:** The NBA's approval is required for **applications for Intellectual Property Rights** (IPR) related to biological

resources, ensuring that these resources are not exploited without appropriate benefit-sharing agreements, especially when it comes to traditional and indigenous knowledge.

**Thus, option (c) is the correct answer.**

**80.** *(b)* Promoting transboundary collaboration for the conservation of the greater one-horned rhino and expansion of rhino habitats.

The **New Delhi Declaration** underscores **transboundary collaboration** among Asian rhino range countries, particularly India, Nepal and **Bhutan**, for the conservation of the **greater one-horned rhino**. It also includes expanding rhino habitats and strengthening efforts to protect all Asian rhino species. This choice reflects the comprehensive conservation and collaboration goals stated in the declaration.

**Thus, option (b) is the correct answer.**

**81.** *(b)* Only two

- **Statement 1 is correct:** The **Greater one-horned rhino** populations in both **India** and **Nepal** have seen significant recovery over recent years due to enhanced **protection efforts** such as effective **anti-poaching measures, community involvement,** and better **habitat management with various projects like Project Rhino, India Rhino Vision 2020,** etc. The population of **Greater one-horned rhinos** is currently estimated at over **3,700** individuals, with a majority in **India** (especially in **Kaziranga** and **Pobitora**) and some in **Nepal (Chitwan National Park)**.
- **Statement 2 is correct:** Assam has developed a linked corridor connecting key protected areas such as **Kaziranga National Park, Manas National Park, Orang National Park,** and other wildlife sanctuaries to allow the free movement of rhinos.
- **Statement 3 is incorrect:** The **DNA profiling project** for rhinos in India was primarily introduced to **combat poaching** and provide evidence of wildlife crimes, rather than to track migration patterns.

**Thus, option (b) is the correct answer.**

**82.** *(d)* Promoting transboundary collaboration among Asian rhino range countries, particularly India, Nepal, and Bhutan, for the conservation and protection of the Greater one-horned rhino.

- The **New Delhi Declaration** highlights the importance of **transboundary collaboration** among **India, Nepal** and **Bhutan** to protect and conserve the **Greater one-horned rhino.** The declaration also includes broader efforts for rhino conservation across other Asian rhino range countries, including Indonesia and Malaysia, but specifically underscores collaboration for the conservation of the greater one-horned rhino.
- Additionally, while the Javan and Sumatran rhinos are critically endangered, the Greater one-horned rhino is classified as vulnerable, making this cooperative effort crucial for its continued recovery.

**Thus, option (d) is the correct answer.**

**83.** *(d)* 1, 2, 3 and 4

- **Ex-situ conservation** involves the protection of components of biodiversity outside their natural habitats. This form of conservation is critical for preserving species at risk of extinction and maintaining genetic diversity. Each of the following methods plays a significant role in conservation:
- **Seed Banks and Gene Banks** store seeds and genetic material, ensuring that species can be regenerated even after natural disasters, habitat destruction, or other environmental changes. In **Long-term Captive Breeding** animals are bred in controlled environments like zoos or breeding centers.
- **Cryopreservation of Gametes and Embryos:** Cryopreservation involves freezing biological material at extremely low temperatures (-80°C to -196°C) to preserve cells, gametes and embryos.
- **Zoological Gardens (Zoos):** Zoos act as custodians of endangered species, providing controlled environments where animals can live, reproduce, and be studied.

**Thus, option (d) is the correct answer.**

**84.** *(b)* 1 and 3 only

- **Statement 1 is correct:** Seed banks store genetic material, primarily seeds, to protect species from extinction due to natural disasters, human-induced habitat destruction, or environmental degradation. The seeds can be stored for decades, if not centuries, in controlled conditions, ensuring that species can be regenerated if they are lost in the wild. This acts as an insurance policy against biodiversity loss.
- **Statement 2 is incorrect:** While the **Svalbard Global Seed Vault** is located in the Arctic and serves as a global backup for seed banks worldwide, the **Indian Seed Vault** is located in **Chang La, Ladakh.** It is a high-altitude facility designed to preserve India's plant genetic resources.
- **Statement 3 is correct:** The Indian Seed Vault is a joint initiative between the **National Bureau of Plant Genetic Resources** (NBPGR), which is under the **Indian Council of Agricultural Research (ICAR)** and the **Defence Institute of High Altitude Research (DIHAR)**, part of **DRDO.** It houses over **5000 seed accessions**, which serve as a critical resource for ensuring future food security.

**Thus, option (b) is the correct answer.**

**85.** *(a)* 1 and 2 only

- **Statement 1 is correct: Cryopreservation** is a method that involves cooling cells, tissues, or embryos to extremely low temperatures (between **–80°C and –196°C**) in liquid nitrogen. By lowering the temperature, biological samples are preserved in a suspended state, halting cellular activity and metabolism.
- **Statement 2 is correct:** Cryopreservation can indeed preserve biological samples indefinitely, as the metabolic processes of the cells are effectively halted. This technique is especially useful in the conservation of endangered species by freezing sperm, eggs, or embryos for future breeding efforts. It is also critical in medical research for storing genetic material and stem cells.
- **Statement 3 is incorrect:** Cryopreservation is used in both **animal and plant conservation.** For plants, cryopreservation involves freezing seeds, embryos, or other tissues that can be regenerated later. It is an essential tool for conserving plant genetic diversity, especially for rare or endangered species that are difficult to store in seed banks.

**Thus, option (a) is the correct answer.**

**86.** *(b)* Only two

- **Statement 1 is incorrect:** National Parks in India can be declared by both the **State and Central Governments.** The purpose is to provide legal protection to areas of ecological, floral, faunal, geomorphological, or zoological importance.
- **Statement 2 is incorrect: No grazing or other human activities** are permitted inside National Parks except for activities explicitly allowed by the **Chief Wildlife Warden** under strict regulations outlined in the **Wildlife Protection Act of 1972.** This ensures that the natural habitat remains undisturbed.
- **Statement 3 is correct:** National Parks in India are part of **Category II** of the **IUCN Protected Areas** classification, which are areas set aside to protect large-scale ecological processes, along with the species and ecosystems they support.
- **Statement 4 is correct:** The first national park in India was **Hailey National Park**, later renamed **Jim Corbett National Park** in honour of the British hunter-turned-conservationist. It was established in **1936** in Uttarakhand to protect endangered species like tigers and elephants.

**Thus, option (b) is the correct answer.**

**87.** *(b)* 1 and 3 only

- **Statement 1 is correct:** A **wildlife sanctuary** can be upgraded to a **National Park** if deemed necessary by the government. This upgrade provides the area with stricter protections and more stringent regulations on human activities. For example, some wildlife sanctuaries like **Bandipur** have been upgraded to national parks.

- **Statement 2 is incorrect:** Both the **State and Central Governments** can declare an area a wildlife sanctuary to protect endangered species and their habitats. The declaration is based on the ecological significance of the area.
- **Statement 3 is correct:** Sanctuaries are part of **Category IV** of the **IUCN Protected Areas,** which are managed for habitat and species conservation with some degree of human involvement, such as limited resource use or tourism.

**Thus, option (b) is the correct answer.**

***88.*** *(d)* 2-1-4-3

- **National Parks** are provided the highest level of protection, with no human activity such as grazing or hunting allowed, except under exceptional circumstances.
- **Wildlife Sanctuaries** offer protection to wildlife and their habitats, but certain activities like tourism may be permitted.
- **Reserved Forests** offer a lower level of protection compared to national parks and sanctuaries, with limited human activity allowing for resource extraction.
- **Protected Forests** receive the least protection, with more human involvement and resource use permitted compared to the other categories.

**Thus, option (d) is the correct answer.**

***89.*** *(c)* 1 and 3 only

- **Activity 1 is permitted : Ongoing agricultural or horticultural practices** are permitted in **Ecologically Sensitive Zones (ESZ),** as these activities are often part of the livelihood of local communities. However, care is taken to ensure that such activities are sustainable and do not harm the ecosystem.
- **Activity 2 is not permitted :** The establishment of hotels and resorts is a **regulated** activity in ESZs. These activities are not outright banned but are subject to strict guidelines to minimise their impact on the environment.
- **Activity 3 is permitted : Organic farming** is encouraged in ESZs because it avoids the use of harmful chemicals and pesticides, which can negatively affect biodiversity and ecosystems.
- **Activity 4 is not permitted : The erection of electrical cables** is classified as a **regulated** activity and requires specific approval. This is because such infrastructure can interfere with the natural habitats of species living in these zones.

**Thus, option (c) is the correct answer.**

***90.*** *(a)* 1 and 2 only

- **Statement 1 is correct: Sacred groves** are small patches of forests protected by local communities due to their **religious, spiritual and cultural significance.** The trees and wildlife within these groves are considered sacred and are traditionally conserved by the local people, who believe that disturbing the grove would invite misfortune.
- **Statement 2 is correct:** Sacred groves are protected under the **Wildlife (Protection) Amendment Act, of 2002,** which introduced the concept of **Community Reserves.** This category allows for government protection of lands held by communities, which may include sacred groves.
- **Statement 3 is incorrect:** Sacred groves are not limited to the Khasi Hills of Meghalaya. They are found in several regions across India, including the **Aravalli Hills of Rajasthan,** the **Western Ghats of Karnataka and Maharashtra** and the **Bastar areas of Chhattisgarh.**

**Thus, option (a) is the correct answer.**

***91.*** *(a)* 1 only

- **Statement 1 is correct:** The **Gharial (Gavialis gangeticus),** known for its long, **narrow snout,** is critically endangered and primarily found in clean river systems, such as the **National Chambal Sanctuary** in India. The Gharial population has suffered due to habitat loss and declining fish populations.
- **Statement 2 is incorrect:.** The **Mugger Crocodile (Crocodylus palustris)** is **not extinct** and is widely distributed across India, including lakes, rivers and marshes. It is classified as Vulnerable, but not extinct.
- **Statement 3 is incorrect:** The **Saltwater Crocodile (Crocodylus porosus)** is the largest living reptile and is found in saltwater habitats, including the **Andaman and**

**Nicobar Islands, the Sundarbans,** and along India's coastal regions. It is listed as Least Concern on the IUCN Red List, but it is included in **Appendix I of CITES.**

**Thus, option (a) is the correct answer.**

***92.*** *(b)* 1 and 2 only

- **Statement 1 is correct:** West Bengal leads in terms of elephant corridors, **with 26 corridors, constituting 17% of the total.** These corridors are essential for facilitating the migration of elephants between fragmented habitats, reducing human-elephant conflict and ensuring genetic diversity.
- **Statement 2 is correct:** In central India, **coal mining and iron ore mining are identified as major threats to elephant corridors.** These activities lead to habitat fragmentation, loss of traditional migration routes and increased human-wildlife conflicts.
- **Statement 3 is incorrect:** Southern India has more **corridors (21% of the total)** than northern India, which has the fewest (12%). The North and North-East regions also have a significant share of elephant corridors, with a concentration of 35% in east-central India and 32% in the North-East.

**Thus, option (b) is the correct answer.**

## Past Learning (Answers)

| | | | | | | | | | |
|---|---|---|---|---|---|---|---|---|---|
| **1** (d) | **2** (d) | **3** (b) | **4** (a) | **5** (c) | **6** (c) | **7** (c) | **8** (a) | **9** (a) | **10** (d) |
| **11** (c) | **12** (a) | **13** (a) | **14** (b) | **15** (a) | **16** (d) | **17** (d) | **18** (b) | **19** (c) | **20** (a) |
| **21** (a) | **22** (a) | **23** (b) | **24** (b) | **25** (b) | **26** (a) | **27** (a) | | | |

CHAPTER 05

# Climate Change and Mitigation Strategies

## Assessment Round

***1.*** Regarding the impacts of climate change, consider the following statements:

1. Ocean deoxygenation, a lesser-known effect of human-induced climate change, is primarily caused by eutrophication, nitrogen deposition from fossil fuel combustion and ocean warming.
2. Climate change disrupts the ocean food chain by altering ocean circulation and reducing productivity due to surface warming.
3. Rising greenhouse gas emissions have caused significant increases in global surface temperatures, leading to mass coral bleaching events and threatening coral reef ecosystems.
4. Climate change increases the frequency of floods and droughts, adversely affecting food production, public health, ecosystems and infrastructure.

Which of the statements given above are correct?

(a) 1 and 2 only
(b) 1, 2 and 4 only
(c) 3 and 4 only
(d) 1, 2, 3 and 4

***2.*** Regarding greenhouse gases, consider the following statements:

1. Nitrogen dioxide is a greenhouse gas, naturally present as part of the nitrogen cycle.
2. Carbon monoxide is a greenhouse gas produced from the incomplete combustion of organic matter.
3. Water vapour is a significant contributor to the greenhouse effect, with its atmospheric concentration influenced by $CO_2$ and other greenhouse gases.
4. Ammonia is a greenhouse gas produced from animal wastes and the nitrogen cycle.

Which of the statements given above is/are correct?

(a) 1 and 2 only
(b) 2 and 3 only
(c) 3 only
(d) 1, 2 and 4 only

***3.*** Which of the following correctly describes a key characteristic of Soil Organic Carbon (SOC) in the context of land degradation and climate?

(a) SOC levels are highest in arid regions due to low rainfall and limited biomass production.
(b) SOC is a minor indicator of Land Degradation Neutrality (LDN) and has limited sensitivity to land management practices.
(c) The largest SOC stocks are typically found in areas with high temperatures and minimal vegetation cover, such as deserts.
(d) SOC levels are highly variable and are often concentrated in 'hot-spot' areas such as wetlands, peatlands and permafrost regions.

**4.** Which of the following best describes the impact of climate change on arable land and agricultural productivity?

(a) Thawing of snow in high-latitude regions will reduce arable land availability in these areas.

(b) Rising sea levels will lead to a reduction of arable land along coastlines due to inundation and increased salinity in coastal water tables.

(c) Crop yields in tropical and sub-tropical regions are expected to increase due to improved water availability and reduced pest incidence.

(d) Rising temperatures will have no impact on the salinity levels in coastal groundwater resources.

**5.** In the context of global warming and its impacts, which of the following scenarios are directly associated with rising global temperatures?

1. Increased occurrence of extreme weather events, including heatwaves, floods and hurricanes, as seen in events like the Chennai floods.
2. Melting of glaciers leads to phenomena such as glacial lake outbursts, similar to the Chamoli incident in Uttarakhand.
3. Expansion of the ecotone, resulting in a wider range of vector-borne diseases like malaria.
4. Changes in global rainfall patterns due to disrupted wind movements are influenced by temperature differences.

Select the correct answer using the codes given below:

(a) 1, 2 and 3 only
(b) 2, 3 and 4 only
(c) 1, 2 and 4 only
(d) 1, 2, 3 and 4

**6.** With reference to the greenhouse effect and Earth's atmospheric composition, consider the following statements:

1. Greenhouse gases in the Earth's atmosphere, such as carbon dioxide, methane and nitrous oxide, trap infrared radiation emitted from the Earth's surface, leading to the greenhouse effect.
2. All gases in the atmosphere contribute to the greenhouse effect by absorbing heat and warming the Earth's surface.
3. The greenhouse effect occurs in the stratosphere, where greenhouse gases trap heat and contribute to the warming of the planet.
4. The term 'Goldilocks planet' describes Earth's ideal temperature, which allows life to exist due to the balanced impact of greenhouse gases.

Which of the statements given above are correct?

(a) 1 and 2 only (b) 1, 2 and 3 only
(c) 2, 3 and 4 only (d) 1 and 4 only

**7.** What is the 'Greenhouse Gas Protocol'?

(a) It is an international accounting tool for government and business leaders to understand, quantify and manage greenhouse gas emissions.

(b) It is an initiative of the United Nations to offer financial incentives to developing countries to reduce greenhouse gas emissions and adopt eco-friendly technologies.

(c) It is an inter-governmental agreement ratified by all the member countries of the United Nations to reduce greenhouse gas emissions to specified levels by the year 2022.

(d) It is one of the multilateral REDD+ initiatives hosted by the World Bank.

**8.** With reference to global environmental challenges and the LiFE initiative, consider the following statements:

1. The triple planetary crisis includes climate change, pollution and biodiversity loss.
2. The LiFE initiative was launched by the United Nations at COP26 to encourage individual climate-friendly actions worldwide.
3. According to the UNEP, more than two-thirds of greenhouse gas emissions can be attributed to household consumption and lifestyles.

How many of the statements given above is/are correct?

(a) Only one
(b) Only two
(c) All three
(d) None

**9.** Match the following terms with their definitions related to the Blue Ocean Event (BOE):

| | Terms | | Definitions |
|---|---|---|---|
| A. | Albedo Effect | 1. | A process in which a system amplifies the initial changes, in this case, causing additional warming in the Arctic. |
| B. | Positive Feedback Loop | 2. | When a surface reflects sunlight, especially ice, it results in less heat being absorbed by the Earth. |
| C. | Blue Ocean Event | 3. | A situation where the Arctic Ocean becomes mostly ice-free during the warm season, absorbing more sunlight and heating the region faster. |
| D. | Refreezing Phenomenon | 4. | The process where Arctic waters freeze again during the cold season after being ice-free for a period during the warm season. |

Choose the correct pair from the codes given below:

(a) A-1, B-3, C-2, D-4
(b) A-2, B-1, C-3, D-4
(c) A-3, B-2, C-1, D-4
(d) A-4, B-3, C-2, D-1

**10.** Identify the concept based on the following statements:

1. It is a market-based mechanism developed by the 2030 Water Resources Group (WRG).
2. It allows the trading of economic instruments across sectors like industrial, municipal and agricultural users to meet water reuse targets.
3. The system issues units equivalent to a certain volume of reused water, which can be sold or purchased.
4. It overcomes geographical constraints in the reclaimed water market and aims to incentivise the reuse of treated wastewater.

Choose the correct answer from the options given below:

(a) Carbon Credits
(b) Water Trading Credits
(c) Renewable Energy Certificates
(d) Emission Trading System

**11.** Identify the phenomenon based on the following descriptions:

1. It refers to the depletion of ozone molecules in the stratosphere, primarily over the Antarctic region.
2. It results from the presence of ozone-depleting substances (ODS) such as chlorofluorocarbons (CFCs) and halons.
3. It is measured in Dobson Units, where a significant drop indicates its presence.
4. Polar stratospheric clouds play a role in the chemical reactions that lead to the formation of this phenomenon.

Choose the correct answer from the options given below:

(a) Global Warming (b) Ozone Hole
(c) Polar Vortex (d) Acid Rain

**12.** Which of the following best describes the role of ozone in Earth's atmosphere?
(a) It absorbs all forms of solar radiation, protecting Earth from extreme temperatures.
(b) It absorbs ultraviolet rays from the Sun, protecting living organisms from harmful radiation.
(c) It traps greenhouse gases in the troposphere, thereby regulating Earth's temperature.
(d) It helps in the formation of clouds and precipitation in the lower atmosphere.

**13.** Consider the following statements regarding the cryosphere:
**Statement I:** The cryosphere helps regulate Earth's temperature due to its high albedo, reflecting sunlight away from the planet.
**Statement II:** Melting of the cryosphere releases large amounts of carbon stored in permafrost, contributing to climate change.
Which one of the following is correct in respect of the above statements?
(a) Both Statement I and Statement II are correct and Statement II is the correct explanation for Statement I.
(b) Both Statement I and Statement II are correct, but Statement II is not the correct explanation for Statement I.
(c) Statement I is correct, but Statement II is incorrect.
(d) Statement I is incorrect, but Statement II is correct.

**14.** Identify the greenhouse gas based on the following statements:
1. It is a synthetic fluorinated gas, mainly used in electrical installations for insulation and switching the flow of electrical current.
2. It is the strongest known greenhouse gas with a Global Warming Potential (GWP) of 25,200 in a 100-year perspective.
3. It contributes to stratospheric ozone depletion and has an atmospheric lifetime of 3,200 years.

Choose the correct answer from the options given below:
(a) Methane ($CH_4$)
(b) Nitrous oxide ($N_2O$)
(c) Sulfur hexafluoride ($SF_6$)
(d) Chlorofluorocarbons (CFCs)

**15.** Arrange the gases in order of their Global Warming Potential (GWP) from lowest to highest.
1. Carbon dioxide ($CO_2$)
2. Methane ($CH_4$)
3. Nitrous oxide ($N_2O$)
4. Perfluorocarbons (PFCs)
5. Sulfurexafluoride ($SF_6$)

Choose the correct sequence from the codes given below.
(a) 1-2-3-4-5 (b) 1-3-2-5-4
(c) 1-3-2-4-5 (d) 1-2-5-3-4

**16.** Which of the following best defines 'Carbon Neutrality'?
(a) It refers to the condition in which carbon emissions from a country are eliminated.
(b) It is the condition in which anthropogenic $CO_2$ emissions are balanced by anthropogenic $CO_2$ removals, assessed over the life cycle or a specified period.
(c) It means offsetting all carbon emissions produced by fossil fuels.
(d) It refers to an individual's or entity's decision to stop using carbon-emitting energy sources.

**17.** Regarding 'carbon credits,' which of the following statements is incorrect?
(a) The carbon credit system was ratified in conjunction with the Kyoto Protocol.
(b) Carbon credits are awarded to countries or groups that have reduced greenhouse gases below their emission quota.
(c) The goal of the carbon credit system is to limit the increase in carbon dioxide emissions.
(d) Carbon credits are traded at a price fixed from time to time by the United Nations Environment Programme (UNEP).

**18.** The formation of the ozone hole in the Antarctic region has been a major cause of concern. What is the primary reason for the formation of this hole?
(a) Presence of prominent tropospheric turbulence and inflow of chlorofluorocarbons (CFCs).
(b) Presence of prominent polar front and stratospheric clouds, along with the inflow of chlorofluorocarbons (CFCs).
(c) Absence of polar front and stratospheric clouds, along with the inflow of methane and chlorofluorocarbons (CFCs).
(d) Increased temperature in the polar region due to global warming.

**19.** Which of the following is associated with the control and phasing out of the use of ozone-depleting substances?
(a) Bretton Woods Conference
(b) Montreal Protocol
(c) Kyoto Protocol
(d) Nagoya Protocol

**20.** The 'Climate Action Tracker', which monitors the emission reduction pledges of different countries, is:
(a) A database created by a coalition of research organisations
(b) A wing of the International Panel on Climate Change
(c) A committee under the United Nations Framework Convention on Climate Change
(d) An agency promoted and financed by the United Nations Environment Programme and the World Bank

**21.** Which of the following best distinguishes Biodiversity Credits from Carbon Credits?
(a) Biodiversity credits are primarily used to offset carbon emissions, while carbon credits focus on biodiversity conservation.
(b) Biodiversity credits are government-issued permits, while carbon credits are only issued by private organisations.
(c) Both biodiversity credits and carbon credits are identical and used interchangeably in environmental conservation efforts.
(d) Biodiversity credits are a financial instrument aimed at funding biodiversity conservation, whereas carbon credits are designed to reduce greenhouse gas emissions by offsetting carbon footprints.

**22.** Which of the following statements correctly describes the factors contributing to the formation of the ozone hole?
1. Human-generated chemicals, such as chlorofluorocarbons (CFCs), lead to ozone depletion.
2. Ozone depletion is most pronounced in the Arctic region.
3. Seasonal variations in the Southern Hemisphere contribute to the formation of the ozone hole.
4. Chlorine and bromine atoms released in the stratosphere break down ozone molecules.

Select the correct answer using the codes given below:
(a) 1, 2 and 3 only
(b) 1, 3 and 4 only
(c) 2, 3 and 4 only
(d) 1 and 4 only

**23.** In the context of geo-engineering techniques, which of the following approaches are used for Carbon Dioxide Removal (CDR)?
1. Afforestation and Reforestation
2. Biochar Production
3. Ocean Acidification
4. Bioenergy with Carbon Capture and Storage (BECCS)

Select the correct answer using the codes given below:
(a) 1, 2 and 4 only
(b) 1, 2, 3 and 4
(c) 2, 3 and 4 only
(d) 1 and 4 only

**24.** With reference to the impact of climate change on plant-pollinator interactions, consider the following statements:

1. Warmer temperatures in the Himalayan region have caused early flowering, which coincides with lower pollinator availability, reducing fruit production.
2. Increased atmospheric carbon dioxide leads to higher production of carbohydrates in plants, making them more attractive to pollinators.
3. The introduction of invasive species due to climate change provides opportunities for better pollinator nutrition and strengthens native pollination dynamics.

How many of the above statements is/are correct?

(a) Only one
(b) Only two
(c) All three
(d) None

**25.** In the context of ozone depletion, which of the following factors contributes to the formation of the ozone hole?

1. Emission of ozone-depleting substances such as chlorofluorocarbons (CFCs) and halons.
2. Decrease in ultraviolet radiation reaching the stratosphere.
3. Breakdown of ozone molecules due to released chlorine and bromine atoms.
4. Seasonal variations in the Southern Hemisphere.

Select the correct answer using the codes given below:

(a) 1, 3 and 4 only
(b) 2 and 3 only
(c) 1, 2 and 4 only
(d) 1, 2, 3 and 4

**26.** In the context of climate phenomena, which of the following impacts or processes can be associated with Arctic Amplification (AA) and Arctic Oscillation (AO)?

1. Jet stream shift influences colder winters in mid-latitude regions, such as the Great Lakes.
2. Increased absorption of solar radiation due to decreasing albedo in the Arctic, contributes to faster warming.
3. Release of methane from melting ice, enhancing the greenhouse effect.
4. Strengthening of the jet stream, keeping colder polar air confined to the Arctic during positive AO phases.

Select the correct answer using the codes given below:

(a) 1 and 2 only
(b) 1, 3 and 4 only
(c) 2 and 3 only
(d) 1, 2, 3 and 4

**27.** With reference to covers, consider the following statements:

1. Biocovers are porous material layers laid directly on top of a landfill and covered by an oxidising layer of compost.
2. They control methane emissions by providing optimal conditions for methanotrophic bacteria to convert methane into carbon dioxide ($CO_2$).
3. Biocovers have potential applications in road construction and land reclamation.

How many of the statements given above is/are correct?

(a) Only one
(b) Only two
(c) All three
(d) None

**28.** Which of the following best describes carbon offsets?

(a) They are credits that allow businesses to increase their $CO_2$ emissions.
(b) They represent reductions in greenhouse gas emissions made at another location, which businesses can purchase to compensate for their emissions.
(c) They are financial credits issued to businesses that use fossil fuels.
(d) They are government-mandated regulations that force companies to reduce emissions by a specific percentage each year.

**29.** What is meant by the term 'Emissions Gap'?

(a) The difference between the emissions levels required to meet global economic goals and current industrial output.

(b) The difference between the emissions levels countries have pledged to achieve under international agreements and the levels necessary to limit global warming to well below 2°C.

(c) The gap between carbon dioxide emissions in developing and developed countries.

(d) The difference in emissions levels before and after the adoption of the Paris Agreement.

**30.** Regarding Coking Coal and its role in steel production, consider the following statements:

1. Coking coal has a higher carbon content than steam coal and lower levels of sulfur, phosphorus and alkalis.
2. Coke, produced from coking coal, is an essential input in steelmaking, specifically used to produce pig iron in blast furnaces.
3. Around 1 tonne (1000 kg) of coke is required to produce 1 tonne of steel.
4. By-products of coke production, such as tar, benzole and coke oven gas, are used in chemical manufacturing and power generation.

Which of the statements given above are correct?

(a) 1 and 2 only (b) 1, 2 and 4 only
(c) 2 and 3 only (d) 1, 2, 3 and 4

**31.** Identify the phenomenon based on the following statements.

1. It refers to sea ice that persists through multiple years, remaining at the end of summer.
2. It is considerably thicker than seasonal sea ice.
3. It acts as a barrier to the transfer of both moisture and heat between the ocean, and the atmosphere.
4. Over the past 40 years, its extent has decreased from around 7 million sq. km to 4 million sq. km.

Choose the correct option:

(a) Blue Ocean Event
(b) Multiyear Sea Ice
(c) Seasonal Sea Ice
(d) Polar Amplification

**32.** With reference to Atmospheric Rivers (AR), consider the following statements:

1. Atmospheric Rivers (AR) are long, narrow regions in the atmosphere that transport water vapour from the tropics to the poles.
2. ARs are part of extra-tropical cyclones and are typically located within low-level jet streams.
3. Atmospheric Rivers are responsible for transferring 50% of moisture from the tropics to the poles.

Which of the statements given above are correct?

(a) 1 and 2 only (b) 2 and 3 only
(c) 1 and 3 only (d) 1, 2 and 3

**33.** Match the following geoengineering techniques with their descriptions:

| | Geo-engineering Technique | | Description |
|---|---|---|---|
| A. | Stratospheric Aerosol Injection (SAI) | 1. | Spraying particles into marine clouds increases their reflectivity and blocks solar radiation. |
| B. | Marine Cloud Brightening (MCB) | 2. | Injecting gas into the stratosphere to create aerosols that block incoming solar radiation. |
| C. | Cirrus Cloud Thinning | 3. | Reducing the thickness of high-altitude ice clouds to allow more heat to escape Earth's atmosphere. |

Select the correct pair from the codes given below.

(a) A-1, B-2, C-3 (b) A-2, B-1, C-3
(c) A-3, B-1, C-2 (d) A-2, B-3, C-1

**34.** What is the key difference between Green Carbon and Blue Carbon?

(a) Green carbon is stored in coastal ecosystems, while blue carbon is stored in terrestrial forests and grasslands.

(b) Green carbon is removed from the atmosphere through marine organisms, while blue carbon is stored in forest biomass.

(c) Green carbon refers to carbon stored in terrestrial ecosystems such as forests and soil, while blue carbon refers to carbon stored in coastal and marine ecosystems.

(d) Green carbon is stored in aquatic ecosystems, while blue carbon is removed from the atmosphere through photosynthesis by crops and plants.

**35.** Which of the following statements about peatlands and their role in climate change is accurate?

(a) Peatlands store less carbon than forests and their degradation has minimal impact on climate change.

(b) Peatlands, though small in global coverage, store significant carbon and their degradation can lead to large greenhouse gas emissions.

(c) Peatlands are mostly found in deserts and play a minor role in global carbon storage.

(d) Drained peatlands are primarily used for urban development and do not contribute to greenhouse gas emissions.

**36.** What is the key difference between carbon dioxide ($CO_2$) and black carbon (BC) in terms of their impact on climate change?

(a) $CO_2$ is the second-largest contributor to climate change, while black carbon is the largest contributor.

(b) $CO_2$ remains in the atmosphere for only a few weeks, while black carbon remains in the atmosphere for centuries.

(c) Black carbon has a shorter atmospheric lifetime and cutting its emissions would have an immediate effect on reducing warming, while $CO_2$ stays in the atmosphere for much longer and its reduction takes decades to stabilise the climate.

(d) Black carbon is mainly produced by natural processes, while $CO_2$ is primarily the result of human activities.

**37.** Which of the following statements correctly describes the process of desertification in India?

1. Desertification is primarily caused by climatic changes and droughts.
2. Increased agricultural activities contribute to desertification.
3. The total area undergoing land degradation in India is 105.48 million hectares.

Select the correct answer from the codes given below:

(a) 1 only (b) 1 and 3 only
(c) 1 and 2 only (d) 2 and 3 only

**38.** In the context of carbon dioxide ($CO_2$) dynamics in the atmosphere, which of the following statements are correct?

1. Volcanic eruptions release $CO_2$ into the atmosphere by emitting gases from deep within the Earth.
2. The decomposition of dead organic matter contributes to the release of $CO_2$.
3. Ocean absorption of $CO_2$ contributes to atmospheric $CO_2$ as it acts as a carbon source.
4. Photosynthesis removes $CO_2$ from the atmosphere, reducing its levels.

Select the correct answer using the codes given below:

(a) 1, 2 and 4 only (b) 2 and 3 only
(c) 1, 3 and 4 only (d) 1, 2, 3 and 4

**39.** Which of the following correctly describes the Fujiwhara effect?

(a) A phenomenon where two nearby cyclonic vortices move around each other, eventually merging into one larger cyclone.

(b) A weather pattern that occurs only when two cyclones of equal size collide head-on and dissipate.

(c) A process where cyclones merge and move towards the equator due to gravity.

(d) A phenomenon where two cyclones repel each other and move away in opposite directions due to their wind circulations.

**40.** With reference to the impact of climate change on food security in tropical countries, consider the following statements:

1. Rising global temperatures are causing changes in growing seasons, leading to food shortages for humans and animals that rely on specific crops.
2. Countries like India and Indonesia, which rely heavily on marine fisheries, are facing threats to their nutrition security due to ocean warming, and acidification.
3. Climate change-induced loss of arable land in coastal regions is mitigated by increased availability of freshwater for irrigation.

How many of the above statements is/are correct?

(a) Only one
(b) Only two
(c) All three
(d) None

**41.** How many pairs given below are correctly matched?

| | Cloud Seeding Techniques | Description |
|---|---|---|
| 1. | Hygroscopic Seeding | Enhances the formation of larger droplets by seeding substances that act as condensation nuclei. |
| 2. | Glaciogenic Seeding | Involves dispersing salts to enhance the size of liquid droplets in warm clouds. |
| 3. | Dry Ice Seeding | Introduces dry ice into clouds to create ice particles and induce rainfall. |

Choose the correct answer from the options given below:

(a) Only one
(b) Only two
(c) All three
(d) None

**42.** Match the following cloud-seeding agents with their functions:

| | List I (Seeding Agents) | | List II (Functions) |
|---|---|---|---|
| 1. | Silver Iodide | A. | Enhances the condensation and collision-coalescence process |
| 2. | Potassium Iodide | B. | Enhances ice particle production and increases rainfall |
| 3. | Dry Ice | C. | Induces precipitation by acting as cloud condensation nuclei |
| 4. | Hygroscopic Salts | D. | Acts as an ice nuclei to induce glaciogenic cloud seeding |

Select the correct answer using the codes given below:

(a) 1-D, 2-C, 3-B, 4-A
(b) 1-A, 2-B, 3-D, 4-C
(c) 1-B, 2-D, 3-C, 4-A
(d) 1-C, 2-A, 3-D, 4-B

**43.** What is the difference between Hygroscopic Cloud Seeding and Glaciogenic Cloud Seeding?

(a) Hygroscopic cloud seeding targets ice formation, while Glaciogenic cloud seeding focuses on enhancing droplet condensation.
(b) Hygroscopic cloud seeding introduces dry ice into warm clouds, while Glaciogenic cloud seeding disperses salts into cold clouds.
(c) Hygroscopic cloud seeding enhances droplet formation by introducing salts in warm clouds, while Glaciogenic cloud seeding promotes ice production by introducing ice nuclei in cold clouds.
(d) There is no difference between the two; both techniques aim at forming large water droplets through condensation nuclei.

**44.** Consider the following statements regarding the Global Biofuel Alliance (GBA):

**Statement I:** The Global Biofuel Alliance is an initiative led by India during its G20 presidency to foster global collaboration on biofuels.

**Statement II:** The Global Biofuel Alliance includes only G20 member countries as participants.

Which one of the following is correct in respect of the above statements?

(a) Both Statement I and Statement II are correct and Statement II is the correct explanation for Statement I.

(b) Both Statement I and Statement II are correct, but Statement II is not the correct explanation for Statement I.

(c) Statement I is correct, but Statement II is incorrect.

(d) Statement I is incorrect, but Statement II is correct.

**45.** Consider the following statements about the Global Biofuel Alliance (GBA):

1. The Global Biofuel Alliance aims to foster global collaboration on the advancement and adoption of biofuels.
2. One of its key goals is to promote the usage of fossil fuels by blending them with biofuels.
3. The GBA is led by India, Brazil and the United States, which are the largest global producers and consumers of ethanol.

How many of the above statements is/are correct?

(a) Only one
(b) Only two
(c) All three
(d) None

**46.** Which of the following statements best describes the Global Cooling Pledge?

(a) A commitment to increase global cooling efficiency and reduce cooling emissions.

(b) An international initiative to phase out the use of fossil fuels in the cooling industry.

(c) A framework developed by the United Nations to regulate air conditioner manufacturing.

(d) A programme aimed at reducing water consumption in air cooling systems.

**47.** With reference to the Global Green Credit Initiative (GGCI), consider the following statements:

1. The initiative aims to establish a digital and tradable green credit system focused on environmental sustainability.
2. It is aligned with the Green Credit Programme and supports voluntary environmental actions by industries, and communities.
3. The initiative has been launched exclusively by India for domestic environmental improvement.

Which of the above statements is/are correct?

(a) 1 and 2 only
(b) 2 and 3 only
(c) 1 and 3 only
(d) 1, 2 and 3

**48.** Identify the global initiative based on the following statements:

1. It is a global network of nearly 100 mayors from major cities worldwide, working together to address climate change.
2. Six Indian cities, including Delhi, Mumbai and Bengaluru, are members of this initiative.
3. The initiative supports city-level climate action plans, such as the Bengaluru Climate Action Plan and Delhi's City of Lakes Project.

Select the correct answer from the options given below:

(a) United Nations Framework Convention on Climate Change (UNFCCC)

(b) C40 Cities

(c) Global Covenant of Mayors for Climate & Energy

(d) Cities Climate Finance Leadership Alliance

**49.** With reference to the Carbon Credit Trading Scheme (CCTS), which of the following statements are correct?

1. The CCTS allows only obligated entities to trade Carbon Credit Certificates (CCCs) based on their greenhouse gas emission reductions.
2. Obligated entities participate in the compliance mechanism, where they are legally required to reduce emissions to meet set targets.
3. CCCs can be earned only by obligated entities and non-obligated entities are excluded from generating and trading CCCs.
4. Non-obligated entities can voluntarily reduce their carbon footprint, earn Cs and trade them on the carbon market.

Select the correct answer using the codes given below:

(a) 2 and 4 only (b) 1 and 2 only
(c) 1, 3 and 4 only (d) 1 and 4 only

**50.** With reference to the EU's Carbon Border Adjustment Mechanism (CBAM), consider the following statements:

1. CBAM requires importers to purchase carbon certificates equivalent to the EU's carbon pricing rules for carbon-intensive goods.
2. It is designed to be compatible with WTO rules to prevent it from being considered a trade barrier.
3. CBAM covers goods such as iron, steel, cement, aluminum and natural gas.

Which of the statements given above are correct?

(a) 1 and 2 only
(b) 2 and 3 only
(c) 1 and 3 only
(d) 1, 2 and 3

**51.** Which of the following describes the 'Fit for 55' package of the European Union?

(a) It refers to the EU's goal to reduce net greenhouse gas emissions by at least 55% by 2030 from 1990 levels and achieve net-zero emissions by 2050.
(b) It refers to a plan to replace all fossil fuels in Europe by 2030.
(c) It is a programme aimed solely at supporting low-income households in Europe with clean energy transitions.
(d) It is a financial package designed to aid developing countries in achieving climate goals.

**52.** Consider the following statements. regarding the International Maritime Organisation's (IMO) Strategy for the Reduction of GHG Emissions from Ships:

1. The IMO's strategy targets reducing $CO_2$ emissions from international shipping by at least 40% by 2030, compared to 2008 levels.
2. The Marine Environment Protection Committee (MEPC) is responsible for the adoption of the IMO's Strategy for the Reduction of GHG Emissions from Ships.
3. The strategy includes a periodic review of its progress every five years, with the first review scheduled for 2028.
4. India has committed to developing certain ports as hydrogen hubs by 2030 as part of its efforts to align with the IMO's strategy.

How many of the above statements is/are correct?

(a) Only one (b) Only two
(c) Only three (d) All four

**53.** Consider the following statements regarding the Green Credit Programme:

1. It is a part of the government's LIFE Movement initiative.
2. The programme focuses solely on $CO_2$ emission reduction.
3. The Indian Council of Forestry Research and Education is responsible for administering the programme.
4. The programme covers activities such as tree plantation, water conservation and waste management.

Which of the statements given above are correct?

(a) 1 and 2 only (b) 2 and 3 only
(c) 1, 3 and 4 only (d) 1, 2, 3 and 4

**54.** With reference to the IPCC 6th Assessment Report, consider the following statements:

1. Human influence has been identified as the primary cause of warming in the atmosphere, oceans and land.
2. Global surface temperatures have already increased by over 2°C compared to pre-industrial levels.
3. Methane reduction ($CH_4$) emissions can help mitigate warming and improve air quality.

How many of the statements given above is/are incorrect?

(a) Only one (b) Only two
(c) All three (d) None

**55.** Identify the organisation or initiative based on the following statements:

1. It is a global platform for countries that are highly vulnerable to climate change.
2. It was established in 2009 and functions as a South-South cooperation platform.
3. It is currently chaired by Ghana and has a membership of 58 countries across Africa, Asia, the Caribbean, Latin America and the Pacific.

Choose the correct answer from the options below:

(a) Global Shield Initiative
(b) International Panel on Climate Change (IPCC)
(c) Climate Vulnerable Forum (CVF)
(d) United Nations Framework Convention on Climate Change (UNFCCC)

**56.** Identify the report based on the following statements:

1. It was launched by UNEP and acknowledges the necessity of rapid growth in cooling due to rising global temperatures.
2. It supports a global initiative jointly hosted by the UAE and the Cool Coalition as part of COP28.
3. The report focuses on reducing the power consumption of cooling equipment to mitigate emissions and improve energy efficiency by 2050.

Choose the correct answer from the options given below:

(a) Global Climate Risk Report
(b) Global Cooling Watch Report
(c) Emissions Gap Report
(d) State of Global Air Report

**57.** Identify the environmental tribunal based on the following features:

1. It is a statutory body established under an Act of Parliament in 2010.
2. It aims for the effective and expeditious disposal of cases relating to environmental protection and conservation.
3. It does not deal with cases under the Wildlife (Protection) Act of 1972.
4. It has its principal Bench in Delhi and four zonal Benches across India.

Choose the correct option from the codes given below:

(a) National Environmental Appellate Authority (NEAA)
(b) National Green Tribunal (NGT)
(c) Central Pollution Control Board (CPCB)
(d) National Biodiversity Authority (NBA)

**58.** Which of the following statements is correct regarding the 2023 hydrological extremes?

(a) The East coast of Africa faced below-normal discharge and droughts throughout the year.
(b) The Amazon basin experienced above-normal river discharge despite severe drought conditions in South America.
(c) The North Island of New Zealand and the Philippines showed much above-normal annual discharge conditions.
(d) The Ganges, Brahmaputra and Mekong river basins experienced above-normal water levels throughout 2023.

**59.** Which of the following inequities are highlighted by the study on IPCC Reports and Climate Change Mitigation?

1. By 2050, regions encompassing 60% of the world's population, such as Sub-Saharan Africa and South, West and East Asia (except China), are projected to still have below-average per-capita GDP.
2. The Global South is expected to consume more energy and fossil fuels than the Global North in future emissions scenarios.
3. Developing nations are projected to bear a heavier burden of carbon sequestration and Carbon Capture and Storage (CCS) technologies.
4. The IPCC scenarios adequately address the historical responsibility of wealthier nations for climate change.

Choose the correct answer from the options given below:

(a) 1 and 3 only (b) 2 and 4 only
(c) 1, 2 and 3 only (d) 1, 3 and 4 only

**60.** Which one of the following statements is correct regarding India's Clean Energy Transition?

(a) India is the largest producer of renewable energy in the world, ahead of all other countries.
(b) India's installed renewable energy capacity has remained constant from 2014 to 2024.
(c) India stands 1st globally in wind power capacity and 4th in solar power capacity.
(d) India has set a target to achieve a non-fossil fuel energy capacity of 500 GW by 2030 and fulfill at least half of its energy requirements through renewable energy by 2030.

**61.** Consider the following pairs regarding Heat Wave Warning Colour Codes:

| | Colour Code | Alert Description |
|---|---|---|
| 1. | Green | Temperatures are near normal |
| 2. | Yellow | Severe heat wave persists for more than 2 days |
| 3. | Orange | Heat wave conditions at isolated pockets persist |
| 4. | Red | Total number of heat/severe heat wave days exceeding 6 days |

Which of the pairs given above are incorrectly matched?

(a) 1 and 2 only (b) 1 and 4 only
(c) 2, 3 and 4 only (d) 2 and 3 only

**62.** Which of the following correctly describes a norm for fly ash usage and disposal issued by the Ministry of Environment, Forest and Climate Change (MoEFCC)?

(a) Power plants are required to sell fly ash at market rates to industries within a 300 kilometer radius.
(b) Cement industries within a 300 kilometer radius of a coal or lignite-based thermal power plant are required to use fly ash for cement manufacturing and the cost of transportation is shared by the thermal power plant, and the industry.
(c) Construction agencies are required to purchase fly ash bricks from thermal power plants regardless of the distance from the power plant.
(d) Construction agencies must use fly ash only within 100 kilometers of thermal power plants.

**63.** Arrange the following environmental laws in India in the correct chronological order of their enactment:

1. The Air (Prevention and Control of Pollution) Act
2. The Forest (Conservation) Act
3. The Water (Prevention and Control of Pollution) Act
4. The Environment (Protection) Act

Select the correct sequence from the codes given below :

(a) 3 - 2 - 1 - 4
(b) 2 - 3 - 1 - 4
(c) 3 - 1 - 2 - 4
(d) 1 - 3 - 2 - 4

**64.** Which one of the following statements is correct about the Atomic Energy (Safe Disposal of Radioactive Waste) Rules, 1987?

(a) The rules are enforced by the Central Pollution Control Board under the Air (Prevention and Control of Pollution) Act, 1981.

(b) The Chairman of the Atomic Energy Regulatory Board (AERB) is designated as the Competent Authority to enforce the rules.

(c) The rules only apply to medical institutions using radioactive materials for diagnosis and treatment.

(d) The Water (Prevention and Control of Pollution) Act, of 1974 outlines the procedures for radioactive waste disposal under these rules.

**65.** With reference to Short-Lived Climate Pollutants (SLCPs), consider the following statements:

1. Black carbon, methane and tropospheric ozone are the main contributors to the human enhancement of the greenhouse effect.
2. Short-Lived Climate Pollutants have a relatively long lifetime in the atmosphere, lasting decades to centuries.
3. SLCPs not only contribute to climate change but also have harmful impacts on human health, agriculture and ecosystems.

How many of the statements given above is/are correct?

(a) Only one (b) Only two
(c) All three (d) None

**66.** With reference to the Emissions Gap Report, consider the following statements:

1. The Emissions Gap Report is published annually by the World Health Organisation (WHO).
2. The report measures the gap between anticipated emissions and the levels needed to limit global warming to below 2°C or pursue 1.5°C, as per the Paris Agreement.

Which of the statements given above is/are correct?

(a) 1 only (b) 2 only
(c) Both 1 and 2 (d) Neither 1 nor 2

**67.** Which of the following statements correctly describes Green Contracts?

(a) Green contracts are environmental agreements between governments to reduce emissions in their industrial sectors.

(b) Green contracts mandate that contracting parties cut down greenhouse gas (GHG) emissions at different stages of goods or services delivery.

(c) Green contracts refer to government policies that enforce the use of renewable energy in public projects.

(d) Green contracts are used exclusively in the agricultural sector to promote sustainable farming practices.

**68.** What is the difference between the Carbon Footprint and Ecological Footprint?

(a) The carbon footprint measures the emission of gases contributing to global warming, while the ecological footprint measures the use of bio-productive space.

(b) The carbon footprint is related to human activities, while the ecological footprint measures the amount of water consumed.

(c) There is no real difference between the two.

(d) Both are used to measure the same thing in different contexts.

**69.** With reference to the Climate Change Performance Index (CCPI), consider the following statements:

1. The CCPI was first published in 2024.
2. India's rank in the 2024 edition improved to 7th, up from the 8th position in 2023.
3. The CCPI tracks performance across four key categories, Greenhouse Gas (GHG) emissions, Renewable Energy, Energy Use and Climate Policy.
4. It is published by Germanwatch, the New Climate Institute and Climate Action Network International.

How many of the statements given above is/are correct?

(a) Only one
(b) Only two
(c) Only three
(d) All four

**70.** Which of the following statements correctly describes an Urban Heat Island?

(a) It is an urban or industrial area with temperatures significantly lower than its surrounding rural areas.

(b) It is an urban area that traps heat due to the replacement of natural vegetation with concrete, asphalt and buildings.

(c) It refers to a rural area experiencing heat waves due to urban development.

(d) It is an area with high levels of vegetation that cools down urban regions.

**71.** With reference to marine heat waves, consider the following statements:

1. Marine heat waves have resulted in large-scale coral bleaching, which can take more than 15 years for corals to recover.
2. Marine heat waves reduce the supply of oxygen and nutrients for marine life by decreasing mixing between water layers.
3. The Atlantic Meridional Overturning Circulation (AMOC) has strengthened, reducing the frequency of marine heat waves.

Which of the statements given above are correct?

(a) 1 and 2 only

(b) 1 and 3 only

(c) 2 and 3 only

(d) 1, 2 and 3

**72.** With reference to the shrinking cryosphere, which of the following statements is correct?

1. Glaciers from almost half of the natural World Heritage sites, such as the Khumbu Glacier in the Himalayas, may disappear entirely by 2100.
2. The cryosphere, including glaciers and ice caps, has a high albedo, which helps reflect heat from the Sun.
3. The cryosphere is resilient to climate shifts and plays no role in the Earth's heat budget.

Select the correct answer using the codes given below:

(a) 1 and 2 only (b) 2 and 3 only

(c) 1 and 3 only (d) 1, 2 and 3

**73.** With reference to the shrinking cryosphere, consider the following statements:

1. The cryosphere's high albedo helps reflect heat from the Sun, contributing to the Earth's heat budget.
2. As the cryosphere shrinks, it results in the loss of coastal wetlands and threatens major cities.
3. The shrinking cryosphere has no impact on water resources and freshwater supplies.

Which of the statements given above are correct?

(a) 1 and 2 only

(b) 1 and 3 only

(c) 2 and 3 only

(d) 1, 2 and 3

**74.** With reference to Arctic (Polar) Amplification, consider the following statements:

1. Arctic Amplification refers to the ratio of warming differential between the poles and the tropics.
2. The average annual temperature of the Arctic region has increased by about 3.1°C between 1971 and 2019.
3. The warming of the Arctic is slower compared to the global average due to the higher net radiation balance.

Which of the statements given above are correct?

(a) 1 and 2 only

(b) 2 and 3 only

(c) 1 and 3 only

(d) 1, 2 and 3

**75.** What does the term 'Biorock technology' refer to in coral restoration?

(a) A biological substance used to clean coral reefs.

(b) An electro-accumulated calcium carbonate formed on steel structures to help restore coral reefs.

(c) A chemical is sprayed onto coral reefs to increase their growth rate.

(d) A genetically engineered coral species developed to withstand warmer waters.

# OMR SHEET

**Assessment Round**

| | | | | | | | |
|---|---|---|---|---|---|---|---|
| 1 | a b c d | 31 | a b c d | 61 | a b c d | 91 | a b c d |
| 2 | a b c d | 32 | a b c d | 62 | a b c d | 92 | a b c d |
| 3 | a b c d | 33 | a b c d | 63 | a b c d | 93 | a b c d |
| 4 | a b c d | 34 | a b c d | 64 | a b c d | 94 | a b c d |
| 5 | a b c d | 35 | a b c d | 65 | a b c d | 95 | a b c d |
| 6 | a b c d | 36 | a b c d | 66 | a b c d | 96 | a b c d |
| 7 | a b c d | 37 | a b c d | 67 | a b c d | 97 | a b c d |
| 8 | a b c d | 38 | a b c d | 68 | a b c d | 98 | a b c d |
| 9 | a b c d | 39 | a b c d | 69 | a b c d | 99 | a b c d |
| 10 | a b c d | 40 | a b c d | 70 | a b c d | 100 | a b c d |
| 11 | a b c d | 41 | a b c d | 71 | a b c d | 101 | a b c d |
| 12 | a b c d | 42 | a b c d | 72 | a b c d | 102 | a b c d |
| 13 | a b c d | 43 | a b c d | 73 | a b c d | 103 | a b c d |
| 14 | a b c d | 44 | a b c d | 74 | a b c d | 104 | a b c d |
| 15 | a b c d | 45 | a b c d | 75 | a b c d | 105 | a b c d |
| 16 | a b c d | 46 | a b c d | 76 | a b c d | 106 | a b c d |
| 17 | a b c d | 47 | a b c d | 77 | a b c d | 107 | a b c d |
| 18 | a b c d | 48 | a b c d | 78 | a b c d | 108 | a b c d |
| 19 | a b c d | 49 | a b c d | 79 | a b c d | 109 | a b c d |
| 20 | a b c d | 50 | a b c d | 80 | a b c d | 110 | a b c d |
| 21 | a b c d | 51 | a b c d | 81 | a b c d | 111 | a b c d |
| 22 | a b c d | 52 | a b c d | 82 | a b c d | 112 | a b c d |
| 23 | a b c d | 53 | a b c d | 83 | a b c d | 113 | a b c d |
| 24 | a b c d | 54 | a b c d | 84 | a b c d | 114 | a b c d |
| 25 | a b c d | 55 | a b c d | 85 | a b c d | 115 | a b c d |
| 26 | a b c d | 56 | a b c d | 86 | a b c d | 116 | a b c d |
| 27 | a b c d | 57 | a b c d | 87 | a b c d | 117 | a b c d |
| 28 | a b c d | 58 | a b c d | 88 | a b c d | 118 | a b c d |
| 29 | a b c d | 59 | a b c d | 89 | a b c d | 119 | a b c d |
| 30 | a b c d | 60 | a b c d | 90 | a b c d | 120 | a b c d |

## Calculate Your Score

| | |
|---|---|
| **Correct (✓)** | |
| **Incorrect (✓)** | |
| **Unattempted** | |
| **Total Score** | |
| **Accuracy (%)** | |

## Reasons for Incorrect Answers?

| | |
|---|---|
| 1. Lack of Knowledge/Existing Source Insufficient | |
| 2. Lack of Multiple Revision | |
| 3. Common Sense Mistakes | |

**Note :**

1. Calculate total score as correct answers carry 2 marks each 1/3rd marks will deducted for **Incorrect** Answers.
2. Calculate Accuracy (%) by dividing the number of correct answers to the total number of attempted questions.

## Past Learning

**1.** Consider the following activities: **(2023)**

1. Spreading finely ground basalt rock on farmlands extensively
2. Increasing the alkalinity of oceans by adding lime
3. Capturing carbon dioxide released by various industries and pumping it into abandoned subterranean mines in the form of carbonated waters

How many of the above activities are often considered and discussed for carbon capture and sequestration?

(a) Only one (b) Only two
(c) All three (d) None

**2.** Consider the following statements : **(2023)**

**Statement I:** Carbon markets are likely to be one of the most widespread tools in the fight against climate change.

**Statement II:** Carbon markets transfer resources from the private sector to the state.

Which one of the following is correct in respect of the above statements?

(a) Both Statement I and Statement II are correct, and Statement II is the correct explanation for Statement I.
(b) Both Statement I and Statement II are correct, and Statement II is not the correct explanation for Statement I.
(c) Statement I is correct, but Statement II is incorrect.
(d) Statement I is incorrect, Statement II is correct.

**3.** Which one of the following statements best describes the term 'Social Cost of Carbon'? It is a measure, in monetary value, of the **(2020)**

(a) Long-term damage done by a tonne of $CO_2$ emissions in a given year.
(b) Requirement of fossil fuels for a country to provide goods and services to its citizens, based on the burning of those fuels.
(c) Efforts put in by a climate refugee to adapt to live in a new place.
(d) Contribution of an individual person to the carbon footprint on the planet Earth.

**4.** In rural road construction, the use of which of the following is preferred for ensuring environmental sustainability or to reduce carbon footprint? **(2020)**

1. Copper slag
2. Cold mix asphalt technology
3. Geotextiles
4. Hot mix asphalt technology
5. Portland cement

Select the correct answer using the codes given below :

(a) 1, 2 and 3 only
(b) 2, 3 and 4 only
(c) 4 and 5 only
(d) 1 and 5 only

**5.** Which of the following statements are correct about the deposits of methane hydrate? **(2019)**

1. Global warming might trigger the release of methane gas from these deposits
2. Large deposits of 'methane hydrate' are found in Arctic Tundra and under the seafloor
3. Methane in atmosphere oxidises to carbon dioxide after a decade or two

Select the correct answer using the codes given below:

(a) 1 and 2 only (b) 2 and 3 only
(c) 1 and 3 only (d) 1, 2 and 3

**6.** In the context of which of the following do some scientists suggest the use of cirrus cloud thinning technique and the injection of sulphate aerosol into stratosphere? **(2019)**

(a) Creating the artificial rains in some regions
(b) Reducing the frequency and intensity of tropical cyclones
(c) Reducing the adverse effects of the solar wind on the Earth
(d) Reducing the global warming

**7.** Which of the following statements best describes 'carbon fertilisation'? **(2018)**

(a) Increased plant growth due to increased concentration of carbon dioxide in the atmosphere
(b) Increased temperature of Earth due to increased concentration of carbon dioxide in the atmosphere
(c) Increased acidity of oceans as a result of increased concentration of carbon dioxide in the atmosphere
(d) Adaptation of all living beings on Earth to the climate change brought about by the increased concentration of carbon dioxide in the atmosphere.

**8.** The term 'sixth mass extinction/sixth extinction' is often mentioned in the news in the context of the discussion of **(2018)**

(a) Widespread monoculture practices in agriculture and large-scale commercial farming with indiscriminate use of chemicals in many parts of the world that may result in the loss of good native ecosystems.
(b) Fears of a possible collision of a meteorite with the Earth in the near future in the manner it happened 65 million years ago that caused the mass extinction of many species including those of dinosaurs.
(c) Large-scale cultivation of genetically modified crops in many parts of the world and promoting their cultivation in other parts of the world which may cause the disappearance of good native crop plants and the loss of food biodiversity.
(d) 'Mankind's over-exploitation/misuse of natural resources, fragmentation/loss of natural habitats, destruction of ecosystems, pollution and global climate change.

**9.** Consider the following statements: **(2017)**

1. Climate and Clean Air Coalition (CCAC) to reduce Short Lived Climate Pollutants is a unique initiative of G20 group of countries.
2. The CCAC focuses on methane, black carbon and hydrofluorocarbons.

Which of the statements given above is/are correct?

(a) 1 only (b) 2 only
(c) Both 1 and 2 (d) Neither 1 nor 2

**10.** In the context of mitigating the impending global warming due to anthropogenic emissions of carbon dioxide, which of the following can be the potential sites for carbon sequestration? **(2017)**

1. Abandoned and uneconomic coal seams
2. Depleted oil and gas reservoirs
3. Subterranean deep saline formations

Select the correct answer using the codes given below:

(a) 1 and 2 only (b) 3 only
(c) 1 and 3 only (d) 1, 2 and 3

**11.** Consider the following statements regarding 'Earth Hour': **(2014)**

1. It is an initiative of UNEP and UNESCO.
2. It is a movement in which the participants switch off the lights for one hour on a certain day every year.
3. It is a movement to raise the awareness about the climate change and the need to save the planet.

Which of the statements given above is/are correct?

(a) 1 and 3 only (b) 2 only
(c) 2 and 3 only (d) 1, 2 and 3

**12.** The scientific view is that the increase in global temperature should not exceed 2 °C above pre-industrial level. If the global temperature increases beyond 3 °C above the preindustrial level, what can be its possible impact/impacts on the world? **(2014)**

1. Terrestrial biosphere tends toward a net carbon source.
2. Widespread coral mortality will occur.
3. All the global wetlands will permanently disappear.
4. Cultivation of cereals will not be possible anywhere in the world.

Select the correct answer using the codes given below.

(a) 1 only
(b) 1 and 2 only
(c) 2, 3 and 4 only
(d) 1, 2, 3 and 4

***13.*** The acidification of oceans is increasing. Why is this phenomenon a cause of concern? **(2012)**

1. The growth and survival of calcareous phytoplankton will be adversely affected.
2. The growth and survival of coral reefs will be adversely affected.
3. The survival of some animals that have phytoplanktonic larvae will be adversely affected.
4. The cloud seeding and formation of clouds will be adversely affected.

Which of the statements given above is/are correct?

(a) 1, 2 and 3 only (b) 2 only
(c) 1 and 3 only (d) 1, 2, 3 and 4

***14.*** Human activities in the recent past have caused the increased concentration of carbon dioxide in the atmosphere, but a lot of it does not remain in the lower atmosphere because of **(2011)**

1. Its escape into the outer stratosphere.
2. The photosynthesis by phytoplankton in the oceans.
3. The trapping of air in the polar ice caps.

Which of the statements given above is/are correct?

(a) 1 and 2 (b) 2 only
(c) 2 and 3 (d) 3 only

***15.*** Consider the following: **(2011)**

1. Carbon dioxide
2. Oxides of Nitrogen
3. Oxides of Sulfur

Which of the above is/are the emission/emissions from coal combustion at thermal power plants?

(a) 1 only (b) 2 and 3 only
(c) 1 and 3 only (d) 1, 2 and 3

***16.*** Due to their extensive rice cultivation, some regions may be contributing to global warming. To what possible reason/reasons is this attributable? **(2010)**

1. The anaerobic conditions associated with rice cultivation cause the emission of methane.
2. When nitrogen-based fertilisers are used, nitrous oxide is emitted from the cultivated soil.

Which of the statements given above is/are correct?

(a) 1 only
(b) 2 only
(c) Both 1 and 2
(d) Neither 1 nor 2

***17.*** Consider the following which can be found in the ambient atmosphere : **(2010)**

1. Soot
2. Sulfur hexafluoride
3. Water vapour

Which of the above contributes to the warming up of the atmosphere?

(a) 1 and 2 only (b) 3 only
(c) 2 and 3 only (d) 1, 2 and 3

***18.*** What are the possible limitations of India in mitigating the global warming at present and in the immediate future? **(2010)**

1. Appropriate alternate technologies are not sufficiently available.
2. India cannot invest huge funds in research and development.
3. Many developed countries have already set up their polluting industries in India.

Which of the statements given above is/are correct?

(a) 1 and 2 only (b) 2 only
(c) 1 and 3 only (d) 1, 2 and 3

# Detailed Solutions

## Assessment Round

**1.** *(d)* 1, 2, 3 and 4

- **Statement 1 is correct: Ocean deoxygenation** refers to the reduction in oxygen levels in the ocean. It is driven by **eutrophication** (due to nutrient runoff), **nitrogen deposition** from **fossil fuel combustion**, and **ocean warming**. Warmer waters hold **less dissolved oxygen**, and **increased nutrient inputs** from agriculture and fossil fuel emissions contribute to eutrophication, reducing oxygen availability.
- **Statement 2 is correct: Climate change** impacts **ocean circulation patterns,** affecting nutrient distribution, which in turn affects **marine productivity** ultimately disrupting the food chain. **Surface warming** can reduce **upwelling** (the process by which nutrient-rich deep water rises to the surface), leading to a decrease in **primary productivity** and disrupting the entire **ocean food chain.**
- **Statement 3 is correct: Greenhouse gas emissions** have led to warming, which has increased **global surface temperatures**. This warming is directly responsible for **mass coral bleaching events.** When ocean temperatures are too high, **corals expel their symbiotic zooxanthellae,** causing them to bleach and making them more susceptible to disease and death.
- **Statement 4 is correct: Climate change** increases the **frequency** and **severity** of **extreme weather events** such as **floods** and **droughts**. These events negatively impact **food production** (disrupting agriculture), **public health** (increasing disease outbreaks), **ecosystems** (affecting biodiversity), and **infrastructure** (damaging roads, bridges, and buildings).

**Thus, option (d) is the correct answer.**

**2.** *(c)* 3 only

- **Statement 1 is incorrect: Nitrogen dioxide** ($NO_2$) is not a **major greenhouse gas,** although it plays a role in **air pollution** and **acid rain.** The **nitrogen cycle** involves nitrogen compounds like **nitrates** and **nitrites,** but $NO_2$ is not a significant contributor to the **greenhouse effect.**
- **Statement 2 is incorrect: Carbon monoxide** (CO) is produced during **incomplete combustion of fossil fuels** or other **organic matter.** However, **carbon monoxide** is **not** considered a **greenhouse gas.** Instead, it can indirectly affect the **atmospheric concentration** of **methane** and **ozone** by influencing **chemical reactions** in the atmosphere.
- **Statement 3 is correct:** The concentration of water vapour in the atmosphere is largely influenced by **temperature,** which, in turn, is affected by other **greenhouse gases** like $CO_2$. **This leads to a positive feedback loop** that amplifies warming.
- **Statement 4 is incorrect: Ammonia** ($NH_3$) is produced from **animal waste** and is a part of the **nitrogen cycle.** However, **ammonia** is not considered a **greenhouse gas.** It contributes to **air pollution** and can lead to **eutrophication** and **acidification** of ecosystems, but it does not have a significant role in trapping heat in the atmosphere.

**Thus, option (c) is the correct answer.**

**3.** *(d)* SOC levels are highly variable and are often concentrated in 'hot-spot' areas such as wetlands, peatlands, and permafrost regions.

- Soil Organic Carbon (SOC) is the carbon component of organic compounds found in soil, and it plays a crucial role in the **carbon cycle, land productivity, and climate regulation**. The distribution of SOC is not uniform across landscapes and ecosystems but varies widely depending on factors such as temperature, moisture, vegetation and land management practices.
- SOC levels are indeed highly variable across different ecosystems. Wetlands, peatlands,

and **permafrost regions** are known as SOC **'hot spots'** because they store large amounts of carbon in the form of organic matter. Wetlands and peatlands have waterlogged conditions that slow the decomposition of organic material, allowing SOC to accumulate over time. Similarly, **permafrost soils in cold regions** store significant amounts of carbon because low temperatures prevent the breakdown of organic matter. These ecosystems are critical for **carbon storage,** and disturbances (such as draining wetlands or thawing permafrost) can release large amounts of carbon into the atmosphere, contributing to climate change.

**Thus, option (d) is the correct answer.**

**4.** *(b)* Rising sea levels will lead to a reduction of arable land along coastlines due to inundation and increased salinity in coastal water tables.

**Rising sea levels** caused by **climate change** lead to **inundation** of coastal areas, which reduces **arable land** along coastlines. Rising sea levels can also increase the **salinity** of **coastal water tables,** making the soil less suitable for agriculture due to increased salt content.

**Thus, option (b) is the correct answer.**

**5.** *(d)* 1, 2, 3 and 4

- **Statement 1 is correct: Rising global temperatures** are associated with increased **extreme weather events.** It includes **heatwaves, heavy rainfall** leading to **floods,** and **intensified storms** like **hurricanes.** The **Chennai floods** and other extreme weather incidents can be attributed to changes in weather patterns due to **global warming.**
- **Statement 2 is correct: Rising temperatures** have accelerated the **melting of glaciers,** which increases the risk of **glacial lake outburst floods (GLOFs).** These floods occur when water breaches glacial lakes formed due to melting. The **Chamoli incident** in Uttarakhand is an example of glacial melt and subsequent flooding linked to **global warming.**
- **Statement 3 is correct:** An **ecotone** is a transitional zone between different ecosystems. With **global warming,** temperature changes can expand these zones, allowing **vectors** such as mosquitoes to thrive in regions that were previously too cold for them. This can lead to a **wider range** of **vector-borne diseases** like **malaria,** making **disease transmission** more prevalent in new regions.
- **Statement 4 is correct: Global warming** disrupts **wind patterns** due to changes in **temperature gradients** between land and oceans. This can lead to altered **rainfall patterns,** with some regions experiencing more rainfall while others face prolonged **droughts.** Changes in **monsoons** and **global precipitation** can be directly linked to these disrupted wind movements influenced by **rising temperatures.**

**Thus, option (d) is the correct answer.**

**6.** *(d)* 1 and 4 only

- **Statement 1 is correct: Greenhouse gases** like **carbon dioxide ($CO_2$), methane ($CH_4$),** and **nitrous oxide ($N_2O$)** absorb **infrared radiation** emitted from the Earth's surface and trap heat, contributing to the **greenhouse effect.** This process warms the **lower atmosphere.**
- **Statement 2 is incorrect:** Not all gases in the atmosphere contribute to the **greenhouse effect.** Gases like **oxygen ($O_2$)** and **nitrogen ($N_2$),** which make up a large portion of the atmosphere, are **not** significant contributors because they do **not absorb infrared radiation.** Only **greenhouse gases** (such as $CO_2$, $CH_4$, $N_2O$, and **water vapour**) are responsible for trapping heat and warming the Earth.
- **Statement 3 is incorrect:** The **greenhouse effect** primarily occurs in the **troposphere,** which is the lowest layer of the atmosphere, where **greenhouse gases** trap heat. The **stratosphere** contains the **ozone layer,** which absorbs **ultraviolet** (UV) radiation, but the **greenhouse effect is not significant in the stratosphere.**
- **Statement 4 is correct:** The term **'Goldilocks planet'** is used to describe a planet that has conditions that are **'just right'** for life—not

too hot, not too cold, but suitable for sustaining **liquid water** and life. This concept applies to Earth due to the **balanced impact** of **greenhouse gases,** which maintain a temperature suitable for life.

**Thus, option (d) is the correct answer.**

**7.** *(a)* It is an international accounting tool for government and business leaders to understand, quantify, and manage greenhouse gas emissions.

The **Greenhouse Gas Protocol** is a widely used international accounting tool that helps governments, businesses, and organisations quantify and manage their **greenhouse gas (GHG) emissions.** It was developed through a partnership between the **World Resources Institute (WRI)** and the **World Business Council for Sustainable Development (WBCSD).** The protocol provides frameworks to measure and report GHG emissions, enabling better climate strategies and regulatory compliance.

**Thus, option (a) is the correct answer.**

**8.** *(b)* Only two

- **Statement 1 is correct:** The triple planetary crisis indeed refers to **climate change, pollution** and **biodiversity loss.** These three interrelated crises are causing severe environmental degradation and are often mentioned in global discussions on sustainability and environmental action.
- **Statement 2 is incorrect:** The **Life (Lifestyle for Environment)** initiative was not launched by the United Nations but by **India's Prime Minister Narendra Modi** at COP26 in 2021. The initiative encourages individuals to adopt environment-friendly lifestyles and reduce their environmental impact. Therefore, the initiative is India-driven, though it encourages global participation.
- **Statement 3 is correct:** According to the UN **Environment Programme** (UNEP), more than two-thirds of **greenhouse gas emissions** are attributed to **household consumption and lifestyles.** This indicates that changes in everyday consumption patterns can significantly reduce emissions, aligning with the goals of the LiFE initiative, which promotes small, individual actions to protect the environment.

**Thus, option (b) is the correct answer.**

**9.** *(b)* A-2, B-1, C-3, D-4

- **Albedo Effect:** Refers to the reflection of sunlight, particularly by white surfaces like ice, reducing heat absorption.
- **Positive Feedback Loop:** Describes a cycle where initial warming causes further warming, as is the case with the BOE.
- **Blue Ocean Event:** Refers to the Arctic Ocean becoming mostly ice-free during the warm season, absorbing more sunlight and accelerating warming.
- **Refreezing Phenomenon:** Describes the process of the Arctic Ocean refreezing during the cold season after being ice-free during the warm season.

**Thus, option (b) is the correct answer.**

**10.** *(b)* Water Trading Credits

- The concept described in the statements refers to **Water Trading Credits (WRCs).** This market mechanism, developed by the **2030 Water Resources Group (WRG),** promotes the trading of water reuse credits across various sectors, encouraging water sustainability and reuse.
- Each WRC represents a specified quantity of **reused water (e.g., 1000 cubic meters)** and is **graded based on water quality,** allowing users with surplus credits to sell them in the market. This system aims to encourage the responsible use and recycling of water resources.

**Thus, option (b) is the correct answer.**

**11.** *(b)* Ozone Hole

- The term **'ozone hole'** refers to a **localised and severe depletion of ozone** in the **stratosphere,** typically observed over **polar regions** like **Antarctica.** This phenomenon is largely caused by the release of **ozone-depleting substances (ODS),** such as **chlorofluorocarbons (CFCs)** and **halons.**
- These compounds rise to the stratosphere, where **UV-C radiation** breaks them down, releasing **chlorine** and **bromine atoms.** These

atoms catalytically destroy **ozone molecules**, thinning the **ozone layer** and allowing increased levels of **harmful UV radiation** to reach the Earth's surface, leading to significant **environmental** and **health risks**.

**Thus, option (b) is the correct answer.**

***12.*** *(b)* It absorbs ultraviolet rays from the sun, protecting living organisms from harmful radiation.

**Ozone** ($O_3$) in the **Earth's stratosphere** plays a critical role by absorbing the majority of the **Sun's harmful ultraviolet (UV) radiation**, particularly **UV-B** and **UV-C** rays. This absorption protects living organisms, including humans, from DNA damage that can lead to health issues like skin cancer and cataracts.

**Thus, option (b) is the correct answer.**

***13.*** *(b)* Both Statement I and Statement II are correct, but Statement II is not the correct explanation for Statement I.

- **Statement I is correct:** The **cryosphere** refers to the portions of the Earth's surface where **water exists in solid form**. This includes **snow, ice, glaciers, ice caps, ice sheets, sea ice, frozen ground**, and **permafrost**. It has a high albedo, which means it reflects a significant portion of solar radiation, helping to regulate Earth's temperature.
- **Statement II is correct:** The cryosphere, specifically the permafrost, contains large amounts of carbon. When the cryosphere melts, it releases carbon in the form of greenhouse gases like carbon dioxide and methane, which contribute to climate change. However, statement II does not explain statement I.

**Thus, option (b) is the correct answer.**

***14.*** *(c)* Sulfur hexafluoride ($SF_6$)

- $SF_6$ is commonly used in the electrical industry, especially in **high-voltage circuit breakers, gas-insulated switchgear**, and other electrical equipment. It has excellent insulating properties, making it ideal for preventing electrical discharges and safely switching electrical currents. It has an exceptionally high **Global Warming Potential (GWP)** of **25,200**, meaning that 1 ton of $SF_6$ has the same warming effect as **25,200 tonnes of $CO_2$ over 100 years.** This makes it the most potent greenhouse gas known to science. Due to its potency, even small emissions of $SF_6$ can have a significant impact on global warming.
- $SF_6$ does not directly deplete the ozone layer, but it is a long-lived gas in the atmosphere with a **lifetime of around 3,200 years.** Once released, it remains in the atmosphere for millennia, contributing to the enhanced greenhouse effect. Due to its long lifetime, $SF_6$ persists and accumulates in the atmosphere, exacerbating its environmental impact.

**Thus, option (c) is the correct answer.**

***15.*** *(a)* 1-2-3-4-5

- **Global Warming Potential** (GWP) is a measure used to compare the **ability of different greenhouse gases** to trap heat in the Earth's atmosphere over a specific period, typically **100 years.** It indicates how much **heat** a greenhouse gas can absorb relative to **carbon dioxide** ($CO_2$), which has a GWP of 1.

**Global warming potential of different gases:**

| | |
|---|---|
| Carbon Dioxide ($CO_2$) | GWP of 1 (baseline reference) |
| Methane ($CH_4$) | GWP of 28-36 (depending on the time horizon) |
| Nitrous Oxide ($N_2O$) | GWP of 298 |
| Perfluorocarbons (PFCs) | GWP varies but is significantly higher (ranging from 7,000 to 12,000) |
| Sulfur Hexafluoride ($SF_6$) | GWP of 25,200 |

**Thus, option (a) is the correct answer.**

***16.*** *(b)* It is the condition in which anthropogenic $CO_2$ emissions are balanced by anthropogenic $CO_2$ removals, assessed over the life cycle or a specified period.

**Carbon neutrality** refers to balancing out the emissions by an equivalent amount of removals. This can apply to countries, organisations, activities, or commodities, and is often assessed over the entire life cycle of the emissions and removals. The goal is not necessarily to eliminate all emissions but to balance them with measures such as carbon sequestration or offsetting.

**Thus, option (b) is the correct answer.**

**17.** *(d)* Carbon credits are traded at a price fixed from time to time by the United Nations Environment Programme.

- **Statement (a) is correct:** The **Kyoto Protocol** (adopted in 1997) introduced mechanisms like the carbon credit system to reduce greenhouse gas emissions globally.
- **Statement (b) is correct:** Under the **Kyoto Protocol,** countries or entities that reduce their emissions below their allocated quotas are awarded carbon credits, which they can trade with other entities that exceed their quotas.
- **Statement (c) is correct:** The primary objective of the carbon credit system is to provide economic incentives to reduce emissions of carbon dioxide and other greenhouse gases, thus limiting their increase.
- **Statement (d) is incorrect:** The price of carbon credits is determined by **market forces** in carbon trading markets, such as the European Union Emission Trading System (EU ETS). The **United Nations Environment Programme (UNEP)** does not set or regulate the price of carbon credits.

**Thus, option (d) is the correct answer.**

**18.** *(b)* Presence of prominent polar front and stratospheric clouds, along with the inflow of chlorofluorocarbons (CFCs).

- The primary reason for the formation of the **ozone hole** in the **Antarctic region** is the combination of the following factors:
- **Polar Front:** The strong polar vortex isolates the Antarctic air, creating conditions for ozone depletion.
- **Stratospheric Clouds:** In the extreme cold of the Antarctic winter, **polar stratospheric clouds (PSCs)** form. These clouds provide surfaces for chemical reactions that involve **chlorine** and **bromine,** primarily released from **chlorofluorocarbons (CFCs).**
- When sunlight returns in the Antarctic spring, these reactions result in the **breakdown of ozone molecules,** leading to the **ozone hole.**

**Thus, option (b) is the correct answer.**

**19.** *(b)* Montreal Protocol

- The **Montreal Protocol** is an international treaty that was adopted in **1987** and is specifically aimed at controlling and **phasing out the production and use of ozone-depleting substances (ODS),** such as **chlorofluorocarbons (CFCs), halons,** and other chemicals that damage the **ozone layer** in the stratosphere.
- The protocol has been highly successful and is considered one of the most effective environmental agreements. Its enforcement has led to significant reductions in the release of ODS, helping the ozone layer gradually recover.o ozone-depleting substances.

**Thus, option (b) is the correct answer.**

**20.** *(a)* A database created by a coalition of research organisations

- The **Climate Action Tracker** (CAT) is an independent scientific analysis produced by a coalition of research organisations, including **Climate Analytics** and the **New Climate Institute.**
- It tracks the progress of different countries in reducing their greenhouse gas emissions and evaluates whether these efforts align with global climate goals, such as the **Paris Agreement** targets. CAT provides an objective assessment of the progress being made by countries and offers insights into the effectiveness of their climate policies.

**Thus, option (a) is the correct answer.**

**21.** *(d)* Biodiversity credits are a financial instrument aimed at funding biodiversity conservation, whereas carbon credits are designed to reduce greenhouse gas emissions by offsetting carbon footprints.

- **Biodiversity credits** are a **financial instrument** intended to attract investment for the **conservation, restoration,** and

**sustainable use of biodiversity-rich areas.** These credits aim to protect and restore biodiversity, as outlined by international agreements like the **Kunming-Montreal Global Biodiversity Framework** (KMGBF) under the CBD.

- Carbon credits are a mechanism that allows entities to 'offset' their carbon footprint by purchasing credits that represent emissions reductions achieved by other projects.

**Thus, option (d) is the correct answer.**

**22.** *(b)* 1, 3 and 4 only

- **Statement 1 is correct: Chlorofluorocarbons** (CFCs) and other **ozone-depleting substances** (ODS), such as **halons**, are human-generated chemicals that release **chlorine** and **bromine** atoms in the **stratosphere**. These atoms break down **ozone** ($O_3$) molecules, leading to **ozone depletion.** The use of **CFCs** in refrigeration, aerosols, and other products was a major factor in the depletion of the **ozone layer.**
- **Statement 2 is incorrect: Ozone depletion** is most pronounced over the **Antarctic region,** not the **Arctic.** The **Antarctic ozone hole** is more severe due to the extreme **cold temperatures** and **polar stratospheric clouds (PSCs),** which facilitate the release of **chlorine** and **bromine** that break down ozone. The **Arctic** also experiences **ozone depletion,** but it is generally less severe than in the **Antarctic** due to milder winter conditions and fewer PSCs.
- **Statement 3 is correct:** The **ozone hole** over the **Antarctic** is largely a result of **seasonal variations.** During the **Antarctic winter,** the **polar vortex** forms, isolating the air over the continent and creating conditions for **PSC** formation. When **sunlight** returns in **spring,** the **chlorine** and **bromine** released from PSCs cause rapid **ozone destruction,** leading to the formation of the **ozone hole.** This seasonal pattern makes **ozone depletion** more pronounced during the **Southern Hemisphere spring** (September to November).
- **Statement 4 is correct: Chlorine** and **bromine** atoms released in the **stratosphere** react with **ozone molecules,** breaking them down into **oxygen molecules** ($O_2$) and reducing the overall concentration of **ozone.** These reactions are facilitated by **sunlight,** which provides the energy needed to break down **CFCs** and release **chlorine** and **bromine.**

**Thus, option (b) is the correct answer.**

**23.** *(a)* 1, 2 and 4 only

- **Option 1 is correct: Afforestation** (planting trees in an area where there were no trees) and **reforestation** (planting trees in areas where they were previously present) are effective **Carbon Dioxide Removal (CDR) techniques** as **trees absorb** $CO_2$ during photosynthesis.
- **Option 2 is correct: Biochar** is **produced by burning organic material in a low-oxygen environment,** creating a stable form of carbon that can be buried in the soil to sequester carbon. This process **effectively captures carbon** from the atmosphere, making it a **CDR** approach.
- **Option 3 is incorrect: Ocean acidification is not a CDR approach.** It is a negative consequence of excess $CO_2$ in the atmosphere dissolving in seawater, which leads to a decrease in ocean pH and impacts marine life. It is a problem rather than a solution to carbon removal.
- **Option 4 is correct:** BECCS involves **growing biomass (such as plants) to absorb** $CO_2$, then burning that biomass for energy while capturing and storing the resulting $CO_2$. This allows for negative emissions, making it a CDR technique.

**Thus, option (a) is the correct answer.**

**24.** *(a)* Only one

- **Statement 1 is correct:** Warmer temperatures due to climate change have led to **earlier flowering** in apple-producing areas of the Himalayan region. However, this **early flowering often coincides with reduced pollinator availability, causing a decrease in fruit production and yield quality.**
- **Statement 2 is incorrect:** While **increased atmospheric** $CO_2$ **indeed boosts**

**carbohydrate production in plants, this does not necessarily make them more attractive to pollinators.** The opposite can occur. The rise in $CO_2$ can alter plant nutritional quality in a way that attracts herbivores (like fruit flies and grasshoppers) rather than pollinators.

- **Statement 3 is incorrect:** The introduction of **invasive species** due to climate change tends to **disrupt native ecosystems** rather than strengthen them. Invasive species often **compete with native plant species**, potentially shifting pollinators away from traditional plants and negatively affecting native pollination dynamics.

**Thus, option (a) is the correct answer.**

**25.** *(a)* 1, 3 and 4 only

- **Statement 1 is correct: Chlorofluorocarbons (CFCs)** and **halons** are **ozone-depleting substances (ODS)** that release **chlorine** and **bromine** atoms when they break down in the **stratosphere.** These released atoms react with **ozone ($O_3$), leading to its destruction and contributing** to the formation of the **ozone hole.**
- **Statement 2 is incorrect:** The **formation of the ozone hole** is primarily caused by **ozone-depleting substances** that break down **ozone molecules.** It is **not caused** by a decrease in **ultraviolet (UV) radiation** reaching the **stratosphere. UV radiation** is crucial for breaking down **CFCs** and releasing **chlorine** and **bromine,** which then destroy ozone. Therefore, a decrease in **UV radiation** would not contribute to ozone depletion; rather, **UV radiation** drives the process.
- **Statement 3 is correct: Chlorine** and **bromine** atoms released from **CFCs** and other ozone-depleting substances in the **stratosphere** break down **ozone molecules,** leading to the formation of the **ozone hole.** These atoms catalytically destroy **ozone,** converting it to **oxygen molecules ($O_2$)** and reducing the overall concentration of ozone in the **stratosphere.**
- **Statement 4 is correct:** The **ozone hole** over **Antarctica** is influenced by **seasonal variations.** During the **Antarctic winter,** the **polar vortex** forms, trapping air and creating extremely cold conditions that lead to the formation of **polar stratospheric clouds (PSCs).** When **sunlight** returns in the **spring,** the **chlorine** and **bromine** released from **PSCs** cause rapid **ozone destruction,** resulting in the formation of the **ozone hole.** This is why ozone depletion is most pronounced in the **Southern Hemisphere spring.**

**Thus, option (a) is the correct answer.**

**26.** *(d)* 1, 2, 3 and 4

- **Statement 1 is correct:** This statement is related to the Arctic Oscillation (AO). In its negative phase, the jet stream becomes weaker and wavier, allowing cold air from the Arctic to extend southward, which can lead to colder winters in regions like the Great Lakes.
- **Statement 2 is correct:** This is a key feature of Arctic Amplification (AA). As ice melts and is replaced by darker water or land, the lower albedo increases the absorption of solar radiation, amplifying warming.
- **Statement 3 is correct:** Arctic Amplification also includes the release of methane and other greenhouse gases trapped in melting ice. When these gases are released, they contribute to the warming of the atmosphere, further accelerating climate change.
- **Statement 4 is correct:** This relates to the Arctic Oscillation. During its positive phase, the jet stream strengthens and moves northward, confining cold air to the Arctic and leading to milder winter conditions in mid-latitudes.

**Thus, option (d) is the correct answer.**

**27.** *(b)* Only two

- **Statement 1 is correct: Biocovers** are used in **landfills** to mitigate the emission of **methane.** They are made of **porous materials** (such as soil or compost) that promote **methane oxidation.** The **oxidising layer** helps to create conditions suitable for **methanotrophic bacteria** to convert **methane** to **carbon dioxide.**
- **Statement 2 is correct: Methanotrophic bacteria** are microorganisms that utilize **methane** as an energy source, converting it

into **carbon dioxide. Biocovers** provide the optimal conditions for these bacteria, including sufficient **oxygen** and **moisture,** which help reduce **methane emissions** from landfills.

- **Statement 3 is incorrect: Biocovers** are primarily used for **methane mitigation** at **landfills.** Their primary function is to reduce **greenhouse gas emissions** rather than for use in **road construction** or **land reclamation.** There is no significant evidence that **covers** are used or have potential applications in **road construction** or **land reclamation.** Their characteristics are more suitable for environmental control rather than for construction or reclamation purposes.

**Thus, option (b) is the correct answer.**

**28.** *(b)* They represent reductions in greenhouse gas emissions made at another location, which businesses can purchase to compensate for their emissions.

**Carbon offsets** allow businesses to purchase credits that represent **emission reductions** achieved at another location, such as through renewable energy projects like **wind farms** or **solar panel installations.** This enables businesses to compensate for their $CO_2$ **emissions,** contributing to overall reductions in greenhouse gases.

**Thus, option (b) is the correct answer.**

**29.** *(b)* The difference between the emissions levels countries have pledged to achieve under international agreements and the levels necessary to limit global warming to well below 2°C.

The term **'Emissions Gap'** refers to the **difference between the emissions levels** that countries have **pledged to achieve under international agreements,** such as the **Paris Agreement,** and the **levels consistent with limiting global warming** to well below 2°C (preferably 1.5°C) above pre-industrial levels. This gap highlights the **shortfall in current climate actions** compared to what is needed to prevent catastrophic climate impacts.

**Thus, option (b) is the correct answer.**

**30.** *(b)* 1, 2 and 4 only

- **Statement 1 is correct: Coking coal** (also known as **metallurgical coal**) has a **higher carbon content** compared to **steam coal** (used for power generation). It also has **lower levels of impurities** like **sulfur, phosphorus,** and **alkalis,** which makes it suitable for use in **steel production.** These lower impurity levels are important to avoid compromising the quality of the **steel** produced.
- **Statement 2 is correct: Coke** is produced by heating **coking coal** in the absence of oxygen, a process called **carbonization. Coke** is an essential input in the production of **pig iron** in **blast furnaces,** as it serves as both a **fuel** and a **reducing agent** to convert **iron ore** into **pig iron,** which is then used to produce **steel.**
- **Statement 3 is incorrect:** The typical requirement for **coke** to produce **1 tonne of steel** is **around 0.5 to 0.7 tonnes** (500 to 700 kg), depending on the efficiency of the **blast furnace** and the quality of the **coal.**
- **Statement 4 is correct:** The production of **coke** generates several **by-products,** including **coal tar, benzole,** and **coke oven gas.** They have widespread use **Coal tar** is used in the **chemical industry** to produce **paints, dyes,** and **pesticides. Benzole** is used as a **solvent** and in the production of other chemicals. **Coke oven gas** can be used for **power generation** and as a **fuel** in industrial processes.

**Thus, option (b) is the correct answer.**

**31.** *(b)* Multiyear Sea Ice

- **Multiyear sea ice** refers to ice that **persists for multiple years,** surviving the annual melting cycle and remaining at the end of summer.
- **Multiyear sea ice is considerably thicker** than **seasonal sea ice** because it accumulates more layers over time, making it more resilient to melting.
- Acting as a **barrier to the transfer of moisture and heat** between the ocean and atmosphere is a key characteristic of **multiyear sea ice,** helping to regulate climatic conditions.

- The **shrinkage** of **multiyear sea ice** from **7 million sq. km to 4 million sq. km** over the past **40 years** underscores the impact of global warming on Arctic ice persistence.

**Thus, option (b) is the correct answer.**

***32.*** *(a)* 1 and 2 only

- **Statement 1 is correct: Atmospheric rivers** are long, narrow bands of **concentrated water vapour** in the atmosphere that transport significant **amounts of moisture from tropical regions to mid-latitudes.** They act like 'rivers in the sky,' **carrying vast quantities of water vapour** and are **capable of producing heavy rainfall** or snowfall when they make landfall.
- **Statement 2 is correct:** ARs are part of larger systems like **extratropical cyclones** and are typically located within the **low-level jet,** an area of strong winds in the lower atmosphere.
- **Statement 3 is incorrect:** ARs are responsible for transferring **90%** of moisture from the tropics to the poles, not 50%.

**Thus, option (a) is the correct answer.**

***33.*** *(b)* A-2, B-1, C-3

- **Stratospheric Aerosol Injection (A-2):** It involves **injecting gases into the stratosphere,** which then form aerosols capable of reflecting part of the incoming solar radiation. According to the **IPCC Special Report, SAI** is seen as a **rapid intervention method** to **temporarily offset climate impacts** during periods of excessive emissions, thereby extending the time available for mitigation efforts to reduce atmospheric $CO_2$ concentrations.
- **Marine Cloud Brightening (B-1):** It involves **spraying** sea salt or **similar particles into marine clouds** to **enhance their reflectivity,** thereby reducing the amount of incoming solar radiation. However, MCB carries potential risks, including altering regional rainfall patterns, decreasing hurricane intensity, and causing minor crop failures.
- **Cirrus Cloud Thinning (C-3):** It aims to **reduce the thickness of ice clouds** located 4-8 miles (6-13 kilometers) above Earth's surface. Since cirrus clouds trap more heat than they reflect, thinning them could help release more heat from Earth's atmosphere, leading to a cooling effect.

**Thus, option (b) is the correct answer.**

***34.*** *(c)* Green carbon refers to carbon stored in terrestrial ecosystems such as forests and soil, while blue carbon refers to carbon stored in coastal and marine ecosystems.

- **Green Carbon:** Green carbon refers to **carbon** stored in **terrestrial ecosystems,** particularly in forests, grasslands, and soils. E.g. Carbon is stored in the **Amazon rainforest, Temperate woodlands,** and **Tropical forests.** It is sequestered through **photosynthesis by trees and plants,** and stored in **biomass** (such as trunks, branches, and roots) and **soil organic matter.** Forests act as major **carbon sinks,** absorbing large amounts of **carbon dioxide** ($CO_2$) from the atmosphere, thereby playing a key role in **mitigating climate change.**
- **Blue Carbon:** Blue carbon refers to **carbon captured and stored in coastal and marine ecosystems.** These include mangroves, salt marshes, seagrasses, and tidal wetlands. Eg-Mangrove forests in coastal areas, seagrass meadows along coastlines, and salt marshes. Blue carbon is sequestered by **marine plants and sediments. Coastal ecosystems** play a critical role in **carbon sequestration** and **climate regulation.** In addition to storing carbon, they provide habitat for marine organisms, protect coastlines, and enhance biodiversity.

**Thus, option (c) is the correct answer.**

***35.*** *(b)* Peatlands, though small in global coverage, store significant carbon, and their degradation can lead to large greenhouse gas emissions.

- **Peatlands** are a type of **wetland** that contains partially decayed organic matter, primarily peat, and they are one of the most important carbon sinks on the planet.
- Peatlands cover only a small portion of the Earth's surface, but they are **highly effective at storing carbon**—they store around 30% of the world's soil carbon. When peatlands are degraded, drained, or burned, the stored

carbon is released into the atmosphere as $CO_2$, contributing significantly to greenhouse gas emissions.

**Thus, option (b) is the correct answer.**

**36.** *(c)* Black carbon has a shorter atmospheric lifetime and cutting its emissions would have an immediate effect on reducing warming, while $CO_2$ stays in the atmosphere for much longer and its reduction takes decades to stabilise the climate.

- **Black carbon** is primarily produced by **incomplete combustion** of **fossil fuels, biomass** and other human-related activities, such as **burning wood** and **diesel engines**. It can also be produced by **natural processes** like **wildfires,** but most emissions are human-driven. $CO_2$ is produced by **both human activities** (e.g., burning fossil fuels, deforestation) and **natural processes** (e.g., respiration, volcanic activity).
- **Black carbon** remains in the atmosphere for a **short period** (days to weeks), but it is highly effective in **absorbing sunlight** and **warming the atmosphere**. Cutting **black carbon emissions** would have an **immediate impact** on reducing global warming. $CO_2$, however, has a **longer atmospheric lifetime** (decades to centuries), meaning that reducing $CO_2$ emissions takes **much longer** to stabilise the climate and mitigate warming.

**Thus, option (c) is the correct answer.**

**37.** *(d)* 2 and 3 only

- **Statement 1 is incorrect:** While climatic changes and droughts do contribute to desertification, it is primarily driven by human activities such as overgrazing, deforestation, and unsustainable agricultural practices rather than natural climatic changes alone. In India, these human-induced factors play a significant role.
- **Statement 2 is correct:** Increased agricultural activities, such as over-cultivation, improper irrigation practices, and excessive use of chemical fertilisers, are significant contributors to desertification by degrading soil quality and leading to erosion and loss of productive land.
- **Statement 3 is correct:** According to reports, the total area undergoing land degradation in India is approximately 105.48 million hectares, highlighting the scale of desertification and land degradation across the country.

**Thus, option (d) is the correct answer.**

**38.** *(a)* 1, 2 and 4 only

- **Statement 1 is correct:** Volcanic eruptions release **water vapour and gases, including** $CO_2$, $SO_2$, etc., from deep within the Earth. This is a natural source of $CO_2$, as volcanic gases contribute to atmospheric carbon through magma degassing during eruptions.
- **Statement 2 is correct:** When dead organic matter (such as plants or animals) decomposes, **microbes break down the material, releasing $CO_2$ into the atmosphere.** Decomposition is a significant part of the carbon cycle, contributing to the natural flux of $CO_2$.
- **Statement 3 is incorrect:** Ocean absorption refers to the process by which oceans absorb $CO_2$ from the atmosphere. The **oceans act as a carbon sink**, meaning they help remove $CO_2$ from the atmosphere rather than acting as a carbon source. The absorption of $CO_2$ by the ocean helps **reduce atmospheric carbon levels.** However, under specific conditions, oceans can release $CO_2$, but primarily, they function as a net carbon sink.
- **Statement 4 is correct:** Photosynthesis is the process by which **plants, algae, and cyanobacteria use $CO_2$ along with sunlight to produce glucose and oxygen.** This process **removes $CO_2$** from the atmosphere, significantly contributing to the regulation of atmospheric carbon levels.

**Thus, option (a) is the correct answer.**

**39.** *(a)* A phenomenon where two nearby cyclonic vortices move around each other, eventually merging into one larger cyclone.

- The Fujiwhara effect occurs when **two cyclonic systems** (such as **tropical cyclones or hurricanes**) come close enough to each other that their **rotational influences** cause them to **orbit around a common center.** If the two systems are close enough, they may eventually merge into a larger cyclone. This effect is named after the Japanese meteorologist **Sakuhei Fujiwara**, who first described it.

- The Fujiwhara effect does not necessarily involve **equal-sized** cyclones colliding head-on. The Fujiwhara effect involves **rotation around a common center** and sometimes merging, but it does not describe repulsion between two cyclones.

**Thus, option (a) is the correct answer.**

**40.** *(b)* Only two

- **Statement 1 is correct:** Rising global temperatures are disrupting growing seasons, causing plants and trees to produce fruit earlier or later than usual, affecting food availability for both humans and animals that rely on specific crops.
- **Statement 2 is correct:** Tropical countries like India, Indonesia, and Malaysia, which are dependent on marine fisheries, are seeing their **nutrition security threatened** due to **ocean warming** and **acidification**, which affect fish habitats and breeding patterns.
- **Statement 3 is incorrect:** Climate change is leading to a loss of arable land in coastal regions due to **sea-level rise, saltwater intrusion,** and **coastal erosion,** but this is not mitigated by the increased availability of freshwater. **Water scarcity** is a major issue due to the lack of irrigation infrastructure and varia

**Thus, option (b) is the correct answer.**

**41.** *(b)* Only two

- **Pair 1 is correct: Hygroscopic seeding** involves the introduction of **hygroscopic particles,** such as **calcium chloride** or **sodium chloride,** which act as **condensation nuclei.** These particles absorb water vapour, enhancing the formation of larger droplets, which can eventually lead to **precipitation.**
- **Pair 2 is incorrect: Glaciogenic seeding** involves dispersing **silver iodide** or similar substances to **supercool** water droplets, leading to the formation of **ice crystals.** This is typically done in **cold clouds** to initiate the process of **ice crystal growth** and precipitation. It does **not** involve **salts** to enhance the size of droplets in **warm clouds.**
- **Pair 3 is correct: Dry ice seeding** involves the use of **solid carbon dioxide (dry ice),** which, when introduced into **supercooled clouds,** lowers the temperature and encourages the formation of **ice particles,** eventually leading to **precipitation.**

**Thus, option (b) is the correct answer.**

**42.** *(a)* 1-D, 2-C, 3-B, 4-A

- **Silver Iodide (1-D):** Commonly used in cloud seeding because it effectively acts as an ice nucleus due to its structural similarity to ice. This property allows it to catalyse ice particle formation in clouds, which can lead to increased precipitation as ice nuclei, typically used for glaciogenic cloud seeding to induce ice formation in clouds.
- **Potassium Iodide (2-C):** While potassium iodide can be used in weather modification, its function as an ice nucleus is less typical than silver iodide. It is more commonly associated with inducing rainfall through other mechanisms like acting as cloud condensation nuclei.
- **Dry Ice (3-B):** When used in cloud seeding, dry ice serves to cool cloud particles, promoting the freezing of water droplets and the formation of ice, which can then lead to precipitation.
- **Hygroscopic Salts (4-A):** These materials attract moisture and are used to encourage the condensation and coalescence of water droplets in clouds, which can increase the likelihood of rain.

**Thus, option (a) is the correct answer.**

**43.** *(c)* Hygroscopic cloud seeding enhances droplet formation by introducing salts in warm clouds, while Glaciogenic cloud seeding promotes ice production by introducing ice nuclei in cold clouds.

| Hygroscopic Cloud Seeding | Glaciogenic Cloud Seeding |
| --- | --- |
| **Hygroscopic Cloud Seeding is about growing larger water droplets in warm clouds, which are typically not cold enough to support ice processes.** | **Glaciogenic seeding aims to initiate and accelerate ice processes in clouds that are cold enough to sustain them.** |
| **Focus:** This method is used primarily in warm clouds. It does not aim to form ice but rather to increase the size and number of water droplets. | **Focus:** This technique is used in cold clouds, where temperatures are below freezing. |
| **Agents Used:** Common materials include salts like sodium chloride or calcium chloride. | **Agents Used:** Common ice-nucleating agents include silver iodide and dry ice (solid CO2). |
| **Mechanism:** The hygroscopic materials attract water vapour, which condenses into droplets around these particles. This helps the droplets grow larger and more likely to combine and fall as precipitation. | **Mechanism:** These agents facilitate the formation of ice by providing a structure similar to natural ice, which can attract supercooled water to freeze around it. This process can initiate a chain reaction that leads to the growth of ice particles, which may then melt into raindrops as they fall or contribute to snowfall. |

**Thus, option (c) is the correct answer.**

**44.** *(c)* Statement I is correct, but Statement II is incorrect.

- **Statement I is correct: The Global Biofuel Alliance** (GBA) was recently launched by world leaders to expedite the global uptake of biofuels, under **India's G20 presidency**. It is to promote biofuels and foster global collaboration. The alliance was launched with **nine initiating members: India, the US, Brazil, Argentina, Bangladesh, Italy, Mauritius, South Africa, and the United Arab Emirates.** It is supported by international organisations like the World Bank, Asian Development Bank, World Economic Forum, World LPG organisation, UN-Energy for All, UNIDO, Biofutures Platform, International Civil Aviation organisation, International Energy Agency, etc.
- **Statement II is incorrect:** Apart from G20 member countries, non-G20 countries like Iceland, Kenya, and Guyana, and several international organisations, are also part of the alliance.

**Thus, option (c) is the correct answer.**

**45.** *(b)* Only two

- **Statement 1 is correct:** The **Global Biofuel Alliance** (GBA) aims to foster global cooperation to promote the **advancement** and **adoption of biofuels.** It seeks to bring together countries, international organisations, and industry players to increase the use of **biofuels** in the global energy mix.
- **Statement 2 is incorrect:** The **Global Biofuel Alliance** does not aim to promote the usage of **fossil fuels**; instead, it aims to reduce the **dependence** on fossil fuels by increasing the use of **biofuels.** While the blending of biofuels with **fossil fuels** is a practice promoted by the alliance, the intent is to **reduce** the carbon footprint of fossil fuels, not to promote their usage.
- **Statement 3 is correct:** The **Global Biofuel Alliance** is led by **India, Brazil,** and the **United States.** These countries are among the **largest producers and consumers of ethanol** globally and are working together to promote the use of **biofuels.**

**Thus, option (b) is the correct answer.**

**46.** *(a)* A commitment to increase global cooling efficiency and reduce cooling emissions.

- **Global Cooling Pledge** is a joint initiative led by the **United Arab Emirates** (host of COP28) and **UNEP's Cool Coalition,** it is the first global initiative focused on **reducing energy emissions** from the cooling sector. It aims to cut **cooling emissions** by at least **68% by 2050.**
- It promotes actions like **insulation, natural shading, ventilation, reflective surfaces,** higher **energy efficiency standards,** and phasing out **hydrofluorocarbon** (HFC) **refrigerants.** It Could reduce projected 2050

emissions by **3.8 billion tons of $CO_2$ equivalent**, preventing significant climate impacts. India is not a Signatory.

**Thus, option (a) is the correct answer.**

***47.*** *(a)* 1 and 2 only

- **Statement 1 is correct:** The **Global Green Credit Initiative (GGCI)** aims to establish a **digital** and **tradable green credit system** that emphasises **environmental sustainability** by creating **incentives** for entities that undertake **environmentally positive actions.**
- **Statement 2 is correct:** The **GGCI** is aligned with the **Green Credit Programme** and aims to support **voluntary environmental actions** by various stakeholders, including **industries** and **communities** which encourages **sustainable practices** and rewards positive contributions to the environment.
- **Statement 3 is incorrect:** The **GGCI** is a **global initiative** and not exclusive to **India.** It involves international collaboration to promote **sustainable practices** and **green credits** on a **global scale.**

**Thus, option (a) is the correct answer.**

***48.*** *(b)* C40 Cities

- C40 is an **international network** of nearly **100 mayors** from major cities worldwide, working together to tackle the **climate crisis.** C40 cities pledge to take **inclusive, science-based** and **collaborative approaches** to reduce emissions, and build **healthy, equitable,** and **resilient communities.**
- **Aims:**
- Cut emissions by **half by 2030.**
- Help limit global temperature rise to **1.5°C.**
- Achieve **carbon neutrality by 2050.**
- Six cities from India—**Delhi, Ahmedabad, Mumbai, Chennai, Bengaluru** and **Kolkata**—are part of the **C40 network,** committed to reducing **$CO_2$ emissions** by 2030 and achieving **carbon neutrality** by 2050.

**Thus, option (b) is the correct answer.**

***49.*** *(a)* 2 and 4 only

- **Statement 1 is incorrect:** The **Carbon Credit Trading Scheme (CCTS)** does not limit the trading of Carbon Credit Certificates (CCCs) to only obligated entities. Both **obligated** and **non-obligated entities** are eligible to participate in CCC trading. **Non-obligated entities** can **voluntarily engage** in projects that reduce greenhouse gas emissions, allowing them to generate and trade Cs as well.
- **Statement 2 is correct:** Obligated entities are part of the **compliance mechanism,** where they must meet specific **legal emission reduction targets.** These entities are allocated a certain number of credits representing their allowed emissions, and they can trade these credits if they either exceed or fall short of their targets.
- **Statement 3 is incorrect:** Cs can be earned by both obligated and non-obligated entities. Non-obligated entities can participate through the **offset mechanism,** which allows them to generate Cs by voluntarily reducing emissions. This mechanism enables them to trade these certificates in the carbon market.
- **Statement 4 is correct:** Non-obligated entities are allowed to **voluntarily reduce their carbon footprint,** earn Cs through approved projects, and trade these certificates. This provides an opportunity for **entities without legal Obligations** to contribute to emission reduction efforts and benefit from the carbon market.

**Thus, option (a) is the correct answer.**

***50.*** *(a)* 1 and 2 only

- **Statement 1 is correct:** The EU's **Carbon Border Adjustment Mechanism (CBAM)** requires importers to purchase **carbon certificates** to account for the carbon emissions of imported goods. This aligns with the EU's **carbon pricing rules,** ensuring that imports meet the same standards as domestically produced goods under the EU's **Emissions Trading System (ETS).**
- **Statement 2 is correct:** CBAM is designed to comply with **World Trade Organisation (WTO) rules** to avoid being classified as a **trade barrier.** It aims to ensure fairness in climate policies without distorting trade.

- **Statement 3 is incorrect:** CBAM currently covers goods such as **iron, steel, cement, aluminum, fertilisers, and electricity**, but it **does not yet include natural gas.**

**Thus, option (a) is the correct answer.**

**51.** *(a)* It refers to the EU's goal to reduce net greenhouse gas emissions by at least 55% by 2030 from 1990 levels and achieve net-zero emissions by 2050.

The '**Fit for 55**' package is a comprehensive policy initiative by the **European Union** aiming to **reduce greenhouse gas emissions by 55% by 2030, as compared to 1990** levels, with the ultimate goal of achieving net-zero emissions by 2050. It also includes reforms such as the Social Climate Fund and the revision of the Emission Trading System (ETS) to help industries and individuals transition to a greener economy.

**Thus, option (a) is the correct answer.**

**52.** *(d)* All four

- **Statement 1 is correct:** The **IMO's Initial Strategy** sets a target of reducing **carbon dioxide ($CO_2$) emissions per transport work** by at least **40% by 2030**, compared to **2008 levels** which is a part of the strategy to combat greenhouse gas (GHG) emissions from shipping.
- **Statement 2 is correct:** The **Marine Environment Protection Committee (MEPC)** of the **International Maritime Organisation (IMO)** is indeed responsible for adopting and implementing the **Strategy for the Reduction of GHG Emissions from Ships.** The MEPC oversees regulatory matters regarding environmental protection, including GHG emissions.
- **Statement 3 is correct:** The **IMO's Strategy for the Reduction of GHG Emissions** is subject to **periodic reviews** subject to a **five-yearly review with the first review due in 2028.**
- **Statement 4 is correct: India** has made commitments to develop certain ports as **hydrogen hubs** by **2030** in its efforts to align with various **green initiatives,** including the **IMO's Strategy** to reduce GHG emissions from shipping. This is part of broader efforts to promote **green hydrogen** as a cleaner fuel and support the decarbonization of the shipping sector.

**Thus, option (d) is the correct answer.**

**53.** *(c)* 1, 3 and 4 only

- **Statement 1 is correct:** The **Green Credit Programme** is a market-based initiative introduced by **Green Credit Rules, 2023,** to incentivise environmental actions like **tree plantation, water conservation, sustainable agriculture,** and **waste management** by assigning **tradable green credits** to these activities. The Green Credit Programme is an initiative under the Lifestyle for Environment (LIFE) movement.
- **Statement 2 is incorrect:** Unlike the domestic carbon market, which focuses on $CO_2$ emission reductions, the Green Credit Programme addresses a broader range of environmental actions.
- **Statement 3 is correct:** The Indian Council of Forestry Research and Education (ICFRE) administers the programme.
- **Statement 4 is correct:** The programme supports activities such as tree plantation, water conservation, waste management, and others related to environmental sustainability.

**Thus, option (c) is the correct answer.**

**54.** *(a)* Only one

- **Statement 1 is correct:** The **IPCC 6th Assessment Report** confirms that **human influence** is the **primary cause** of **warming in the atmosphere, oceans, and land.** Human activities, especially the emission of **greenhouse gases** such as carbon dioxide, methane, and nitrous oxide, are driving global warming.
- **Statement 2 is incorrect:** The report indicates that **global surface temperatures** have **increased by approximately** 1.1°C above **pre-industrial levels,** not over 2°C. Crossing the 2°C threshold is a future projection if emissions continue unabated.
- **Statement 3 is correct: Methane reduction ($CH_4$) emissions** can indeed help mitigate warming and **improve air quality.** Methane is a potent greenhouse gas with a much higher

warming potential than $CO_2$ over a short timeframe, and reducing it can lead to relatively quick climate and air quality benefits.

**Thus, option (a) is the correct answer.**

***55.*** *(c)* Climate Vulnerable Forum (CVF)

- The **Climate Vulnerable Forum (CVF)** is indeed a **global platform** for countries that are **highly vulnerable to climate change.** It aims to promote cooperation and bring attention to the specific needs of countries that face heightened risks from climate impacts. The CVF was established in **2009** in the **Maldives** as a means to highlight and promote cooperation among vulnerable nations.
- It functions as a **South-South cooperation platform**, which emphasises collaboration between developing countries to address climate challenges. The **CVF** is currently **chaired by Ghana** and includes **58 member countries** from diverse regions, including **Africa, Asia, the Caribbean, Latin America, and the Pacific.** These countries are particularly susceptible to the impacts of climate change, such as rising sea levels, extreme weather events, and other related challenges.

**Thus, option (c) is the correct answer.**

***56.*** *(b)* Global Cooling Watch Report 2023

**Global Cooling Watch Report** monitors progress and challenges in reducing global temperatures and mitigating the effects of **global warming** through cooling technologies and strategies. The **Global Cooling Watch Report** titled 'Keeping It Chill: How to Meet Cooling Demands While Cutting Emissions,' highlights the importance of sustainable cooling solutions to reduce emissions and support global climate goals. It was launched in partnership with the Global Cooling Pledge at COP28, hosted by the UAE and the Cool Coalition.

**Thus, option (b) is the correct answer.**

***57.*** *(b)* National Green Tribunal (NGT)

- The NEAA was established under the **National Environment Appellate Authority Act of 1997**, and was responsible for hearing appeals regarding environmental clearances. It was replaced by the NGT in 2010. The NGT was established under the **National Green Tribunal Act, of 2010.**
- It aims to provide speedy environmental justice and help reduce the burden of litigation in higher courts. The NGT specifically does **not** have jurisdiction over matters about the **Wildlife (Protection) Act of 1972.** It deals with cases under the following Acts: Water (Prevention and Control of Pollution) Act, 1974, Water (Prevention and Control of Pollution) Cess Act, 1977, Forest (Conservation) Act, 1980, Air (Prevention and Control of Pollution) Act, 1981, Environment (Protection) Act, 1986, Public Liability Insurance Act, 1991, Biological Diversity Act, 2002.

**Thus, option (b) is the correct answer.**

***58.*** *(c)* The North Island of New Zealand and the Philippines showed much above-normal annual discharge conditions.

- **Hydrological extremes** refer to extreme variations in the water cycle, typically involving events of **flooding** or **drought** that are beyond the normal range of variability. These extremes can be caused by both natural climatic patterns (such as El Nino or La Nina) and human-induced factors, particularly **climate change.** They have significant impacts on ecosystems, communities and economies.
- The **North Island of New Zealand** and the **Philippines** experienced **much above-normal annual discharge conditions,** as highlighted in the 2023 State of Global Water Resources report.

**Thus, option (c) is the correct answer.**

***59.*** *(a)* 1 and 3 only

- **Statement 1 is correct:** Studies indicate that many regions in the **Global South,** including **Sub-Saharan Africa** and parts of **Asia,** are likely to continue experiencing below-average **per-capita GDP** by **2050** due to climate-related challenges and uneven economic growth.
- **Statement 2 is incorrect:** The **Global North** is still expected to have higher per capita

energy consumption compared to the **Global South**. However, the **Global South** is projected to increase its energy consumption as it seeks to achieve economic growth and development, but it may not surpass the **Global North** in terms of total energy or fossil fuel consumption.

- **Statement 3 is correct:** Some concerns developing nations may be expected to take on a larger share of **carbon sequestration** and **CCS technologies** as part of climate mitigation strategies, even though they have contributed less historically to climate change.
- **Statement 4 is incorrect:** There has been criticism that the **IPCC scenarios** and international climate mitigation frameworks do not adequately address the **historical responsibility** of wealthier nations, which have contributed disproportionately to **greenhouse gas emissions.**

**Thus, option (a) is the correct answer.**

**60.** *(d)* India has set a target to achieve a non-fossil fuel energy capacity of 500 GW by 2030 and fulfill at least half of its energy requirements through renewable energy by 2030.

- India's installed renewable energy capacity has **significantly increased** from 2014 to 2024. In 2014, the capacity was around 35 GW, and by 2023, it had increased to around 174 GW, showing substantial growth rather than remaining constant.
- India has set an ambitious target to achieve **500 GW of non-fossil fuel energy capacity by 2030.** Additionally, India aims to meet at least **50% of its energy requirements from renewable sources** by the same year, as announced during the **COP26** summit.
- India ranks **4th globally in wind power** and **5th in solar power capacity.**

**Thus, option (d) is the correct answer.**

**61.** *(c)* 2, 3 and 4 only

- **Pair 1 is correct: Green** is used as an indication that **temperatures are normal** or that there is **no significant weather warning.**
- **Pair 2 is incorrect:** The **Yellow** warning indicates that people should be aware of **heatwave conditions** or **severe weather** that requires caution. It typically represents **heat wave conditions** but does not mean that they are severe or have persisted for a certain number of days.
- **Pair 3 is incorrect:** The **Orange** warning is issued when a **severe heat wave** is expected, and **temperatures are dangerous,** warranting caution and preparedness. It is used when **heat wave conditions** could be widespread, not just in **isolated pockets.**
- **Pair 4 is incorrect:** The **Red** warning represents **extreme danger** with **persistent severe heatwave conditions,** indicating that significant precautions are necessary. However, it is not specifically associated with **6 days;** rather, it indicates an urgent situation that may have a broad and lasting impact.

**Thus, option (c) is the correct answer.**

**62.** *(b)* Cement industries within a 300 kilometer radius of a coal or lignite-based thermal power plant are required to use fly ash for cement manufacturing, and the cost of transportation is shared by the thermal power plant and the industry.

The norms require **cement industries** located within a **300 kilometer radius** of a thermal power plant to utilise **fly ash** for manufacturing. The **cost of transportation** is often shared between the **thermal power plant** and the **cement industry,** promoting the use of fly ash in a sustainable manner.

**Thus, option (b) is the correct answer.**

**63.** *(a)* 3 - 2 - 1 - 4

- **The Water (Prevention and Control of Pollution) Act, 1974:** This was the first major environmental law in India aimed at **preventing and controlling water pollution.** It established the **Central and State Pollution Control Boards** to enforce laws related to water pollution and maintain water quality.
- **The Forest (Conservation) Act, 1980:** Enacted to conserve and protect **India's forests,** this act restricts the deforestation of forest land for non-forest purposes. It mandates **prior central government approval** for clearing forested land and seeks to preserve biodiversity by protecting forest cover.

- **The Air (Prevention and Control of Pollution) Act, 1981:** This law addresses **air pollution** by establishing regulations for air quality standards. The **Pollution Control Boards** were also tasked with monitoring and enforcing air quality, including industrial emissions and vehicular pollution control.
- **The Environment (Protection) Act, 1986:** This act was enacted in response to the **Bhopal Gas Tragedy** and provides an umbrella framework for environmental protection in India. It empowers the government to coordinate efforts, set standards for pollutants, and enforce actions across air, water, and land.

**Thus, option (a) is the correct answer.**

**64.** *(b)* The Chairman of the Atomic Energy Regulatory Board (AERB) is designated as the Competent Authority to enforce the rules.

The **Atomic Energy (Safe Disposal of Radioactive Waste) Rules, 1987**, are enforced by the **Chairman of the AERB**, who is designated as the **Competent Authority**. These rules outline the safe disposal of radioactive waste and include surveillance procedures, standards, and guides for implementation under the **Atomic Energy Act of 1962**.

**Thus, option (b) is the correct answer.**

**65.** *(b)* Only two

- **Statement 1 is correct:** Short-Lived Climate Pollutants (SLCPs), particularly **black carbon, methane,** and **tropospheric ozone,** are major contributors to global warming after $CO_2$. **Black carbon** is a fine particulate matter produced by incomplete combustion from diesel engines, cookstoves, and wildfires. **Methane,** a potent greenhouse gas, is released from natural gas systems, livestock, and agricultural activities, while **tropospheric ozone** is a secondary pollutant formed by reactions involving methane and other volatile organic compounds (VOCs) under sunlight.
- **Statement 2 is incorrect:** Unlike $CO_2$, **which remains in the atmosphere for centuries, SLCPs like black carbon and tropospheric ozone have a short atmospheric lifetime, ranging from days to a few decades.** This characteristic makes them more manageable in terms of mitigation since reducing emissions could lead to quicker improvements in the climate.
- **Statement 3 is correct:** SLCPs are not just climate pollutants; they also have **adverse effects on human health and agriculture.** For example, **black carbon** exposure is linked to respiratory and cardiovascular diseases, while **tropospheric ozone** damages crops, reducing agricultural yields. The impacts of SLCPs extend beyond global warming to ecosystems, where they exacerbate issues like air pollution, leading to further environmental degradation.

**Thus, option (b) is the correct answer.**

**66.** *(b)* 2 only

- **Statement 1 is incorrect:** The **Emissions Gap Report** is an annual publication of the **United Nations Environment Programme (UNEP),** not the **World Health organisation (WHO).** The report has been published every year since 2010 and provides critical insights into the difference between **current national pledges** and the emissions levels needed to meet the **Paris Agreement** targets.
- **Statement 2 is correct:** The Emissions Gap Report specifically measures the gap between the **projected emissions** based on current **nationally determined contributions** (NDCs) and the **emission levels required** to limit global temperature rise to **below 2°C** or ideally to **1.5°C,** as outlined in the **Paris Agreement.** The report shows that the world is currently **off-track,** and more ambitious measures are needed to meet these targets.

**Thus, option (b) is the correct answer.**

**67.** *(b)* Green contracts mandate that contracting parties cut down greenhouse gas (GHG) emissions at different stages of goods or services delivery.

- **Green contracts** are **commercial contracts** that require the parties involved to **reduce GHG emissions** during the various stages of goods and services delivery. These contracts can be enforced in a range of sectors, from **construction** to **transportation**, and promote sustainability by integrating **environmental obligations** into the contractual process.

- The implementation of green contracts may begin at the **bidding stage**, where companies are selected based on their **green qualifications** and commitment to cutting emissions. Green contracts help drive the **transition to a low-carbon economy** by embedding **sustainability** in supply chains, ensuring that companies adopt **environmentally friendly practices** and reduce their overall carbon footprint.

**Thus, option (b) is the correct answer.**

**68.** *(a)* The carbon footprint measures the emission of gases contributing to global warming, while the ecological footprint measures the use of bio-productive space.

- The **carbon footprint** is a measure of the **total amount of greenhouse gases (GHGs)**, primarily $CO_2$, **emitted directly or indirectly by human activities. These emissions are quantified in terms of $CO_2$ equivalent** ($CO_2e$) and represent the impact of various activities like burning fossil fuels for transportation, energy use in buildings, and industrial processes, which contribute to **global warming**. The **carbon footprint** is an essential tool in understanding the **climate impact** of individual, corporate, and national actions and is critical in the effort to reduce emissions to combat climate change.
- The **ecological footprint**, on the other hand, is a broader measure that assesses the **demand for natural resources** by human activities. It includes not just carbon emissions but also the consumption of **land, water**, and **biological resources** like forests and fisheries. The ecological footprint is expressed in terms of **global hectares** and calculates the amount of **bio-productive space** needed to sustain human consumption and absorb the waste generated. It serves as a measure of sustainability, comparing humanity's resource use with the Earth's capacity to regenerate those resources.

**Thus, option (a) is the correct answer.**

**69.** *(c)* Only three

- **Statement 1 is incorrect:** The **Climate Change Performance Index** (CCPI) has been published annually since **2005**, not 2024. It serves as an independent monitoring tool that tracks countries' climate protection performance and aims to enhance **transparency in international climate policy** by comparing the climate actions of individual countries.
- **Statement 2 is correct:** India's **rank** improved to **7th** place in the **2024 edition** of the CCPI, moving up from **8th position** in 2023. This improvement reflects progress in renewable energy deployment and climate policies.
- **Statement 3 is correct:** The **CCPI** evaluates countries across four main categories: **GHG emissions, Renewable Energy, Energy Use,** and **Climate Policy**. Each category is assigned a percentage weight, with GHG emissions accounting for the largest share at 40%.
- **Statement 4 is correct:** The CCPI is published by **Germanwatch**, the **New Climate Institute**, and **Climate Action Network International**. These organisations collaborate to provide an accurate assessment of global climate protection efforts.

**Thus, option (c) is the correct answer.**

**70.** *(b)* It is an urban area that traps heat due to the replacement of natural vegetation with concrete, asphalt, and buildings.

- An **Urban Heat Island** (UHI) occurs when a metropolitan or industrial area experiences **significantly higher temperatures** than its surrounding **rural areas** due to human activities. This phenomenon is primarily caused by the **replacement of natural vegetation** with materials like **concrete, asphalt**, and **buildings**, which have a **low albedo** (reflectivity) and absorb large amounts of heat. These surfaces release the stored heat slowly, causing urban areas to remain warmer even at night.

- Urban heat islands can exacerbate the effects of heat waves and increase energy demand for **cooling appliances** like **air conditioners.** Moreover, they contribute to **air pollution** by creating a local atmosphere that traps **greenhouse gases** and **particulate matter.** Urban planners and environmentalists often advocate for increasing **green spaces, cool roofs,** and **permeable pavements** to mitigate the UHI effect.

**Thus, option (b) is the correct answer.**

***71.*** *(a)* 1 and 2 only

- **Statement 1 is correct:** Marine heat waves are periods of unusually high sea surface temperatures lasting for days to months. These waves have led to **large-scale coral bleaching,** where corals expel the symbiotic algae (zooxanthellae) living in their tissues due to stress caused by the elevated temperatures. Without the algae, corals lose their colour and are at risk of dying. Recovery from bleaching can take **15 years or more,** and repeated bleaching events, which are becoming more frequent due to climate change, can result in the permanent loss of coral ecosystems.
- **Statement 2 is correct:** Marine heat waves reduce the mixing of water layers, which diminishes the **supply of oxygen and nutrients** necessary for marine life. The **stratification of water** becomes more pronounced as warmer surface waters create a barrier that prevents the cooler, nutrient-rich waters from rising to the surface. This can negatively impact marine productivity and the entire food chain.
- **Statement 3 is incorrect:** The **Atlantic Meridional Overturning Circulation** (AMOC), a crucial component of Earth's climate system, has been **weakening,** not strengthening. A weakening AMOC reduces the transport of warm, salty water from the tropics to the North Atlantic, leading to colder conditions in Europe and increasing the risk of **marine heat waves** in other regions, particularly in the **North Atlantic.**

**Thus, option (a) is the correct answer.**

***72.*** *(a)* 1 and 2 only

- **Statement 1 is correct:** The **cryosphere,** which includes glaciers, ice caps, and permafrost, is one of the Earth's most sensitive systems to **climate change.** As per estimates by **2100,** glaciers from **almost half** of the natural World Heritage sites, including prominent ones like the **Khumbu Glacier** in the **Himalayas,** could disappear completely due to rising global temperatures.
- **Statement 2 is correct:** The cryosphere has a **high albedo,** meaning it reflects a significant portion of solar radiation into space. This helps regulate the Earth's temperature by preventing excess heat absorption. As ice and snow diminish, more heat is absorbed by the darker surfaces of the Earth, accelerating global warming through a positive feedback loop.
- **Statement 3 is incorrect:** The cryosphere plays a **crucial role in the Earth's heat budget** and is highly vulnerable to **climate shifts.** The loss of ice and snow alters weather patterns, disrupts ecosystems, and accelerates global warming by reducing the Earth's reflective capacity.

**Thus, option (a) is the correct answer.**

***73.*** *(a)* 1 and 2 only

- **Statement 1 is correct:** The cryosphere, which includes all frozen water on Earth (ice caps, glaciers, snow), has a **high albedo,** meaning it reflects a large proportion of incoming solar radiation. This reflection helps to cool the planet and regulate the **Earth's heat budget.** As the cryosphere shrinks due to global warming, more sunlight is absorbed by the Earth's surface, leading to further warming and exacerbating climate change through a **positive feedback loop.**
- **Statement 2 is correct:** As the cryosphere shrinks, **sea levels rise** due to melting glaciers and ice sheets. This leads to the **loss of**

**coastal wetlands**, increases the risk of **flooding**, and poses significant threats to **major coastal cities** around the world. The loss of protective wetlands and the increasing frequency of extreme weather events, such as storms and storm surges, place these cities at a higher risk of environmental disasters.

- **Statement 3 is incorrect:** The shrinking cryosphere has a profound impact on **water resources**. Many regions, especially in South Asia and South America, rely on glaciers for **freshwater**. As glaciers shrink, they release less water, threatening the availability of freshwater for **agriculture, drinking water**, and **hydroelectric power generation**. The melting of permafrost also releases stored carbon, which further accelerates climate change.

**Thus, option (a) is the correct answer.**

**74.** *(a)* 1 and 2 only

- **Statement 1 is correct: Arctic Amplification** refers to the phenomenon where the **Arctic region** is warming at a faster rate compared to the **tropics**. This is due to the **warming differential** between the poles and tropical regions, primarily caused by the loss of **sea ice** and **snow cover** that once reflected solar energy into space.
- **Statement 2 is correct:** Between **1971 and 2019**, the average annual temperature of the **Arctic** rose by **3.1°C**, compared to a global average increase of about 1°C during the same period. This rapid warming is a clear indication of **polar amplification**, where changes in the **Arctic climate** occur at a faster rate than elsewhere on the planet.
- **Statement 3 is incorrect:** The **Arctic** is warming **faster**, not slower, than the global average. The **net radiation balance** is higher in the Arctic compared to tropical areas, leading to an increased retention of heat. This is partly because the loss of **ice cover** reduces the region's ability to reflect heat (albedo effect), causing the Arctic to absorb more solar radiation and warm more quickly.

**Thus, option (a) is the correct answer.**

**75.** *(b)* An electro-accumulated calcium carbonate formed on steel structures to help restore coral reefs.

- **Biorock** is a technology used in coral reef restoration, where **electro-accumulation** of minerals such as **calcium carbonate** takes place on **steel structures** placed in the ocean. These structures are connected to a low-voltage electrical current, which triggers the formation of **calcium carbonate** (**$CaCO_3$**) from the naturally occurring **carbonate ions** in seawater. This **electro-accumulated calcium carbonate** forms a stable surface where **coral larvae** can attach and grow faster than they would on natural reefs. The process encourages the growth of corals by providing a solid foundation for the corals to build upon without expending their energy to create the calcium carbonate skeletons themselves.
- This technology has been successfully used to **restore degraded coral reefs**, particularly in areas like the **Gulf of Kutch** in India. **Biorock** structures can significantly improve coral recovery rates and enhance the survival of coral reefs under the stress of **climate change** and **ocean acidification**.

**Thus, option (b) is the correct answer.**

## Past Learning (Answers)

| | | | | | | | | | |
|---|---|---|---|---|---|---|---|---|---|
| 1 (c) | 2 (b) | 3 (a) | 4 (a) | 5 (d) | 6 (d) | 7 (a) | 8 (d) | 9 (b) | 10 (a) |
| 11 (c) | 12 (d) | 13 (d) | 14 (c) | 15 (d) | 16 (c) | 17 (d) | 18 (a) | | |

# CHAPTER 06 International Conventions and Treaties

## Assessment Round

**1.** With reference to the definition of a convention, protocol and agreement, consider the following statements:

1. Conventions establish detailed obligations and specific actions required from parties.
2. Protocols typically outline specific obligations, targets, or actions required of the parties and are usually non-binding.
3. Agreements are always legally binding documents between two or more parties.

Which of the above statements are correct?

(a) 1 and 2 only (b) 2 and 3 only
(c) 1 and 3 only (d) None of these

**2.** Consider the following statements regarding the Ramsar Convention on Wetlands:

1. The Montreux Record includes wetlands that have fully restored their ecological character.
2. Ramsar sites are only designated for wetlands important for migratory bird populations.
3. India has two wetlands listed on the Montreux Record: Keoladeo National Park and Loktak Lake.

Which of the above statements is/are correct?

(a) 2 and 3 only (b) 3 only
(c) 1 and 2 only (d) 2 only

**3.** Consider the following statements regarding the Basel Convention:

1. It covers hazardous wastes that are explosive, flammable, poisonous, infectious, corrosive, toxic, or eco-toxic.
2. It includes household waste and incinerator ash under the category of 'other wastes.'
3. The Convention strictly prohibits all transboundary movements of hazardous wastes without exception.
4. India, after ratifying the Convention, implemented the Hazardous and Other Wastes (Management & Transboundary Movement) Rules, in 2016.

Which of the statements given above are correct?

(a) 1, 2 and 4 only (b) 1 and 3 only
(c) 2 and 4 only (d) 1, 2, 3 and 4

**4.** What is the fundamental difference between the Basel Convention and the Rotterdam Convention?

(a) The Basel Convention mandates a complete ban on hazardous waste movement, whereas the Rotterdam Convention allows the free trade of hazardous chemicals without restrictions.

(b) The Basel Convention addresses the regulation of greenhouse gas emissions, whereas the Rotterdam Convention focuses on ozone layer depletion.

(c) The Basel Convention focuses on the transboundary movement and disposal of hazardous wastes, while the Rotterdam Convention deals with the prior informed consent procedure for the international trade of certain hazardous chemicals and pesticides.

(d) There is no significant difference; both conventions address the same issues with identical mechanisms.

**5.** Which of the following best describes the concept of Prior Informed Consent (PIC) under the Rotterdam Convention?

(a) It is a process where exporting countries inform importing countries about the shipment of any goods.

(b) It is a mechanism for formally obtaining and disseminating decisions of importing countries on whether they wish to receive future shipments of certain hazardous chemicals listed in Annex III of the Convention, ensuring compliance by exporting countries.

(c) It allows exporting countries to ship hazardous chemicals freely unless the importing country objects.

(d) It mandates that all international trade of chemicals be approved by a global regulatory body before shipment.

**6.** Consider the following statements concerning the Convention on International Trade in Endangered Species (CITES):

1. CITES is an international agreement that is non-legally binding on the parties.
2. Appendix I of CITES contains species that are not yet threatened but need close monitoring.
3. CITES classifies species into three appendices based on their conservation status and the extent of control required over their trade.

Which of the above statements is/are correct?

(a) 2 and 3 only
(b) 1 and 3 only
(c) 3 only
(d) 1 and 2 only

**7.** Consider the following chemicals:

1. Chlordane
2. Methoxychlor
3. hexachlorobenzene
4. heptachlor
5. Perfluorohexane Sulphonic Acid (PFHxS)

Which of the chemicals given above are among the seven Persistent Organic Pollutants (POPs) that were approved for ratification by the Union Cabinet of India under the Stockholm Convention?

(a) 1, 3 and 4 only (b) 2, 4 and 5 only
(c) 1, 3, 4 and 5 only (d) 1, 2, 3, 4 and 5

**8.** Identify the international environmental convention based on the following statements:

1. It aims at eliminating or reducing the release of Persistent Organic Pollutants (POPs) into the environment.
2. Under this convention, chemicals are categorised for Elimination (Annex A), Restriction (Annex B), or Unintentional Production (Annex C).
3. India has ratified only the initial 12 POPs under this convention but is in the process of ratifying additional chemicals.
4. The convention currently lists 26 chemicals recognised as POPs.

Choose the correct answer from the options given below:

(a) Basel Convention
(b) Rotterdam Convention
(c) Stockholm Convention
(d) Minamata Convention

**9.** Under the Convention on Biological Diversity (CBD), what does Access and Benefit-Sharing (ABS) refer to?

(a) The mechanism by which developed countries provide financial aid to developing countries for biodiversity conservation.

(b) The way genetic resources are accessed and how the benefits from their use are shared between users, and providers.

(c) A global agreement to share technological advancements in genetic engineering among member nations.

(d) The process of cataloging and patenting all biological species discovered within a country's borders.

**10.** Consider the following given below statements :

**Statement I:** Prior Informed Consent (PIC) is the permission granted by a competent national authority of a provider country to a user before accessing genetic resources, following an appropriate national legal framework.

**Statement II:** Mutually Agreed Terms (MAT) are agreements reached between providers and users of genetic resources on the conditions of access and use, including benefit-sharing.

Which one of the following is correct in respect of the above statements?

(a) Both Statement I and Statement II are correct, and Statement II is the correct explanation for Statement I.

(b) Both Statement I and Statement II are correct, but Statement II is not the correct explanation for Statement I.

(c) Statement I is correct, but Statement II is incorrect.

(d) Statement I is incorrect, but Statement II is correct.

**11.** Consider the following statements regarding the Kunming Declaration:

1. The Kunming Declaration calls for immediate and comprehensive action in all areas of the global economy to reflect biodiversity concerns.
2. China established the Kunming Biodiversity Fund with a budget of around USD 230 million to fund programmes that safeguard biodiversity in underdeveloped nations.
3. The Declaration includes a commitment by all participating countries to protect 30% of their land and sea areas by 2030, known as the '30 by 30' objective.
4. The Global Environment Facility, UNDP and UNEP have pledged to expedite financial, and technical assistance to developing countries to help them implement the Global Biodiversity Framework.

How many of the above statements is/are correct?

(a) Only one (b) Only two
(c) Only three (d) All four

**12.** Under the Cartagena Protocol on Biosafety, what does the Advance Informed Agreement (AIA) procedure entail?

(a) A mandatory inspection of all LMOs before they are exported to any country.

(b) A requirement for exporting countries to obtain consent from importing countries before the first intentional transboundary movement of LMOs intended for environmental release.

(c) A system where LMOs can be freely traded without any regulatory oversight once approved by the Biosafety Clearing House.

(d) An agreement that allows countries to bypass national regulations for the import of LMOs.

**13.** Identify the international environmental treaty based on the following statements:

1. It is a supplementary agreement to the Convention on Biological Diversity (UNCBD).
2. The treaty establishes the Advance Informed Agreement (AIA) procedure for the import of living modified organisms (LMOs).
3. It includes provisions for liability and redress in the event of damage caused by LMOs.

Select the correct answer from the options given below:

(a) Nagoya-Kuala Lumpur Supplementary Protocol

(b) Cartagena Protocol on Biosafety

(c) Stockholm Convention on Persistent Organic Pollutants

(d) Rotterdam Convention

**14.** Which of the following best describes the Precautionary Principle as referenced in the Cartagena Protocol on Biosafety?

(a) It mandates that all LMOs must be approved by an international body before any transboundary movement.

(b) It emphasises taking preventive action in the face of scientific uncertainty to avoid potential environmental harm.

(c) It allows countries to waive safety measures if economic benefits are substantial.

(d) It focuses solely on the conservation of genetic resources without considering human health.

**15.** Match the following Conventions with their Objectives:

| List I (Conventions) | List II (Objectives) |
|---|---|
| 1. Cartagena Protocol on Biosafety | A. Regulates the transboundary movement of hazardous wastes. |
| 2. Stockholm Convention | B. Regulates persistent organic pollutants that bioaccumulate and are toxic. |
| 3. Rotterdam Convention | C. Prior informed consent procedure for hazardous chemicals and pesticides. |
| 4. Basel Convention | D. Regulates the safe handling and transboundary movement of living modified organisms. |

Choose the correct pair from the codes given below

(a) 1-A, 2-C, 3-B, 4-D
(b) 1-D, 2-B, 3-C, 4-A
(c) 1-B, 2-A, 3-D, 4-C
(d) 1-C, 2-A, 3-B, 4-D

**16.** Consider the following statements regarding Agenda 21:

1. Agenda 21 was produced at the Earth Summit in 1992 as a non-binding action plan for achieving sustainable development.
2. Agenda 21 involves stakeholders from local and national governments, businesses, international organisations and Non-Governmental Organisations (NGOs).
3. India is not a signatory to Agenda 21 and has not aligned any part of its development infrastructure to its goals.
4. The World Summit on Sustainable Development in 2002 reviewed and promoted global partnerships for the implementation of Agenda 21.

How many of the above statements is/are correct?

(a) Only one (b) Only two
(c) Only three (d) All four

**17.** Which of the following statements correctly describes the 'Fire Ready Formula' proposed by UNEP?

(a) It is a new international agreement aimed at banning the use of fire as a land management tool in all forested areas.
(b) It is a formula that advises governments to spend 66% of their wildfire-related budget on planning, prevention, preparedness and recovery and 34% on response efforts.
(c) It is a guideline for establishing forest fire brigades, with 34% of the budget dedicated to response and 66% dedicated to global awareness campaigns.
(d) It is a joint UNEP and World Bank initiative to fund post-fire recovery efforts in developing countries.

**18.** Under which of the following international agreements was the concept of carbon trading first introduced?

(a) Paris Agreement, 2015
(b) Montreal Protocol, 1987
(c) Earth Summit, 1992
(d) Kyoto Protocol, 1997

**19.** Consider the following statements regarding international protocols under the Convention on Biological Diversity (CBD):

1. The Nagoya Protocol focuses on the fair and equitable sharing of benefits arising from the use of genetic resources.
2. The Cartagena Protocol aims to ensure the safe handling and transport of living-modified organisms (LMOs) that may impact biodiversity.
3. Both the Nagoya Protocol and the Cartagena Protocol are independent agreements unrelated to the CBD.

How many of the statements given above is/are correct?

(a) Only one
(b) Only two
(c) All three
(d) None

**20.** Which of the following describes the Aichi Biodiversity Targets?

(a) A set of legally binding goals for all United Nations member states specifically focused on reducing greenhouse gas emissions by 2020.

(b) A series of 20 targets adopted under the Convention on Biological Diversity (CBD) aimed at reducing biodiversity loss and promoting sustainable biodiversity management during 2011-2020.

(c) A list of environmental regulations set by the World Health Organisation to combat water pollution.

(d) A framework of trade agreements on genetic resources developed under the Nagoya Protocol.

**21.** Which of the following correctly describes the Cartagena Protocol on Biosafety?

(a) It is an agreement focusing on the protection of migratory bird species and their habitats.

(b) It is a protocol that regulates the movement of living-modified organisms (LMOs) across international borders, ensuring countries have the necessary information to make decisions about their import.

(c) It is an international agreement that aims to reduce carbon emissions by restricting the use of fossil fuels.

(d) It focuses on the sustainable management of marine ecosystems and resources in the high seas.

**22.** What is the primary purpose of the Loss and Damage (L&D) Fund established at COP28?

(a) To fund renewable energy projects in developing countries.

(b) To compensate countries impacted by climate change, particularly Least Developed Countries and Small Island Developing States.

(c) To provide financial support for coal-based energy projects in developing nations.

(d) To fund research on reducing methane emissions in agriculture.

**23.** Which of the following actions was first agreed upon by almost 200 countries at COP28?

(a) Phasing out nuclear energy to prevent environmental degradation.

(b) Accelerating the phase-out of unabated coal power across all regions.

(c) Transitioning away from fossil fuels in energy systems globally.

(d) Reducing methane emissions by 50% by 2030.

**24.** Which of the following best describes the aim of the Bonn Convention?

(a) To protect habitats of endangered species by promoting habitat connectivity across different countries.

(b) To establish financial assistance programs for migratory species conservation in developing nations.

(c) To protect only marine migratory species under legally binding international agreements.

(d) To ensure migratory species of wild animals and their habitats are conserved through global cooperation, and agreements.

**25.** What global pledge related to methane emissions was introduced at COP26 in Glasgow, but is not part of the COP28 agreement?

(a) The Global Methane Pledge

(b) The Global Carbon Capture Pledge

(c) The Sustainable Livestock Pledge

(d) The Zero Waste Agriculture Pledge

**26.** How does the Global Stocktake mechanism contribute to the goals of the Paris Agreement as discussed at COP28?

(a) By reviewing and providing guidelines on how countries can promote economic growth while ignoring climate change.

(b) By mandating all countries to reduce methane emissions by 50% by 2030.

(c) By focusing only on technological advancements in developed countries to achieve net-zero emissions.

(d) By periodically reviewing progress towards limiting global temperature rise to 1.5 degrees Celsius and recommending strategies such as tripling renewable energy capacity, and phasing out coal.

**27.** Identify the global treaty based on the following statements:

1. It aims at safeguarding human health and the environment from persistent organic pollutants (POPs).
2. The treaty was ratified by India in 2006, allowing the country to maintain a default 'opt-out' status.
3. Amendments to the treaty's Annexes do not apply to India unless the country explicitly deposits an instrument with the UN depositary.

Choose the correct answer from the codes given below:

(a) Kyoto Protocol
(b) Stockholm Convention
(c) Basel Convention
(d) Paris Agreement

**28.** Identify the international treaty based on the following statements:

1. It is a legally binding international treaty on climate change.
2. It was adopted by 196 countries at the Conference of the Parties (COP 21) in December 2015.
3. Its main goal is to limit global warming to well below 2°C, preferably 1.5°C, compared to pre-industrial levels.
4. India reaffirmed its commitment to this treaty by submitting an updated Nationally Determined Contribution (NDC) in August 2022.

Choose the correct answer from the options given below:

(a) Kyoto Protocol
(b) Paris Climate Accord
(c) Montreal Protocol
(d) Rio Declaration

**29.** Identify the international environmental treaty based on the following statements:

1. It aims to protect human health and the environment from the adverse effects of mercury, and its compounds.
2. It was agreed upon during the fifth session of the Intergovernmental Negotiating Committee in Geneva, Switzerland, in 2013.
3. It includes obligations to control the anthropogenic release of mercury throughout its lifecycle.

Select the correct answer from the options given below:

(a) Paris Agreement (b) Minamata Convention
(c) Montreal Protocol (d) Kyoto Protocol

**30.** Consider the following statements:

**Statement I:** The Tiger Landscapes Investment Fund is a blended financial mechanism developed by the UNDP to catalyse nature-positive businesses that positively impact tigers, biodiversity and people.

**Statement II:** The Asian Development Bank is exploring Tiger Bonds as innovative financing instruments to engage private sector investors and promote nature-based solutions.

Which one of the following is correct in respect of the above statements?

(a) Both Statement I and Statement II are correct, and Statement II is the correct explanation for Statement I.
(b) Both Statement I and Statement II are correct and Statement II is not the correct explanation for Statement I.
(c) Statement I is correct, but Statement II is incorrect.
(d) Statement I is incorrect, but Statement II is correct.

**31.** Identify the initiative launched at UNFCCC COP27 based on the following statements:

1. It was launched by the United Nations High-Level Climate Champions and the Global Mangrove Alliance.
2. The initiative aims to secure the future of over 15 million hectares of mangroves globally by 2030, supported by $4 billion of sustainable finance.
3. Its key actions include halting mangrove loss, restoring half of recent losses and doubling the protection of mangroves globally.

Choose the correct answer from the options given below:

(a) Mangrove for the Future Initiative
(b) Global Mangrove Conservation Framework
(c) Mangrove Breakthrough Initiative
(d) Blue Carbon Initiative

**32.** Consider the following pairs related to global initiatives on e-waste management:

| List I (Initiative) | | List II (Description) |
|---|---|---|
| 1. Basel Convention | A. | Reduces the movement of hazardous waste, including e-waste, between countries |
| 2. Global E-waste Statistics Partnership (GESP) | B. | A collaboration to monitor and report e-waste data globally |
| 3. E-waste Challenge | C. | A UN-backed initiative to address the global e-waste problem |
| 4. E-waste Coalition 2018 | D. | A non-binding Letter of Intent signed by seven UNorganisations addressing e-waste |

Which of the pairs given above are correctly matched?

(a) 1 and 2 only (b) 1, 2 and 3 only
(c) 1, 2 and 4 only (d) 1, 2, 3 and 4

**33.** With reference to the Paris Agreement reached at the UNFCCC Meeting in 2015, which of the following statements is/are correct?

1. The Agreement was signed by all the member countries of the UN and it was set to go into effect in 2017.
2. The Agreement aims to limit greenhouse gas emissions to ensure the rise in average global temperature by the end of this century does not exceed 2°C or ideally 1.5°C above pre-industrial levels.
3. Developed countries acknowledged their historical responsibility for global warming and committed to donating $1000 billion annually from 2020 to help developing countries cope with climate change.

Select the correct answer using the codes given below:

(a) 1 and 3 only (b) 2 only
(c) 2 and 3 only (d) 1, 2 and 3

**34.** What is/are the importance(s) of the United Nations Convention to Combat Desertification (UNCCD)?

1. It aims to promote effective action through innovative national programs and supportive international partnerships.
2. It has a particular focus on South Asia and North Africa and its Secretariat facilitates the allocation of a major portion of financial resources to these regions.
3. It is committed to a bottom-up approach, encouraging the participation of local people in combating desertification.

Select the correct answer using the codes given below:

(a) 1 only (b) 2 and 3 only
(c) 1 and 3 only (d) 1, 2 and 3

**35.** Arrange the following environmental treaties in chronological order of their occurrence:

1. Montreal Protocol
2. Vienna Convention
3. Kigali Agreement

Choose the correct sequence from the codes given below:

(a) 2-1-3
(b) 1-2-3
(c) 3-1-2
(d) 2-3-1

**36.** Consider the following pairs regarding key environmental treaties:

| | Treaty | Focus Area |
|---|---|---|
| 1. | Vienna Convention | Ozone Layer Protection |
| 2. | Montreal Protocol | Global Warming Mitigation |
| 3. | Kigali Agreement | Phasing Out HFCs |

Which of the pairs given above is/are correctly matched?

(a) 1 only (b) 1 and 3 only
(c) 2 and 3 only (d) 1, 2 and 3

**37.** With reference to the REDD+ mechanism under the UNFCCC, consider the following statements:

1. REDD+ provides results-based payments for emission reductions achieved in the forestry sector.
2. The REDD+ mechanism includes actions like deforestation, reforestation and forest degradation.
3. The Lima REDD+ Information Hub aims to increase the transparency of information on REDD+ results-based actions.

How many of the statements given above is/are correct?

(a) Only one (b) Only two
(c) All three (d) None

**38.** Consider the following statements with reference to the Brundtland Commission Report, 'Our Common Future':

1. The Brundtland Report defined sustainable development as development that meets present needs without compromising future generations' ability to meet their needs.
2. It played a pivotal role in introducing the term 'sustainable development' to international discussions.
3. It shifted focus to environmental strategies only, without consideration of economic and social development.

Which of the above statements is/are correct?

(a) 1 and 2 only (b) 2 and 3 only
(c) 1 and 3 only (d) None

**39.** With reference to the 1992 United Nations Conference on Environment and Development (UNCED), consider the following:

1. It was held in Rio de Janeiro, Brazil and focused on sustainable development.
2. Agenda 21 was one of the key outcomes of the conference, providing a comprehensive plan of action for achieving sustainable development.
3. The conference led to the establishment of the Green Climate Fund to support climate change mitigation in developing countries.

Which of the above statements are correct?

(a) 1 and 2 only
(b) 2 and 3 only
(c) 1 and 3 only
(d) 1, 2 and 3

**40.** Consider the following statements with reference to the Rio Declaration on Environment and Development:

1. It consists of 27 principles that serve as a roadmap for sustainable development.
2. The declaration states that countries can exploit their natural resources as long as it does not harm other countries' environments.
3. The declaration links long-term economic growth exclusively to industrial development.

Which of the above statements are correct?

(a) 1 and 2 only
(b) 2 and 3 only
(c) 1 and 3 only
(d) 1, 2 and 3

**41.** Arrange the following major events on climate change in the correct chronological order:

1. Establishment of the Kyoto Protocol
2. Adoption of the Paris Agreement
3. The Marrakesh Accords
4. COP21

Select the correct sequence from the codes given below:

(a) 4 - 3 - 1 - 2 (b) 1 - 2 - 3 - 4
(c) 3 - 1 - 4 - 2 (d) 1 - 3 - 4 - 2

# OMR SHEET

**Assessment Round**

| | | | | | | | | | | | | | | | | | | | |
|---|---|---|---|---|---|---|---|---|---|---|---|---|---|---|---|---|---|---|---|
| 1 | a | b | c | d | 31 | a | b | c | d | 61 | a | b | c | d | 91 | a | b | c | d |
| 2 | a | b | c | d | 32 | a | b | c | d | 62 | a | b | c | d | 92 | a | b | c | d |
| 3 | a | b | c | d | 33 | a | b | c | d | 63 | a | b | c | d | 93 | a | b | c | d |
| 4 | a | b | c | d | 34 | a | b | c | d | 64 | a | b | c | d | 94 | a | b | c | d |
| 5 | a | b | c | d | 35 | a | b | c | d | 65 | a | b | c | d | 95 | a | b | c | d |
| 6 | a | b | c | d | 36 | a | b | c | d | 66 | a | b | c | d | 96 | a | b | c | d |
| 7 | a | b | c | d | 37 | a | b | c | d | 67 | a | b | c | d | 97 | a | b | c | d |
| 8 | a | b | c | d | 38 | a | b | c | d | 68 | a | b | c | d | 98 | a | b | c | d |
| 9 | a | b | c | d | 39 | a | b | c | d | 69 | a | b | c | d | 99 | a | b | c | d |
| 10 | a | b | c | d | 40 | a | b | c | d | 70 | a | b | c | d | 100 | a | b | c | d |
| 11 | a | b | c | d | 41 | a | b | c | d | 71 | a | b | c | d | 101 | a | b | c | d |
| 12 | a | b | c | d | 42 | a | b | c | d | 72 | a | b | c | d | 102 | a | b | c | d |
| 13 | a | b | c | d | 43 | a | b | c | d | 73 | a | b | c | d | 103 | a | b | c | d |
| 14 | a | b | c | d | 44 | a | b | c | d | 74 | a | b | c | d | 104 | a | b | c | d |
| 15 | a | b | c | d | 45 | a | b | c | d | 75 | a | b | c | d | 105 | a | b | c | d |
| 16 | a | b | c | d | 46 | a | b | c | d | 76 | a | b | c | d | 106 | a | b | c | d |
| 17 | a | b | c | d | 47 | a | b | c | d | 77 | a | b | c | d | 107 | a | b | c | d |
| 18 | a | b | c | d | 48 | a | b | c | d | 78 | a | b | c | d | 108 | a | b | c | d |
| 19 | a | b | c | d | 49 | a | b | c | d | 79 | a | b | c | d | 109 | a | b | c | d |
| 20 | a | b | c | d | 50 | a | b | c | d | 80 | a | b | c | d | 110 | a | b | c | d |
| 21 | a | b | c | d | 51 | a | b | c | d | 81 | a | b | c | d | 111 | a | b | c | d |
| 22 | a | b | c | d | 52 | a | b | c | d | 82 | a | b | c | d | 112 | a | b | c | d |
| 23 | a | b | c | d | 53 | a | b | c | d | 83 | a | b | c | d | 113 | a | b | c | d |
| 24 | a | b | c | d | 54 | a | b | c | d | 84 | a | b | c | d | 114 | a | b | c | d |
| 25 | a | b | c | d | 55 | a | b | c | d | 85 | a | b | c | d | 115 | a | b | c | d |
| 26 | a | b | c | d | 56 | a | b | c | d | 86 | a | b | c | d | 116 | a | b | c | d |
| 27 | a | b | c | d | 57 | a | b | c | d | 87 | a | b | c | d | 117 | a | b | c | d |
| 28 | a | b | c | d | 58 | a | b | c | d | 88 | a | b | c | d | 118 | a | b | c | d |
| 29 | a | b | c | d | 59 | a | b | c | d | 89 | a | b | c | d | 119 | a | b | c | d |
| 30 | a | b | c | d | 60 | a | b | c | d | 90 | a | b | c | d | 120 | a | b | c | d |

## Calculate Your Score

| | |
|---|---|
| **Correct (✓)** | |
| **Incorrect (✓)** | |
| **Unattempted** | |
| **Total Score** | |
| **Accuracy (%)** | |

## Reasons for Incorrect Answers?

1. Lack of Knowledge/Existing Source Insufficient
2. Lack of Multiple Revision
3. Common Sense Mistakes

**Note :**

1. Calculate total score as correct answers carry 2 marks each 1/3rd marks will deducted for **Incorrect** Answers.
2. Calculate Accuracy (%) by dividing the number of correct answers to the total number of attempted questions.

## Past Learning

**1.** Consider the following statements: **(2023)**

1. In India, the Biodiversity Management Committees are key to the realisation of the objectives of the Nagoya Protocol.
2. The Biodiversity Management Committees have important functions in determining access and benefit sharing, including the power to levy collection fees on the access of biological resources within its jurisdiction.

Which of the statements given above is/are correct?

(a) 1 only
(b) 2 only
(c) Both 1 and 2
(d) Neither 1 nor 2

**2.** Consider the following statements: **(2023)**

**Statement 1:** The United Nations Capital Development Fund (UNCDF) and the Arbor Day Foundation have recently recognised Hyderabad as 2020 Tree City of the World.

**Statement 2:** Hyderabad was selected for the recognition for a year following its commitment to grow and maintain the urban forests.

Which one of the following is correct in respect of the above statements?

(a) Both Statement 1 and Statement 2 are correct, and Statement 2 is the correct explanation for Statement 1.
(b) Both Statement 1 and Statement 2 are correct, but Statement 2 is not the correct explanation for Statement 1.
(c) Statement 1 is correct, but Statement 2 is not correct.
(d) Statement 1 is not correct, but Statement 2 is correct.

**3.** 'Climate Action Tracker' which monitors the emission reduction pledges of different countries is a : **(2022)**

(a) Database created by a coalition of research organisations
(b) Wing of 'International Panel of Climate Change'
(c) Committee under 'United Nations Framework Convention on Climate Change'
(d) Agency promoted and financed by United Nations Environment Programme and World Bank

**4.** With reference to the 'New York, Declaration on Forests', which of the following statements are correct? **(2021)**

1. It was first endorsed at the United Nations Climate Summit in 2014.
2. It endorses a global timeline to end the loss of forests.
3. It is a legally binding international declaration.
4. It is endorsed by governments, big companies and indigenous communities.
5. India was one of the signatories at its inception.

Select the correct answer using the codes given below.

(a) 1, 2 and 4 only
(b) 1, 3 and 5 only
(c) 3 and 4 only
(d) 2 and 5 only

**5.** The 'Common Carbon Metric', supported by UNEP, had been developed for **(2021)**

(a) Assessing the carbon footprint of building operations around the world
(b) Enabling commercial farming entities around the world to enter carbon emission trading
(c) Enabling governments to assess the overall carbon footprint caused by their countries
(d) Assessing the overall carbon footprint caused by the use of fossil fuels by the world in a unit time

**6.** Consider the following statements : **(2019)**

1. Under Ramsar Convention, it is mandatory on the part of the Government of India to protect and conserve all the wetlands in the territory of India.
2. The Wetlands (Conservation and Management) Rules, 2010 were framed by the Government of India based on the recommendations of Ramsar Convention.
3. The Wetlands (Conservation and Management) Rules, 2010 also encompass the drainage area or catchment regions of the wetlands as determined by the authority.

Which of the statements given above is/are correct?

(a) 1 and 2 only
(b) 2 and 3 only
(c) 3 only
(d) 1, 2 and 3

**7.** The Partnership for Action on Green Economy (PAGE), a UN mechanism to assist countries transition towards greener and more inclusive economies, emerged in **(2018)**

(a) The Earth Summit on Sustainable Development 2002, Johannesburg
(b) The United Nations Conference on Sustainable Development 2012, Rio de Janeiro
(c) The United Nations Framework Convention on Climate Change 2015, Paris
(d) The World Sustainable Development Summit 2016, New Delhi

**8.** 'Momentum for Change: Climate Neutral Now' is an initiative launched by **(2018)**

(a) The Intergovernmental Panel on Climate Change
(b) The UNEP Secretariat
(c) The UNFCCC Secretariat
(d) The World Meteorological Organisation

**9.** Consider the following statements in respect of Trade Related Analysis of Fauna and Flora in Commerce (TRAFFIC): **(2017)**

1. TRAFFIC is a bureau under the United Nations Environment Programme (UNEP).
2. The mission of TRAFFIC is to ensure that trade in wild plants and animals is not a threat to the conservation of nature.

Which of the above statements is/are correct?

(a) 1 only
(b) 2 only
(c) Both 1 and 2
(d) Neither 1 nor 2

**10.** With reference to the 'Global Climate Change Alliance', which of the following statements is/are correct? **(2017)**

1. It is an initiative of the European Union.
2. It provides technical and financial support to targeted developing countries to integrate climate change into their development policies and budgets.
3. It is coordinated by World Resources Institute (WRI) and World Business Council for Sustainable Development (WBCSD).

Select the correct answer using the codes given below:

(a) 1 and 2 only
(b) 3 only
(c) 2 and 3 only
(d) 1, 2 and 3

**11.** With reference to an initiative called 'The Economics of Ecosystems and Biodiversity (TEEB)', which of the following statements is/are correct? **(2016)**

1. It is an initiative hosted by UNEP, IMF and World Economic Forum.
2. It is a global initiative that focuses on drawing attention to the economic benefits of biodiversity.
3. It presents an approach that can help decision-makers recognise, demonstrate and capture the value of ecosystems, and biodiversity.

Select the correct answer using the codes given below.

(a) 1 and 2 only
(b) 3 only
(c) 2 and 3 only
(d) 1, 2 and 3

**12.** What is/are the importance/importances of the 'United Nations Convention to Combat Desertification'? **(2016)**

1. It aims to promote effective action through innovative national programs and supportive inter-national partnerships.
2. It has a special/particular focus on South Asia and North Africa regions and its Secretariat facilitates the allocation of major portion of financial resources to these regions.
3. It is committed to bottom-up approach, encouraging the participation of local people in combating the desertification.

Select the correct answer using the codes given below.

(a) 1 only (b) 2 and 3 only
(c) 1 and 3 only (d) 1, 2 and 3

**13.** The term 'Intended Nationally Determined Contributions' is sometimes seen in the news in the context of **(2016)**

(a) Pledges made by the European countries to rehabilitate refugees from the war-affected Middle East.
(b) Plan of action outlined by the countries of the world to combat climate change.
(c) Capital contributed by the member countries in the establishment of Asian Infrastructure Investment Bank.
(d) Plan of action outlined by the countries of the world regarding Sustainable Development Goals.

**14.** With reference to the Agreement at the UNFCCC Meeting In Paris in 2015, which of the following statements is/are correct? **(2016)**

1. The Agreement was signed by all the member countries of the UN and it will go into effect in 2017.
2. The Agreement aims to limit the greenhouse gas emissions so that the rise in average global temperature by the end of this century does not exceed 2 °C or even 1.5 °C above pre-industrial levels.
3. Developed countries acknowledged their historical responsibility in global warming and committed to donate $ 1000 billion a year from 2020 to help developing countries to cope with climate change.

Select the correct answer using the code given below.

(a) 1 and 3 only (b) 2 only
(c) 2 and 3 only (d) 1, 2 and 3

**15.** Consider the following pairs : **(2016)**

Terms sometimes seen in the news Their origin

1. Annex-I Countries: Cartagena Protocol
2. Certified Emissions Reductions: Nagoya Protocol
3. Clean Development Mechanism: Kyoto Protocol

Which of the pairs given above is/are correctly matched?

(a) 1 and 2 only (b) 2 and 3 only
(c) 3 only (d) 1, 2 and 3

**16.** Which of the following statements is/are correct? **(2016)**

Proper design and effective implementation of UN-REDD+ Programme can significantly contribute to

1. Protection of biodiversity
2. Resilience of forest ecosystems
3. Poverty reduction

Select the correct answer using the codes given below.

(a) 1 and 2 only (b) 3 only
(c) 2 and 3 only (d) 1, 2 and 3

**17.** What is 'Greenhouse Gas Protocol'? **(2016)**

(a) It is an international accounting tool for government and business leaders to understand, quantify and manage greenhouse gas emissions.
(b) It is an initiative of the United Nations to offer financial incentives to developing countries to reduce greenhouse gas emissions and to adopt eco-friendly technologies.
(c) It is an inter-governmental agreement ratified by all the member countries of the United Nations to reduce greenhouse gas emissions to specified levels by the year 2022.
(d) It is one of the multilateral REDD+ initiatives hosted by the World Bank.

**18.** With reference to 'Agenda 21', sometimes seen in the news, consider the following statements : **(2016)**

1. It is a global action plan for sustainable development
2. It originated in the World Summit on Sustainable Development held in Johannesburg in 2002.

Which of the statements given above is/are correct?

(a) 1 only
(b) 2 only
(c) Both 1 and 2
(d) Neither 1 nor 2

**19.** With reference to the International Union for Conservation of Nature and Natural Resources (IUCN), and the Convention on International Trade in Endangered Species of Wild Fauna and Flora (CITES), which of the following statements is/are correct? **(2015)**

1. IUCN is an organ of the United Nations and CITES is an international agreement between governments.
2. IUCN runs thousands of field projects around the world to better manage natural environments.
3. CITES is legally binding on the States that have joined it, but this Convention does not take the place of national laws.

Select the correct answer using the codes given below :

(a) 1 only
(b) 2 and 3 only
(c) 1 and 3 only
(d) 1, 2 and 3

**20.** Which one of the following is associated with the issue of control and phasing out of the use of ozone-depleting substances? **(2015)**

(a) Bretton Woods Conference
(b) Montreal Protocol
(c) Kyoto Protocol
(d) Nagoya Protocol

**21.** What is Rio+20 Conference, often mentioned in the news? **(2015)**

(a) It is the United Nations Conference on Sustainable Development
(b) It is a Ministerial Meeting of the World Trade Organisation
(c) It is a Conference of the Inter-governmental Panel on Climate Change
(d) It is a Conference of the Member Countries of the Convention on Biological Diversity

**22.** With reference to 'Forest Carbon Partnership Facility', which of the following statements is/ are correct? **(2015)**

1. It is a global partnership of governments, businesses, civil society, and indigenous peoples.
2. It provides financial aid to universities, individual scientists, and institutions involved in scientific forestry research to develop eco-friendly, and climate adaptation technologies for sustainable forest management.
3. It assists the countries in their 'REDD+ (Reducing Emissions from Deforestation and Forest Degradation+)' efforts by providing them with financial and technical assistance.

Select the correct answer using the codes given below :

(a) 1 only (b) 2 and 3 only
(c) 1 and 3 only (d) 1, 2 and 3

**23.** Which of the following statements regarding 'Green Climate Fund' is/are correct? **(2015)**

1. It is intended to assist the developing countries in adaptation and mitigation practices to counter climate change.
2. It is founded under the aegis of UNEP, OECD, Asian Development Bank and World Bank.

Select the correct answer using the codes given below:

(a) 1 only (b) 2 only
(c) Both 1 and 2 (d) Neither 1 nor 2

**24.** With reference to an organisation known as 'Birdlife International', which of the following statements is/are correct? **(2015)**

1. It is a Global Partnership of Conservation organisations.
2. The concept of 'biodiversity hotspots' originated from this organisation.
3. It identifies the sites known/referred to as 'Important Bird and Biodiversity Areas'.

Select the correct answer using the codes given below:

(a) 1 only (b) 2 and 3 only
(c) 1 and 3 only (d) 1, 2 and 3

**25.** Consider the following international agreements : **(2014)**

1. The International Treaty on Plant Genetic Resources for Food and Agriculture
2. The United Nations Convention to Combat Desertification
3. The World Heritage Convention

Which of the above has/have a bearing on biodiversity?

(a) 1 and 2 only
(b) 3 only
(c) 1 and 3 only
(d) 1, 2 and 3

**26.** If a wetland of international importance is brought under the 'Montreux Record', what does it imply? **(2014)**

(a) Changes in ecological character have occurred, are occurring, or are likely to occur in the wetland as a result of human interference.
(b) The country in which the wetland is located should enact a law to prohibit any human activity within five kilometres from the edge of the wetland.
(c) The survival of the wetland depends on the cultural practices and traditions of certain communities living in its vicinity, and therefore the cultural diversity therein should not be destroyed.
(d) It is given the status of 'World Heritage Site'.

**27.** With reference to a conservation organisation called 'Wetlands International', which of the following statements is/ are correct? **(2014)**

1. It is an intergovernmental organisation formed by the countries which are signatories to Ramsar Convention.
2. It works at the field level to develop and mobilise knowledge, and use the practical experience to advocate for better policies.

Select the correct answer using the codes given below.

(a) 1 only
(b) 2 only
(c) Both 1 and 2
(d) Neither 1 nor 2

**28.** The 'Red Data Books' published by the International Union for Conservation of Nature and Natural resources (IUCN) contain lists of? **(2011)**

1. Endemic plant and animal species present in the biodiversity hotspots.
2. Threatened plant and animal species.
3. Protected sites for conservation of nature and natural resources in various countries.

Select the correct answer using the codes given below:

(a) 1 and 3
(b) 2 only
(c) 2 and 3
(d) 3 only

**29.** Regarding 'carbon credits', which one of the following statements is not correct? **(2011)**

(a) The carbon credit system was ratified in conjunction with the Kyoto Protocol.
(b) Carbon credits are awarded to countries or groups that have reduced greenhouse gases below their emission quota.
(c) The goal of the carbon credit system is to limit the increase of carbon dioxide emission.
(d) Carbon credits are traded at a price fixed from time to time by the United Nations Environment Programme.

# Detailed Solutions

## Assessment Round

1. *(d)* None of the above
   - **Statement 1 is incorrect: Conventions** do not typically establish detailed obligations. Instead, they set broad principles and frameworks for further detailed action. They provide general guidelines for addressing issues like climate change but leave specific measures to be decided in later agreements or protocols.
   - **Statement 2 is incorrect: Protocols** are usually **legally binding** and outline detailed and specific obligations, targets, or actions required of the parties. They supplement conventions with more concrete commitments. An example is the **Kyoto Protocol.**
   - **Statement 3 is incorrect.** Depending on their nature, **Agreements** can be **legally binding** or **non-binding.** They can range from formal treaties to informal accords. Not all agreements have the force of law.

   **Thus, option (d) is the correct answer.**

2. *(b)* Only 3
   - **Statement 1 is incorrect:** The **Montreux Record** does not include wetlands that have fully restored their ecological character. Instead, it lists wetlands facing or at risk of significant ecological changes due to human activity or other factors. The record helps prioritise such sites for conservation measures.
   - **Statement 2 is incorrect:** While many **Ramsar sites** are designated because they are important for migratory birds, they are not limited to such areas. Ramsar sites can include any wetlands that are important for biodiversity, water filtration, flood control, or other ecological functions. Wetlands of national or international significance may also be included for their broader ecological roles.
   - **Statement 3 is correct: India** has two Ramsar sites listed in the Montreux Record: **Keoladeo National Park** and **Loktak Lake.** Both wetlands are facing ecological challenges and are prioritized for restoration efforts.

   **Thus, option (b) is the correct answer.**

3. *(a)* 1, 2 and 4 only
   - **Statement 1 is correct:** The Basel Convention covers hazardous wastes exhibiting characteristics such as being explosive, flammable, poisonous, infectious, corrosive, toxic, or eco-toxic.
   - **Statement 2 is correct:** The Convention extends its scope to include two types of 'other wastes'—household waste and incinerator ash.
   - **Statement 3 is incorrect:** The Convention restricts transboundary movements of hazardous wastes but does not strictly prohibit them in all cases. Movements are allowed under the principle of environmentally sound management (ESM) when certain conditions are met.
   - **Statement 4 is correct:** India, after ratifying the Basel Convention in 1992, notified the Hazardous and Other Wastes (Management & Transboundary Movement) Rules in 2016 to manage hazardous wastes effectively and comply with its obligations under the Convention.

   **Thus, option (a) is the correct answer.**

4. *(c)* The Basel Convention focuses on the transboundary movement and disposal of hazardous wastes, while the Rotterdam Convention deals with the prior informed consent procedure for the international trade of certain hazardous chemicals and pesticides.

   The **Basel Convention** is concerned with **controlling and reducing the transboundary movement of hazardous wastes** to protect human health and the environment from their adverse effects. It emphasises the environmentally sound management of hazardous wastes and allows movement under specific conditions. On the other hand, the **Rotterdam Convention** introduces the **Prior**

Informed Consent (PIC) procedure, which requires exporting countries to obtain consent from importing countries before proceeding with the trade of certain hazardous chemicals and pesticides listed in Annex III of the Convention.

**Thus, option (c) is the correct answer.**

**5.** *(b)* It is a mechanism for formally obtaining and disseminating decisions of importing countries on whether they wish to receive future shipments of certain hazardous chemicals listed in Annex III of the Convention, ensuring compliance by exporting countries.

**Prior Informed Consent (PIC)** is a key provision of the **Rotterdam Convention**. It serves as a mechanism to: **Formally obtain and disseminate the decisions of importing countries (Parties)** regarding their willingness to receive future shipments of certain hazardous chemicals that are listed in **Annex III** of the Convention, and it **ensures compliance** with these decisions by exporting countries (Parties).

**Thus, option (b) is the correct answer.**

**6.** *(c)* 3 only

- **Statement 1 is incorrect: CITES** is a **legally binding** international agreement, meaning that the parties that sign and ratify it are obligated to enforce its provisions through national legislation. The convention helps ensure that international trade does not threaten the survival of wild animals and plants.
- **Statement 2 is incorrect: Appendix I** of CITES lists species that are most endangered and threatened by international trade. Trade in these species is only allowed under exceptional circumstances, and such species require the highest level of protection. **Appendix II** includes species that are not necessarily threatened but may become so unless trade is closely controlled.
- **Statement 3 is correct: CITES** classifies species into **three appendices**: Appendix I (highest level of protection), Appendix II (controlled trade), and Appendix III (species protected in at least one country). These appendices determine the degree of control required over trade to ensure species survival.

**Thus, option (c) is the correct answer.**

**7.** *(a)* 1, 3 and 4 only

- The **Stockholm Convention on Persistent Organic Pollutants (POPs)** is a global treaty aimed at protecting human health and the environment from chemicals that remain intact in the environment for long periods, become widely distributed, accumulate in the fatty tissue of humans and wildlife, and have harmful impacts.
- The 12 POPs, sometimes called the 'dirty dozen,' include pesticides: aldrin, chlordane, DDT, dieldrin, endrin, heptachlor, mirex, and toxaphene; industrial chemicals: hexachlorobenzene and PCBs; and. unintentionally produced POPs: dioxins and furans.

**Thus, option (a) is the correct answer.**

**8.** *(c)* Stockholm Convention

The **Stockholm Convention on Persistent Organic Pollutants (POPs)** is a global treaty aimed at eliminating or reducing the production and environmental release of **POPs**, which are chemicals that persist in the environment, bioaccumulate in humans and wildlife, and pose risks to health and ecosystems. The convention categorizes chemicals for **elimination**, **restriction**, or **unintentional production**, targeting substances such as DDT, PCBs, and dioxins.

**Thus, option (c) is the correct answer.**

**9.** *(b)* The way genetic resources are accessed and how the benefits from their use are shared between users and providers.

**Access and Benefit-Sharing (ABS)** under the **CBD** refers to the system governing how genetic resources are accessed and how the benefits arising from their use are shared fairly and equitably between the users (those who utilise the resources) and the providers (those who supply the resources). This mechanism ensures that providers, including indigenous and local communities, receive a fair share of the benefits, which can be monetary or non-monetary, thus promoting conservation and sustainable use of biodiversity.

**Thus, option (b) is the correct answer.**

**10.** *(b)* Both Statement I and Statement II are correct, but Statement II is not the correct explanation for Statement I.

- **Statement I is correct.** Prior Informed Consent (PIC) is a core component of the **Nagoya Protocol** under the **Convention on Biological Diversity (CBD)**. It ensures that a provider country's national authority grants permission before users access genetic resources. This is part of the global framework to ensure that the use of these resources is legal and ethical, with permission granted before access takes place.
- **Statement II is also correct.** Mutually Agreed Terms (MAT) are indeed negotiated agreements between users and providers of genetic resources, outlining the conditions for their use and how benefits (monetary or non-monetary) will be shared. However, **MAT is a separate concept from PIC**, and while both are related to access and benefit-sharing, MAT is not an explanation for PIC. Instead, MAT deals with the conditions of use **after** access is granted.

**Thus, option (b) is the correct answer.**

**11.** *(c)* Only three

- **Statement 1 is correct:** The **Kunming Declaration**, adopted during the UN Biodiversity Conference (COP15), indeed calls for urgent and comprehensive action across various sectors of the global economy to integrate biodiversity concerns into all areas of decision-making and development.
- **Statement 2 is correct:** China has committed to establishing the Kunming Biodiversity Fund, with an initial pledge of USD 230 million, to support biodiversity conservation in developing countries.
- **Statement 3 is incorrect:** The '30 by 30' target is a significant goal discussed under the **Global Biodiversity Framework**, but it is **not explicitly part of the Kunming Declaration** itself. This commitment is a key element under ongoing negotiations for the post-2020 framework, but it was not formalised in the Kunming Declaration.
- **Statement 4 is correct:** The **Global Environment Facility** (GEF), along with UNDP and UNEP, has committed to fast-tracking financial, and technical support to developing countries to help them implement the goals of the **Global Biodiversity Framework**, which is critical for safeguarding global biodiversity.

**Thus, option (c) is the correct answer.**

**12.** *(b)* A requirement for exporting countries to obtain consent from importing countries before the first intentional transboundary movement of LMOs intended for environmental release.

- The **Advance Informed Agreement (AIA)** procedure under the Cartagena Protocol on Biosafety is a fundamental mechanism that ensures countries are informed about and consent to the import of LMOs intended for intentional introduction into their environment. **Exporting countries** must obtain **prior consent from importing countries** before conducting the first intentional transboundary movement of LMOs for environmental release.
- **Purpose of AIA:** To provide importing countries with the necessary information to make informed decisions about the import of LMOs and to ensure that LMOs are only introduced into the environment after careful consideration of potential risks to biological diversity and human health.
- **Living Modified Organisms (LMOs)** are organisms whose genetic material has been altered through modern biotechnology, such as genetic engineering, to introduce traits like pest resistance or improved yield. LMOs are widely used in agriculture, research, medicine and industry. Unlike naturally occurring organisms, their genetic changes are scientifically engineered. The **Cartagena Protocol on Biosafety** regulates the safe handling, transport and use of LMOs, focusing on minimising risks to biodiversity and human health.

**Thus, option (b) is the correct answer.**

**13.** *(b)* Cartagena Protocol on Biosafety

- The **Cartagena Protocol on Biosafety** is an international treaty that serves as a **supplementary agreement** to the **Convention on Biological Diversity (CBD)**.

It aims to protect biological diversity from the potential risks posed by **living modified organisms (LMOs)**, resulting from modern biotechnology.

- The Cartagena Protocol establishes the **Advance Informed Agreement (AIA)** procedure, which is a key mechanism under the treaty. This procedure requires exporting countries to provide detailed information to importing countries before the first intentional transboundary movement of LMOs. The importing country must consent to the import based on a risk assessment, ensuring that the LMOs do not negatively impact biodiversity or human health. The Cartagena Protocol includes provisions for **liability and redress** in the event of damage caused by LMOs to biodiversity or human health.

**Thus, option (b) is the correct answer.**

**14.** *(b)* It emphasises taking preventive action in the face of scientific uncertainty to avoid potential environmental harm.

The **Precautionary Principle**, as referenced in the **Cartagena Protocol on Biosafety**, underscores the need to take preventive action when there is **scientific uncertainty** about the potential risks that **living modified organisms (LMOs)** may pose to biodiversity and human health. This principle allows countries to **restrict or prohibit the import** of LMOs if there is insufficient scientific evidence to prove their safety.

**Thus, option (b) is the correct answer.**

**15.** *(b)* 1-D, 2-B, 3-C, 4-A

- **Cartagena Protocol (1-A):** It is a supplementary agreement to the Convention on Biological Diversity (CBD) that focuses on the **safe handling and transboundary movement of living-modified organisms (LMOs)**, particularly to prevent risks to biodiversity, and human health.
- **Stockholm Convention (2-B):** It addresses **Persistent Organic Pollutants (POPs)**, which are persistent hazardous chemicals, bioaccumulated in organisms, and pose serious health and environmental risks.
- **Rotterdam Convention (3-C):** It promotes **Prior Informed Consent (PIC)** procedures, requiring that countries exporting hazardous chemicals or pesticides inform and obtain consent from the importing country.
- **Basel Convention (4-A):** It regulates the **transboundary movement of hazardous wastes** and promotes environmentally sound waste management practices, aiming to prevent the illegal dumping of hazardous waste, especially in developing countries.

**Thus, option (b) is the correct answer.**

**16.** *(c)* Only three

- **Statement 1 is correct: Agenda 21** was produced at the **Earth Summit** in **1992** in Rio de Janeiro as a **non-binding action plan** to promote sustainable development across the globe.
- **Statement 2 is correct: Agenda** 21 involves a wide array of **stakeholders**, including **local and national governments, businesses, international organisations, citizen groups, and Non-Governmental Organisations** (NGOs).
- **Statement 3 is incorrect: India** is a signatory to **Agenda 21** and has aligned various parts of its development infrastructure, such as **energy, transport, climate change policy, forests, biodiversity, ecosystems, and urban governance**, to the goals of Agenda 21.
- **Statement 4 is correct:** The **World Summit on Sustainable Development** in **2002** (held in Johannesburg) reviewed progress and forged global partnerships to promote the continued implementation of Agenda 21.

**Thus, option (c) is the correct answer.**

**17.** *(b)* It is a formula that advises governments to spend 66% of their wildfire-related budget on planning, prevention, preparedness and recovery, and 34% on response efforts.

The **Fire Ready Formula**, proposed by **UNEP**, is designed to address the growing threat of **wildfires**. The formula recommends that **66%** of government spending should be allocated towards **planning, prevention, preparedness and recovery**, while the remaining **34%** should be focused on **response efforts**. This approach emphasises proactive measures to reduce the occurrence and impact of wildfires, rather than relying solely on reactive firefighting measures.

**Thus, option (b) is the correct answer.**

**18.** *(d)* Kyoto Protocol, 1997

Carbon trading was **introduced under the Kyoto Protocol of 1997 (which came into force in 2005)**. Under this framework, **Certified Emission Reductions (CERs) were issued** to entities that implemented projects reducing emissions, such as wind, solar, or energy efficiency initiatives. **Countries unable to meet their emissions reduction targets could purchase carbon credits** to comply. The Paris Agreement also facilitates voluntary trading between nations to achieve their Nationally Determined Contributions (NDCs). If a country reduces more greenhouse gas (GHG) emissions than required, it can sell the surplus as an 'internationally traded mitigation outcome' to another country.

**Thus, option (d) is the correct answer.**

**19.** *(b)* Only two

- **Statement 1 is correct.** The **Nagoya Protocol**, adopted under the Convention on Biological Diversity (CBD), emphasises the fair and equitable sharing of benefits arising from the utilisation of genetic resources. It promotes access to genetic resources while ensuring that benefits (e.g., knowledge, profits) are shared fairly between users and providers.
- **Statement 2 is correct.** The **Cartagena Protocol** is also a protocol under the CBD. It focuses on ensuring the safe handling, transport and use of **living-modified organisms** (LMOs) resulting from biotechnology that may negatively impact biodiversity, and human health.
- **Statement 3 is incorrect.** Both the **Nagoya Protocol** and the **Cartagena Protocol** are not independent agreements. They are associated directly with the **CBD** and aim to complement the overarching objectives of the Convention.

**Thus, option (b) is the correct answer.**

**20.** *(b)* A series of 20 targets adopted under the Convention on Biological Diversity (CBD) aimed at reducing biodiversity loss and promoting sustainable biodiversity management from 2011 to 2020.

- The **Aichi Biodiversity Targets** were adopted at the **10th COP of the Convention on Biological Diversity in Nagoya, Japan, in 2010.** Comprising **20 targets,** they aimed to guide global biodiversity conservation and sustainable use from **2011 to 2020.** This framework served as a global roadmap for biodiversity management, encouraging countries and organisations to take coordinated actions to reduce biodiversity loss and promote sustainable ecosystems across the United Nations and international platforms.

**Thus, option (b) is the correct answer.**

**21.** *(b)* It is a protocol that regulates the movement of living modified organisms (LMOs) across international borders, ensuring countries have the necessary information to make decisions about their import.

- **The Cartagena Protocol on Biosafety,** adopted **in 2000 under the Convention on Biological Diversity,** provides a framework for **regulating the international movement of living-modified organisms (LMOs).**
- It ensures that countries are given all the necessary information about LMOs through **an advance informed agreement (AIA) procedure,** enabling them to make informed decisions about their import. The protocol also established the Biosafety Clearing House to facilitate the exchange of information related to LMOs.

**Thus, option (b) is the correct answer.**

**22.** *(b)* To compensate countries impacted by climate change, particularly Least Developed Countries and Small Island Developing States.

The **Loss and Damage (L&D) Fund** was established at **COP28** to help countries, especially **Least Developed Countries** and **Small Island Developing States,** deal with the impacts of **climate change.** It aims to provide compensation for losses and damages due to climate-related disasters, with the **World Bank** serving as the interim host.

**Thus, option (b) is the correct answer.**

**23.** *(c)* Transitioning away from fossil fuels in energy systems globally.

- At **COP28** in Dubai, nearly 200 countries reached an unprecedented agreement to initiate a transition away from fossil fuels across global energy systems. This agreement calls for a 'just, orderly, and equitable' transition, emphasising a global shift to achieve **net-zero emissions by 2050**. It also includes commitments to triple renewable energy capacity by 2030, phase down coal usage, and significantly reduce non-$CO_2$ emissions like methane by 2030. This historic decision marks the first time that a COP agreement explicitly includes language regarding transitioning away from fossil fuels, responding to urgent climate goals and the Paris Agreement targets.
- At **COP28**, for the first time, almost **200 countries** agreed to **transition away from fossil fuels** in energy systems. This is a significant shift toward breaking away from fossil fuel dependence and moving towards cleaner energy sources.

**Thus, option (c) is the correct answer.**

**24.** *(d)* To ensure migratory species of wild animals and their habitats are conserved through global cooperation, and agreements.

The **Bonn Convention,** formally known as the **Convention on the Conservation of Migratory Species of Wild Animals** (CMS), is the only global treaty aimed explicitly at the conservation of **migratory species** and their habitats, working under the **United Nations Environment Programme.** It uses legally binding agreements and non-binding Memoranda of Understanding (MoUs) to cater to the conservation needs of these species. The **two appendixes** of the Convention categorise species requiring urgent conservation efforts and those benefiting from international cooperation.

**Thus, option (d) is the correct answer.**

**25.** *(a)* The Global Methane Pledge

**The Global Methane Pledge:** Launched at **COP26** by the US and the European Union, this pledge commits countries to reduce **methane emissions by 30% from 2020 levels by 2030**. Methane, a potent greenhouse gas, is targeted here to rapidly lower global warming potential. Over 100 countries have joined, focusing on major methane sources, including energy, agriculture and waste.

**Thus, option (a) is the correct answer.**

**26.** *(d)* By periodically reviewing progress towards limiting global temperature rise to 1.5 degrees Celsius and recommending strategies such as tripling renewable energy capacity, and phasing out coal.

- The 28th **United Nations Climate Change Conference (COP28)**, held in Dubai from 30th November to December 12th, 2023, focuses on limiting global temperature **rise to 1.5°C**, achieving net-zero emissions by 2050 and supporting climate-vulnerable communities. A key feature is the **Global Stocktake** (GST), a five-year review process under the Paris Agreement assessing progress toward climate goals.
- At COP28, recommendations include tripling renewable energy capacity and phasing out coal. A UN technical report from September 2023 notes some progress but highlights gaps, with the temperature **rise already at 1.2°C** since pre-industrial levels. The first stocktake, initiated at COP21, will conclude at COP28, emphasising the need for increased ambition in emissions reduction and adaptation efforts.

**Thus, option (d) is the correct answer.**

**27.** *(b)* Stockholm Convention

The **Stockholm Convention** is an international treaty that addresses the elimination or restriction of **persistent organic pollutants (POPs)**, which pose significant risks to human health and the environment. India ratified the Stockholm Convention in **2006**. Countries that ratify the convention can choose a default 'opt-out' status regarding amendments to the annexes, which list harmful chemicals. Amendments to the convention's annexes (which add new POPs) do not apply automatically to all parties. Countries must explicitly agree (by depositing an instrument) to the amendments for them to apply within their borders.

**Thus, option (b) is the correct answer.**

**28.** *(b)* Paris Climate Accord

The **Paris Climate Accord**, also known as the **Paris Agreement**, is a legally binding international treaty adopted at **COP 21** in Paris in **2015**. It aims to **limit global warming** to well below 2°C, preferably 1.5°C above pre-industrial levels, with India reaffirming its commitment by updating its **NDC** in **2022**.

**Thus, option (b) is the correct answer.**

**29.** *(b)* Minamata Convention

The **Minamata Convention on Mercury** is an international treaty adopted in **2013** to protect human health and the environment from **mercury emissions** and releases. Named after the Minamata tragedy in Japan, the convention addresses the life cycle of mercury, including its mining, trade and disposal, aiming to reduce, and eliminate the use of mercury in various industrial products and processes.

**Thus, option (b) is the correct answer.**

**30.** *(b)* Both Statement I and Statement II are correct, and Statement II is not the correct explanation for Statement I

- **Statement I is correct:** The Tiger Landscapes Investment Fund is an initiative presented by the United Nations Development Programme (UNDP). It is a **new blended financial mechanism** under development aimed at **catalysing nature-positive businesses** with positive impacts on tigers, biodiversity and people. The fund focuses on **businesses that adopt innovative strategies** to not only minimise environmental harm but also actively enhance ecosystems.
- **Statement II is correct:** The **Asian Development Bank (ADB)** intends to explore innovative financing instruments such as **Tiger Bonds.** These bonds are designed to engage private sector investors and promote nature-based solutions, channeling investments into projects that support biodiversity conservation, particularly in tiger habitats.
- **However, Statement II is not the explanation for Statement I:** Both statements refer to separate initiatives by different organisations (UNDP and ADB) aiming to promote conservation and sustainable development.

**Thus, option (b) is the correct answer.**

**31.** *(c)* Mangrove Breakthrough Initiative

The **Mangrove Breakthrough Initiative**, launched at **UNFCCC COP27** by the **United Nations High-Level Climate Champions** and the **Global Mangrove Alliance**, focuses on securing **15 million hectares of mangroves globally by 2030**, supported by **$4 billion** of sustainable finance. The initiative emphasises halting mangrove loss, restoring recent losses, and doubling mangrove protection globally.

**Thus, option (c) is the correct answer.**

**32.** *(c)* 1, 2 and 4 only

- **Pair 1 is correct:** The Basel Convention is a global treaty that aims to reduce the movement of hazardous waste, including e-waste, between countries to protect human health and the environment.
- **Pair 2 is correct:** The Global E-waste Statistics Partnership (GESP) is a collaboration between the United Nations University and the International Telecommunication Union to improve the monitoring, and reporting of e-waste data worldwide.
- **Pair 3 is incorrect:** The E-waste Challenge is not a UN-backed initiative but rather a World Economic Forum initiative aimed at creating a circular economy for electronics.
- **Pair 4 is correct:** The E-waste Coalition 2018 involved a non-binding Letter of Intent signed by seven UN organisations working to tackle the global e-waste challenge.

**Thus, option (c) is the correct answer.**

**33.** *(b)* 2 only

- **Statement 1 is incorrect.** While the **Paris Agreement** was widely adopted by many countries, it was **not signed by all UN member countries.** Additionally, it came into effect on **November 4, 2016,** after being ratified by enough countries to meet the required threshold, not in 2017.
- **Statement 2 is correct.** The key objective of the Paris Agreement is to **limit global warming to well below 2°C**, with efforts to

**limit it to 1.5°C** above pre-industrial levels, recognising that the latter goal would significantly reduce the risks and impacts of climate change.

- **Statement 3 is incorrect.** The Paris Agreement includes a commitment by developed countries to mobilise **$100 billion annually by 2020** to help developing countries with climate change adaptation and mitigation, not $1000 billion.

**Thus, option (b) is the correct answer.**

***34.*** *(c)* 1 and 3 only

- **Statement 1 is correct**: The **UNCCD** promotes action to combat desertification through **national action plans** supported by **international cooperation**. It encourages partnerships between governments, Non-Governmental Organisations and other stakeholders to address land degradation, and desertification.
- **Statement 2 is incorrect**: While **South Asia and North Africa** are regions affected by desertification, the UNCCD does not exclusively focus on these areas or allocate most of its financial resources to them. The convention is global in scope and addresses desertification issues in all affected regions.
- **Statement 3 is correct:** The UNCCD promotes a **bottom-up approach**, emphasising the participation of local communities and stakeholders in the decision-making process to ensure sustainable land management practices.

**Thus, option (c) is the correct answer.**

***35.*** *(a)* 2-1-3

- **Vienna Convention** (1985): It was the first global agreement to address the protection of the ozone layer. It created a framework for international efforts to protect the ozone but did not include legally binding targets to reduce ozone-depleting substances.
- **Montreal Protocol** (1987): It was established under the framework of the Vienna Convention. It is a legally binding international treaty aimed at phasing out the production and consumption of ozone-depleting substances (ODS).
- **Kigali Agreement** (2016): It was an amendment to the Montreal Protocol was agreed upon to phase down **hydrofluorocarbons** (HFCs), potent greenhouse gases that contribute to climate change. It builds on the Montreal Protocol but focuses specifically on addressing HFCs.

**Thus, option (a) is the correct answer.**

***36.*** *(b)* 1 and 3 only

- **Pair 1 is correct.** The **Vienna Convention (1985)** is an international treaty designed to protect the **ozone layer** by establishing frameworks for cooperation, research, and monitoring of ozone depletion.
- **Pair 2 is incorrect.** The **Montreal Protocol** (1987) primarily addresses the **phasing out of ozone-depleting substances** (ODS), such as chlorofluorocarbons (CFCs). While it indirectly contributes to climate change mitigation by eliminating substances that also act as potent greenhouse gases, its primary focus is ozone protection.
- **Pair 3 is correct.** The **Kigali Agreement** (2016) is an amendment to the **Montreal Protocol** that aims to phase down the use of **hydrofluorocarbons** (HFCs), which are potent greenhouse gases but do not deplete the ozone layer.

**Thus, option (b) is the correct answer.**

***37.*** *(b)* Only two

- **Statement 1 is correct.** REDD+ (Reducing Emissions from Deforestation and Forest Degradation) is a global initiative under the UNFCCC that provides **results-based payments** to countries for achieving verified emission reductions in the forestry sector through activities like reducing deforestation and forest degradation.
- **Statement 2 is incorrect.** REDD+ does not include **deforestation** itself as an activity. It focuses on reducing **deforestation and forest degradation**, promoting conservation, sustainable management of forests, and enhancing forest carbon stocks (reforestation).
- **Statement 3 is correct.** The **Lima REDD+ Information Hub** was established to enhance transparency in the implementation of

REDD+ activities by sharing information on the results of these actions and the payments received by countries for verified emission reductions.

**Thus, option (b) is the correct answer.**

***38.*** *(a)* Only 1 and 2

- **Statement 1 is correct:** The **Brundtland Commission**, formally known as the **World Commission on Environment and Development (WCED)**, introduced the concept of **sustainable development** in its 1987 report 'Our Common Future.' The report defines sustainable development as development that meets the needs of the present without compromising the ability of future generations to meet their own needs.
- **Statement 2 is correct:** The **Brundtland Report** was significant because it brought the term 'sustainable development' to the forefront of global policy discussions. It connected environmental preservation with economic and social dimensions, thus presenting a more holistic approach. The report also laid the groundwork for the 1992 **Earth Summit** in Rio de Janeiro, which resulted in key environmental agreements.
- **Statement 3 is incorrect:** The report did not focus solely on environmental strategies. Instead, it emphasised the importance of a **balanced approach** that integrates **economic growth, social equity,** and **environmental protection.** This three-pillar model of sustainable development is now widely accepted.

**Thus, option (a) is the correct answer.**

***39.*** *(a)* Only 1 and 2

- **Statement 1 is correct:** The **1992 Earth Summit** was a landmark event held in **Rio de Janeiro, Brazil,** with a central focus on sustainable development. It is officially known as the **United Nations Conference on Environment and Development** (UNCED). The summit brought together world leaders to address pressing environmental challenges and set the stage for subsequent global efforts on climate change, biodiversity, and sustainability.
- **Statement 2 is correct:** One of the major outcomes of the Earth Summit was **Agenda 21,** a comprehensive action plan that outlines strategies for promoting sustainable development at global, national, and local levels. It covers various aspects such as combating poverty, changing consumption patterns, conserving natural resources, and strengthening institutional frameworks for sustainable development.
- **Statement 3 is incorrect:** The **Green Climate Fund** (GCF) was not established at the 1992 Earth Summit but much later, in 2010, at the **COP16 negotiations in Cancun.** The GCF aims to support developing countries in mitigating and adapting to the effects of climate change.

**Thus, option (a) is the correct answer.**

***40.*** *(a)* Only 1 and 2

- **Statement 1 is correct:** The **Rio Declaration on Environment and Development** was one of the key documents adopted at the **1992 Earth Summit.** It lays down **27 principles** that emphasise the need for integrating **environmental protection** with **economic development.** These principles serve as a guiding framework for achieving sustainable development.
- **Statement 2 is correct:** One of the core principles of the Rio Declaration is the recognition of the **sovereign rights** of states to **exploit their natural resources.** However, it also emphasises that this exploitation should not cause environmental harm to other states or regions. This principle highlights the need for **global cooperation** in environmental protection, respecting national sovereignty while ensuring that actions within one country do not negatively impact others.
- **Statement 3 is incorrect:** The Rio Declaration does not promote long-term economic growth through industrial development alone. Instead, it underscores that **sustainable economic growth** is only achievable when it is closely linked to **environmental protection.** The declaration advocates for a balanced approach that considers social, economic and environmental aspects.

**Thus, option (a) is the correct answer.**

**41.** *(d)* 1 – 3 – 4 – 2

- **Kyoto Protocol** (1997): The **Kyoto Protocol** was the first legally binding agreement aimed at reducing greenhouse gas emissions in developed countries. It set specific emission reduction targets for industrialised nations.
- **Marrakesh Accords** (2001): The **Marrakesh Accords** followed the adoption of the Kyoto Protocol. They established detailed rules for the implementation of the Protocol, including provisions for carbon trading and the Clean Development Mechanism (CDM).
- **COP21** (2015): **COP21** refers to the **21st Conference of the Parties** to the UNFCCC, held in **Paris**. This conference led to the **adoption of the Paris Agreement**.
- **Paris Agreement** (2015): The **Paris Agreement** was a landmark international accord aimed at limiting global temperature rise to well below 2°C, with efforts to limit the rise to 1.5°C. It was adopted during **COP21** and brought almost all countries together to combat climate change.

**Thus, option (d) is the correct answer.**

## Past Learning (Answers)

| | | | | | | | | | |
|---|---|---|---|---|---|---|---|---|---|
| **1** (c) | **2** (d) | **3** (a) | **4** (a) | **5** (a) | **6** (c) | **7** (b) | **8** (c) | **9** (b) | **10** (a) |
| **11** (c) | **12** (c) | **13** (b) | **14** (b) | **15** (c) | **16** (d) | **17** (a) | **18** (a) | **19** (b) | **20** (b) |
| **21** (a) | **22** (c) | **23** (a) | **24** (c) | **25** (d) | **26** (a) | **27** (b) | **28** (b) | **29** (d) | |

CHAPTER

# 07 Organisations, Funds, Acts and Policies

## Assessment Round

**1.** Identify the international environmental fund based on the following statements:

1. It was established at the time of the 1992 Rio Earth Summit to address critical global environmental issues such as biodiversity loss, climate change and pollution.
2. It provides financial assistance to support international conventions, including the UNFCCC, UNCBD and the Stockholm Convention.
3. It has a unique governance structure consisting of an Assembly, Council, Secretariat, 18 agencies, and an Evaluation Office, and it includes 184 member countries.

Which of the following is correct?

(a) Green Climate Fund
(b) Global Environment Facility
(c) Adaptation Fund
(d) Climate Investment Funds

**2.** With reference to the Special Climate Change Fund (SCCF), consider the following statements:

1. The SCCF was established in 2001 under the UNFCCC to finance adaptation projects in vulnerable developing countries.
2. The fund supports a wide range of adaptation activities, including water resource management, agriculture, and health.
3. SCCF funding is also directed towards technology transfer to help countries adopt climate-resilient technologies for adaptation and mitigation.
4. The SCCF primarily funds mitigation projects in the transportation and energy sectors.

How many of the statements given above is/are correct?

(a) Only one (b) Only two
(c) Only three (d) All four

**3.** In the context of the Least Developed Countries Fund (LDCF), which of the following activities are prioritised to support climate resilience in vulnerable nations?

1. Implementation of National Adaptation Programs of Action (NAPAs) to address immediate adaptation needs.
2. Development of climate change early warning systems to enable rapid responses to extreme weather events.
3. Restoration of coastal mangrove forests as a nature-based adaptation solution.
4. Exclusive funding for high-tech industrial infrastructure for economic growth.

Select the correct answer using the codes given below:

(a) 1, 2 and 3 only (b) 1 and 4 only
(c) 2, 3 and 4 only (d) 1, 2, 3 and 4

**4.** With reference to the Adaptation Fund, consider the following statements:

1. The Adaptation Fund was established under the Kyoto Protocol to support adaptation projects in developing countries vulnerable to climate change.
2. The Adaptation Fund is primarily funded through a share of proceeds from the Clean Development Mechanism (CDM) and other sources.
3. The Adaptation Fund pioneered Direct Access, allowing countries to access funding through accredited national implementing entities.
4. The National Bank for Agriculture and Rural Development (NABARD) serves as the trustee of the Adaptation Fund.

How many of the statements given above is/are correct?

(a) Only one
(b) Only two
(c) Only three
(d) All four

**5.** With reference to the National Adaptation Fund for Climate Change (NAFCC), consider the following statements:

1. NAFCC was established in 2015–16 as a Central Sector Scheme to support climate adaptation initiatives.
2. NAFCC funds adaptation projects across sectors such as agriculture, water, forestry and tourism.
3. The National Bank for Agriculture and Rural Development (NABARD) serves as the national implementing entity for NAFCC.

How many of the statements given above is/are correct?

(a) Only one
(b) Only two
(c) All three
(d) None

**6.** With reference to the Land Degradation Neutrality Fund (LDN Fund), consider the following statements:

1. The LDN Fund is managed by the United Nations Convention to Combat Desertification (UNCCD).
2. The LDN Fund focuses on private investment for sustainable land management and landscape restoration projects globally.
3. It invests in areas like sustainable agriculture, forestry and renewable energy.

Which of the given statements are correct?

(a) 1 and 2 only
(b) 2 and 3 only
(c) 1 and 3 only
(d) 1, 2 and 3

**7.** Which of the following correctly describes the Green Climate Fund?

1. It is designed to help developing countries in adaptation and mitigation efforts to combat climate change.
2. It was established under the guidance of UNEP, OECD, Asian Development Bank and World Bank.

Select the correct answer using the codes given below:

(a) 1 only
(b) 2 only
(c) Both 1 and 2
(d) Neither 1 nor 2

**8.** Consider the following statements regarding the Antarctic Treaty:

1. The treaty allows countries to establish military bases in Antarctica as long as they are used for peaceful purposes.
2. Under the treaty, freedom of scientific investigation is promoted without restriction.
3. The Antarctic Treaty permits the disposal of radioactive waste under strict guidelines.
4. Countries are prohibited from claiming sovereignty over Antarctic territories by establishing research stations.

How many of the above statements is/are correct?

(a) Only one (b) Only two
(c) Only three (d) All four

**9.** Consider the following statements about the Tropical Forest Alliance (TFA):

1. The TFA was founded by the World Economic Forum (WEF) in 2012 during the Rio+20 summit.
2. The alliance focuses on supporting private-sector commitments to eliminate deforestation from the supply chains of key commodities like palm oil, beef, soy and pulp/paper.
3. It includes a broad range of partners, such as governments, companies, civil society organisations, and indigenous peoples.

How many of the above statements is/are correct?

(a) Only one (b) Only two
(c) All three (d) None

**10.** Regarding the One Trillion Trees Initiative, consider the following statements:

1. It was launched by the World Economic Forum (WEF) to restore 1 trillion trees globally by 2030.
2. The initiative is focused solely on reforestation in tropical regions.
3. The initiative is part of the UN Decade on Ecosystem Restoration (2021-2030) and involves mobilising the private sector.

Which of the statements given above are correct?

(a) 1 and 3 only (b) 2 and 3 only
(c) 1 and 2 only (d) 1, 2 and 3

**11.** What is the Global Forest Finance Pledge?

(a) A financial commitment made by developing countries to invest $12 billion for forest restoration.
(b) A pledge by 12 developed countries to provide $12 billion in public finance for forest-related climate actions in ODA-eligible countries between 2021-2025.
(c) A United Nations-led programme to promote sustainable forest management.
(d) A trade agreement between developed and developing countries to prevent deforestation.

**12.** Which of the following accurately describes the International Energy Agency (IEA) and its roles?

1. The IEA was established in response to the oil crisis of the mid-1970s and focuses on energy policies, including energy security and environmental protection.
2. Membership in the IEA is open to all countries, with India being a member country.
3. The IEA provides key reports such as the World Energy Outlook and India Energy Outlook Report.
4. The IEA plays a significant role in responding to disruptions in the international oil market.

Which of the statements given above are correct?

(a) Only 1, 3 and 4 (b) Only 1 and 3
(c) Only 2, 3 and 4 (d) All of the above

**13.** Consider the following statements with regard to the Green Climate Fund (GCF):

1. The GCF functions as the main fund for global climate change finance, accountable to the COP.
2. The GCF Board comprises an equal number of members from both developed and developing countries.
3. The GCF aims to mobilise USD 100 billion annually by 2020, primarily for mitigation projects.

How many of the above statements is/are correct?

(a) Only one (b) Only two
(c) All three (d) None

**14.** Under the Biological Diversity Act, 2002, which of the following correctly describes a Biodiversity Heritage Site (BHS)?

(a) An area designated exclusively for the conservation of endangered wildlife species under the Wildlife Protection Act.
(b) A well-defined area with unique, ecologically fragile ecosystems rich in biodiversity, comprising wild and domesticated species, high endemism, or significant cultural or aesthetic values.
(c) A marine protected area established for the conservation of coral reefs and marine life.
(d) A biosphere reserve declared under UNESCO's Man and the Biosphere Programme to promote sustainable development.

**15.** Consider the following statements:

**Statement I**: The Biological Diversity (Amendment) Act, 2023 simplifies the patent acquisition process for Indian residents and companies not controlled by foreign entities by requiring them to seek approval from the National Biodiversity Authority only before the grant of a patent.

**Statement II**: The Act aims to reduce bureaucratic hurdles and promote innovation within India by expanding the scope of approval required from the National Biodiversity Authority.

Which one of the following is correct in respect of the above statements?

(a) Both Statement I and Statement II are correct, and Statement II is the correct explanation for Statement I.

(b) Both Statement I and Statement II are correct, but Statement II is not the correct explanation for Statement I.

(c) Statement I is correct, but Statement II is incorrect.

(d) Statement I is incorrect, but Statement II is correct.

**16.** Which one of the following statements is correct regarding the Biological Diversity (Amendment) Act, 2023?

(a) The Act introduces new criminal penalties, including imprisonment, for unauthorised access to biological resources.

(b) The Act removes the requirement for benefit-sharing arrangements when biological resources are commercialised.

(c) The Act decriminalises offenses related to biological resources, focusing on imposing fines rather than criminal sanctions.

(d) The Act eliminates the role of State Biodiversity Boards in regulating access to biological resources.

**17.** Which of the following statements correctly describes the Animal Welfare Board of India (AWBI)?

(a) It is a statutory advisory body established in 1962 under the Wildlife Protection Act, 1972.

(b) It is a non-governmental organisation functioning under the Ministry of Environment, Forest and Climate Change.

(c) It is a statutory advisory body established in 1962 under the Prevention of Cruelty to Animals Act, 1960.

(d) It is an executive body under the Ministry of Fisheries, Animal Husbandry and Dairying, headquartered in Chennai, Tamil Nadu.

**18.** Consider the following statements regarding the provisions of the Wild Life (Protection) Amendment Act, 2022:

1. The Central Government can declare an area as a conservation reserve.
2. The amendment defines Invasive Alien Species as species of animals or plants not native to India, whose introduction or spread may threaten or adversely impact wildlife or its habitat.
3. The amendment empowers State Governments to constitute Standing Committees of the State Board for Wildlife.
4. The term 'Zoo' includes establishments of licensed dealers in captive animals.

How many of the above statements is/are correct?

(a) Only one

(b) Only two

(c) Only three

(d) All four

**19.** With reference to the provisions regarding animal ownership under the Wild Life (Protection) Amendment Act, 2022, consider the following statements:

1. If any government property is a live animal that cannot be released into its natural habitat, the State Government shall ensure it is housed and cared for by a recognised zoo or rescue centre.
2. Any person possessing a certificate of ownership for a captive animal or animal article can surrender it to the Chief Wildlife Warden and will receive compensation for the surrender.
3. Transfer or transport of a captive elephant by a person having a valid certificate of ownership is permitted without any conditions imposed by the Central Government.
4. Any animal article, trophy, uncured trophy, or meat derived from any wild animal can be disposed of by the State Government or Central Government in a manner prescribed by the State Government.

How many of the statements given above is/are correct?

(a) Only one
(b) Only two
(c) Only three
(d) All four

**20.** Consider the following pairs regarding the Schedules under the Wild Life (Protection) Amendment Act, 2022:

| | Animal/Plant | Schedule |
|---|---|---|
| 1. | Blackbuck | Schedule I |
| 2. | Nilgai | Schedule II |
| 3. | Neel Kurinji | Schedule III |
| 4. | Vermins | Schedule V |

Which of the above pairs are correctly matched?

(a) 1 and 2 only (b) 1, 2 and 3 only
(c) 1, 2, 3 and 4 (d) 2 and 4 only

**21.** Consider the following statements regarding the Genetic Engineering Appraisal Committee (GEAC):

1. GEAC was established under the Ministry of Environment, Forest and Climate Change (MoEFCC).
2. The Chairman of GEAC is the Minister of Environment, Forest and Climate Change.
3. The Vice-Chairman of GEAC is the Joint Secretary, MoEFCC.
4. GEAC is responsible for approving activities involving large-scale use of hazardous microorganisms and recombinants from an environmental perspective.

Which of the statements given above are correct?

(a) 1 and 3 only
(b) 2 and 4 only
(c) 1, 3 and 4 only
(d) All of the above

**22.** Identify the committee based on the following statements:

1. It is established under the Ministry of Environment, Forest and Climate Change (MoEFCC) in India.
2. The committee is responsible for approving activities involving the large-scale use of hazardous microorganisms and recombinants from an environmental perspective.
3. The Chairman of this committee is the Additional/Special Secretary, MoEFCC.
4. The committee operates under the Rules of 1989.

Select the correct answer using the codes given below:

(a) Genetic Engineering Appraisal Committee (GEAC)
(b) National Biodiversity Authority (NBA)
(c) Central Pollution Control Board (CPCB)
(d) Indian Council of Agricultural Research (ICAR)

**23.** In the context of the Environment Protection Act, 1986 (EPA, 1986) and its amendments, which of the following scenarios would be penalised under the proposed Environment (Protection) Amendment Rules, 2021?

1. A company fails to submit its environmental impact reports on time.
2. A factory releases pollutants into a river, leading to a local community's water source contamination.
3. A manufacturing plant violates the air quality standards set under EPA 1986 but rectifies it within a day.
4. An individual illegally cuts down protected forest trees but claims ignorance of environmental laws.

Select the correct answer using the codes given below:

(a) 1 and 2 only (b) 2 and 3 only
(c) 1, 2 and 4 only (d) 1, 2, 3 and 4

**24.** The Botanical Survey of India (BSI) and the Zoological Survey of India (ZSI) are two important institutions set up by the Government of India. What is the key difference between the BSI and the ZSI?

(a) BSI focuses on the identification of plant resources, while ZSI focuses on the exploration and research of fauna.
(b) BSI was established in 1916, while ZSI was established in 1890.
(c) BSI is under the Ministry of Agriculture, while ZSI is under the Ministry of Environment, Forest and Climate Change (MoEFCC).
(d) BSI's headquarters is in Delhi, while ZSI's headquarters is in Kolkata.

**25.** With reference to the National Transit Pass System (NTPS), consider the following statements:

1. NTPS is designed to facilitate seamless transit of timber, bamboo, and other forest produce across the country.
2. NTPS operates under the concept of 'One Nation, One Pass', allowing the issuance of transit passes for inter-state and intra-state transportation.
3. NTPS exempts all species grown on private lands from requiring a transit permit.

How many of the above statements is/are correct?

(a) Only one (b) Only two
(c) All three (d) None

**26.** In the context of the National Transit Pass System (NTPS), which of the following actions would require a No-Objection Certificate (NOC) for the transportation of exempted species?

1. Transporting timber that is exempted from a transit pass in the originating state but not in the destination state.
2. Transporting bamboo that is not exempted from a transit pass in the originating state.
3. Transporting timber that is exempted in the originating state but not in the en-route state.

Select the correct answer using the codes given below:

(a) 1 and 3 only (b) 2 and 3 only
(c) 1 and 2 only (d) 1, 2 and 3

**27.** Consider the following statements regarding the National Forest Policy, 1988:

1. The principal aim of the National Forest Policy, 1988, is to ensure environmental stability and maintain ecological balance.
2. The National Forest Policy emphasises that the derivation of direct economic benefits must take precedence over environmental stability.
3. Since the introduction of the policy, the forest and tree cover in India has increased from 19.7% to 23.4% of the geographical area.

How many of the above statements is/are correct?

(a) Only one (b) Only two
(c) All three (d) None

**28.** Consider the following aspects of the Environment (Protection) Act, 1986:

1. The Act empowers the Central Government to take necessary measures to protect and improve the quality of the environment.
2. It provides the Central Government with the authority to prohibit or restrict the setting and/or operation of any industrial facility based on environmental grounds.
3. The Act was last amended in 1991, and it extends to the whole of India.

How many of the above statements is/are correct?

(a) Only one
(b) Only two
(c) All three
(d) None

**29.** Which of the following statements regarding the Composite Water Management Index (CWMI) are correct?

1. The CWMI was launched by NITI Aayog to provide an annual snapshot of the water sector status in India.
2. The index assesses states and union territories based on nine themes and 28 indicators, including water augmentation, irrigation practices, and rural drinking water.
3. The first edition of the CWMI was launched in 2020 and focused on the water management performance of states and UTs during the Covid-19 pandemic.
4. The CWMI has experienced delays in subsequent editions due to the unavailability of updated data caused by the Covid-19 pandemic.

Select the correct answer from the codes given below :

(a) Only 1 and 2
(b) Only 2 and 3
(c) Only 1, 2 and 4
(d) All of the above

**30.** How does the Composite Water Management Index (CWMI) help address India's water challenges?

(a) By providing detailed, real-time water data for each district across India.
(b) By assessing the water management performance of states based on key indicators like irrigation practices, water augmentation, and rural drinking water, and offering a comparison to encourage improvement.
(c) By ensuring that water resources are allocated equally to all regions, regardless of their current water management practices.
(d) By setting legal restrictions on water usage for industries to reduce over-extraction.

**31.** Which of the following statements regarding the Plastic Waste Management (Amendment) Rules, 2024 are correct?

1. The rules have introduced a definition of biodegradable plastics as materials capable of degrading without leaving any microplastics.
2. Microplastics are defined as plastic particles with dimensions between 1 micron and 1,000 microns.
3. The definition of 'Importer' now includes only those who import finished plastic products for commercial purposes.
4. The scope of 'Producer' now extends to include intermediate materials used in plastic packaging and contract manufacturing for brand owners.

Which of the statements given above are correct?

(a) 1 and 3 only
(b) 2 and 4 only
(c) 1, 2 and 4 only
(d) 1, 2, 3 and 4

**32.** Which of the following correctly describes a provision under the Water (Prevention and Control of Pollution) Cess Act?

(a) The cess is levied on water consumed by industries, with the aim of raising funds for the Central and State Pollution Control Boards to prevent and control water pollution.
(b) The act imposes a cess on water used by individuals in residential areas to augment water resources.
(c) The act was last amended in 2021 to regulate water purification systems and ensure compliance with environmental standards.
(d) The cess is imposed on water used only for agricultural purposes to ensure the sustainability of water resources.

**33.** Under the Forest Rights Act, 2006, which of the following rights are granted to Forest Dwelling Scheduled Tribes (FDST) and Other Traditional Forest Dwellers (OTFD)?

1. Title rights, including ownership of land being cultivated, up to a maximum of 4 hectares.
2. Use rights, including extraction of minor forest produce, grazing areas, and access to pastoralist routes.
3. Relief and development rights, including rehabilitation in case of illegal eviction or forced displacement, and access to basic amenities.
4. Forest management rights, including the right to protect, regenerate, conserve or manage any community forest resource traditionally protected.
5. Rights to claim new lands for cultivation beyond those currently being farmed.

Select the correct answer using the codes given below:

(a) 1, 2, 3 and 4 only
(b) 1, 2 and 5 only
(c) 2, 3 and 5 onl
(d) 1, 3, 4 and 5 only

**34.** Under the Environment Protection Act, 1986, the powers of the Central Government to issue directions include:

1. Ordering the closure of any industry, operation, or process.
2. Prohibiting or regulating the supply of electricity or water to any industry.
3. Directing the stoppage of any service, such as gas or telephone, to polluting industries.
4. Issuing directions to individuals or officers to comply with environmental standards and procedures.

How many of the above is/are included in the Central Government's power to issue directions under the Act?

(a) Only one
(b) Only two
(c) Only three
(d) All four

**35.** Consider the following definitions under the Environment Protection Act, 1986:

1. 'Environment' includes water, air, land and the inter-relationship among them and with human beings, other living creatures, plants, microorganisms, and property.
2. 'Environmental Pollutant' means any solid, liquid, or gaseous substance present in such concentration as may be, or tend to be, injurious to the environment.
3. 'Hazardous Substance' includes any substance or preparation which, by reason of its chemical or physico-chemical properties or handling, is liable to cause harm to human beings, other living creatures, plants, microorganisms, property or the environment.
4. 'Occupier' refers to a person who has ultimate control over the affairs of the factory or premises, including the owner in the case of a firm or association.

How many of the above definitions is/are correctly stated according to the Environment Protection Act, 1986?

(a) Only one
(b) Only two
(c) Only three
(d) All four

**36.** Which one of the following statements is correct regarding the Central Ground Water Authority (CGWA)?

(a) The CGWA is a statutory body established under the Environment (Protection) Act, 1986.
(b) The CGWA functions under the Ministry of Environment, Forest and Climate Change.
(c) The CGWA was formed in 1996 by an executive order under the Environment (Protection) Act, 1986.
(d) The CGWA regulates groundwater management in all Indian States and Union Territories without exception.

**37.** Consider the following statements regarding the Mines and Minerals (Development & Regulation) Amendment Act, 2023:

**Statement I**: The Amendment Act removed six minerals, including lithium and titanium, from the list of atomic minerals to allow private sector participation in their exploration and mining.

**Statement II**: Prior to the amendment, mining and exploration of atomic minerals specified in Part B of the First Schedule of the MMDR Act were exclusively reserved for Public Sector Undertakings (PSUs), leading to limited exploration and mining of these minerals.

Which one of the following is correct in respect of the above statements?

(a) Both Statement I and Statement II are correct, and Statement II is the correct explanation for Statement I.

(b) Both Statement I and Statement II are correct, but Statement II is not the correct explanation for Statement I.

(c) Statement I is correct, but Statement II is incorrect.

(d) Statement I is incorrect, but Statement II is correct.

**38.** Which of the following minerals were removed from the list of atomic minerals specified in Part B of the First Schedule of the MMDR Act by the Mines and Minerals (Development & Regulation) Amendment Act, 2023?

(a) Uranium and Thorium

(b) Lithium, Beryllium, Titanium, Niobium, Tantalum and Zirconium

(c) Molybdenum, Rhenium, Tungsten and Cadmium

(d) Copper, Gold, Silver and Diamond

**39.** Which one of the following statements is correct regarding the provisions of the Mines and Minerals (Development & Regulation) Amendment Act, 2023?

(a) The State Governments exclusively auction mining leases and composite licences for critical minerals such as lithium and cobalt.

(b) The Amendment Act allows private sector participation in the exploration and mining of certain minerals by removing them from the list of atomic minerals.

(c) The Amendment Act introduced a new mineral concession called Exploration Licence, which is granted without any auction process.

(d) The rate of royalty for lithium has been notified as 1% by the Union Ministry of Mines.

**40.** Consider the following statements regarding the process of notifying Critical Wildlife Habitats (CWH) under the Forest Rights Act, 2006:

1. The Chief Wildlife Warden of a state will notify an Expert Committee for the identification of CWH in a national park or sanctuary.
2. To notify a CWH, the Act requires state governments to establish that the presence of right-holders is causing irreversible damage to wildlife and their habitats.
3. The Expert Committee must issue a public notice to notify CWH, which includes details of areas required to be kept inviolate, criteria adopted for CWH identification, implications of the notification on existing rights, and all options of resettlement and rehabilitation schemes, if applicable.

How many of the above statements is/are correct?

(a) Only one (b) Only two
(c) All three (d) None

**41.** Which of the following best describes the Bureau of Energy Efficiency (BEE)?

(a) It is a statutory body established under the Energy Conservation Act, 2001, responsible for implementing policies to improve energy intensity in India.

(b) It is a non-governmental organisation working on promoting renewable energy technologies in India.

(c) It is a regulatory authority under the Ministry of Environment, responsible for climate change mitigation and adaptation strategies.

(d) It is an autonomous body under the Ministry of Finance, managing energy tariffs and subsidies.

# OMR SHEET

**Assessment Round**

| | | | | | | | | | | | | | | | | | | | |
|---|---|---|---|---|---|---|---|---|---|---|---|---|---|---|---|---|---|---|---|
| 1 | a | b | c | d | 31 | a | b | c | d | 61 | a | b | c | d | 91 | a | b | c | d |
| 2 | a | b | c | d | 32 | a | b | c | d | 62 | a | b | c | d | 92 | a | b | c | d |
| 3 | a | b | c | d | 33 | a | b | c | d | 63 | a | b | c | d | 93 | a | b | c | d |
| 4 | a | b | c | d | 34 | a | b | c | d | 64 | a | b | c | d | 94 | a | b | c | d |
| 5 | a | b | c | d | 35 | a | b | c | d | 65 | a | b | c | d | 95 | a | b | c | d |
| 6 | a | b | c | d | 36 | a | b | c | d | 66 | a | b | c | d | 96 | a | b | c | d |
| 7 | a | b | c | d | 37 | a | b | c | d | 67 | a | b | c | d | 97 | a | b | c | d |
| 8 | a | b | c | d | 38 | a | b | c | d | 68 | a | b | c | d | 98 | a | b | c | d |
| 9 | a | b | c | d | 39 | a | b | c | d | 69 | a | b | c | d | 99 | a | b | c | d |
| 10 | a | b | c | d | 40 | a | b | c | d | 70 | a | b | c | d | 100 | a | b | c | d |
| 11 | a | b | c | d | 41 | a | b | c | d | 71 | a | b | c | d | 101 | a | b | c | d |
| 12 | a | b | c | d | 42 | a | b | c | d | 72 | a | b | c | d | 102 | a | b | c | d |
| 13 | a | b | c | d | 43 | a | b | c | d | 73 | a | b | c | d | 103 | a | b | c | d |
| 14 | a | b | c | d | 44 | a | b | c | d | 74 | a | b | c | d | 104 | a | b | c | d |
| 15 | a | b | c | d | 45 | a | b | c | d | 75 | a | b | c | d | 105 | a | b | c | d |
| 16 | a | b | c | d | 46 | a | b | c | d | 76 | a | b | c | d | 106 | a | b | c | d |
| 17 | a | b | c | d | 47 | a | b | c | d | 77 | a | b | c | d | 107 | a | b | c | d |
| 18 | a | b | c | d | 48 | a | b | c | d | 78 | a | b | c | d | 108 | a | b | c | d |
| 19 | a | b | c | d | 49 | a | b | c | d | 79 | a | b | c | d | 109 | a | b | c | d |
| 20 | a | b | c | d | 50 | a | b | c | d | 80 | a | b | c | d | 110 | a | b | c | d |
| 21 | a | b | c | d | 51 | a | b | c | d | 81 | a | b | c | d | 111 | a | b | c | d |
| 22 | a | b | c | d | 52 | a | b | c | d | 82 | a | b | c | d | 112 | a | b | c | d |
| 23 | a | b | c | d | 53 | a | b | c | d | 83 | a | b | c | d | 113 | a | b | c | d |
| 24 | a | b | c | d | 54 | a | b | c | d | 84 | a | b | c | d | 114 | a | b | c | d |
| 25 | a | b | c | d | 55 | a | b | c | d | 85 | a | b | c | d | 115 | a | b | c | d |
| 26 | a | b | c | d | 56 | a | b | c | d | 86 | a | b | c | d | 116 | a | b | c | d |
| 27 | a | b | c | d | 57 | a | b | c | d | 87 | a | b | c | d | 117 | a | b | c | d |
| 28 | a | b | c | d | 58 | a | b | c | d | 88 | a | b | c | d | 118 | a | b | c | d |
| 29 | a | b | c | d | 59 | a | b | c | d | 89 | a | b | c | d | 119 | a | b | c | d |
| 30 | a | b | c | d | 60 | a | b | c | d | 90 | a | b | c | d | 120 | a | b | c | d |

## Calculate Your Score

| | |
|---|---|
| **Correct (✓)** | |
| **Incorrect (✓)** | |
| **Unattempted** | |
| **Total Score** | |
| **Accuracy (%)** | |

## Reasons for Incorrect Answers?

| | |
|---|---|
| 1. Lack of Knowledge/Existing Source Insufficient | |
| 2. Lack of Multiple Revision | |
| 3. Common Sense Mistakes | |

**Note :**

1. Calculate total score as correct answers carry 2 marks each 1/3rd marks will deducted for **Incorrect** Answers.
2. Calculate Accuracy (%) by dividing the number of correct answers to the total number of attempted questions.

## Past Learning

**1.** Consider the following statements: **(2024)**

**Statement I:** The Indian Flying Fox is placed under the 'vermin' category in the Wild Life (Protection) Act, 1972.

**Statement II:** The Indian Flying Fox feeds on the blood of other animals.

Which one of the following is correct in respect of the above statements?

(a) Both Statement I and Statement II are correct, and Statement II explains Statement I.

(b) Both Statement I and Statement II are correct, but Statement II does not explain Statement I.

(c) Statement I is correct, but Statement II is incorrect.

(d) Statement I is incorrect, but Statement II is correct.

**2.** Invasive Species Specialist Group (that develops Global Invasive Species Database) belongs to which one of the following organisations? **(2023)**

(a) The International Union for Conservation of Nature

(b) The United Nations Environment Programme

(c) The United Nations World Commission for Environment and Development

(d) The World Wide Fund for Nature

**3.** With reference to Indian laws about wildlife protection, consider the following statements: **(2022)**

1. Wild animals are the sole property of the government.
2. When a wild animal is declared protected, such animal is entitled for equal protection whether it is found in protected areas or outside.
3. Apprehension of a protected wild animal becoming a danger to human life is sufficient ground for its capture or killing.

Which of the statements given above is/are correct?

(a) 1 and 2 only (b) 2 only

(c) 1 and 3 only (d) 3 only

**4.** Consider the following statements: **(2022)**

1. 'The Climate Group' is an international non-profit organisation that drives climate action by building large networks and runs them.
2. The International Energy Agency in partnership with the Climate Group launched a global initiative 'EP100'.
3. EP100 brings together leading companies committed to driving innovation in energy efficiency and increasing competitiveness while delivering on emission reduction goals.
4. Some Indian companies are members of EP100.
5. The International Energy Agency is the Secretariat to the 'Under2 Coalition'.

Which of the statements given above are correct?

(a) 1, 2, 4 and 5

(b) 1, 3 and 4 only

(c) 2, 3 and 5 only

(d) 1, 2, 3, 4 and 5

**5.** Which one of the following has been constituted under the Environment (Protection) Act, 1986? **(2022)**

(a) Central Water Commission

(b) Central Ground Water Board

(c) Central Ground Water Authority

(d) National Water Development Agency

**6.** Consider the following statements: **(2020)**

1. 36% of India's districts are classified as 'overexploited' or 'critical' by the Central Ground Water Authority (CGWA).
2. CGWA was formed under the Environment (Protection) Act.
3. India has the largest area under groundwater irrigation in the world.

Which of the statements given above is/are correct?

(a) 1 only (b) 2 and 3 only

(c) 2 only (d) 1 and 3 only

**7.** If a particular plant species is placed under Schedule VI of The Wildlife Protection Act, 1972, what is the implication? **(2020)**

(a) A license is required to cultivate that plant.

(b) Such a plant cannot be cultivated under any circumstances.

(c) It is a Genetically Modified crop plant.

(d) Such a plant is invasive and harmful to the ecosystem.

**8.** As per the Solid Waste Management Rules, 2016 in India, which one of the following statements is correct? **(2019)**

(a) Waste generator has to segregate waste into five categories.

(b) The Rules are applicable to notified urban local bodies, notified towns, and all industrial townships only.

(c) The Rules provide for exact and elaborate criteria for the identification of sites for landfills and waste processing facilities.

(d) It is mandatory on the part of waste generator that the waste generated in one district cannot be moved to another district.

**9.** Consider the following statements : **(2019)**

The Environment Protection Act, 1986 empowers the Government of India to

1. state the requirement of public participation in the process of environmental protection, and the procedure and manner in which it is sought
2. lay down the standards for emission discharge or environmental pollutants various sources of from

Which of the statements given above is/are correct?

(a) 1 only (b) 2 only
(c) Both 1 and 2 (d) Neither 1 nor 2

**10.** In India, 'extended producer responsibility' was introduced as an important feature in which of the following? **(2019)**

(a) The Bio-medical Waste (Management and Handling) Rules, 1998

(b) The Recycled Plastic (Manufacturing and Usage) Rules, 1999

(c) The e-Waste (Management and Handling) Rules, 2011

(d) The Food Safety and Standard Regulations, 2011

**11.** Consider the following statements: **(2019)**

1. As per law, the Compensatory Afforestation Fund Management and Planning Authority exists at both National and State levels.
2. People's participation is mandatory in the compensatory afforestation programmes carried out under the Compensatory Afforestation Fund Act, of 2016.

Which of the statements given above is/are correct?

(a) 1 only
(b) 2 only
(c) Both 1 and 2
(d) Neither 1 nor 2

**12.** How is the National Green Tribunal (NGT) different from the Central Pollution Control Board **(2018)**

1. The NGT has been established by an Act whereas the CPCB has been created by an executive order of the Government.
2. The NGT provides environmental justice and helps reduce the burden of litigation in the higher courts whereas the CPCB promotes cleanliness of streams and wells, and aims to improve the quality of air in the country.

Which of the statements given above is/are correct:

(a) 1 only (b) 2 only
(c) Both 1 and 2 (d) Neither 1 nor 2

**13.** Consider the following statements: **(2018)**

1. The definition of 'Critical Wildlife Habitat' is incorporated in the Forest Rights Act, 2006.
2. For the first time in India, Baigas have been given Habitat Rights.
3. Union Ministry of Environment, Forest and Climate Change officially decides and declares Habitat Rights for Primitive and Vulnerable Tribal Groups in any part of India.

Which of the statements given above is/are correct?

(a) 1 and 2 only (b) 2 and 3 only
(c) 3 only (d) 1, 2 and 3

**14.** In India, if a species of tortoise is declared protected under Schedule I of the Wildlife (Protection) Act, 1972, what does it imply? **(2017)**

(a) It enjoys the same level of protection as the tiger.

(b) It no longer exists in the wild, a few individuals are under captive protection, and now it is impossible to prevent its extinction.

(c) It is endemic to a particular region of India.

(d) Both (b) and (c) stated above are correct in this context.

**15.** According to the Wildlife (Protection) Act, 1972, which of the following animals cannot be hunted by any person except under some provisions provided by law? **(2017)**

1. Gharial
2. Indian wild ass
3. Wild buffalo

Select the correct answer using the codes given below:

(a) 1 only (b) 2 and 3 only
(c) 1 and 3 only (d) 1, 2 and 3

**16.** Which of the following best describes/describes the aim of the 'Green India Mission' of the Government of India? **(2016)**

1. Incorporating environmental benefits and costs into the Union and State Budgets thereby implementing the 'green accounting'
2. Launching the second green revolution to enhance agricultural output so as to ensure food security to one and all in the future
3. Restoring and enhancing forest cover and responding to climate change by a combination of adaptation and mitigation measures

Select the correct answer using the codes given below :

(a) 1 only (b) 2 and 3 only
(c) 3 only (d) 1, 2 and 3

**17.** The FAO accords the status of 'Globally Important Agricultural Heritage System (GIAHS)' to traditional agricultural systems. What is the overall goal of this initiative? **(2016)**

1. To provide modern technology, training in modern farming methods, and financial support to local communities of identified GIAHS so as to greatly enhance their agricultural productivity
2. To identify and safeguard eco-friendly traditional farm practices and their associated landscapes, agricultural biodiversity, and knowledge systems of the local communities.
3. To provide Geographical Indication status to all the varieties of agricultural produce in such identified GIAHS

Select the correct answer using the codes given below :

(a) 1 and 3 only (b) 2 only
(c) 2 and 3 only (d) 1, 2 and 3

**18.** On which of the following can you find the Bureau of Energy Efficiency Star Label? **(2016)**

1. Ceiling fans
2. Electric geysers
3. Tubular fluorescent lamps

Select the correct answer using the codes given below :

(a) 1 and 2 only (b) 3 only
(c) 2 and 3 only (d) 1, 2 and 3

**19.** Which of the following are the key features of 'National Ganga River Basin Authority (NGRBA)'? **(2016)**

1. River basin is the unit of planning and management.
2. It spearheads the river conservation efforts at the national level.
3. One of the Chief Ministers of the States through which the Ganga flows becomes the Chairman of NGRBA on a rotation basis.

Select the correct answer using the codes given below :

(a) 1 and 2 only (b) 2 and 3 only
(c) 1 and 3 only (d) 1, 2 and 3

**20.** 'BioCarbon Fund Initiative for Sustainable Forest Landscapes' is managed by the **(2015)**

(a) Asian Development Bank
(b) International Monetary Fund
(c) United Nations Environment Programme
(d) World Bank

**21.** The Genetic Engineering Appraisal Committee is constituted under the **(2015)**

(a) Food Safety and Standards Act, 2006

(b) Geographical Indications of Goods (Registration and Protection) Act, 1999

(c) Environment (Protection) Act, 1986

(d) Wildlife (Protection) Act, 1972

**22.** With reference to Bombay Natural History Society (BNHS), consider the following statements : **(2014)**

1. It is an autonomous organisation under the Ministry of Environment and Forests.
2. It strives to conserve nature through action-based research, education and public awareness.
3. It organises and conducts nature trails and camps for the general public.

Which of the statements given above is/are correct?

(a) 1 and 3 only

(b) 2 only

(c) 2 and 3 only

(d) 1, 2 and 3

**23.** With reference to 'Global Environment Facility', which of the following statements is/are correct? **(2014)**

(a) It serves as financial mechanism for 'Convention on Biological Diversity' and 'United Nations Framework Convention on Climate Change'.

(b) It undertakes scientific research on environmental issues at global level.

(c) It is an agency under OECD to facilitate the transfer of technology and funds to underdeveloped countries with specific aim to protect their environment.

(d) Both (a) and (b)

**24.** With reference to 'Eco-Sensitive Zones', which of the following statements is/are correct? **(2014)**

1. Eco-sensitive zones are the areas that are declared under the Wildlife (Protection) Act, 1972.
2. The purpose of the declaration of Eco-Sensitive Zones is to prohibit all kinds of human activities in those zones except agriculture.

Select the correct answer using the codes given below:

(a) 1 only

(b) 2 only

(c) Both 1 and 2

(d) Neither 1 nor 2

**25.** Consider the following statements : **(2014)**

1. Animal Welfare Board of India is established under the Environment (Protection) Act, 1986.
2. National Tiger Conservation Authority is a statutory body.
3. National Ganga River Basin Authority is chaired by the Prime Minister.

Which of the statements given above is/are correct?

(a) 1 only

(b) 2 and 3 only

(c) 2 only

(d) 1, 2 and 3

**26.** The National Green Tribunal Act, 2010 was enacted in consonance with which of the following provisions of the Constitution of India? **(2012)**

1. Right to a healthy environment, construed as a part of Right to life under Article 21
2. Provision of grants for raising the level of administration in the Scheduled Areas for the welfare of Scheduled Tribes under Article 275(1)
3. Powers and functions of Gram Sabha as mentioned under Article 243 (A)

Select the correct answer using the codes given below :

(a) 1 only

(b) 2 and 3 only

(c) 1 and 3 only

(d) 1, 2 and 3

# Detailed Solutions

## Assessment Round

**1.** *(b)* Global Environment Facility

The **Global Environment Facility (GEF)** was created around the 1992 Rio Earth Summit to address global environmental challenges. It supports five major environmental conventions, including the **UNFCCC, UNCBD** and **Stockholm Convention.** The GEF is known for its structured governance, including an Assembly, Council and Secretariat, and comprises 184 member countries.

**Thus, option (b) is the correct answer.**

**2.** *(c)* Only three

- The **Special Climate Change Fund (SCCF)** was established in 2001 at the United Nations Framework Convention on Climate Change (UNFCCC) COP7 to help vulnerable developing countries address the impacts of climate change. Managed by the **Global Environment Facility (GEF)**, the SCCF provides targeted support for adaptation and technology transfer to build climate resilience.
- **Statement 1 is correct :** The **Special Climate Change Fund** (SCCF) was indeed established in **2001** under the **UNFCCC** to finance adaptation measures in vulnerable developing countries.
- **Statement 2 is correct :** The SCCF supports a broad range of **adaptation activities** such as water resource management, agriculture health and more.
- **Statement 3 is correct:** The SCCF also facilitates **technology transfer,** helping countries adopt climate-resilient technologies for both **adaptation** and **mitigation.**
- **Statement 4 is incorrect:** While the SCCF does support certain mitigation activities, its primary focus is on **adaptation** and resilience-building, not exclusively on sectors like transportation and energy.

**Thus, option (c) is the correct answer.**

**3.** *(a)* 1, 2 and 3 only

- The **Least Developed Countries Fund (LDCF)** was established under the United Nations Framework Convention on Climate Change (UNFCCC) in 2001 to specifically support Least Developed Countries (LDCs) in adapting to the impacts of climate change. Managed by the **Global Environment Facility (GEF),** the LDCF focuses on helping these nations address their most urgent climate adaptation needs.
- **Option 1 is correct:** The **LDCF** prioritizes the implementation of **National Adaptation Programs of Action (NAPAs)** to address the immediate adaptation needs of least developed countries.
- **Option 2 is correct:** The LDCF supports the development of **early warning systems** for climate change to improve responses to extreme weather events.
- **Option 3 is correct:** The LDCF promotes **nature-based adaptation solutions,** such as restoring mangrove forests to protect coastal areas.
- **Option 4 is incorrect:** The LDCF focuses on adaptation needs rather than high-tech industrial infrastructure for economic growth.

**Thus, option (a) is the correct answer.**

**4.** *(c)* Only three

- **Statement 1 is correct :** The **Adaptation Fund** was indeed established under the **Kyoto Protocol** to finance adaptation projects in developing countries vulnerable to climate change.
- **Statement 2 is correct:** The fund is financed through a **share of proceeds from Clean Development Mechanism (CDM) project activities** and other sources, specifically with a 2% share of Certified Emission Reductions (CERs).

- **Statement 3 is correct:** The **Adaptation Fund** introduced the concept of **Direct Access**, enabling countries to access funding through **accredited national implementing entities.**
- **Statement 4 is incorrect:** The **World Bank**, not NABARD, serves as the **trustee** of the Adaptation Fund on an interim basis, whereas NABARD serves as the national implementing entity for India's **National Adaptation Fund for Climate Change** (NAFCC).

**Thus, option (c) is the correct answer.**

**5.** *(c)* All three

- **Statement 1 is correct:** The **National Adaptation Fund for Climate Change** (NAFCC) was established as a **Central Sector Scheme** in 2015-16 with the aim to support adaptation initiatives that reduce climate change impacts.
- **Statement 2 is correct:** NAFCC funds projects across various sectors impacted by climate change, including **agriculture, water resources, forestry and tourism.**
- **Statement 3 is correct: NABARD** acts as the **national implementing entity** for the NAFCC, facilitating the implementation of climate adaptation projects.

**Thus, option (c) is the correct answer.**

**6.** *(b)* 2 and 3 only

The **Land Degradation Neutrality** (LDN) **Fund** is an investment vehicle established by the **United Nations Convention to Combat Desertification** (UNCCD). It aims to support **sustainable land management** projects that help achieve **land degradation neutrality**, a target under the **Sustainable Development Goals (SDGs)**. The fund mobilises **public and private investments** to finance projects that restore degraded land, improve ecosystems, enhance food security and combat desertification. By promoting sustainable practices, the **LDN Fund** seeks to generate both **environmental** and **financial returns**, while mitigating the impacts of climate change.

- **Statement 1 is incorrect :** The **LDN Fund** is **not directly managed by the UNCCD**, but rather it was established in collaboration with the UNCCD. It is **managed by Mirova**, a subsidiary of Natixis Investment Managers, with technical support from the **UNCCD.**
- **Statement 2 is correct :** The **LDN Fund** focuses on **private investment** for **sustainable land management** and **landscape restoration** projects globally, aiming to achieve **land degradation neutrality.**
- **Statement 3 is correct:** The fund invests in areas such as **sustainable agriculture, forestry, land restoration**, and also supports projects related to **renewable energy**, aligning with efforts to mitigate climate change and enhance biodiversity.

**Thus, option (b) is the correct answer.**

**7.** *(a)* 1 only

- **Statement 1 is correct:** The **Green Climate Fund** (**GCF**) was established to support developing countries in implementing adaptation and mitigation projects to address the challenges of climate change. The fund aims to assist these nations in achieving low-emission and climate-resilient development.
- **Statement 2 is incorrect:** The GCF was established under the framework of the **United Nations Framework Convention on Climate Change** (UNFCCC), specifically as part of the **Copenhagen Accord** and further detailed in the **Cancún Agreements.** It was not created under the guidance of the UNEP, OECD, Asian Development Bank, or World Bank though it may collaborate with these institutions for project implementation.

**Thus, option (a) is the correct answer.**

**8.** *(b)* Only two

- **Statement 1 is incorrect :** The Antarctic Treaty **prohibits** any military activities, including the establishment of military bases, regardless of their purpose. All activities must be peaceful, and no military installations are allowed.
- **Statement 2 is correct :** The treaty **promotes freedom of scientific investigation** in Antarctica, allowing researchers to conduct scientific studies without undue restrictions, provided they adhere to the treaty's regulations.

- **Statement 3 is incorrect** : The treaty **prohibits** the disposal of **radioactive waste** in Antarctica. Any nuclear explosions or disposal of radioactive materials are strictly banned to protect the pristine environment.
- **Statement 4 is correct** :The treaty **prevents countries from claiming sovereignty** over Antarctic territories based solely on establishing research stations. Sovereignty claims are not recognised under the treaty framework.

**Thus, option (b) is the correct answer.**

**9.** *(c)* All three

- **Statement 1 is correct:** The **Tropical Forest Alliance (TFA)** was indeed founded by the **World Economic Forum (WEF)** in 2012 during the **Rio+20 summit**. It was established to address deforestation, particularly linked to commodity supply chains.
- **Statement 2 is correct:** The TFA focuses on supporting **private-sector commitments** to **eliminate deforestation** from the supply chains of key commodities such as **palm oil, beef, soy and pulp/paper**, which are major drivers of deforestation globally.
- **Statement 3 is correct** : The TFA includes a **broad range of partners** such as **governments, companies, civil society organisations, and indigenous peoples**, all collaborating to reduce deforestation and promote sustainable land use.

**Thus, option (c) is the correct answer.**

**10.** *(a)* 1 and 3 only

- **Statement 1 is correct:** The **One Trillion Trees Initiative** was launched by the **World Economic Forum** (WEF) to grow, restore, and conserve 1 trillion trees globally by **2030**.
- **Statement 2 is incorrect:** The initiative is **global** and not restricted to tropical regions.
- **Statement 3 is correct:** The initiative is part of the **UN Decade on Ecosystem Restoration** and involves **mobilising the private sector,** facilitating partnerships, and inspiring eco-preneurship.

**Thus, option (a) is the correct answer.**

**11.** *(b)* A pledge by 12 developed countries to provide $12 billion in public finance for forest-related climate actions in ODA-eligible countries between 2021-2025.

- The **Global Forest Finance Pledge** is an international commitment to mobilise financial resources for the protection and restoration of forests worldwide. Announced at the **COP26 climate summit** in 2021, the pledge brought together over 20 countries that committed to allocate **$12 billion between 2021 and 2025** to support forest conservation and sustainable land use, particularly in tropical regions.
- This initiative aims to prevent deforestation, enhance reforestation, and promote sustainable land management practices, with a particular emphasis on assisting **developing nations** facing severe environmental and social impacts from forest degradation. By providing financial assistance, the pledge seeks to empower local communities, including **indigenous peoples**, who play a critical role in forest stewardship, to adopt sustainable practices.
- Emphasising **transparency and accountability**, the pledge ensures funds are used effectively to achieve long-term climate and biodiversity goals, aligning with the **Paris Agreement** and **Sustainable Development Goals (SDGs).**

**Thus, the correct answer is (b).**

**12.** *(a)* Only 1, 3 and 4

- **Statement 1 is correct:**The **International Energy Agency (IEA)** was founded in response to the 1970s oil crisis and focuses on **energy policies, including economic development, energy security, and environmental protection.**
- **Statement 2 is incorrect:** Membership in the IEA is open only to **OECD member countries,** but India is an **association country,** not a full member.
- **Statement 3 is correct:** The IEA publishes important reports, including the **World Energy Outlook** and the **India Energy Outlook Report.**

- **Statement 4 is correct:**The IEA provides critical information on the **international oil market** and can take action against **physical disruptions** in oil supply.

**Thus, option (a) is the correct answer.**

**13.** *(b)* Only two

- The **Green Climate Fund** (**GCF**), established in **2010** under the **UNFCCC**, is a global financial mechanism aimed at helping **developing countries** mitigate and adapt to the impacts of **climate change**. It provides funding for projects that reduce greenhouse gas emissions and enhance climate resilience. The GCF mobilises financial resources from developed nations to support sustainable development, clean energy, and adaptation strategies in vulnerable regions. Its goal is to achieve **low-emission** and **climate-resilient** development, contributing to global efforts to combat climate change.
- **Statement 1 is correct**: The GCF functions under the guidance of the COP and serves as the primary fund for climate change finance.
- **Statement 2 is correct**: The GCF's governing Board consists of 24 members, equally representing developed and developing countries.
- **Statement 3 is incorrect**: The GCF aims to mobilise USD 100 billion by 2020, but not solely for mitigation projects; it is intended for both mitigation and adaptation to climate change.

**Thus, option (b) is the correct answer.**

**14.** *(b)* A well-defined area with unique, ecologically fragile ecosystems rich in biodiversity, comprising wild and domesticated species, high endemism, or significant cultural or aesthetic values.

- **Option (a) is incorrect** : This describes wildlife sanctuaries or national parks under the Wildlife Protection Act, 1972, not Biodiversity Heritage Sites under the Biological Diversity Act, 2002.
- **Option (b) is correct** : Under Section 37 of the Biological Diversity Act, 2002, Biodiversity Heritage Sites are areas of biodiversity importance notified by the State Government in consultation with local bodies. These sites are characterised by:
  - Richness of wild and domesticated species.
  - High levels of endemism (species unique to a specific location).
  - Presence of rare and threatened species.
  - Significant ecological, cultural or aesthetic values.
  - Unique or fragile ecosystems (terrestrial, coastal, inland waters or marine).
- **Option (c) is incorrect** : While some BHS may include marine areas, this option is too specific and refers generally to marine protected areas, which are designated under different provisions.
- **Option (d) is incorrect** : Biosphere reserves are areas designated by UNESCO to promote sustainable development, combining conservation of biodiversity with sustainable use. They are not the same as BHS under the Biological Diversity Act.

**Thus, option (b) is the correct answer.**

**15.** *(c)* Statement I is correct, but Statement II is incorrect:

- **Statement I is correct**: The **Biological Diversity (Amendment) Act, 2023** simplifies the patent acquisition process for Indian residents and companies not controlled by foreign entities. They are now required to seek approval from the **National Biodiversity Authority (NBA) only before the grant of a patent**, rather than at earlier stages. This change is intended to streamline the process and reduce unnecessary delays in patent acquisition.
- **Statement II is incorrect**: The Act does aim to reduce bureaucratic hurdles and promote innovation within India; however, it does so by **narrowing**, not expanding, the scope of approval required from the NBA. The requirement is now limited to approval before the grant of a patent, simplifying the process. Therefore, the statement that the Act is **expanding** the scope of approval is incorrect:

**Thus, option (c) is the correct answer.**

**16.** *(c)* The Act decriminalises offenses related to biological resources, focusing on imposing fines rather than criminal sanctions.

- **Option (a) is incorrect:** Contrary to introducing new criminal penalties, the Act actually **decriminalises** offenses, removing criminal sanctions such as imprisonment for violations related to biological resources.
- **Option (b) is incorrect:** The Act does not remove the requirement for benefit-sharing arrangements. In fact, it **mandates fair and equitable benefit-sharing** to ensure that benefits arising from the commercialisation of biological resources are shared fairly with appropriate stakeholders.
- **Option (c) is correct:**The **Biological Diversity (Amendment) Act, 2023** introduces a significant change by **completely decriminalising offenses related to biological resources.** Previously, violations could result in criminal sanctions, including imprisonment. The amendment shifts the regulatory approach to impose **penalties in the form of fines,** aiming to deter violations without resorting to criminal punishment. This change reflects a move towards a more compliance-oriented framework rather than punitive measures.
- **Option (d) is incorrect:**The Act does not eliminate the role of State Biodiversity Boards. Instead, it amends their composition and functions to enhance their capacity to make informed decisions related to benefit-sharing and biodiversity conservation at the state level.

**Thus, option (c) is the correct answer.**

**17.** *(c)* It is a statutory advisory body established in 1962 under the Prevention of Cruelty to Animals Act, 1960.

- **Option (a) is incorrect** : This option is incorrect because the AWBI was established under the **Prevention of Cruelty to Animals Act, 1960,** not the **Wildlife Protection Act,** 1972. The Wildlife Protection Act was enacted later and deals primarily with the protection of wildlife and their habitats, whereas the Prevention of Cruelty to Animals Act focuses on the welfare of animals and prevention of cruelty towards them.
- **Option (b) is incorrect** : The AWBI is not a **Non-Governmental Organisation (NGO);** it is a **statutory advisory body** established by an Act of Parliament. Furthermore, it functions under the **Ministry of Fisheries, Animal Husbandry and Dairying (Department of Animal Husbandry and Dairying),** not under the Ministry of Environment, Forest and Climate Change.
- **Option (c) is correct** : The **Animal Welfare Board of India (AWBI)** is a **statutory advisory body** established in **1962** under **Section 4 of the Prevention of Cruelty to Animals Act, 1960.** Its primary role is to advise the government on animal welfare laws and promote animal welfare in the country. The AWBI ensures that animal welfare laws are diligently followed and provides grants to Animal Welfare Organisations. It also advises the Government of India on animal welfare issues.
- **Option (d) is correct** : While the AWBI does function under the Ministry of Fisheries, Animal Husbandry and Dairying, it is a **statutory advisory body, not an executive body.** Additionally, its headquarters have been shifted from **Chennai, Tamil Nadu,** to **Ballabhgarh, Faridabad, Haryana.**

Therefore, stating that it is headquartered in Chennai is incorrect:

**Thus, option (c) is the correct answer.**

**18.** *(c)* Only three

- **Statement 1 is correct:** As per the **Wild Life (Protection) Amendment Act, 2022,** the **Central Government** now has the authority to declare any area as a conservation reserve. Previously, only the State Governments had this power, but the amendment extends this authority to the Central Government as well.
- **Statement 2 is correct:** The amendment introduces a definition for **Invasive Alien Species,** which was previously undefined in the Act. It defines them as species of animals or plants that are **not native to India** and whose introduction or spread may **threaten or adversely impact wildlife or its habitat.**
- **Statement 3 is correct:** Prior to the amendment, only the **National Board for**

Wildlife had the power to constitute a **Standing Committee**. The amendment empowers State Governments to constitute Standing Committees for their respective **State Boards for Wildlife**. The Standing Committee is to be headed by the Vice-Chairperson, who is the State Minister in charge of Wildlife or Forests, and will have no more than 10 members.

- **Statement 4 is incorrect** : The amendment defines **'Zoo'** as an establishment, whether stationary or mobile, where captive animals are kept for exhibiting to the public or for **ex-situ conservation.** It includes circuses and off-exhibit facilities such as rescue centres and conservation breeding centres. However, it **explicitly excludes** establishments of **licensed dealers in captive animals.** Therefore, licensed dealers' establishments are **not** included in the definition of a zoo.

**Thus, option (c) is the correct answer.**

***19.*** *(a)* Only one

- **Statement 1 is correct** : The Act specifies that if any government property is a live animal and it cannot be released back into its natural habitat, the **State Government** is responsible for ensuring that the animal is housed and cared for by a **recognised zoo or rescue centre.**
- **Statement 2 is incorrect** : While a person holding a certificate of ownership can **surrender** the captive animal, trophy, or animal article to the **Chief Wildlife Warden, no compensation** is paid for such surrender. The surrendered item becomes the property of the **State Government.**
- **Statement 3 is incorrect:** The transfer or transport of a captive elephant by a person with a valid certificate of ownership is **subject to terms and conditions prescribed by the Central Government.** It is not permitted unconditionally.
- **Statement 4 is incorrect** : Such items can be disposed of by the **State Government or Central Government,** but **in the manner prescribed by the Central Government,** not the State Government.

**Thus, option (a) is the correct answer.**

***20.*** *(b)* 1, 2 and 3 only

- **Pair 1 is correct :**
  - **Blackbuck** (Antilope cervicapra) is listed under **Schedule I** of the Act.
  - Schedule I includes animals accorded the highest level of protection.
  - Under the category **'Antelopes'**, Schedule I lists species such as Blackbuck, Chinkara, Four-Horned Antelope, Tibetan Antelope (Chiru) and Tibetan Gazelle.
- **Pair 2 is correct:**
  - **Nilgai** (Boselaphus tragocamelus), also known as the blue bull, is included in **Schedule II.**
  - Schedule II provides protection to animals with lesser protection compared to Schedule I.
  - Other animals in Schedule II include Chitals, Bats, Badgers, Hares, Hedgehogs, Rodents, Pigs, Hanuman Langur, Shrews, Squirrels and Tree Mice.
- **Pair 3 is correct:**
  - **Neel Kurinji** (Strobilanthes kunthiana) is a plant species listed under **Schedule III.**
  - Schedule III specifies plants that are protected.
  - Other plants in Schedule III include Gold Threat, Mishmi Teeta, Tree Turmeric, Common Yew, Blue Vanda, Pitcher Plant, Red Vanda, Daffodil Orchid, Indian Podophyllum and Kuth.
- **Pair 4 is incorrect:**
  - **Schedule V** has been **removed** in the Wild Life (Protection) Amendment Act, 2022.
  - Previously, Schedule V related to **vermins,** which are species that could be hunted.
  - Under the amendment, vermins are now defined as any wild animal specified by the **Central Government** for any period and any area, rather than being listed in a separate schedule.
  - Therefore, there is no Schedule V under the amended Act, making this pair incorrect:

**Thus, option (b) is the correct answer.**

**21.** *(c)* 1, 3 and 4 only

- **Statement 1 is correct:** GEAC was indeed established under the **Ministry of Environment, Forest and Climate Change** (MoEFCC). It functions as the apex body for the appraisal of activities involving genetic engineering in India.
- **Statement 2 is incorrect:** The **Chairman** of GEAC is the **Additional/Special Secretary, MoEFCC**, not the Minister of Environment, Forest and Climate Change.
- **Statement 3 is correct:** The **Vice-Chairman** of GEAC is the **Joint Secretary, MoEFCC.** This aligns with the committee's structured hierarchy as outlined in the rules.
- **Statement 4 is correct:** GEAC is responsible for **approving activities** that involve the large-scale use of **hazardous microorganisms and recombinants** in research and industrial production from an environmental standpoint. This ensures that genetic engineering activities comply with environmental safety standards.

**Thus, option (c) is the correct answer.**

**22.** *(a)* Genetic Engineering Appraisal Committee (GEAC)

The **Genetic Engineering Appraisal Committee (GEAC)** is the apex regulatory body in India responsible for the approval, appraisal, and oversight of activities related to the use of **genetically modified organisms** (GMOs) and **living modified organisms** (LMOs). It operates under the **Ministry of Environment, Forest and Climate Change** (MoEFCC) and is mandated by the **Rules for Manufacture, Use, Import, Export, and Storage of Hazardous Microorganisms/ Genetically Engineered Organisms or Cells,** 1989 under the **Environment Protection Act,** 1986.

- **Statement 1 is correct:** The **Genetic Engineering Appraisal Committee (GEAC)** is established under the **Ministry of Environment, Forest and Climate Change** (MoEFCC).
- **Statement 2 is correct:** GEAC is tasked with **approving activities** that involve the **large-scale use of hazardous microorganisms and recombinants,** ensuring they meet environmental safety standards.
- **Statement 3 is correct:** The **Chairman** of GEAC is the **Additional/Special Secretary, MoEFCC.**
- **Statement 4 is correct:** GEAC operates under the **Rules of 1989,** which outline its functions and authority in regulating genetic engineering activities.

**Thus, option (a) is the correct answer.**

**23.** *(c)* 1, 2 and 4 only

- **Scenario 1 is correct: Failure to submit environmental impact reports** on time would be penalised, as the 2021 amendments propose that companies failing to comply with reporting and information-sharing requirements face penalties rather than imprisonment.
- **Scenario 2 is correct: Contamination of water sources** due to pollutant release is a serious violation that could result in severe penalties under EPA 1986, especially if it endangers public health or the environment.
- **Scenario 3 is incorrect:** Minor violations that are promptly addressed may not attract strict penalties under the new amendment rules, as compliance within a reasonable timeframe is encouraged.
- **Scenario 4 is correct: Illegal cutting of protected trees** is penalised under EPA 1986, as ignorance of the law is generally not a defense for violating environmental protection standards.

**Thus, option (c) is the correct answer.**

**24.** *(a)* BSI focuses on the identification of plant resources, while ZSI focuses on the exploration and research of fauna.

- **Option (a) is correct: Botanical Survey of India (BSI)** focuses on the **identification and documentation of plant resources** in India. It was established in **1890.**
- **Zoological Survey of India (ZSI),** established in **1916,** is responsible for the **exploration and research of the fauna** in the country.
- Both institutions are under the **Ministry of Environment, Forest and Climate Change**

(MoEFCC), and both have their **headquarters in Kolkata.**

- **Option *(b)* is incorrect:** The establishment dates are reversed-BSI was set up in 1890, and ZSI in 1916.
- **Option (c) is incorrect:** Both BSI and ZSI are under the **Ministry of Environment, Forest and Climate Change** (MoEFCC), not the Ministry of Agriculture.
- **Option *(d)* is incorrect:** Both institutions are headquartered in **Kolkata**, not in Delhi.

**Thus, option (a) is the correct answer.**

**25.** *(b)* Only two

- **Statement 1 is correct :** NTPS was introduced to enable the seamless transit of **timber, bamboo and other forest** produce across the country.
- **Statement 2 is correct :** NTPS follows the **'One Nation, One Pass'** system, enabling the issuance of transit permits for both **inter-state and intra-state** transportation.
- **Statement 3 is incorrect :** While NTPS allows the exemption of **some species** grown on private lands from transit permits, not **all species** are exempted. Certain species still require permits even if they are grown on private land.

**Thus, option (b) is the correct answer.**

**26.** *(a)* 1 and 3 only

Under the **National Transit Pass System** (NTPS) in India, a **No-Objection Certificate** (NOC) is required in specific cases to ensure compliance with transit regulations across states for exempted species.

- **Statement 1 is correct:** An NOC is required because, although timber is exempted in the originating state, the destination state requires a **transit pass** for this species. Thus, an NOC facilitates smooth transport across state lines.
- **Statement 2 is incorrect:** Since bamboo is not exempted in the originating state, a transit pass is required rather than an NOC. The transit pass will cover its transportation across states, so an additional NOC is not needed.
- **Statement 3 is correct:** An NOC is required for transporting timber that, while exempted in the originating state, must pass through an en-route state where it is not exempted. The NOC ensures compliance with the en-route state's regulations.

**Thus, option (a) is the correct answer.**

**27.** *(b)* Only two

- **Statement 1 is correct:**The **principal aim** of the National Forest Policy, 1988, is to ensure **environmental stability** and maintain **ecological balance.**
- **Statement 2 is incorrect:** The policy states that **economic benefits** must be **subordinate** to the aim of environmental stability, not take precedence.
- **Statement 3 is correct:** Since the introduction of the policy, forest and tree cover has increased from **19.7%** to **23.4%** of the geographical area.

**Thus, option (b) is the correct answer.**

**28.** *(c)* All three

- **Statement 1 is correct:** The Environment (Protection) Act, 1986, empowers the Central Government to protect and improve environmental quality.
- **Statement 2 is correct:** The Act authorizes the government to **prohibit or restrict** industrial activities based on environmental concerns.
- **Statement 3 is correct :** The Act was last amended in **1991** and extends to the whole of India.

**Thus, option (c) is the correct answer.**

**29.** *(c)* Only 1, 2 and 4

- **Statement 1 is correct:** The **CWMI** was launched by **NITI Aayog** to provide an **annual snapshot** of the water sector and evaluate the performance of states and union territories in managing water resources.
- **Statement 2 is correct:** The CWMI evaluates states based on **nine themes** and **28 indicators**, including factors like **water augmentation, irrigation practices** and **rural drinking water.**

- **Statement 3 is incorrect:** The first edition of the **CWMI** was launched in **2018**, not **2020**, and it covered data from **2015-16** and **2016-17**.
- **Statement 4 is correct:**The **Covid-19 pandemic** caused delays in subsequent editions of the CWMI due to the **unavailability of updated data.**

**Thus, option (c) is the correct answer.**

***30.*** *(b)* By assessing the water management performance of states based on key indicators like irrigation practices, water augmentation, and rural drinking water, and offering a comparison to encourage improvement.

- The **Composite Water Management Index** (CWMI), launched by **NITI Aayog**, provides an annual overview of the status and performance of water management across States and Union Territories in India.

**Genesis and Evolution:**

- The CWMI was first introduced in **June 2018** to address India's water challenges, evaluating states across **28 parameters** using data from **2015-16** and **2016-17**. The **second edition**, released in **August 2019**, assessed data from **2017-18**. This initiative was a collaborative effort involving **NITI Aayog** and the **Ministries of Water Resources, Drinking Water and Sanitation** and **Rural Development.**
- The CWMI helps tackle India's **water challenges by providing an annual assessment of how states and union territories are managing their water resources** based on key indicators.

**Thus,option (b) is the correct answer.**

***31.*** *(c)* 1, 2 and 4 only

- **Statement 1 is correct :** Biodegradable plastics are defined as those capable of degrading without leaving microplastics.
- **Statement 2 is correct:** Microplastics are defined as particles between 1 micron and 1,000 microns.
- **Statement 3 is incorrect :** The definition of 'Importer' includes imports of various plastic-related materials, not just finished products.
- **Statement 4 is correct :** The definition of 'Producer' now includes the production of intermediate materials used in plastic packaging and contract manufacturing for brand owners.

**Thus, option (c) is the correct answer.**

***32.*** *(a)* The cess is levied on water consumed by industries, with the aim of raising funds for the Central and State Pollution Control Boards to prevent and control water pollution.

**The Water (Prevention and Control of Pollution) Cess Act**, enacted in 1977, imposes a cess on water consumed by specific industries. The collected funds are used to support the activities of the **Central Pollution Control Board (CPCB)** and **State Pollution Control Boards (SPCBs)** in their efforts to **prevent and control water pollution.**

**Thus, option (a) is the correct answer.**

***33.*** *(a)* 1, 2, 3 and 4 only

- **Statement 1 is correct:** The Act grants **Title Rights** to FDST and OTFD, allowing them ownership of land that they have been cultivating, subject to a maximum of 4 **hectares.** Ownership is limited to land **currently being cultivated** by the concerned family as of December 13, 2005. **No new lands** are granted under this provision.
- **Statement 2 is correct:** The Act provides **Use Rights** to FDST and OTFD.

  These rights include:

  – **Extraction of Minor Forest Produce (MFP):** Such as fruits, flowers, seeds, medicinal plants, and other non-timber forest products.

  – Access to **grazing areas** for livestock.

  – Use of **pastoralist routes** traditionally followed.
- **Statement 3 is correct:** The Act ensures **Relief and Development Rights** for FDST and OTFD.

  These rights include:

  – **Rehabilitation** in case of **illegal eviction** or **forced displacement.**

  – Access to **basic amenities** and development facilities (e.g., health care, education, infrastructure), subject to forest protection measures.

- **Statement 4 is correct:** The Act grants **Forest Management Rights** to FDST and OTFD. These rights empower communities to:
  - **Protect, regenerate, conserve,** or **manage** any community forest resource.
  - Recognise and support traditional practices of sustainable forest management.
- **Statement 5 is incorrect :** The Act **does not** grant rights to claim **new lands** for cultivation.
  - **Title Rights** are limited to land that is **already being cultivated** by the concerned family.
  - The Act explicitly states that **no new lands will be granted** under its provisions.

**Thus, option (a) is the correct answer.**

**34.** *(c)* Only three

- **Statement 1 is correct:** The Central Government has the power to **order the closure** of any industry, operation, or process contributing to environmental pollution.
- **Statement 2 is correct:** The government can **prohibit or regulate** the supply of **electricity or water** to any industry as a measure to enforce compliance.
- **Statement 3 is incorrect:** The Act specifically mentions the **stoppage or regulation of the supply of electricity or water,** but does not explicitly include services like **gas** or **telephone.**
- **Statement 4 is correct:** The Central Government can **issue directions in writing** to any person or officer, and they are bound to comply.

**Thus, option (c) is the correct answer.**

**35.** *(c)* Only three

- **Statement 1 is correct:** The Act defines 'Environment' as inclusive of water, air, land, and the inter-relationship among them and with human beings, other living creatures, plants, microorganisms, and property.
- **Statement 2 is incorrect:** The correct definition of **'Environmental Pollutant'** is any **solid, liquid, or gaseous substance** present in such concentration as may be **injurious to the environment.** However, the Act defines **'Environmental Pollutant'** as any substance in solid, liquid, or gaseous form **which is injurious to health.**
- **Statement 3 is correct: 'Hazardous Substance'** is defined as any substance or preparation which, by reason of its chemical or physico-chemical properties or handling, is liable to cause harm to human beings, other living creatures, plants, microorganisms, property, or the environment.
- **Statement 4 is correct: 'Occupier'** relates to a factory or premises and means a person who has ultimate control over the affairs, including the owner in the case of a firm or association

**Thus, option (c) is the correct answer.**

**36.** *(c)* The CGWA was formed in 1996 by an executive order under the Environment (Protection) Act, 1986.

- **Option (a) is incorrect:** While the CGWA was established under the provisions of the Environment (Protection) Act, 1986, it was formed through an **executive order,** not by an Act of Parliament specifically creating it as a statutory body.
- **Option (b) is incorrect :** The CGWA functions under the **Ministry of Jal Shakti,** specifically under the **Department of Water Resources, River Development, and Ganga Rejuvenation.**
- **Option (c) is correct:** The **Central Ground Water Authority (CGWA)** was established in **1996** by an **executive order** of the Government of India under the powers conferred by **Section 3(3) of the Environment (Protection) Act, 1986.**
- **Option (d) is incorrect :** The CGWA frames guidelines for sustainable groundwater management in **22 States and Union Territories,** particularly where groundwater development is **not regulated by the respective State or UT Governments.**

**Thus, option (c) is the correct answer.**

**37.** *(a)* Both Statement I and Statement II are correct, and Statement II is the correct explanation for Statement I.

- **Statement I is correct:** The **Mines and Minerals (Development & Regulation) Amendment Act, 2023** removed **six minerals**—lithium, beryllium, titanium, niobium, tantalum, and zirconium—from the list of atomic minerals specified in Part B of the First Schedule of the MMDR Act.
- **Statement II is correct:** Before the amendment, the mining and exploration of atomic minerals listed in Part B of the First Schedule were conducted **exclusively by Public Sector Undertakings (PSUs).**
- **Statement II explains Statement I:** The limitation in exploration and mining due to PSU exclusivity (Statement II) was a key reason for amending the Act to remove these minerals from the atomic minerals list (Statement I).

**Thus, option (a) is the correct answer.**

**38.** *(b)* Lithium, Beryllium, Titanium, Niobium, Tantalum and Zirconium

- **Option (a) is incorrect:** Uranium and Thorium minerals remain classified as atomic minerals due to their radioactive properties and strategic importance.
- **Option (b) is correct:** The Amendment Act removed six minerals from the list of atomic minerals to open them up for private sector exploration and mining:
  - **Lithium** – **Beryllium** – **Titanium**
  - **Niobium** – **Tantalum** – **Zirconium**
- **Option (c) is incorrect:** Molybdenum, Rhenium, Tungsten and Cadmium are considered critical minerals but were not part of the six minerals removed from the atomic minerals list.
- **Option (d) is incorrect:** Copper, Gold, Silver and Diamond are valuable minerals included in the 7th Schedule for exploration licences but were not removed from the atomic minerals list.

**Thus, option (b) is the correct answer.**

**39.** *(b)* The Amendment Act allows private sector participation in the exploration and mining of certain minerals by removing them from the list of atomic minerals.

- **Option (a) is incorrect,** because the **Central Government** is empowered to exclusively auction mining leases and composite licences for certain critical minerals.
- **Option (b) is correct:**The Amendment Act **removed six minerals** from the list of atomic minerals, including **lithium, beryllium, titanium, niobium, tantalum** and **zirconium.**
- **Option (c) is incorrect,** as the **Exploration Licence** introduced by the Amendment Act is granted through an **auction process.**
- **Option (d) is incorrect,** because the **rate of royalty** for **lithium** has been notified as **3%**, not 1%, by the Union Ministry of Mines.

**Thus, option (b) is the correct answer.**

**40.** *(c)* All three

- **Statement 1 is correct:** As per the guidelines for notifying CWH under the Forest Rights Act, 2006, the **Chief Wildlife Warden** is responsible for notifying an **Expert Committee.** This committee is tasked with identifying Critical Wildlife Habitats within national parks or sanctuaries.
- **Statement 2 is correct:** The Forest Rights Act stipulates that before a CWH can be notified, it must be **scientifically and objectively established** that the presence of rights-holders (FDST and OTFD) is causing **irreversible damage** to wildlife and their habitats. Additionally, it must be shown that **co-existence is not a reasonable option** for conservation in that area.
- **Statement 3 is correct:** The guidelines require the Expert Committee to issue a **public notice** when notifying CWH.The public notice must contain **details of the areas** required to be kept inviolate, **criteria adopted** for the identification of CWH, **implications on existing rights** of the forest dwellers and **options for resettlement and rehabilitation schemes**, if applicable.

**Thus, option (c) is the correct answer.**

**41.** *(a)* It is a statutory body established under the Energy Conservation Act, 2001, responsible for implementing policies to improve energy intensity in India.

**Bureau of Energy Efficiency** (BEE):The Bureau of Energy Efficiency (BEE) is a statutory body functioning under the Ministry of Power, focusing on reducing energy intensity through regulatory and promotional measures as per the Energy Conservation Act, 2001.

- **Established:** 1st March, 2002, under the **Energy Conservation Act, 2001**, under the **Ministry of Power.**
- **Mission:** BEE's primary goal is to assist in **developing policies and strategies** for **energy efficiency**, with the objective of **reducing the energy intensity** of India's economy.
- **Functions:** BEE is tasked with both **regulatory** and **promotional functions** as per the provisions of the **Energy Conservation Act, 2001.**
- **Impact:** BEE has contributed to reducing India's energy consumption by approximately **3.5%** through its initiatives

**Thus, option (a) is the correct answer.**

## Past Learning (Answers)

| | | | | | | | | | |
|---|---|---|---|---|---|---|---|---|---|
| **1** (c) | **2** (a) | **3** (a) | **4** (b) | **5** (c) | **6** (b) | **7** (a) | **8** (c) | **9** (b) | **10** (c) |
| **11** (a) | **12** (b) | **13** (a) | **14** (a) | **15** (d) | **16** (c) | **17** (b) | **18** (d) | **19** (a) | **20** (d) |
| **21** (c) | **22** (c) | **23** (a) | **24** (d) | **25** (b) | **26** (a) | | | | |

CHAPTER 08

# Energy Sector

## Assessment Round

**1.** Arrange the following renewable energy sources in India by their installed power capacity from highest to lowest:

1. Biomass Energy
2. Solar Energy
3. Wind Energy
4. Small Hydro Power

Select the correct option from the codes given below:

(a) 2 - 3 - 1 - 4 (b) 3 - 2 - 4 - 1
(c) 2 - 1 - 3 - 4 (d) 3 - 1 - 2 - 4

**2.** India announced specific targets to address climate change at COP26. Which of the following commitments were part of India's announcements?

1. Achieving net-zero emissions by 2070
2. Reducing carbon intensity of GDP by 45% by 2030
3. Meeting 50% of energy needs from renewable sources by 2030
4. Reducing greenhouse gas emissions by 70% by 2025

Select the correct answer from the codes given below:

(a) 1, 2 and 3 only (b) 2 and 4 only
(c) 1, 3 and 4 only (d) 1, 2, 3 and 4

**3.** With reference to the status of renewable energy in India, consider the following statements:

1. India aims to achieve 500 GW of renewable energy capacity by 2030.
2. The share of renewables in India's total electricity generation mix has crossed 30%.
3. Wind energy has the largest installed capacity among all renewable energy sources in India.

How many of the above statements is/are correct?

(a) Only one (b) Only two
(c) All three (d) None

**4.** Which of the following best describes the objective of the LiFE (Lifestyle for Environment) initiative launched by India?

(a) To encourage people to adopt environmentally sustainable lifestyles and reduce their carbon footprints
(b) To promote economic growth through industrial expansion
(c) To establish a global carbon trading platform
(d) To limit international cooperation on climate action

**5.** With reference to the process of solar energy production, consider the following statements:

1. Photovoltaic cells generate electricity by converting light energy into electric energy through the photovoltaic effect.
2. Solar thermal systems directly convert sunlight into electrical energy without the need for heat.
3. Silicon is commonly used as a semiconductor material in solar cells.

How many of the above statements is/are correct?

(a) Only one (b) Only two
(c) All three (d) None

**6.** Consider the following statements:
1. The photovoltaic effect in solar cells causes the movement of electrons, generating direct current (DC) electricity.
2. The efficiency of solar cells can be affected by temperature, shading and material purity.

Which of the statements given above is/are correct?

(a) 1 only (b) 2 only
(c) Both 1 and 2 (d) Neither 1 nor 2

**7.** Consider the following states:
1. Tamil Nadu 2. Rajasthan
3. West Bengal 4. Andhra Pradesh

How many of the given above states has/have high potential for wind energy production?

(a) Only one (b) Only two
(c) Only three (d) All four

**8.** Which of the following benefits are associated with offshore wind energy?
1. Higher energy output due to strong and stable offshore winds
2. Reduced land use conflicts with agriculture and residential zones
3. Lower initial installation costs compared to onshore wind energy

Select the correct answer from the codes given below:

(a) 1 and 2 only (b) 1 and 3 only
(c) 2 and 3 only (d) 1, 2 and 3

**9.** Which of the following best describes the characteristics of the largest wind power plant?

(a) It primarily serves as an experimental site for hybrid wind-solar energy.
(b) Located in Muppandal, it benefits from high wind speeds from the Western Ghats.
(c) It utilises offshore wind turbines exclusively for consistent power generation.
(d) Established in Tirunelveli, focusing solely on small-scale wind farms.

**10.** India has identified various locations with geothermal energy potential. In this context, which of the following areas are known for geothermal activity suitable for energy development?
1. Puga Valley in Ladakh
2. Cambay Basin in Gujarat
3. Manikaran in Himachal Pradesh

Select the correct answer from the codes given below:

(a) 1 and 2 only (b) 1 and 3 only
(c) 2 and 3 only (d) 1, 2 and 3

**11.** What is the primary goal of the 'Global Geothermal Alliance (GGA)'?

(a) To fund geothermal projects exclusively in developing countries
(b) To increase geothermal energy use globally and support clean energy transitions
(c) To research potential sites for geothermal energy without direct implementation
(d) To regulate geothermal energy tariffs across member countries

**12.** Which of the following best describes the principle behind Ocean Thermal Energy Conversion (OTEC)?

(a) It uses tidal movements to generate electricity.
(b) It relies on temperature differences between warmer surface water and colder deep water to produce power.
(c) It captures wave motion energy through mechanical turbines.
(d) It depends on high-pressure gas extraction from deep-sea reservoirs.

**13.** With reference to 'Renewable Purchase Obligations (RPOs)' in India, consider the following statements:
1. RPOs mandate electricity distribution companies (DISCOMS) and other obligated entities to purchase a certain percentage of their total power from renewable energy sources.
2. The RPO targets are set uniformly for all states across India by the Ministry of New and Renewable Energy (MNRE).
3. Solar power has a specific category under RPOs, known as Solar Purchase Obligations (SPOs).

How many of the above statements is/are correct?

(a) Only one (b) Only two
(c) All three (d) None

**14.** With reference to the 'International Solar Alliance (ISA)', consider the following statements:

1. ISA was launched jointly by India and France in COP21 to mobilise efforts for solar energy adoption worldwide.
2. Membership in ISA is open only to countries located between the Tropic of Cancer and Tropic of Capricorn.
3. ISA aims to reduce the cost of financing solar energy projects for member nations.

How many of the above statements is/are correct?

(a) Only one (b) Only two
(c) All three (d) None

**15.** What is the primary objective of the Global Solar Facility created under 'International Solar Alliance (ISA)'?

(a) To create a centralised global marketplace for solar equipment
(b) To finance and support solar projects in developing countries
(c) To enforce global tariffs on solar energy production
(d) To establish solar research centres in high-income countries

**16.** Match the following renewable energy schemes with their objectives:

| | Scheme | | Description |
|---|---|---|---|
| 1. | National Solar Mission | A. | Encourages farmers to install solar pumps and grid-connected solar power projects |
| 2. | Kisan Urja Suraksha Evam UtthaanMahaab hiyan (KUSUM) | B. | Promotes development of solar parks across India |
| 3. | UJALA Scheme | C. | Distribution of energy-efficient LED bulbs across India |

Select the correct option:

(a) 1-A, 2-B, 3-C
(b) 1-B, 2-A, 3-C
(c) 1-C, 2-B, 3-A
(d) 1-B, 2-C, 3-A

**17.** Which of the following best describes a primary advantage of floating solar panels compared to traditional ground-mounted panels?

(a) Floating panels require no maintenance due to natural water cleaning.
(b) They help reduce water evaporation and algae growth on water bodies.
(c) Floating panels are exclusively used for offshore ocean installations.
(d) They generate double the electricity as ground-mounted solar panels.

**18.** Which of the following statements regarding the Global Renewables and Energy Efficiency Pledge at COP28 is/are correct?

1. The pledge aims to triple the world's installed renewable energy generation capacity by 2030.
2. The pledge calls for doubling the global average annual rate of energy efficiency improvements from around 2% to over 4% every year until 2030.
3. The pledge is mandatory for all countries and includes penalties for non-compliance.

Select the correct answer using the codes given below:

(a) 1 only (b) 1 and 2 only
(c) 2 and 3 only (d) 1, 2 and 3

**19.** Consider the following pairs related to solar energy initiatives:

| | Initiative | Focus |
|---|---|---|
| 1. | One Sun One World One Grid (OSOWOG) | Focuses on building solar energy projects exclusively in Africa. |
| 2. | Solar Technology Application Resource Centre (STAR-C) | Focuses on capacity-building and institutional strengthening in the solar energy sector. |
| 3. | Global Solar Facility | Aims to catalyse solar investments in underserved regions, particularly across Africa. |

How many above pairs is/are correctly matched?

(a) Only one (b) Only two
(c) All three (d) None

**20.** With reference to the Green Energy Open Access Rules (GOAR) 2022, consider the following statements:

1. Open Access (OA) means non-discriminatory access to electricity transmission and distribution systems for eligible consumers, generators, and state distribution companies (DISCOMs).
2. The minimum transaction limit for green energy open access has been reduced from 1 MW to 100 kW.
3. DISCOMs are obligated to procure and supply green power to consumers only on a mandatory basis.

Which of the statements given above are correct?

(a) 1 and 2 only (b) 2 and 3 only
(c) 1 and 3 only (d) 1, 2 and 3

**21.** With reference to Biofuels, consider the following statements:

1. First-generation biofuels are derived from edible feedstock such as sugarcane and beets.
2. Second-generation biofuels are produced from non-food crops and waste biomass like Jatropha and Pongamia.
3. Third-generation biofuels are derived from genetically modified microorganisms.
4. Fourth-generation biofuels are produced from algal biomass.

How many of the statements given above is/are correct?

(a) Only one (b) Only two
(c) Only three (d) All four

**22.** Match the following biofuels with their description:

| Biofuel | Description |
|---|---|
| 1. Ethanol | A. Produced from vegetable oils and animal fats |
| 2. Biodiesel | B. Can be blended with petrol and produced from sugarcane |
| 3. Compressed Biogas (CBG) | C. Methane-rich fuel produced from agricultural and organic waste |

Select the correct option:

(a) 1-A, 2-B, 3-C
(b) 1-B, 2-A, 3-C
(c) 1-C, 2-A, 3-B
(d) 1-B, 2-C, 3-A

**23.** In the context of the Compressed Bio Gas (CBG) Blending Obligation (CBO) introduced by the Ministry of Petroleum & Natural Gas, which of the following actions aligns with the goals of the CBO Roadmap?

1. Mandatory blending of CBG in CNG/PNG begins from FY 2025-26.
2. The blending percentage of CBG in CNG/PNG will gradually increase to 5% from FY 2028-29 onwards.
3. The blending obligation is optional for companies up to FY 2028-29.

Select the correct answer using the codes given below:

(a) 1 and 2 only
(b) 2 and 3 only
(c) 1 and 3 only
(d) 1, 2 and 3

**24.** Consider the following statements about 'Sustainable Alternative Towards Affordable Transportation (SATAT)' initiative:

1. The SATAT initiative was launched in 2018 to encourage the setting up of Compressed Bio Gas (CBG) plants by entrepreneurs.
2. Oil Marketing Companies (OMCs) purchase CBG from entrepreneurs and supply it as an automotive and industrial fuel.
3. Ministry of New and Renewable Energy (MNRE) is the nodal ministry responsible for implementing the SATAT initiative.

How many of the statements given above is/are correct?

(a) Only one
(b) Only two
(c) All three
(d) None

**25.** Which of the following best describes Methanol Diesel-15 (MD15) developed by Indian Railways' Research Design and Standards Organisation (RDSO) and Indian Oil Corporation Ltd. (IOCL)?
(a) MD15 is a special fuel blend consisting of 15% methanol, 71% biodiesel, and 14% water.
(b) MD15 is a blend that includes 15% methanol, 71% mineral diesel and 14% coupler additives.
(c) MD15 is a synthetic fuel made entirely from methanol for use in diesel engines.
(d) MD15 is a fuel mix of 85% ethanol and 15% mineral diesel.

**26.** Which of the following correctly describes 'Reference Fuel'?
(a) It refers to alternative fuels derived from biomass for testing fuel efficiency.
(b) It represents high-value premium fuels, such as petrol and diesel, used for vehicle calibration and testing by automotive manufacturers.
(c) It is a blend of biofuels used for reducing vehicle emissions.
(d) It refers to aviation-grade fuels used in jet engine testing.

**27.** Which of the following statements best describes bio-diesel?
(a) Bio-diesel is made only from edible oils such as soybean or rapeseed oil and is widely used in India for fuel blending.
(b) Bio-diesel is made from non-edible oils or used cooking oil in India and is environmentally friendly with no sulphur and about 10% built-in oxygen.
(c) Bio-diesel requires specialised infrastructure for storage and dispensing and cannot be blended with conventional diesel.
(d) Bio-diesel is unsafe to handle because its flash points are lower than those of conventional diesel.

**28.** Which of the following best describes bio-jet fuel used in India's first-ever bio-jet fuel flight?
(a) It is a synthetic fuel produced from coal and used exclusively in military aircraft.
(b) It is a biofuel made from biomass sources such as jatropha, used in combination with Air Turbine Fuel (ATF) to power aircraft.
(c) It is a renewable energy source derived from wind energy, used to supplement traditional fuels in aviation.
(d) It is a type of fuel produced from nuclear energy, aimed at reducing carbon emissions in aviation.

**29.** With reference to e-Fuels, consider the following statements:
1. e-Fuels are produced using electricity from renewable sources, water and $CO_2$ extracted from the air.
2. e-Fuels release additional $CO_2$ into the atmosphere during combustion.
3. e-Fuels can be used in existing internal combustion engines without requiring modifications.

Which of the statements given above are correct?
(a) 1 and 3 only (b) 1 and 2 only
(c) 2 and 3 only (d) 1, 2 and 3

**30.** Which of the following best describes the primary composition of biogas?
(a) Mainly carbon monoxide and oxygen
(b) Primarily methane and carbon dioxide
(c) High levels of nitrogen and ammonia
(d) Equal proportions of methane, hydrogen and carbon monoxide

**31.** With reference to the National Policy on Biofuels, 2018, consider the following statements:
1. The policy promotes the production of biofuels from non-food feedstocks to avoid food security concerns.
2. The policy allows the blending of ethanol with petrol up to 20%.
3. It provides incentives for the production of ethanol from sugarcane only.

How many of the above statements is/are correct?
(a) Only one (b) Only two
(c) All three (d) None

**32.** With reference to 'India's Ethanol Blending Programme (EBP)', consider the following statements:

1. It was first introduced in 2003 with a mandate for 5% blending of ethanol with petrol and now aims to achieve 20% ethanol blending by 2025.
2. The government offers a differential price for ethanol based on its source such as sugarcane juice or surplus grains.
3. India achieved a 10% ethanol blending target with petrol in 2022.

Which of the above statements are correct?

(a) 1 and 2 only (b) 2 and 3 only
(c) 1 and 3 only (d) 1, 2 and 3

**33.** Which of the following raw materials are permitted for biofuel production under the National Policy on Biofuels?

1. Rotten potatoes
2. Excess rice stocks
3. Municipal Solid Waste (MSW)
4. Fresh food grains reserved for the Public Distribution System (PDS)

Select the correct answer using the codes given below:

(a) 1, 2 and 3 only
(b) 1 and 3 only
(c) 2 and 4 only
(d) 1, 2, 3 and 4

**34.** Consider the following statements about the 'Global Biofuel Alliance (GBA)', launched during the G20 Summit held in New Delhi, 2023:

1. Only G20 countries are eligible to join GBA.
2. India, Brazil and the United States jointly initiated the Alliance.
3. The Alliance exclusively promotes first-generation biofuels.

How many of the statements given above is/are correct?

(a) Only one (b) Only two
(c) All three (d) None

**35.** With reference to the methods of hydrogen production, consider the following processes:

1. Steam Methane Reforming (SMR)
2. Electrolysis of water
3. Biomass gasification
4. Nuclear fusion

How many of the given above methods is/are currently viable for producing hydrogen on a commercial scale?

(a) Only one (b) Only two
(c) Only three (d) All four

**36.** Consider the following statements about different types of hydrogen production:

1. Green hydrogen is produced through electrolysis using renewable energy sources such as solar, wind or hydel, resulting in zero carbon emissions.
2. Grey hydrogen is produced using fossil fuels like natural gas or coal, with carbon emissions released into the air.
3. Pink/Red hydrogen is produced through electrolysis using nuclear energy.
4. Brown hydrogen is produced using coal, with emissions directly released into the atmosphere.

How many of the above statements is/are correct?

(a) Only one (b) Only two
(c) Only three (d) All four

**37.** Consider the following statements:

**Assertion** (A): Hydrogen fuel cell buses can significantly contribute to the decarbonisation of transportation.

**Reason** (R): Hydrogen fuel cells generate electricity through an electrochemical reaction between hydrogen and oxygen, producing water as the only byproduct and no harmful emissions.

Which one of the following is correct?

(a) Both Assertion (A) and Reason (R) are correct, and Reason (R) is the correct explanation of Assertion (A).
(b) Both Assertion (A) and Reason (R) are correct, but Reason (R) is not the correct explanation of Assertion (A).
(c) Assertion (A) is correct, but Reason (R) is incorrect.
(d) Assertion (A) is incorrect, but Reason (R) is correct.

**38.** Which of the following benefits are associated with the use of 'Hydrogen Enriched Compressed Natural Gas (HCNG)' as a fuel?

1. Reduced greenhouse gas emissions
2. Enhanced fuel efficiency
3. Improved engine life by reducing carbon buildup
4. Lower production costs compared to conventional CNG

Select the correct answer from the codes given below:

(a) 1, 2 and 3 only (b) 1 and 3 only
(c) 2, 3, and 4 only (d) 1, 2, 3 and 4

**39.** With reference to 'Green Hydrogen', consider the following statements:

1. It can be used directly as a fuel for internal combustion.
2. It can be blended with natural gas and used as fuel for heat or power generation.
3. It can be used in hydrogen fuel cells to run vehicles.

How many of the above statements is/are correct?

(a) Only one (b) Only two
(c) All three (d) None

**40.** With reference to the 'National Green Hydrogen Mission', consider the following statements:

1. Ministry of New and Renewable Energy (MNRE) is the nodal agency responsible for implementing the mission.
2. The mission includes financial incentives to support the establishment of hydrogen production facilities from coal-based sources.
3. A primary objective of the mission is to achieve 5 million metric tonnes (MMT) of green hydrogen production annually by 2030.

Which of the statements given above are correct?

(a) 1 and 2 only (b) 1 and 3 only
(c) 2 and 3 only (d) 1, 2 and 3

**41.** Regarding the Green Hydrogen and Ammonia policy, consider the following statements:

1. It aims to provide free power transmission for 25 years for new renewable energy facilities built before July 2025.
2. The policy mandates that all energy plants for green hydrogen production be connected to the grid on a priority basis.
3. Green hydrogen and ammonia production will not be allowed in India for export.

Which of the statements given above are correct?

(a) 1 and 2 only (b) 2 and 3 only
(c) 1 and 3 only (d) 1, 2 and 3

**42.** The Green Hydrogen Catapult initiative primarily focuses on which of the following?

(a) Establishing a global network of fossil-fuel-based hydrogen plants.
(b) Supporting infrastructure only for hydrogen-powered vehicles.
(c) Reducing the cost of green hydrogen production to less than $2/kg.
(d) Encouraging investments solely from private sector companies.

**43.** Which of the following best describes the purpose of coal beneficiation?

(a) To increase the ash content of coal for better energy output.
(b) To reduce impurities and enhance the quality of coal.
(c) To decrease the carbon content in coal for use in the steel industry.
(d) To increase moisture in coal to improve transportation safety.

**44.** With reference to 'Coal Gasification', consider the following statements:

1. It is a process that converts coal into syngas.
2. It produces fewer sulphur dioxide and nitrogen oxide emissions compared to traditional coal combustion.
3. The by-products of coal gasification are entirely biodegradable.

Which of the statements given above are correct?

(a) 1 and 2 only (b) 1 and 3 only
(c) 2 and 3 only (d) 1, 2 and 3

**45.** Which of the following describes a primary environmental advantage of supercritical thermal power plants over conventional subcritical plants?
(a) Supercritical plants consume less fuel per unit of electricity produced, resulting in fewer greenhouse gas emissions and a smaller carbon footprint, aligning with global environmental goals.
(b) They operate at lower efficiency levels, requiring increased coal consumption and leading to higher carbon emissions and environmental impact.
(c) Supercritical plants have minimal impact on emission levels and provide limited improvements in fuel efficiency.
(d) They produce fewer by-products, making waste management cheaper but with minimal environmental impact.

**46.** Which of the following best differentiates Flue Gas Desulphurisation (FGD) from Circulating Fluidised Bed Combustion (CFBC)?
(a) FGD focuses on removing sulfur compounds after combustion, while CFBC uses a pre-combustion process to prevent sulfur from entering the emissions.
(b) FGD is a post-combustion process for removing sulfur dioxide from exhaust gases, while CFBC is a combustion technology that reduces the emission of both sulfur oxides and nitrogen oxides during the combustion process.
(c) Both FGD and CFBC operate on the same principle and are used interchangeably in reducing sulfur dioxide emissions from fossil fuel power plants.
(d) FGD removes carbon dioxide from flue gas, while CFBC is a method of improving combustion efficiency without impacting sulfur emissions.

**47.** Regarding the implementation of Carbon Capture, Utilisation, and Storage (CCUS) technology in India, consider the following statements:
1. CCUS involves capturing carbon emissions primarily from large industrial sources such as power plants and refineries.
2. Captured $CO_2$ is only stored underground, and there is no utilisation of $CO_2$ for other industrial purposes.
3. The CCUS process contributes to India's goal of achieving net-zero emissions by 2070, as highlighted by NITI Aayog's policy framework.

Which of the statements given above is/are correct?
(a) 1 and 3 only (b) 2 and 3 only
(c) 1 only (d) 1, 2 and 3

**48.** Which of the following best explains the primary function of an electrostatic precipitator in industrial settings?
(a) It captures particulate matter from exhaust gases by ionising particles, which are then attracted to charged collection plates.
(b) It cools down exhaust gases to prevent the release of hot emissions into the atmosphere.
(c) It removes nitrogen oxides and sulphur dioxides from emissions by chemical scrubbing.
(d) It uses high-pressure water sprays to capture pollutants in industrial exhaust.

**49.** With reference to the 'Bureau of Energy Efficiency (BEE)', consider the following statements:
1. It was established under the Energy Conservation Act, 2001, to promote energy efficiency and conservation in India.
2. The Energy Conservation Building Code (ECBC), implemented by BEE is applicable to residential buildings only.

Which of the given above statements is/are correct?
(a) 1 only (b) 2 only
(c) Both 1 and 2 (d) Neither 1 nor 2

**50.** Consider the following sectors:
1. Iron and Steel
2. Cement
3. IT and Software Services
4. Thermal Power Plants

How many of the above sectors is/are typically designated as consumers under the Energy Conservation Act, 2001?
(a) Only one (b) Only two
(c) Only three (d) All four

**51.** With reference to the 'Energy Saving Certificates (ESCerts)' in India, consider the following statements:

1. ESCerts are issued to industrial units that achieve energy savings beyond their mandated targets under the Perform, Achieve, and Trade (PAT) scheme.
2. ESCerts can only be traded among industrial units within the same sector.
3. These are a part of the National Action Plan on Climate Change, under the National Mission for Enhanced Energy Efficiency (NMEEE).

Which of the statements given above is/are correct?

(a) 1 and 2 only (b) 3 only
(c) 1 and 3 only (d) 1, 2 and 3

**52.** With reference to 'Energy Efficiency Services Limited (EESL)', consider the following statements:

1. It implemented the Smart Meter National Programme (SMNP) to promote the use of smart meters in India.
2. EESL exclusively works in the industrial sector to promote energy efficiency initiatives.
3. It operates under the Ministry of Environment, Forest and Climate Change.

Which of the above statements is/are correct?

(a) 1 only
(b) 1 and 3 only
(c) 2 and 3 only
(d) 1, 2 and 3

**53.** What is the primary purpose of Eco Niwas Samhita (ENS) in the context of building construction standards in India?

(a) To establish guidelines for earthquake-resistant construction practices across residential and commercial buildings
(b) To set energy efficiency standards for residential buildings in order to reduce energy consumption and promote sustainability
(c) To mandate the use of green building materials in urban infrastructure projects exclusively
(d) To provide a framework for water conservation measures in industrial buildings only

**54.** With reference to the Energy Conservation Building Code (ECBC), consider the following statements:

1. The ECBC mandates energy efficiency standards for new commercial and residential buildings in India.
2. It includes guidelines for lighting, ventilation, and building insulation to reduce energy consumption.
3. ECBC implementation varies across states, with each state having the authority to enforce or modify the code.

Which of the above statements are correct?

(a) 1 and 2 only (b) 2 and 3 only
(c) 1 and 3 only (d) 1, 2, and 3

**55.** Consider the following appliances:

1. Ceiling fans
2. LED lamps
3. Room air conditioners
4. Electric irons

How many of the given above appliances are covered under the mandatory standards of the Standards and Labelling Programme?

(a) Only one (b) Only two
(c) Only three (d) All four

**56.** With reference to the 'state Energy Efficiency Index (SEEI)', consider the following statements:

1. It is an initiative launched by the Bureau of Energy Efficiency (BEE) to evaluate states' performance in implementing energy efficiency policies.
2. It ranks Indian states based solely on industrial sector efficiency.
3. It incorporates sectors such as transport, industry, and municipal energy use to assess state performance.

Which of the above statements are correct?

(a) 1 and 2 only
(b) 1 and 3 only
(c) 2 and 3 only
(d)1, 2 and 3

# OMR SHEET

**Assessment Round**

| | | | | | | | |
|---|---|---|---|---|---|---|---|
| 1 | ⓐ ⓑ ⓒ ⓓ | 31 | ⓐ ⓑ ⓒ ⓓ | 61 | ⓐ ⓑ ⓒ ⓓ | 91 | ⓐ ⓑ ⓒ ⓓ |
| 2 | ⓐ ⓑ ⓒ ⓓ | 32 | ⓐ ⓑ ⓒ ⓓ | 62 | ⓐ ⓑ ⓒ ⓓ | 92 | ⓐ ⓑ ⓒ ⓓ |
| 3 | ⓐ ⓑ ⓒ ⓓ | 33 | ⓐ ⓑ ⓒ ⓓ | 63 | ⓐ ⓑ ⓒ ⓓ | 93 | ⓐ ⓑ ⓒ ⓓ |
| 4 | ⓐ ⓑ ⓒ ⓓ | 34 | ⓐ ⓑ ⓒ ⓓ | 64 | ⓐ ⓑ ⓒ ⓓ | 94 | ⓐ ⓑ ⓒ ⓓ |
| 5 | ⓐ ⓑ ⓒ ⓓ | 35 | ⓐ ⓑ ⓒ ⓓ | 65 | ⓐ ⓑ ⓒ ⓓ | 95 | ⓐ ⓑ ⓒ ⓓ |
| 6 | ⓐ ⓑ ⓒ ⓓ | 36 | ⓐ ⓑ ⓒ ⓓ | 66 | ⓐ ⓑ ⓒ ⓓ | 96 | ⓐ ⓑ ⓒ ⓓ |
| 7 | ⓐ ⓑ ⓒ ⓓ | 37 | ⓐ ⓑ ⓒ ⓓ | 67 | ⓐ ⓑ ⓒ ⓓ | 97 | ⓐ ⓑ ⓒ ⓓ |
| 8 | ⓐ ⓑ ⓒ ⓓ | 38 | ⓐ ⓑ ⓒ ⓓ | 68 | ⓐ ⓑ ⓒ ⓓ | 98 | ⓐ ⓑ ⓒ ⓓ |
| 9 | ⓐ ⓑ ⓒ ⓓ | 39 | ⓐ ⓑ ⓒ ⓓ | 69 | ⓐ ⓑ ⓒ ⓓ | 99 | ⓐ ⓑ ⓒ ⓓ |
| 10 | ⓐ ⓑ ⓒ ⓓ | 40 | ⓐ ⓑ ⓒ ⓓ | 70 | ⓐ ⓑ ⓒ ⓓ | 100 | ⓐ ⓑ ⓒ ⓓ |
| 11 | ⓐ ⓑ ⓒ ⓓ | 41 | ⓐ ⓑ ⓒ ⓓ | 71 | ⓐ ⓑ ⓒ ⓓ | 101 | ⓐ ⓑ ⓒ ⓓ |
| 12 | ⓐ ⓑ ⓒ ⓓ | 42 | ⓐ ⓑ ⓒ ⓓ | 72 | ⓐ ⓑ ⓒ ⓓ | 102 | ⓐ ⓑ ⓒ ⓓ |
| 13 | ⓐ ⓑ ⓒ ⓓ | 43 | ⓐ ⓑ ⓒ ⓓ | 73 | ⓐ ⓑ ⓒ ⓓ | 103 | ⓐ ⓑ ⓒ ⓓ |
| 14 | ⓐ ⓑ ⓒ ⓓ | 44 | ⓐ ⓑ ⓒ ⓓ | 74 | ⓐ ⓑ ⓒ ⓓ | 104 | ⓐ ⓑ ⓒ ⓓ |
| 15 | ⓐ ⓑ ⓒ ⓓ | 45 | ⓐ ⓑ ⓒ ⓓ | 75 | ⓐ ⓑ ⓒ ⓓ | 105 | ⓐ ⓑ ⓒ ⓓ |
| 16 | ⓐ ⓑ ⓒ ⓓ | 46 | ⓐ ⓑ ⓒ ⓓ | 76 | ⓐ ⓑ ⓒ ⓓ | 106 | ⓐ ⓑ ⓒ ⓓ |
| 17 | ⓐ ⓑ ⓒ ⓓ | 47 | ⓐ ⓑ ⓒ ⓓ | 77 | ⓐ ⓑ ⓒ ⓓ | 107 | ⓐ ⓑ ⓒ ⓓ |
| 18 | ⓐ ⓑ ⓒ ⓓ | 48 | ⓐ ⓑ ⓒ ⓓ | 78 | ⓐ ⓑ ⓒ ⓓ | 108 | ⓐ ⓑ ⓒ ⓓ |
| 19 | ⓐ ⓑ ⓒ ⓓ | 49 | ⓐ ⓑ ⓒ ⓓ | 79 | ⓐ ⓑ ⓒ ⓓ | 109 | ⓐ ⓑ ⓒ ⓓ |
| 20 | ⓐ ⓑ ⓒ ⓓ | 50 | ⓐ ⓑ ⓒ ⓓ | 80 | ⓐ ⓑ ⓒ ⓓ | 110 | ⓐ ⓑ ⓒ ⓓ |
| 21 | ⓐ ⓑ ⓒ ⓓ | 51 | ⓐ ⓑ ⓒ ⓓ | 81 | ⓐ ⓑ ⓒ ⓓ | 111 | ⓐ ⓑ ⓒ ⓓ |
| 22 | ⓐ ⓑ ⓒ ⓓ | 52 | ⓐ ⓑ ⓒ ⓓ | 82 | ⓐ ⓑ ⓒ ⓓ | 112 | ⓐ ⓑ ⓒ ⓓ |
| 23 | ⓐ ⓑ ⓒ ⓓ | 53 | ⓐ ⓑ ⓒ ⓓ | 83 | ⓐ ⓑ ⓒ ⓓ | 113 | ⓐ ⓑ ⓒ ⓓ |
| 24 | ⓐ ⓑ ⓒ ⓓ | 54 | ⓐ ⓑ ⓒ ⓓ | 84 | ⓐ ⓑ ⓒ ⓓ | 114 | ⓐ ⓑ ⓒ ⓓ |
| 25 | ⓐ ⓑ ⓒ ⓓ | 55 | ⓐ ⓑ ⓒ ⓓ | 85 | ⓐ ⓑ ⓒ ⓓ | 115 | ⓐ ⓑ ⓒ ⓓ |
| 26 | ⓐ ⓑ ⓒ ⓓ | 56 | ⓐ ⓑ ⓒ ⓓ | 86 | ⓐ ⓑ ⓒ ⓓ | 116 | ⓐ ⓑ ⓒ ⓓ |
| 27 | ⓐ ⓑ ⓒ ⓓ | 57 | ⓐ ⓑ ⓒ ⓓ | 87 | ⓐ ⓑ ⓒ ⓓ | 117 | ⓐ ⓑ ⓒ ⓓ |
| 28 | ⓐ ⓑ ⓒ ⓓ | 58 | ⓐ ⓑ ⓒ ⓓ | 88 | ⓐ ⓑ ⓒ ⓓ | 118 | ⓐ ⓑ ⓒ ⓓ |
| 29 | ⓐ ⓑ ⓒ ⓓ | 59 | ⓐ ⓑ ⓒ ⓓ | 89 | ⓐ ⓑ ⓒ ⓓ | 119 | ⓐ ⓑ ⓒ ⓓ |
| 30 | ⓐ ⓑ ⓒ ⓓ | 60 | ⓐ ⓑ ⓒ ⓓ | 90 | ⓐ ⓑ ⓒ ⓓ | 120 | ⓐ ⓑ ⓒ ⓓ |

## Calculate Your Score

| | |
|---|---|
| **Correct (✓)** | |
| **Incorrect (✓)** | |
| **Unattempted** | |
| **Total Score** | |
| **Accuracy (%)** | |

## Reasons for Incorrect Answers?

| | |
|---|---|
| 1. Lack of Knowledge/Existing Source Insufficient | |
| 2. Lack of Multiple Revision | |
| 3. Common Sense Mistakes | |

**Note :**

1. Calculate total score as correct answers carry 2 marks each 1/3rd marks will deducted for **Incorrect** Answers.
2. Calculate Accuracy (%) by dividing the number of correct answers to the total number of attempted questions.

## Past Learning

**1.** Consider the following: **(2024)**

1. Battery storage
2. Biomass generators
3. Fuel cells
4. Rooftop solar photovoltaic units

How many of the above are considered 'Distributed Energy Resources'?

(a) Only one (b) Only two
(c) Only three (d) All four

**2.** Consider the following materials: **(2024)**

1. Agricultural residues
2. Corn grain
3. Wastewater treatment sludge
4. Wood mill waste

Which of the above can be used as feedstock for producing Sustainable Aviation Fuel?

(a) 1 and 2 only (b) 3 and 4 only
(c) 1, 2, 3 and 4 (d) 1, 3 and 4 only

**3.** Consider the following infrastructure sectors: **(2023)**

1. Affordable housing
2. Mass rapid transport
3. Health care
4. Renewable energy

On how many of the above do/does UNOPS Sustainable Investments in Infrastructure and Innovation (S3i) initiative focus for its investments?

(a) Only one (b) Only two
(c) Only three (d) All Four

**4.** With reference to coal-based thermal power plants in India, consider the following statements : **(2023)**

1. None of them uses seawater.
2. None of them is set up in water-stressed district.
3. None of them is privately owned.

How many of the above statements is/are correct?

(a) Only one (b) Only two
(c) All three (d) None

**5.** With reference to 'palm oil', consider the following statements : **(2021)**

1. The palm oil tree is native to South-East Asia.
2. The palm oil is a raw material for some industries producing lipstick and perfumes.
3. The palm oil can be used to produce biodiesel.

Which of the statements given above are correct?

(a) 1 and 2 only (b) 2 and 3 only
(c) 1 and 3 only (d) 1, 2 and 3

**6.** According to India's National Policy on Biofuels, which of the following can be used as raw materials for the production of biofuels? **(2020)**

1. Cassava
2. Damaged wheat grains
3. Groundnut seeds
4. Horse gram
5. Rotten potatoes
6. Sugar beet

Select the correct answer using the codes given below:

(a) 1, 2, 5 and 6 only (b) 1, 3, 4 and 6 only
(c) 2, 3, 4 and 5 only (d) 1, 2, 3, 4, 5 and 6

**7.** In the context of proposals to the use of Hydrogen-enriched CNG (H-CNG) as fuel for buses in public transport, consider the following statements : **(2019)**

1. The main advantage of the use of H-CNG is the elimination of carbon monoxide emissions.
2. H-CNG as fuel reduces carbon dioxide emissions. and hydrocarbon
3. Hydrogen up to one-fifth by volume can be blended with CNG as fuel for buses.
4. H-CNG makes the fuel less expensive than CNG.

Which of the statements given above is/are correct?

(a) 1 only (b) 2 and 3 only
(c) 4 only (d) 1, 2, 3 and 4

**8.** It is possible to produce algae-based biofuels, but what is/are the likely limitation(s) of developing countries in promoting this industry? **(2017)**

1. Production of algae-based biofuels is possible in seas only and not on continents.
2. Setting up and engineering the algae-based biofuel production requires high level of expertise/technology until the construction is completed.
3. Economically viable production necessitates the setting up of large-scale facilities which may raise ecological and social concerns.

Select the correct answer using the codes given below:

(a) 1 and 2 only
(b) 2 and 3 only
(c) 3 only
(d) 1, 2 and 3

**9.** 'Net metering' is sometimes seen in the news in the context of promoting the **(2016)**

(a) production and use of solar energy by the households/consumers
(b) use of piped natural gas in the kitchens of households
(c) installation of CNG kits in motor cars
(d) installation of water meters in urban households.

**10.** Consider the following statements: **(2016)**

1. The Sustainable Development Goals were first proposed in 1972 by a global think tank called the 'Club of Rome'.
2. The Sustainable Development Goals have to be achieved by 2030.

Which of the statements given above is/are correct?

(a) 1 only
(b) 2 only
(c) Both 1 and 2
(d) Neither 1 nor 2

**11.** Consider the following statements: **(2016)**

1. The International Solar Alliance was launched at the United Nations Climate Change Conference in 2015.
2. The Alliance includes all the member countries of the United Nations.

Which of the statements given above is/are correct?

(a) 1 only (b) 2 only
(c) Both 1 and 2 (d) Neither 1 nor 2

**12.** In India, cluster bean (Guar) is traditionally used as a vegetable or animal feed, but recently the cultivation of this has assumed significance. Which one of the following statements is correct in this context? **(2014)**

(a) The oil extracted from seeds is used in the manufacture of biodegradable plastics
(b) The gum made from its seeds is used in the extraction of shale gas
(c) The leaf extract of this plant has the properties of antihistamines
(d) It is a source of high-quality biodiesel

**13.** Biomass gasification is considered to be one of the sustainable solutions to the power crisis in India. In this context, which of the following statements is/are correct? **(2012)**

1. Coconut shells, groundnut shells, and rice husks can be used in biomass gasification.
2. The combustible gases generated from biomass gasification consist of hydrogen and carbon dioxide only.
3. The combustible gases generated from biomass gasification can be used for direct heat generation but not in internal combustion engines.

Select the correct answer using the codes given below :

(a) 1 only (b) 2 and 3 only
(c) 1 and 3 only (d) 1, 2 and 3

# Detailed Solutions

## Assessment Round

**1.** *(a)* 2 - 3 - 1 - 4

- **Solar Energy:** Solar energy has the highest installed capacity among renewable energy sources in India.
- **Wind Energy:** Wind power is the second largest contributor to renewable energy capacity.
- **Biomass Energy:** Biomass energy, while significant, is smaller in capacity compared to solar and wind.
- **Small Hydro Power:** Small hydro power contributes the least among these categories to India's total installed renewable energy capacity.

**Thus, the correct order is (a) 2 - 3 - 1 - 4.**

**2.** *(a)* 1, 2 and 3 only

India's major commitments at COP26 include targets aimed at reducing emissions, promoting renewable energy and achieving climate resilience:

- **Statement 1 is correct:** India pledged to achieve **net-zero emissions by 2070**. This means balancing greenhouse gas emissions with removal measures, signifying India's long-term dedication to climate neutrality.
- **Statement 2 is correct:** India committed to reducing the **carbon intensity of its GDP by 45% by 2030**. This involves decreasing emissions per unit of GDP, thus promoting sustainable economic growth with lower carbon footprints.
- **Statement 3 is correct:** Another key commitment is to **meet 50% of India's energy needs from renewable sources by 2030**, which includes ramping up solar, wind and other green energy capacities.
- **Statement 4 is incorrect:** There was no target to reduce greenhouse gas emissions by 70% by 2025. India's commitments focused on 2030 and 2070 as target years.

**Thus, the correct answer is (a) 1, 2 and 3 only.**

**3.** *(b)* Only two

- **Statement 1 is correct:** India has set a goal to achieve **500 GW of renewable energy capacity by 2030**, which is part of its commitment to reducing carbon emissions and transitioning to clean energy sources.
- **Statement 2 is correct:** As of 2024, the share of renewables (including Hydropower) in India's total electricity generation mix exceeded 40%.
- **Statement 3 is incorrect: Wind energy** was the leading renewable energy source in terms of installed capacity, but in recent years, **solar energy** has gained significant ground, and now **solar energy** surpasses wind in terms of installed capacity.

**Thus, the correct answer is (b) only two.**

**4.** *(a)* To encourage people to adopt environmentally sustainable lifestyles and reduce their carbon footprints

The LiFE initiative, introduced by India, aims to inspire individuals and communities to adopt sustainable practices in daily life to mitigate climate change. It promotes awareness and actionable steps to reduce carbon footprints, enhancing personal responsibility for environmental conservation.

**Thus, option (a) is the correct answer.**

**5.** *(b)* Only two

Solar energy production relies on technologies like photovoltaic cells and solar thermal systems to harness sunlight for electricity generation.

- **Statement 1 is correct:** Photovoltaic cells generate electricity by converting light energy directly into electric energy through the **photovoltaic effect**. When sunlight hits the cell, it excites electrons in the semiconductor material, creating an electric current.
- **Statement 2 is incorrect: Solar thermal systems** do not convert sunlight directly into electricity. Instead, they use sunlight to heat a fluid, which then produces steam to drive a turbine and generate electricity.

- **Statement 3 is correct**: Silicon is widely used as a semiconductor in solar cells due to its availability and effectiveness in converting sunlight into electricity through electron movement.

**Thus, the correct answer is (b) Only two.**

**6.** *(c)* Both 1 and 2

Solar cells convert sunlight into electricity through the photovoltaic effect, where material properties and environmental factors significantly impact efficiency.

- **Statement 1 is correct**: In solar cells, the **photovoltaic effect** causes electron movement within the semiconductor material when exposed to sunlight, creating **direct current (DC) electricity**. This process relies on the semiconductor's ability to convert light energy into electrical energy directly.
- For use in most household and grid applications, this DC electricity must be converted to **alternating current (AC)** using an inverter. AC is the standard form of electricity for most appliances and power grids.
- **Statement 2 is correct**: The efficiency of solar cells is influenced by factors such as **temperature, shading, and material purity**. Higher temperatures can reduce efficiency, while shading interrupts light exposure. High-purity materials enhance electron flow, improving overall performance.

**Thus, the correct answer is (c) Both 1 and 2.**

**7.** *(c)* Only three

India's diverse topography influences its wind energy potential, with specific states leading in wind power due to favourable conditions like high wind speeds and extensive coastal areas.

- **State 1 is correct: Tamil Nadu** has strong coastal winds, particularly around areas like Kanyakumari, and ranks among the top states for wind energy production in India.
- **State 2 is correct: Rajasthan** benefits from high desert wind speeds, particularly in districts like Jaisalmer and Barmer, making it suitable for wind farms.
- **State 3 is incorrect: West Bengal** has limited wind resources compared to coastal and desert states, as it lacks sustained high-speed winds required for effective energy generation.
- **State 4 is correct: Andhra Pradesh** has favourable wind conditions, especially along its extensive coastline near districts like Anantapur and Kadapa, which support significant wind power projects.

**Thus, the correct answer is (c) Only three.**

**8.** *(a)* 1 and 2 only

Offshore wind energy has distinct advantages that enhance its effectiveness and minimise environmental and social conflicts.

- **Statement 1 is correct**: Offshore wind turbines harness strong, consistent winds found over oceans and seas, which can generate higher energy output compared to onshore turbines. This reliability is due to the reduced turbulence and higher wind speeds found offshore, making it highly efficient for electricity production.
- **Statement 2 is correct**: Offshore wind farms reduce the need for land-based installations, thus avoiding conflicts with agricultural and residential zones. This location advantage makes offshore projects less disruptive to populated or cultivated areas.
- **Statement 3 is incorrect**: Offshore wind energy generally has **higher initial installation costs** than onshore projects, as the construction, transportation, and maintenance of offshore turbines are more complex and costly due to the marine environment.

**Therefore, the correct answer is (a) 1 and 2 only.**

**9.** *(b)* Located in Muppandal, it benefits from high wind speeds from the Western Ghats.

**Muppandal Wind Farm** is located in the Muppandal region of Tamil Nadu, leveraging the high wind speeds and favourable wind patterns generated by the **Western Ghats**. This region is ideal for wind energy due to consistent, strong winds.

**Thus, option (b) is the correct answer.**

**10.** *(d)* India has significant geothermal energy potential in specific regions due to its unique geological conditions. The government has identified several key areas suitable for geothermal energy development.

- **Statement 1 is correct: Puga Valley** in Ladakh is one of the most promising sites for geothermal energy in India, with abundant hot springs and surface geothermal activity, indicating strong subsurface heat suitable for power generation.
- **Statement 2 is correct:** The **Cambay Basin** in Gujarat has deep underground geothermal reservoirs due to its geological characteristics, making it suitable for geothermal energy projects.
- **Statement 3 is correct: Manikaran** in Himachal Pradesh is known for its hot springs, making it another viable site for geothermal energy potential, as the presence of thermal springs is conducive to energy extraction.

**Therefore, the correct answer is (d) 1, 2 and 3.**

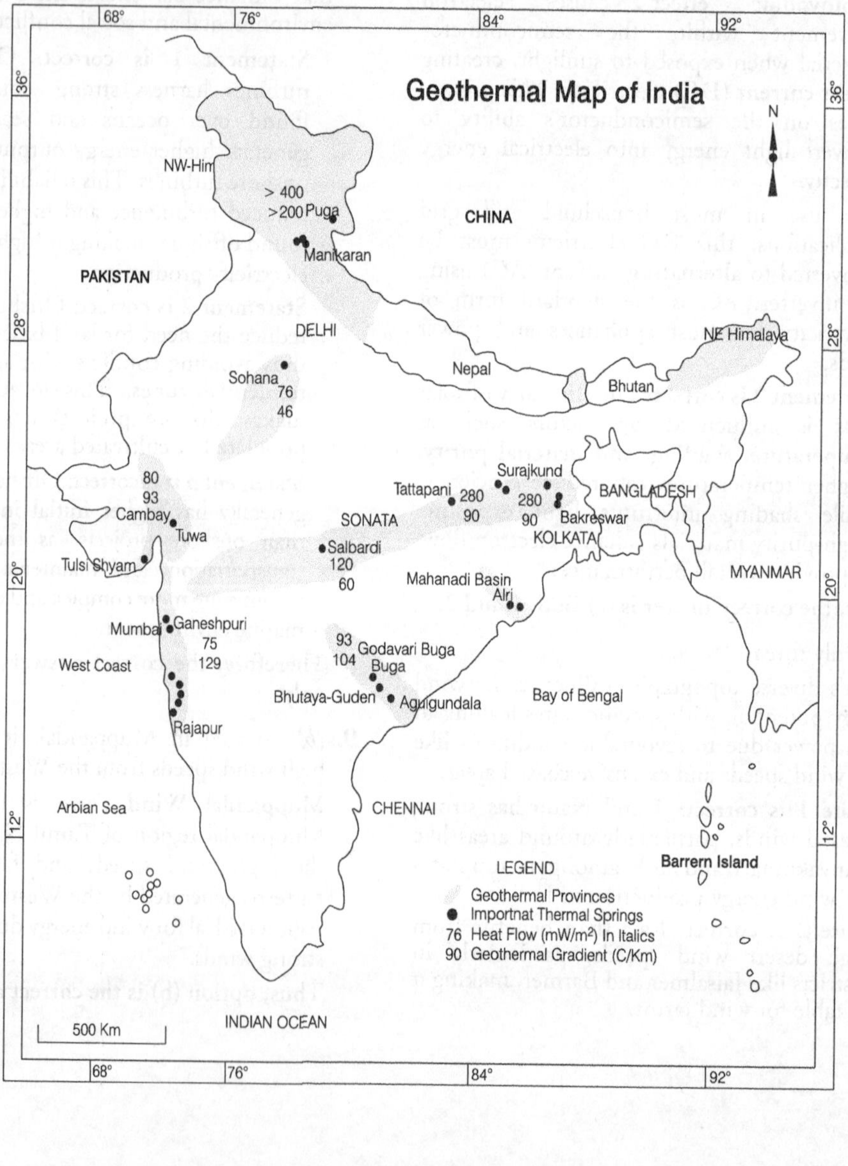

**11.** *(b)* To increase geothermal energy use globally and support clean energy transitions.

The **Global Geothermal Alliance** (**GGA**) is an initiative led by the **International Renewable Energy Agency** (**IRENA**), aiming to accelerate the global adoption of **geothermal energy**. The GGA's mission is to support **clean energy transitions** by facilitating policy frameworks, technical cooperation and investment opportunities to increase geothermal energy's contribution to the global energy mix. It enables members to share **technical expertise, policy frameworks**, and **best practices** to expand geothermal capabilities and promote it as a sustainable, low-emission energy source globally.

**Thus, option (b) is the correct answer.**

**12.** *(b)* It relies on temperature differences between warmer surface warmer and colder deep water to produce power.

- Ocean Thermal Energy Conversion (OTEC) is a technology that generates electricity by utilising the **temperature difference** between warm surface seawater and cold deep seawater.
- This gradient allows for the operation of a heat engine, which produces energy in a sustainable manner, particularly suited for tropical regions.
- 1st such OTEC plant being developed in Kavaratti (Lakshadweep).

**Thus, option (b) is the correct answer.**

**13.** *(b)* Only two

**Renewable purchase obligations** (**RPOs**) are mechanisms designed to compel power procurers in every state through State Electricity Regulatory Commissions (SERC), like distribution companies (DISCOMS), captive power producers and open-access consumers, to annually purchase a certain minimum amount of renewable energy.

- **Statement 1 is correct: RPOs** mandate that **Discoms** and other obligated entities purchase a specific percentage of their total electricity from **renewable energy sources**, such as wind, solar, and bioenergy.
- **Statement 2 is incorrect:** RPO targets are **not uniform** across India. They are determined by each **State Electricity Regulatory Commission** (**SERC**), although there are broad national guidelines issued by the MNRE.
- **Statement 3 is correct: Solar Purchase Obligations** (**SPOs**) are a specific category under RPOs, focusing exclusively on the purchase of **solar energy**.

**Thus, the correct answer is (b) Only two.**

**14.** *(b)* Only two

- **Statement 1 is correct:** The International Solar Alliance (ISA) was launched by India and France during COP21 in 2015 to mobilise global efforts to increase solar energy usage. This initiative aligns with the broader goal of combating climate change by expanding renewable energy adoption worldwide.
- **Statement 2 is incorrect:** Although initially aimed at countries located between the Tropic of Cancer and Tropic of Capricorn, ISA membership was later expanded to include countries from all geographic locations, allowing nations outside the tropics to join. This move was made to strengthen global cooperation on solar energy.
- **Statement 3 is correct:** ISA aims to reduce the financial barriers to solar energy projects for its member nations. By facilitating cooperation, providing technical support, and encouraging innovative financing mechanisms, ISA helps reduce the overall cost of solar projects, making solar energy more accessible.

**Thus, the correct answer is (b) Only two.**

**15.** *(b)* To finance and support solar projects in developing countries.

The **Global Solar Facility** aims to **mobilize resources and provide financing** for solar energy projects, particularly in developing regions. Its primary objective is to enhance solar infrastructure and capacity where it's most needed, helping expand access to clean and sustainable energy.

**Thus, option (b) is the correct answer.**

**16.** *(b)* 1-B, 2-A, 3-C

- **Option 1 is correctly matched with B: National Solar Mission:** Aims to promote the

**development of solar parks** and achieve large-scale deployment of **solar power** across India. The **Solar Energy Corporation of India (SECI)** is the **implementing agency** for the **National Solar Mission.**

- **Option 2 is correctly matched with A:** KUSUM scheme Encourages farmers to set up **solar pumps** and small-scale **grid-connected solar power projects** to ensure reliable power supply and reduce the use of conventional energy sources.
- **Option 3 is correctly matched with C:** The UJALA scheme is aimed at distributing **energy-efficient LED bulbs** to households across India to reduce energy consumption. **Energy Efficiency Services Limited (EESL)** is responsible for implementing the **UJALA scheme.**

**Thus, the correct answer is (b) 1-B, 2-A, 3-C.**

**17.** *(b)* They help reduce water evaporation and algae growth on water bodies.

Floating solar panels are installed on water bodies, providing benefits such as reducing water evaporation, lowering algae growth due to shading, and using otherwise unused water surface. Unlike offshore installations, they are typically used in reservoirs and lakes. This dual benefit of electricity generation and water conservation makes them a promising technology in solar energy.

**Thus, option (b) is the correct answer.**

**18.** *(b)* 1 and 2 only

- **Statement 1 is correct:** The Global Renewables and Energy Efficiency Pledge at **COP28** calls for **tripling the world's installed renewable energy generation capacity** by 2030, aiming for at least **11,000** GW of renewable capacity.
- **Statement 2 is correct:** The pledge also seeks to **double the global average annual rate of energy efficiency improvements** from around **2% to over 4%** every year until 2030, which is a crucial step towards reducing energy consumption and emissions.
- **Statement 3 isincorrect:** The pledge is **voluntary**, not mandatory, and does **not include penalties** for non-compliance. It relies on collective commitment rather than enforcement through penalties.

**Thus, option (b) is the correct answer.**

**19.** *(b)* Only two

- **Pair 1 is incorrect:** OSOWOG is not limited to Africa. It is a global initiative that aims to create an interconnected **global grid** for solar energy, linking countries across different regions to share solar energy. The initiative envisions harnessing solar power and transferring it across time zones globally, not focusing exclusively on Africa.
- **Pair 2 is correct:** The **STAR-C initiative** is focused on **capacity-building** and **institutional strengthening** in the solar energy sector, particularly in developing countries. It helps enhance technical expertise and promotes the deployment of solar technologies.
- **Pair 3 is correct:** This initiative focuses on catalysing **solar investments** in **underserved regions**, particularly in **Africa**. It aims to de-risk investments and promote the growth of solar infrastructure in regions that face investment challenges.

**Thus, option (b) is the correct answer.**

**20.** *(a)* 1 and 2 only

The **Green Energy Open Access Rules 2022**, notified by the Government of India, aim to promote renewable energy generation, purchase, and consumption, supporting India's goal of reducing emissions by **45%** by 2030 as part of its updated **Nationally Determined Contributions** (NDCs). Key features include:

- **Uniform Renewable Purchase Obligation (RPO),** including **Green Hydrogen/Ammonia.**
- **Green Open Access** for consumers, with the minimum transaction limit reduced from **1 MW to 100 kW** to allow smaller consumers to purchase renewable energy.
- **Approval within 15 days** for Green Open Access requests.
- **Voluntary green power purchases** for commercial and industrial consumers.
- This initiative encourages industries and households to shift towards **green energy** and supports India's target of **500 GW** of non-fossil fuel energy by 2030.

- **Statement 1 is correct: Open Access (OA)** refers to non-discriminatory access to electricity transmission and distribution systems.
- **Statement 2 is correct:** The minimum transaction limit for **green energy open access** has indeed been reduced from **1 MW to 100 kW.**
- **Statement 3 is incorrect: DISCOMs** are obligated to procure and supply green power, but consumers can **voluntarily** demand **green power,** not only on a mandatory basis.

**Thus, option (a) is the correct answer.**

**21.** *(b)* Only two

- **Statement 1 is correct:** First-generation biofuels, also known as conventional biofuels, are derived from edible feedstock such as sugarcane, corn, and sugar beets. These biofuels are produced by fermenting these feedstocks to create ethanol, which is then used as a fuel. However, this generation has been criticised for competing with food sources.
- **Statement 2 is correct:** Second-generation biofuels are made from non-food crops and waste biomass, such as Jatropha and Pongamia. This generation includes lignocellulosic biofuels derived from plant materials that don't interfere with food supply.
- **Statement 3 is incorrect: Third-generation biofuels** are derived from **algal biomass,** not genetically modified microorganisms.
- **Statement 4 is incorrect:** Fourth-generation biofuels focus on carbon capture and sequestration technology combined with biofuel production, not simply on algal biomass. They aim to remove $CO_2$ from the atmosphere as part of their production process, contributing positively to carbon neutrality.

**Thus, the correct answer is (b) Only two.**

**22.** *(b)* 1-B, 2-A, 3-C

- **Ethanol:** Ethanol is a **biofuel** that is commonly produced from **sugarcane** or corn and is blended with petrol to reduce carbon emissions.
- **Biodiesel:** Biodiesel is produced from **vegetable oils** or **animal fats** and can be used as a substitute for diesel in engines.
- **Compressed Biogas (CBG):** CBG is a **methane-rich fuel** produced from **organic waste** like agricultural residue and can be used as a substitute for natural gas.

**Therefore, the correct answer is (b) 1-B, 2-A, 3-C.**

**23.** *(a)* 1 and 2 only

**Compressed Bio Gas (CBG)** is a **hydrocarbon gas mixture,** mainly **methane,** produced by **anaerobic decomposition** of animal and plant waste. After the removal of **carbon dioxide** and **hydrogen sulphide,** the biogas is purified and compressed, making it chemically identical to **CNG.**

Unlike CNG, which comes from **petroleum,** CBG can be generated from **biomass,** offering a **sustainable** alternative for **transportation fuel** and **industrial uses.** Its by-products, such as **bio-manure,** improve crop growth and reduce dependence on **chemical fertilisers,** while captured $CO_2$ can be used for **food preservation** and in **fire extinguishers,** promoting **circular economy** growth.

- **Statement 1 is correct: Mandatory blending of CBG** in **CNG/PNG** begins from **FY 2025-26.**
- **Statement 2 is correct:** The blending obligation is set to increase to **5%** of total CNG/PNG consumption from **FY 2028-29** onwards.
- **Statement 3 is incorrect:** The blending obligation is **voluntary** only till **FY 2024-25;** it becomes **mandatory** starting from **FY 2025-26.**

**Thus, option (a) is the correct answer.**

**24.** *(b)* Only two

The Minister of Petroleum and Natural Gas recently handed over the 100th Letter of Intent (LOI) to a Compressed Bio-Gas (CBG) entrepreneur under the **SATAT scheme.**

This initiative aims to utilise over **62 million metric tonnes of waste** annually, reduce **import dependence,** create jobs, and lower vehicular emissions by converting

**agricultural residue, cattle dung and municipal waste** into CBG.

CBG, a renewable fuel with over **90% methane**, is similar to natural gas and can replace CNG in automotive, industrial and commercial uses. This promotes **responsible waste management**, supports **farmers' income** and boosts **rural entrepreneurship** while aligning with **climate goals**.

- **Statement 1 is correct**: The SATAT initiative was indeed launched in 2018 to promote the production and supply of **CBG** by encouraging entrepreneurs to set up plants.
- **Statement 2 is correct**: **Oil Marketing Companies (OMCs)** purchase **CBG** from entrepreneurs and use it as an **automotive and industrial fuel**.
- **Statement 3 is incorrect**: The **Ministry of Petroleum and Natural Gas (MoPNG)**, not the **Ministry of New and Renewable Energy (MNRE)**, is the nodal ministry responsible for the SATAT initiative.

**Thus, option (b) is the correct answer.**

**25.** *(b)* MD15 is a blend that includes 15% methanol, 71% mineral diesel and 14% coupler additives.

- **Methanol Diesel-15 (MD-15)** is a **blended fuel** developed by Indian Railways' **RDSO in collaboration with IOCL**. It consists of **15% methanol, 71% mineral diesel**, and **14% indigenously developed additives**.
- It offers **superior performance** and **reduced emissions** compared to regular diesel, potentially cutting diesel consumption by 15%, resulting in cost savings and environmental benefits.

**Key Facts about Methanol:**

- Also known as **methyl alcohol** or **wood alcohol**.
- Simplest alcohol ($CH_3OH$) that mixes completely with water.
- Produced by steam-reforming natural gas and catalysing the synthesis gas.

**Thus, option (b) is the correct answer.**

**26.** *(b)* It represents high-value premium fuels, such as petrol and diesel, used for vehicle calibration, and testing by automotive manufacturers.

- **Reference Fuel** refers to specialised petrol and diesel used for calibrating and testing vehicles by automotive manufacturers and testing institutions. These fuels have higher specifications than regular or premium fuels, such as improved cetane number, octane number, and purity.
- **Indigenous Production**: India, previously reliant on imports, now produces reference-grade petrol at Indian Oil's Paradip refinery and diesel at its Panipat unit, significantly reducing costs from ₹ 800-850 to ₹ 450 per litre.
- **Benefits**: This lowers costs, ensures faster availability for manufacturers, and supports import substitution, offering substantial advantages to the automotive sector.

**Thus, option (b) is the correct answer.**

**27.** *(b)* Bio-diesel is made from non-edible oils or used cooking oil in India and is environmentally friendly with no sulphur and about 10% built-in oxygen.

**Biodiesel** is a renewable, biodegradable fuel made from **natural oils or fats**, such as vegetable oil, animal fat, or recycled cooking grease. It is produced through a **process called transesterification**, where the oils or fats are chemically reacted with alcohol (usually methanol) to create Fatty Acid Methyl Esters (FAME), commonly known as biodiesel.

**Key Features:**

- **Renewable**: Derived from biological sources, making it a sustainable alternative to fossil fuels.
- **Clean Burning**: Biodiesel reduces emissions of pollutants like carbon dioxide ($CO_2$), particulate matter, and sulfur dioxide ($SO_2$) compared to conventional diesel.
- **Compatible with Diesel Engines**: Biodiesel can be blended with petroleum diesel (e.g., B20 for 20% biodiesel) or used in its pure form (B100) in diesel engines with little or no modification.
- **Environmental Benefits**: Reduces greenhouse gas emissions and reliance on non-renewable resources, supporting cleaner energy and sustainability goals.

- In India, bio-diesel is primarily made from **non-edible oils** or **used cooking oil** (UCO), as edible oil resources are limited. **Bio-diesel** is environmentally friendly, containing almost no **sulfur** and approximately **10% built-in oxygen**, making it suitable for blending with conventional diesel. Additionally, bio-diesel does not require new infrastructure for storage and can be safely handled due to its higher flash points compared to conventional diesel.

**Thus, option (b) is the correct answer.**

**28.** *(b)* It is a biofuel made from biomass sources such as Jatropha, used in combination with Air Rurbine Fuel (ATF) to power aircraft.

Bio-jet fuel is produced from various biomass sources like Jatropha, animal fats, and waste oils. In the case of India's first bio-jet fuel flight, a blend of 75% Air Turbine Fuel (ATF) and 25% bio-jet fuel from Jatropha was used. This initiative aims at reducing carbon emissions and dependence on traditional fuels in aviation.

**Thus, option (b) is the correct answer.**

**29.** *(a)* 1 and 3 only

E-fuels, also known as electro-fuels, are a **type of synthetic fuel that can be used to power vehicles, ships, and aeroplanes.** They are a sustainable alternative to fossil fuels and can be used in existing infrastructure E-fuels are **made from captured carbon dioxide or carbon monoxide, and hydrogen obtained from water split by sustainable electricity sources.** The process uses hydrogen to bind with the CO under high pressure using a catalyst E-fuels are climate-neutral and can be used to reduce $CO_2$ emissions in the transport and heating market.

- **Statement 1 is correct:** e-Fuels are created using electricity from renewable sources, water (through electrolysis), and $CO_2$ captured from the air, making the process climate-friendly.
- **Statement 2 is incorrect:** e-Fuels do not release additional $CO_2$ into the atmosphere. They are considered climate-neutral because they reuse $CO_2$ already present in the air.
- **Statement 3 is correct:** e-Fuels are compatible with existing internal combustion engines, which allows them to be used without the need for engine modifications.

**Thus, option (a) is the correct answer.**

**30.** *(b)* Primarily methane and carbon dioxide

Biogas primarily consists of methane ($CH_4$) and carbon dioxide ($CO_2$), which result from the anaerobic digestion of organic material by microorganisms. Methane is the main component, providing the energy content of biogas, while carbon dioxide is also present in significant proportions.

**Thus, option (b) is the correct answer.**

**31.** *(b)* Only two

- **Statement 1 is correct:** The **National Policy on Biofuels** promotes the production of biofuels from **non-food feedstocks** like agricultural residues and waste, avoiding competition with food production.
- **Statement 2 is correct:** The policy supports **ethanol blending** with petrol, and the target is up to **20% by 2025-26.**
- **Statement 3 is incorrect:** The policy promotes the production of ethanol from **various feedstocks**, including **sugarcane, agricultural waste**, and **non-edible oilseeds**, not sugarcane alone.

The policy categorises biofuels into three main types to streamline their promotion and use:

- **First-generation (1G) biofuels:** Produced from **edible sources** like sugarcane (ethanol), maize, and vegetable oils (biodiesel).
- **Second-generation (2G) biofuels:** Produced from **non-edible sources** such as agricultural waste, forestry residues, and municipal solid waste.
- **Third-generation (3G) biofuels:** Derived from **algae** and other advanced biofuels.

**Thus, the correct answer is (b) Only two.**

**32.** *(d)* 1, 2 and 3

- **Statement 1 is correct:** The **Ethanol Blending Programme** was initially introduced in **2003**, starting with a 5% **blending mandate** of ethanol with petrol. Since than the target has been increased, and the government now aims to achieve **20% ethanol blending (E20)** by 2025.

- **Statement 2 is correct**: The government provides **differential pricing** for ethanol based on its **source**, such as ethanol produced from **sugarcane** juice or **surplus food grains.**
- **Statement 3 is correct**: India **achieved the 10% ethanol blending target** with petrol in **June 2022**, well ahead of its **2023 deadline**, demonstrating strong progress in its ethanol blending initiative.

**Therefore, the correct answer is (d) 1, 2 and 3.**

***33.*** *(a)* 1, 2 and 3 only

- **Rotten potatoes**: Can be used for **biofuel production** as they fall under damaged and surplus food grains.
- **Excess rice stocks**: Allowed for biofuel production, especially in cases where they are **surplus** and stored by the government.
- **Municipal Solid Waste (MSW)**: Used for producing **2nd generation (2G) biofuels.**
- **Fresh food grains reserved for PDS: Not allowed under the policy**, as food grains reserved for **public consumption** cannot be diverted for biofuel production.

**Thus, the correct answer is (a) 1, 2 and 3 only.**

***34.*** *(a)* Only one

The **Global Biofuel Alliance** (**GBA**), launched during the **G20 Summit in New Delhi in 2023**, aims to promote biofuel adoption globally by fostering collaboration and innovation among member countries.

- **Statement 1 is incorrect**: Membership in the Alliance is not restricted to G20 countries; it is open to all interested nations.
- **Statement 2 is correct**: India, Brazil and the United States jointly initiated the alliance, signalling their commitment to advancing biofuel technologies and adoption worldwide.
- **Statement 3 is incorrect**: GBA does not exclusively promote first-generation biofuels. Instead, it supports multiple generations of biofuels, including advanced biofuels, to enhance sustainable energy options.

**Thus, the correct answer is (a) Only one.**

***35.*** *(c)* Only three

Hydrogen production methods vary in feasibility and commercial viability. Currently, three methods are widely adopted for large-scale hydrogen production.

- **Option 1 is correct**: Steam Methane Reforming (SMR) is a primary method where methane reacts with steam to produce hydrogen and $CO_2$. Though cost-effective, it generates carbon emissions.
- **Option 2 is correct**: Electrolysis of water, particularly when powered by renewable energy, produces 'green hydrogen,' a low-emission method becoming more economically viable.
- **Option 3 is correct**: Biomass gasification involves converting organic material into hydrogen, offering a renewable approach, though on a smaller scale.
- **Option 4 is incorrect**: Nuclear fusion is still experimental and not yet viable for commercial hydrogen production.

**Thus, the correct answer is (c) Only three.**

***36.*** *(d)* All four

- **Statement 1 is correct**: Green hydrogen is produced through **electrolysis powered by renewable energy sources like solar, wind, or hydel power.** This process generates hydrogen without carbon emissions, making it environmentally friendly and sustainable.
- **Statement 2 is correct**: Grey hydrogen is produced from fossil fuels, primarily natural gas, through a **process called steam methane reforming.** This method emits carbon dioxide directly into the atmosphere, contributing to greenhouse gas emissions.
- **Statement 3 is correct**: Pink (or red) hydrogen production uses **electrolysis powered by nuclear energy.** This method is considered low-emission because nuclear power does not produce carbon dioxide, although nuclear waste management is a factor.
- **Statement 4 is correct**: Brown hydrogen is generated from coal gasification, where coal is converted into hydrogen with carbon emissions released into the atmosphere, making it one of the least environmentally friendly forms of hydrogen.

**Thus, the correct answer is (d) All four.**

**37.** *(a)* Both Assertion (A) and Reason (R) are correct, and Reason (R) is the correct explanation of Assertion (A).

**Hydrogen Fuel Cell:**

- **Working Principle**: Generates electricity through an **electrochemical reaction** between hydrogen and oxygen, producing water and heat as byproducts.
- **No Harmful Emissions**: Produces **zero carbon emissions**, with **water vapour** as the only output.
- **Energy Efficiency**: More efficient than traditional combustion engines; can achieve up to **60% efficiency** in converting fuel to electricity.
- **Versatile Applications**: Used in **transportation (buses, cars, trains), backup power systems**, and **portable devices.**
- **Fuel Source**: Requires **hydrogen** as the primary fuel, which can be obtained from renewable energy sources or fossil fuels.
- **Decarbonisation Potential**: Plays a critical role in achieving **clean energy** goals.

**Assertion** (A) **is correct:Hydrogen fuel cell buses** can contribute to the **decarbonisation** of transportation because they use **hydrogen** as fuel instead of fossil fuels, which helps in reducing carbon emissions from the transport sector. Hydrogen fuel cells have the potential to replace diesel and gasoline-powered vehicles, making them a promising solution for **zero-emission** transportation.

**Reason** (R) **is correct**: Hydrogen fuel cells generate electricity through an **electrochemical reaction** between **hydrogen** and **oxygen**, with **water** as the only byproduct. This process does not produce any harmful emissions like carbon dioxide or other pollutants, making it a clean energy source.

**Thus, option** (a) **is the correct answer.**

**38.** *(a)* 1, 2 and 3 only

Hydrogen Enriched Compressed Natural Gas (HCNG) is an alternative fuel mixture that combines Compressed Natural Gas (CNG) with hydrogen, bringing multiple benefits in terms of environmental impact and fuel efficiency:

- **Statement 1 is correct**: HCNG reduces greenhouse gas emissions due to hydrogen's cleaner-burning properties, which help minimise pollutants and carbon emissions.
- **Statement 2 is correct**: The higher hydrogen content in HCNG enhances combustion efficiency, leading to increased fuel efficiency when compared to traditional CNG.
- **Statement 3 is correct**: HCNG produces fewer carbon deposits, which can reduce engine wear and improve overall engine life.
- **Statement 4 is incorrect**: Initial production costs for HCNG can be higher due to hydrogen sourcing and infrastructure modifications.

**Thus, the correct answer is (a) 1, 2 and 3 only.**

**39.** *(c)* All three

- **Statement 1 is correct**: Green hydrogen can be used directly in modified internal combustion engines to power vehicles. However, this application is less common compared to fuel cells due to efficiency issues.
- **Statement 2 is correct**: Green hydrogen can be mixed with **natural gas** in certain proportions and used in existing power plants or heating systems, helping to reduce carbon emissions from fossil fuels.
- **Statement 3 is correct**: Hydrogen fuel cells convert hydrogen into electricity, which can then power electric motors in vehicles, producing only water as a byproduct, making it a clean energy option for transportation.

**Thus, option (c) is the correct answer.**

**40.** *(b)* 1 and 3 only

- **Statement 1 is correct**: The Ministry of New and Renewable Energy (MNRE) is indeed the nodal agency tasked with implementing the National Green Hydrogen Mission.
- **Statement 2 is incorrect**: The mission's focus is on promoting green hydrogen from renewable sources like solar and wind energy, not coal-based hydrogen production, which emits significant carbon.
- **Statement 3 is correct**: One of the mission's main objectives is to establish a production capacity of 5 million metric tonnes of green hydrogen annually by 2030 to help reduce carbon emissions and meet clean energy goals.

**Thus, the correct answer is (b) 1 and 3 only.**

**41.** *(a)* 1 and 2 only

- **Statement 1 is correct:** It aims to provide free **power transmission for 25 years for new renewable energy facilities built before July 2025.** The Green Hydrogen and Ammonia policy includes provisions for free **inter-state power transmission for a period of 25 years** for renewable energy facilities built before July 2025 for the production of green hydrogen and ammonia.
- **Statement 2 is correct:** The policy aims to facilitate the establishment of green hydrogen and ammonia production plants by prioritising grid connectivity.
- **Statement 3 is incorrect:** The policy **allows for the production of green hydrogen and ammonia for both domestic use and export. In fact, promoting exports is one of the key aims of the policy, as green hydrogen can become an** important component of India's renewable energy exports.

**Thus, option (a) is the correct answer.**

**42.** *(c)* Reducing the cost of green hydrogen production to less than \$2/kg

One of the core goals of the Green Hydrogen Catapult is to drive down the production cost of green hydrogen to make it more economically viable at under \$2/kg. This target cost reduction aims to make green hydrogen competitive with other energy sources, helping expand its use across industries for a low-carbon future.

**Thus, option (c) is the correct answer.**

**43.** *(b)* To reduce impurities and enhance the quality of coal

Coal beneficiation involves treating raw coal to improve its quality by removing impurities such as ash and sulfur. This process enhances the combustion efficiency, reduces emissions, and lowers transportation costs, making coal a more environmentally friendly fuel source.

**Thus, option (b) is the correct answer.**

**44.** *(a)* 1 and 2 only

- **Statement 1 is correct:** Coal gasification is a chemical process that converts coal into a mixture of carbon monoxide, hydrogen, carbon dioxide and methane known as syngas, which can be used as a fuel or as a raw material in chemical production.
- **Statement 2 is correct:** Compared to conventional coal combustion, coal gasification generates lower levels of pollutants such as sulphur dioxide ($SO_2$) and nitrogen oxides ($NO_2$), as the process is more controlled and allows for the removal of impurities.
- **Statement 3 is incorrect:** The by-products of coal gasification, like **ash or slag, are not entirely biodegradable.** Some by-products may be repurposed, but they generally require management for disposal or environmental use.

**Thus, the correct answer is (a) 1 and 2 only.**

**45.** *(a)* Super plants consume less fuel per unit of electricity produced, resulting in fewer greenhouse gas emission and a smaller carbon fottpritns, aligning with global environment goals.

Supercritical plants operate at higher temperatures and pressures, allowing more complete and efficient fuel combustion. This results in lower fuel consumption per unit of electricity produced, thereby reducing the total emissions of greenhouse gases such as $CO_2$. By optimising fuel usage, supercritical technology minimises the plant's carbon footprint, contributing positively to environmental sustainability.

**Thus, option (a) is not the correct answer.**

**46.** *(b)* FGD is a post-combustion process for removing sulphur dioxide from exhaust gases, while CFBC is a combustion technology that reduces the emission of both sulfur oxides and nitrogen oxides during the combustion process.

- **Flue Gas Desulfurisation (FGD)** is a **post-combustion** process that removes **sulfur dioxide** ($SO_2$) from the exhaust gases of fossil-fueled power plants by using absorbents, which can eliminate up to 95% of sulfur emissions.
- **Circulating Fluidised Bed Combustion** (CFBC) is a **combustion technology** that involves burning fossil fuels in a fluidised bed, allowing for the injection of lime during combustion to reduce the release of both **sulfur oxides** ($SO_2$) and **nitrogen oxides** ($NO_2$). This helps mitigate pollution **during combustion.**

**Thus, option (b) is the correct answer.**

**47.** *(a)* 1 and 3 only

- **Statement 1 is correct:** CCUS involves capturing **carbon emissions** primarily from large industrial sources such as power plants and refineries.
- **Statement 2 is incorrect:** Apart from storage, the captured $CO_2$ can also be **utilised** for various industrial purposes, such as manufacturing **chemicals, fuels**, or using it in **construction materials** like **concrete**.
- **Statement 3 is correct:** The **CCUS process** plays an essential role in helping India achieve its **net-zero emissions** goal by **2070**, as outlined by **NITI Aayog**.

**Thus, option (a) is the correct answer.**

**48.** *(a)* It captures particulate matter from exhaust gases by ionising particles, which are then attracted to charged collection plates.

Electrostatic Precipitators (ESPs) are widely used in industrial applications to reduce airborne particulate matter from exhaust gases. They work by first charging particles through ionisation as exhaust flows through an electric field. These charged particles are then attracted to oppositely charged collection plates, effectively trapping pollutants and preventing their release into the atmosphere. This process is especially effective for large industries, including cement, steel and power plants.

**Thus, option (a) is the correct answer.**

**49.** *(a)* 1 only

- **Statement 1 is correct:** The **Bureau of Energy Efficiency** (BEE) was established under the **Energy Conservation Act, 2001**, with the mission of promoting **energy efficiency** and **conservation across** various sectors in India.
- **Statement 2 is incorrect:** The **Energy Conservation Building Code** (ECBC) is applicable primarily to **commercial buildings**, not just residential buildings.

The ECBC sets minimum energy performance standards for commercial buildings to promote **energy efficiency** and reduce energy consumption in the building sector, which is one of the largest consumers of energy in India.

**Thus, the correct answer is (a) 1 only.**

**50.** *(c)* Only three

- The Energy Conservation Act of 2001 defines a designated consumer as any consumer that falls under the criteria specified in clause (e) of section 14 of the act.
- The Central Government notified the criteria for designated consumers in 2007, which included industrial units in the following sectors: **Aluminium; Cement; Chlor-Alkali; Fertiliser; Iron & Steel; Paper & Pulp; Railways; Thermal Power and Textile**
- The **IT and Software Services** sector generally **does not fall** under this category as its energy consumption is relatively lower compared to the designated sectors.

**Thus, the correct answer is (c) Only three.**

**51.** *(c)* 1 and 3 only

- **Statement 1 is correct:** Under the Perform, Achieve, and Trade (PAT) scheme, **Energy Saving Certificates** (ESCerts) are issued to units achieving energy savings beyond their targets. These units can trade ESCerts with others that fall short of their targets.
- **Statement 2 is incorrect:** ESCerts can be traded across various designated sectors and are not restricted to units within the same sector. The flexibility of trading ESCerts across sectors helps ensure that energy efficiency goals are achieved broadly.
- **Statement 3 is correct:**ESCerts fall under the **National Mission for Enhanced Energy Efficiency** (NMEEE), which is part of the **National Action Plan on Climate Change** aimed at promoting energy efficiency in energy-intensive sectors through tradeable certificates.

**Thus, option (c) is the correct answer.**

**52.** *(a)* 1 only

- **Statement 1 is correct:** EESL is responsible for the **Smart Meter National Programme** (SMNP), which promotes the installation of **smart meters** to help manage electricity consumption more efficiently.
- **Statement 2 is incorrect:** EESL works across **various sectors**, including industrial, residential, commercial, and municipal sectors, not just in the industrial sector.
- **Statement 3 is incorrect:** EESL operates under the **Ministry of Power**, not the

Ministry of Environment, Forest and Climate Change.

**Thus, the correct answer is (a) 1 only.**

***53.*** *(b)* To set energy efficiency standards for residential buildings in order to reduce energy consumption and promote sustainability

Eco Niwas Samhita (ENS) is aimed at establishing **energy efficiency standards specifically for residential buildings** in India, promoting **sustainable and energy-saving practices.** It focuses on reducing overall energy demand and optimising the design for energy-efficient residential spaces.

**Thus, option (b) is the correct answer.**

***54.*** *(b)* 2 and 3 only

- **Statement 1 is incorrect**: The ECBC mandates energy efficiency standards specifically for new commercial buildings. While there are ongoing efforts to extend energy efficiency standards to the residential sector, the ECBC currently does not enforce mandatory requirements for residential buildings.
- **Statement 2 is correct**: The ECBC provides detailed guidelines on optimising building components such as lighting, ventilation, and insulation to minimise energy consumption and promote sustainable use of resources.
- **Statement 3 is correct**: The code's implementation indeed varies across states, as each state in India has the authority to adopt, enforce, or modify ECBC provisions according to regional needs and priorities, ensuring flexibility and adaptability in line with local conditions.

**Thus, the correct answer is (b) 2 and 3 only.**

***55.*** *(c)* Only three

The Standards and Labelling Programme by the Bureau of Energy Efficiency (BEE) mandates energy efficiency standards for certain appliances to promote energy conservation and reduce electricity consumption.

- **Appliance 1 - Ceiling fans: Covered under mandatory standards.** Ceiling fans are common household appliances, and mandatory labelling helps consumers choose energy-efficient options.
- **Appliance 2 - LED lamps: Covered under mandatory standards.** LED lamps require energy efficiency labelling due to their widespread use and energy-saving potential.
- **Appliance 3 - Room air conditioners: Covered under mandatory standards.** Air conditioners consume significant energy, especially in high-demand months, making them a target for mandatory labelling.
- **Appliance 4 - Electric irons: Not covered under mandatory standards** currently, though other programmes encourage energy-efficient choices.

**Thus, the correct answer is (c) Only three.**

***56.*** *(b)* 1 and 3 only

The State Energy Efficiency Index (SEEI) is a tool used to monitor and encourage energy efficiency efforts across Indian states, **developed by the Bureau of Energy Efficiency (BEE) under the Ministry of Power.** This index considers a range of metrics to assess states' progress in implementing energy conservation measures.

Based on the **progress and accomplishments of states** in energy efficiency implementation, they have been classified into four categories: **Front Runner, Achiever, Contender, and Aspirant.**

- **Statement 1 is correct**: The SEEI was indeed launched by the BEE to help track state performance in line with national energy-saving targets and policies.
- **Statement 2 is incorrect**: The index does not focus solely on industrial efficiency; it evaluates multiple sectors.
- **Statement 3 is correct**: It includes a broad set of sectors such as transport, industry, buildings, and municipal utilities to offer a comprehensive assessment of each state's efforts in energy efficiency.

**Thus, the correct answer is (b) 1 and 3 only.**

## Past Learning (Answers)

| | | | | | | | | | |
|---|---|---|---|---|---|---|---|---|---|
| 1 (d) | 2 (c) | 3 (c) | 4 (d) | 5 (b) | 6 (a) | 7 (b) | 8 (b) | 9 (a) | 10 (a) |
| 11 (b) | 12 (a) | 13 (a) | | | | | | | |

CHAPTER 09

# Sustainable Agriculture Practices

## Assessment Round

**1.** Consider the following factors:

1. Parent material
2. Climate
3. Organisms
4. Time

How many of the factors given above is/are critical in determining the development and characteristics of soil?

(a) Only one (b) Only two
(c) Only three (d) All four

**2.** Which of the following best describes the impact of soil texture on plant growth and soil health?

(a) Coarse-textured soils retain water better than fine-textured soils, increasing nutrient availability.
(b) Fine-textured soils retain more nutrients and water but may lead to poor drainage, affecting root development.
(c) Soil texture only affects the colour of the soil and has minimal impact on plant growth.
(d) Sandy soils are ideal for all crops due to their excellent drainage capabilities.

**3.** Arrange the following soil horizons in the correct order from the surface layer to the deeper layers:

1. O-horizon 2. B-horizon
3. C-horizon 4. A-horizon

Select the correct answer from the codes given below:

(a) 1, 4, 2, 3 (b) 4, 1, 3, 2
(c) 1, 3, 2, 4 (d) 1, 2, 3, 4

**4.** Consider the following processes involved in soil formation with their corresponding effects on soil properties:

| | Process | Effect on Soil |
|---|---|---|
| 1. | Calcification | Accumulation of calcium carbonates in arid regions, affecting soil structure. |
| 2. | Podzolisation | Acidic leaching process causing soil to develop a distinct gray or white subsurface layer. |
| 3. | Laterisation | Intense weathering and leaching in tropical climates, leaving iron and aluminum oxides. |
| 4. | Salinisation | Accumulation of soluble salts, typically in poorly drained arid and semi-arid soils. |

How many of the given pairs is/are correctly matched?

(a) Only one pair (b) Only two pairs
(c) Only three pairs (d) All four pairs

**5.** Which of the following best describes a primary characteristic of Podzol soils?

(a) Highly fertile with a high organic matter content suitable for agriculture
(b) Well-drained soils rich in calcium and magnesium due to calcification
(c) Acidic soils with distinct gray or white sub-surface layers due to intense leaching
(d) Sandy soils predominantly found in tropical rainforests

**6.** Which of the following best describes the process of 'Gleisation' in soil formation?
(a) Accumulation of calcium in arid regions, leading to hard soil layers
(b) Saturation of soil with water, causing reduction and accumulation of iron compounds, often creating a grayish-blue layer
(c) Formation of highly acidic soils in cold climates with high organic matter leaching
(d) Rapid decomposition of organic matter, resulting in fertile, humus-rich topsoil

**7.** Identify the type of soil based on the following characteristics:
1. Known as the 'omnibus group.'
2. Covers about 18.5% of India's total land area.
3. Found in regions of low rainfall, particularly in the Eastern and Southern parts of the Deccan Plateau, along the Western Ghats, and in parts of Odisha, Chhattisgarh and the Southern Middle Ganga Plain.
4. The soil is red due to iron presence and appears yellow in hydrated form.
5. Typically deficient in nitrogen, phosphorus and humus.

Select the correct answer from the codes below:
(a) Alluvial Soil (b) Black Soil
(c) Laterite Soil (d) Red and Yellow Soil

**8.** Consider the following types of soil erosion with their descriptions and prevalent regions in India:

| Type of Erosion | Description | Region |
|---|---|---|
| 1. Sheet Erosion | A Removal of thin layers of soil from sloping land surfaces | i. Western Ghats |
| 2. Gully Erosion | B. Formation of deep channels or gullies on the soil surface due to intense water flow | ii. Chambal Basin |
| 3. Wind Erosion | C. Displacement of topsoil particles by wind, especially in dry areas | iii. Arid regions of Rajasthan |

How many of the pairs given above is/are correctly matched?
(a) Only one pair (b) Only two pairs
(c) All three pairs (d) None

**9.** Which component of soil texture is crucial for aeration and drainage in soils?
(a) Sand, as it consists of larger particles allowing water to drain easily.
(b) Clay, due to its small particles that improve drainage.
(c) Silt, as it binds the soil particles tightly to hold water.
(d) Organic matter, which primarily determines soil texture.

**10.** Consider the types of erosion with their descriptions and prevalent regions:

| Type of Erosion | Description | Region |
|---|---|---|
| 1. Splash Erosion | A. Soil detachment caused by the impact of raindrops on exposed soil | i. Hilly regions of North-East |
| 2. Rill Erosion | B. Formation of small, temporary channels on sloped land | ii. Shivalik Range |
| 3. Coastal Erosion | C. Removal of soil along coast.lines due to tides and wave action | iii. Eastern Coastline of India |

How many of the pairs given above is/are correctly matched?
(a) Only one pair
(b) Only two pairs
(c) All three pairs
(d) None

**11.** With reference to biofertilisers, consider the following statements:

1. Biofertilisers supply nitrogen and phosphorus to plants but do not affect soil fertility.
2. Biofertilisers require careful handling as they contain living microorganisms.
3. They are more eco-friendly compared to chemical fertilisers.

How many of the above statements is/are correct?

(a) Only one
(b) Only two
(c) All three
(d) None

**12.** Consider the following statements regarding biofertilisers:

1. Mycorrhiza helps plants absorb phosphorus and water from the soil.
2. Phosphate solubilizing bacteria convert insoluble phosphorus compounds into forms that plants can use.
3. Cyanobacteria do not play any role in nitrogen fixation.

Which of the statements given above are correct?

(a) 1 and 2 only (b) 2 and 3 only
(c) 1 and 3 only (d) 1, 2 and 3

**13.** Identify the biofertiliser based on the following attributes:

1. Known for its nitrogen-fixing capability within the roots of leguminous plants.
2. Forms visible nodules on the roots as a result of the symbiotic association.
3. It cannot independently fix nitrogen without associating with a host plant.
4. This biofertiliser improves soil nitrogen content specifically in legume-based farming systems.

Which biofertiliser is described from the above characteristics?

(a) Cyanobacteria
(b) Azolla
(c) Rhizobium
(d) Phosphate-solubilizing bacteria

**14.** Consider the following types of biofertilisers with their correct examples:

| | Biofertiliser Type | Example |
|---|---|---|
| 1. | Nitrogen-fixing bacteria | Rhizobium |
| 2. | Phosphate-solubilizing bacteria | Azotobacter |
| 3. | Cyanobacteria | Anabaena |
| 4. | Potassium- solubilizing bacteria | Bacillus mucilaginosus |

How many of the given pairs is/are correctly matched?

(a) Only one pair (b) Only two pairs
(c) Only three pairs (d) All four pairs

**15.** Consider the following statements with reference to the Bio NPK biofertilisers:

1. Bio NPK is composed of bacteria that facilitate the uptake of nitrogen, phosphorus, and potassium by plants.
2. It helps in enhancing germination, early crop emergence, and root development.
3. Bio NPK fertilisers do not contribute to increasing plant resistance to diseases and drought conditions.
4. The use of Bio NPK fertilisers can increase crop yield and quality by 20 to 30 percent.

Which of the statements given above are correct?

(a) 1, 2 and 4 only (b) 1 and 3 only
(c) 2 and 3 only (d) 1, 2, 3 and 4

**16.** With reference to the current status of organic farming in India, consider the following statements:

1. India has the largest area under organic farming in the world.
2. The government provides financial incentives for organic certification to encourage farmers.
3. Organic farming adoption is higher in the states of Sikkim, Uttarakhand and Madhya Pradesh.

Which of the statements given above are correct?

(a) 1 and 2 only (b) 2 and 3 only
(c) 1 and 3 only (d) 1, 2 and 3

**17.** With reference to organic farming, consider the following core components:
1. Crop Rotation
2. Genetic Modification
3. Use of Chemical Fertilisers
4. Biological Pest Control

How many of the above practices is/are considered core components of organic farming?
(a) Only one
(b) Only two
(c) Only three
(d) All four

**18.** Consider the following pairs related to the Principles of Organic Farming:

| Principle of Organic Farming | Key Description |
|---|---|
| 1. Principle of Health | A. Ensures fairness in relationships and environment |
| 2. Principle of Ecology | B. Considers future generations and the environment |
| 3. Principle of Fairness | C. Enhances the health of soil, plants, animals, humans and the planet |
| 4. Principle of Care | D. Balances ecological systems and cycles, works with them, and sustains them |

Which of the above pairs are correctly matched?
(a) 1-C, 2-D, 3-A, 4-B
(b) 1-D, 2-C, 3-B, 4-A
(c) 1-A, 2-D, 3-B, 4-C
(d) 1-B, 2-A, 3-C, 4-D

**19.** With reference to the 'Paramparagat Krishi Vikas Yojana (PKVY)', consider the following statements:
1. It aims to promote organic farming practices through a cluster-based approach.
2. Financial assistance under PKVY is available only to large-scale commercial farms.
3. PKVY includes certification assistance to help farmers label their produce as organic.

Which of the statements given above are correct?
(a) 1 and 2 only
(b) 1 and 3 only
(c) 2 and 3 only
(d) 1, 2 and 3

**20.** In the context of Paramparagat Krishi Vikas Yojana (PKVY), consider the following practices encouraged by the scheme:
1. Crop residue burning
2. Use of vermicompost
3. Intercropping with leguminous crops

Which of the given above practices are promoted under PKVY?
(a) 1 and 2 only (b) 2 and 3 only
(c) 1 and 3 only (d) 1, 2 and 3

**21.** What is a unique aspect of the Participatory Guarantee Scheme (PGS) for organic certification?
(a) It requires third-party certification from government bodies.
(b) It involves community-based verification, where farmers collectively certify each other's organic practices.
(c) It applies only to large commercial farms that export organic products.
(d) It mandates random inspections by international agencies.

**22.** Which of the following statements correctly describes the difference between organic farming and natural farming?
(a) Organic farming allows the use of off-farm inputs like compost, while natural farming prohibits all external inputs.
(b) Organic farming prohibits micronutrient correction, while natural farming permits the use of minerals.
(c) Natural farming involves ploughing and soil tilling, while organic farming mimics ecosystems by avoiding such practices.
(d) Both organic and natural farming allow the use of external inputs, but natural farming allows more synthetic inputs.

**23.** Consider the following principles of natural farming with their descriptions:

| Principle | Description |
|---|---|
| 1. Jeevamrutha | Biofertiliser created from cow dung, cow urine and natural ingredients to enrich soil. |
| 2. Mulching | Covering soil with organic matter to retain moisture and prevent weeds. |
| 3. Intercropping | Growing multiple crops together for pest control and soil fertility. |
| 4. Seed Treatment with Beejamrutha | Treating seeds with a natural mixture to protect against diseases. |

How many of the pairs above is/are correctly matched?

(a) Only one pair (b) Only two pairs
(c) Only three pairs (d) All four pairs

**24.** Which benefits of Zero Budget Natural Farming (ZBNF) help lower farming costs for farmers?

1. Elimination of chemical fertilisers
2. Reduced need for expensive seeds
3. Dependence on locally available resources like cow dung
4. High requirement for synthetic pesticides

Select the correct answer from the codes given below:

(a) 1, 2 and 3 only (b) 1 and 4 only
(c) 2, 3 and 4 only (d) 1, 2, 3 and 4

**25.** What is the primary focus of the Bhartiya Prakritik Krishi Padhati (BPKP) Scheme in Indian agriculture?

(a) To promote chemical-intensive agriculture for high yields
(b) To support natural farming practices that rely on locally available, eco-friendly resources
(c) To establish monoculture farming systems across India
(d) To encourage the use of genetically modified seeds exclusively

**26.** Match the following cropping concepts with their descriptions:

| | Cropping Concept | Description |
|---|---|---|
| 1. | Crop Rotation | Growing two or more crops in the same field simultaneously |
| 2. | Inter-Cropping | Planting different crops in succession to improve soil fertility |
| 3. | Relay Cropping | Sowing a second crop before the first crop has fully matured |
| 4. | Mixed Cropping | Growing different crops in the same field without a specific pattern |

How many of the given above pairs is/are correctly matched?

(a) Only one pair
(b) Only two pairs
(c) Only three pairs
(d) All four pairs

**27.** Which of the following components are typically included in an Integrated Farming System (IFS) to promote sustainable agriculture?

1. Crop production
2. Animal husbandry
3. Fish farming
4. Water harvesting

Select the correct answer from the codes given below:

(a) 1 and 2 only
(b) 1, 2 and 3 only
(c) 1, 3 and 4 only
(d) 1, 2, 3 and 4

# OMR SHEET

**Assessment Round**

| | | | | | | | |
|---|---|---|---|---|---|---|---|
| 1 | (a) (b) (c) (d) | 31 | (a) (b) (c) (d) | 61 | (a) (b) (c) (d) | 91 | (a) (b) (c) (d) |
| 2 | (a) (b) (c) (d) | 32 | (a) (b) (c) (d) | 62 | (a) (b) (c) (d) | 92 | (a) (b) (c) (d) |
| 3 | (a) (b) (c) (d) | 33 | (a) (b) (c) (d) | 63 | (a) (b) (c) (d) | 93 | (a) (b) (c) (d) |
| 4 | (a) (b) (c) (d) | 34 | (a) (b) (c) (d) | 64 | (a) (b) (c) (d) | 94 | (a) (b) (c) (d) |
| 5 | (a) (b) (c) (d) | 35 | (a) (b) (c) (d) | 65 | (a) (b) (c) (d) | 95 | (a) (b) (c) (d) |
| 6 | (a) (b) (c) (d) | 36 | (a) (b) (c) (d) | 66 | (a) (b) (c) (d) | 96 | (a) (b) (c) (d) |
| 7 | (a) (b) (c) (d) | 37 | (a) (b) (c) (d) | 67 | (a) (b) (c) (d) | 97 | (a) (b) (c) (d) |
| 8 | (a) (b) (c) (d) | 38 | (a) (b) (c) (d) | 68 | (a) (b) (c) (d) | 98 | (a) (b) (c) (d) |
| 9 | (a) (b) (c) (d) | 39 | (a) (b) (c) (d) | 69 | (a) (b) (c) (d) | 99 | (a) (b) (c) (d) |
| 10 | (a) (b) (c) (d) | 40 | (a) (b) (c) (d) | 70 | (a) (b) (c) (d) | 100 | (a) (b) (c) (d) |
| 11 | (a) (b) (c) (d) | 41 | (a) (b) (c) (d) | 71 | (a) (b) (c) (d) | 101 | (a) (b) (c) (d) |
| 12 | (a) (b) (c) (d) | 42 | (a) (b) (c) (d) | 72 | (a) (b) (c) (d) | 102 | (a) (b) (c) (d) |
| 13 | (a) (b) (c) (d) | 43 | (a) (b) (c) (d) | 73 | (a) (b) (c) (d) | 103 | (a) (b) (c) (d) |
| 14 | (a) (b) (c) (d) | 44 | (a) (b) (c) (d) | 74 | (a) (b) (c) (d) | 104 | (a) (b) (c) (d) |
| 15 | (a) (b) (c) (d) | 45 | (a) (b) (c) (d) | 75 | (a) (b) (c) (d) | 105 | (a) (b) (c) (d) |
| 16 | (a) (b) (c) (d) | 46 | (a) (b) (c) (d) | 76 | (a) (b) (c) (d) | 106 | (a) (b) (c) (d) |
| 17 | (a) (b) (c) (d) | 47 | (a) (b) (c) (d) | 77 | (a) (b) (c) (d) | 107 | (a) (b) (c) (d) |
| 18 | (a) (b) (c) (d) | 48 | (a) (b) (c) (d) | 78 | (a) (b) (c) (d) | 108 | (a) (b) (c) (d) |
| 19 | (a) (b) (c) (d) | 49 | (a) (b) (c) (d) | 79 | (a) (b) (c) (d) | 109 | (a) (b) (c) (d) |
| 20 | (a) (b) (c) (d) | 50 | (a) (b) (c) (d) | 80 | (a) (b) (c) (d) | 110 | (a) (b) (c) (d) |
| 21 | (a) (b) (c) (d) | 51 | (a) (b) (c) (d) | 81 | (a) (b) (c) (d) | 111 | (a) (b) (c) (d) |
| 22 | (a) (b) (c) (d) | 52 | (a) (b) (c) (d) | 82 | (a) (b) (c) (d) | 112 | (a) (b) (c) (d) |
| 23 | (a) (b) (c) (d) | 53 | (a) (b) (c) (d) | 83 | (a) (b) (c) (d) | 113 | (a) (b) (c) (d) |
| 24 | (a) (b) (c) (d) | 54 | (a) (b) (c) (d) | 84 | (a) (b) (c) (d) | 114 | (a) (b) (c) (d) |
| 25 | (a) (b) (c) (d) | 55 | (a) (b) (c) (d) | 85 | (a) (b) (c) (d) | 115 | (a) (b) (c) (d) |
| 26 | (a) (b) (c) (d) | 56 | (a) (b) (c) (d) | 86 | (a) (b) (c) (d) | 116 | (a) (b) (c) (d) |
| 27 | (a) (b) (c) (d) | 57 | (a) (b) (c) (d) | 87 | (a) (b) (c) (d) | 117 | (a) (b) (c) (d) |
| 28 | (a) (b) (c) (d) | 58 | (a) (b) (c) (d) | 88 | (a) (b) (c) (d) | 118 | (a) (b) (c) (d) |
| 29 | (a) (b) (c) (d) | 59 | (a) (b) (c) (d) | 89 | (a) (b) (c) (d) | 119 | (a) (b) (c) (d) |
| 30 | (a) (b) (c) (d) | 60 | (a) (b) (c) (d) | 90 | (a) (b) (c) (d) | 120 | (a) (b) (c) (d) |

## Calculate Your Score

| | |
|---|---|
| **Correct (✓)** | |
| **Incorrect (✓)** | |
| **Unattempted** | |
| **Total Score** | |
| **Accuracy (%)** | |

## Reasons for Incorrect Answers?

1. Lack of Knowledge/Existing Source Insufficient
2. Lack of Multiple Revision
3. Common Sense Mistakes

**Note :**

1. Calculate total score as correct answers carry 2 marks each 1/3rd marks will deducted for **Incorrect** Answers.
2. Calculate Accuracy (%) by dividing the number of correct answers to the total number of attempted questions.

## Past Learning

**1.** Which one of the following is the correct description of '100 Million Farmers'? **(2024)**

(a) It is a platform for accelerating the transition towards food and water systems that are net-zero (carbon), nature-positive and that aims to increase farmer resilience.

(b) It is an international alliance and a network of individuals and farming organisations interested in supporting and strengthening the development of the organic animal husbandry.

(c) It is a digital platform fully integrated with service providers and built on blockchain that lets buyers, sellers, and third parties trade fertilisers quickly and securely.

(d) It is a platform with the mission of encouraging the farmers to form Farmer Product Organisations or Agribusiness Consortiums, thus facilitating the access to global open markets to sell their products.

**2.** 'System of Rice Intensification' of cultivation, in which alternate wetting and drying of rice fields is practised, results in:

1. Reduced seed requirement **(2022)**
2. Reduced methane production
3. Reduced electricity consumption

Select the correct answer using the codes given below:

(a) 1 and 2 only
(b) 2 and 3 only
(c) 1 and 3 only
(d) 1, 2 and 3

**3.** The 'Miyawaki method' is well known for the: **(2022)**

(a) Promotion of commercial farming in arid and semi-arid areas

(b) Development of gardens using genetically modified flora

(c) Creation of mini forests in urban areas

(d) Harvesting wind energy on coastal areas and on sea surfaces

**4.** 'R2 Code of Practices' constitutes a tool available for promoting the adoption of **(2021)**

(a) Environmentally responsible practices in electronics recycling industry.

(b) Ecological management of 'Wetlands of International Importance' under the Ramsar Convention.

(c) Sustainable practices in the cultivation of agricultural crops in degraded lands.

(d) 'Environmental Impact Assessment' in the exploitation of natural resources.

**5.** In the context of India's preparation for Climate-Smart Agriculture, consider the following statements: **(2021)**

1. The 'Climate-Smart Village' approach in India is a part of a project led by the Climate Change, Agriculture and Food Security (CCAFS), an international research programme.
2. The project of CCAFS is carried out under Consultative Group on International Agricultural Research (CGIAR) headquartered in France.
3. The International Crops Research Institute for the Semi-Arid Tropics (ICRISAT) in India is one of the CGIAR's research centres.

Which of the statements given above are correct?

(a) 1 and 2 only
(b) 2 and 3 only
(c) 1 and 3 only
(d) 1, 2 and 3

**6.** How is permaculture farming different from conventional chemical farming? **(2021)**

1. Permaculture farming discourages monocultural practices but in conventional chemical farming, monoculture practices are pre-dominant.
2. Conventional chemical farming can cause increase in soil salinity but the occurrence of such phenomenon is not observed in permaculture farming.
3. Conventional chemical farming is easily possible in semi-arid regions but permaculture farming is not so easily possible in such regions.
4. Practice of mulching is very important in permaculture farming but not necessarily in conventional chemical farming.

Select the correct answer using the codes given below.

(a) 1 and 3 (b) 1, 2 and 4
(c) 4 only (d) 2 and 3

**7.** What is the use of biochar in farming? **(2020)**

1. Biochar can be used as a part of the growing medium in vertical farming.
2. When biochar is a part of the growing medium, it promotes the growth of nitrogen-fixing microorganisms.
3. When biochar is a part of the growing medium, it enables the growing medium to retain water for longer time.

Which of the statements given above is/are correct?

(a) 1 and 2 only
(b) 2 only
(c) 1 and 3 only
(d) 1, 2 and 3

**8.** What are the advantages of fertigation in agriculture? **(2020)**

1. Controlling the alkalinity of irrigation water is possible.
2. Efficient application of Rock Phosphate and all other phosphatic fertilisers is possible.
3. Increased availability of nutrients to plants is possible.
4. Reduction in the leaching of chemical nutrients is possible.

Select the correct answer using the codes given below:

(a) 1, 2 and 3 only (b) 1, 2 and 4 only
(c) 1, 3 and 4 only (d) 2, 3 and 4 only

**9.** What is/are the advantage/advantages of zero tillage in agriculture? **(2020)**

1. Sowing of wheat is possible without burning the residue of previous crop.
2. Without the need for nursery of rice saplings, direct planting of paddy seeds in the wet soil is possible.
3. Carbon sequestration in the soil is possible.

Select the correct answer using the codes given below:

(a) 1 and 2 only
(b) 2 and 3 only
(c) 3 only
(d) 1, 2 and 3

**10.** In the context of India, which of the following is/are considered to be practice(s) of eco-friendly agriculture? **(2020)**

1. Crop diversification
2. Legume intensification
3. Tensiometer use
4. Vertical farming

Select the correct answer using the codes given below:

(a) 1, 2 and 3 only
(b) 3 only
(c) 4 only
(d) 1, 2, 3 and 4

**11.** With reference to the 'Global Alliance for Climate-Smart Agriculture (GACSA)', which of the following statements is/are correct? **(2018)**

1. GACSA is an outcome of the Climate Summit held in Paris in 2015.
2. Membership of GACSA does not create any binding obligations.
3. India was instrumental in the creation of GACSA.

Select the correct answer using the codes given below:

(a) 1 and 3 only (b) 2 only
(c) 2 and 3 only (d) 1, 2 and 3

**12.** With reference to the circumstances in Indian agriculture, the concept of 'Conservation Agriculture' assumes significance. Which of the following fall under the Conservation Agriculture? **(2018)**

1. Avoiding the monoculture practices
2. Adopting minimum tillage
3. Avoiding the cultivation of plantation crops
4. Using crop residues to cover soil surface
5. Adopting spatial and temporal crop sequencing/crop rotations

Select the correct answer using the codes given below:

(a) 1, 3 and 4
(b) 2, 3, 4 and 5
(c) 2, 4 and 5
(d) 1, 2, 3 and 5

**13.** Which of the following practices can help in water conservation in agriculture? **(2017)**

1. Reduced or zero tillage of the land
2. Applying gypsum before irrigating the field
3. Allowing crop residue to remain in the field

Select the correct answer using the codes given below:

(a) 1 and 2 only (b) 3 only
(c) 1 and 3 only (d) 1, 2 and 3

**14.** Which of the following is/are the advantage/advantages of practising drip irrigation? **(2016)**

1. Reduction in weed
2. Reduction in soil salinity
3. Reduction in soil erosion

Select the correct answer using the codes given below.

(a) 1 and 2 only
(b) 3 only
(c) 1 and 3 only
(d) None of the above is an advantage of practising drip irrigation

**15.** In India, the problem of soil erosion is associated with which of the following? **(2014)**

1. Terrace cultivation
2. Deforestation
3. Tropical climate

Select the correct answer using the codes given below :

(a) 1 and 2 only
(b) 2 only
(c) 1 and 3 only
(d) 1, 2 and 3

**16.** What are the significances of a practical approach to sugarcane production known as 'sustainable Sugarcane Initiative'? **(2014)**

1. Seed cost is very low in this compared to the conventional method of cultivation.
2. Drip irrigation can be practiced very effectively in this.
3. There is no application of chemical/ inorganic fertilisers at all in this.
4. The scope for intercropping is more in this compared to the conventional method of cultivation.

Select the correct answer using the codes given below :

(a) 1 and 3 only
(b) 1, 2 and 4 only
(c) 2, 3 and 4 only
(d) 1, 2, 3 and 4

**17.** Consider the following agricultural practices : **(2012)**

1. Contour bunding
2. Relay cropping
3. Zero tillage

In the context of global climate change, which of the above helps/help in carbon sequestration/storage in the soil?

(a) 1 and 2 only
(b) 3 only
(c) 1, 2 and 3
(d) None of them

# Detailed Solutions

## Assessment Round

**1.** *(d)* The development and characteristics of soil are influenced by multiple critical factors:

- **Parent material** provides the original mineral content from which soil is derived. It determines the soil's mineral composition and influences texture, colour, and nutrient availability.
- **Climate** plays a significant role in soil formation. Temperature and precipitation impact the rate of weathering, organic matter decomposition, and leaching of minerals, shaping the soil's structure and fertility.
- **Organisms** contribute to soil fertility by breaking down organic matter, which adds essential nutrients to the soil. Roots, bacteria, and other microorganisms also improve soil structure and aeration.
- **Time** allows soils to evolve and develop distinct horizons. Over time, ongoing weathering, organic matter accumulation, and microbial activity enrich and mature the soil profile.

All four factors collectively contribute to the physical, chemical, and biological properties of soil, making them crucial in soil development.

**Thus, the correct answer is (d) All four.**

**2.** *(b)* Fine-textured soils retain more nutrients and water but may lead to poor drainage, affecting root development.

Soil texture, determined by particle size, impacts water retention, drainage, and nutrient availability. Fine-textured soils (like clay) hold more water and nutrients but may hinder root growth due to poor drainage. Coarse-textured soils, such as sandy soils, have good drainage but may lack nutrients and retain less water, affecting plant growth.

**Thus, option (b) is the correct answer.**

**3.** *(a)* 1, 4, 2, 3

- **O-horizon:** Organic layer on the soil surface with decomposed organic matter.
- **A-horizon:** Known as the topsoil, it contains minerals mixed with organic material.
- **B-horizon:** Known as the subsoil, where minerals leached from above accumulate.
- **C-horizon:** Composed of weathered parent material and marks the transition to bedrock.

**Soil Horizons**

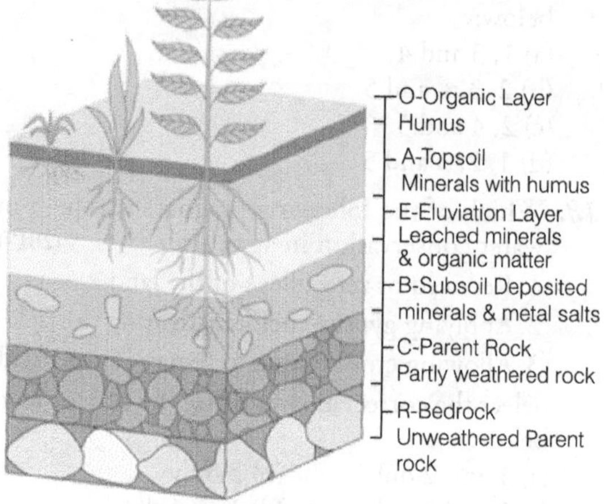


**Thus, the correct order is (a) 1, 4, 2, 3.**

**4.** *(d)* All four pairs

- **Calcification** : In arid and semi-arid regions, calcification leads to the accumulation of calcium carbonate, particularly in subsoil layers, impacting the soil structure by making it more alkaline and often less suitable for agriculture.
- **Podzolisation** : This process typically occurs in cold, humid regions with acidic soils, leading to a distinct white or gray subsurface horizon due to heavy leaching and organic acid buildup. Podzolised soils are often low in nutrients.
- **Laterisation** : In tropical climates with high rainfall, laterisation results in significant leaching, leaving soils enriched in iron and aluminium oxides. Such soils are typically reddish and less fertile due to nutrient loss.

- **Salinisation** : Salinisation is common in poorly drained arid or semi-arid soils where soluble salts accumulate on the soil surface, causing salinity issues that reduce crop yields and degrade soil health.

**Therefore, the correct answer is (d) All four pairs.**

**5.** *(c)* Acidic soils with distinct gray or white subsurface layers due to intense leaching

Podzol soils are typically acidic and form in cold, humid regions with high rainfall. Due to intense leaching, these soils develop a distinct gray or white layer beneath the organic topsoil, often lacking in nutrients and making them less suitable for conventional agriculture.

**Thus, option (c) is the correct answer.**

**6.** *(b)* Saturation of soil with water, causing reduction and accumulation of iron compounds, often creating a grayish-blue layer

- **Gleisation** is a soil-forming process that occurs primarily in waterlogged environments with limited drainage and oxygen supply. In these saturated soils, the lack of oxygen leads to the reduction of iron compounds.
- **Resulting Characteristics**: The reduced iron compounds give the soil a distinctive grayish-blue color, typical of gleised soils, which are commonly found in wetland and lowland areas.
- **Impact on Soil Properties**: Gleisation impacts root growth and fertility due to reduced soil aeration and accumulation of iron, hindering agricultural productivity in affected soils.

**Thus, option (b) is the correct answer.**

**7.** *(d)* **Red and Yellow Soil**

Red and Yellow Soil is characterised by its distinctive colour due to iron content and is commonly found in regions with low rainfall in the Deccan Plateau, Western Ghats, Odisha, and parts of Chhattisgarh. It is also known as the 'omnibus group' and is deficient in essential nutrients like nitrogen and phosphorus.

**Thus, option (d) is the correct answer.**

**8.** *(c)* All three pairs

- **Sheet Erosion**: Involves the gradual removal of thin layers of soil from large areas, particularly on sloped lands. Water runoff from rainfall washes away these thin layers, depleting fertile topsoil.
  - **Region**: Common in the **Western Ghats**, where frequent rainfall on sloped terrains causes soil displacement.
- **Gully Erosion**: Occurs when intense water flow carves out deep channels or gullies, often due to unrestrained rainwater on loose soils.
  - **Region**: Notable in the **Chambal Basin**, where unchecked water flow and soil erosion result in large, eroded gullies.
- **Wind Erosion**: Involves the displacement of soil particles by wind, particularly in dry or barren regions with sparse vegetation. Wind carries loose topsoil away, affecting soil quality.
  - **Region**: Primarily affects **arid regions in Rajasthan**, where high wind speeds and limited vegetation lead to significant soil loss.

**Therefore, the correct answer is (c) All three pairs.**

**9.** *(a)* Soil texture is determined by the relative proportions of three primary particle types: **sand, silt and clay.**

- **Sand** particles are the largest, allowing for good drainage and aeration but poor nutrient retention.
- **Silt** particles are medium-sized, with better nutrient-holding capacity and moderate drainage.
- **Clay** particles are the smallest, offering high nutrient retention but often poor drainage due to their compact nature.

The combination of these particles in different ratios creates various soil textures, such as loam, which is ideal for agriculture due to its balanced properties.

**Thus, option (a) is the correct answer.**

**10.** *(c)* All three pairs

Each type of erosion corresponds to specific conditions and geographic locations in India:

- **Splash Erosion**: This erosion type is caused by raindrop impact, which detaches soil particles from exposed surfaces, especially when there's no vegetation cover to absorb the force of rainfall.
  – **Region**: Often occurs in **Hilly regions of North-East India**, where heavy rainfall and steep slopes make soil susceptible to detachment.
- **Rill Erosion**: Results in the formation of small channels, or rills, on slopes due to surface water runoff. Rills are typically temporary but can become more severe with persistent runoff.
  – **Region**: Common in the **Shivalik Range**, where slopes and runoff conditions encourage the formation of these small channels.
- **Coastal Erosion**: Involves the gradual removal of soil and rock along coastlines due to the action of waves, tides and coastal currents.
  – **Region**: Particularly significant along the **Eastern Coastline of India**, where tidal activity and wave action contribute to soil loss.

**Therefore, the correct answer is (c) All three pairs.**

***11.*** *(b)* Only two

- **Statement 1 is incorrect**: Biofertilisers **not only supply nitrogen and phosphorus to plants but also improve soil fertility**. They enhance the soil's nutrient content and make it biologically active by increasing the population of beneficial microorganisms. Over time, biofertilisers improve soil structure and texture, which is crucial for maintaining long-term soil health.
- **Statement 2 is correct**: Biofertilisers contain living microorganisms, such as bacteria, fungi, and algae that promote plant growth by colonising the root area. These organisms need careful handling during storage and application to maintain their viability. **Extreme temperatures, direct sunlight, and contamination can reduce their effectiveness**, so they must be stored and applied correctly.
- **Statement 3 is correct**: Biofertilisers are generally more eco-friendly compared to chemical fertilisers. They reduce the need for synthetic inputs, which can lead to issues like soil degradation and water pollution. Biofertilisers promote sustainable agriculture by recycling nutrients in the soil and reducing dependency on harmful chemicals.

**Thus, option (b) is the correct answer.**

***12.*** *(a)* 1 and 2 only

- **Statement 1 is correct** : Mycorrhiza is a type of **symbiotic association between fungi and plant roots. The fungi enhance the plant's ability to absorb water and nutrients, especially phosphorus, from the soil.** By extending their hyphae into the soil, mycorrhizal fungi increase the root surface area, allowing plants to take up more nutrients, particularly in phosphorus-deficient soils.
- **Statement 2 is correct**: Phosphate solubilising bacteria (PSB) play a **significant role in converting insoluble phosphorus compounds in the soil into forms that are accessible to plants**. They release organic acids, which help to dissolve the insoluble forms of phosphorus, thereby increasing its availability for plant uptake. This process is crucial for plants as phosphorus is a vital nutrient for their growth and development.
- **Statement 3 is incorrect** : Cyanobacteria, also known as blue-green algae, do play a role in nitrogen fixation. **Certain cyanobacteria, such as Anabaena and Nostoc, are capable of fixing atmospheric nitrogen into forms that plants can use.** This process is essential in nitrogen-poor environments, such as rice paddies, where cyanobacteria contribute to soil fertility by providing a natural source of nitrogen.

**Thus, option (a) is the correct answer.**

***13.*** *(c)* Rhizobium

Rhizobium is a nitrogen-fixing biofertiliser that relies on a symbiotic relationship with leguminous plants, producing root nodules. Unlike free-living nitrogen-fixers, Rhizobium requires a host plant to perform nitrogen fixation, significantly aiding in the growth of legumes by enhancing the soil's nitrogen levels naturally.

**Thus, option (c) is the correct answer.**

**14.** *(c)* Only three pairs

1. **Pair 1 is correct:** Nitrogen-fixing bacteria include **Rhizobium,** which forms symbiotic relationships with leguminous plants to fix atmospheric nitrogen in the soil. This enriches soil nitrogen levels, making it beneficial for plant growth.
2. **Pair 2 is incorrect:** While phosphate-solubilizing bacteria improve phosphorus availability in soil, **Azotobacter** is primarily known as a nitrogen-fixing bacterium rather than a phosphate-solubilizer.
3. **Pair 3 is correct:** Cyanobacteria such as **Anabaena** are known for their nitrogen-fixing abilities and are commonly found in paddy fields and aquatic environments, supporting plant growth by fixing nitrogen.
4. **Pair 4 is correct:** Potassium-solubilising bacteria, like **Bacillus mucilaginosus,** release potassium from insoluble compounds, enhancing its availability to plants.

**Thus, the correct answer is (c) Only three pairs.**

**15.** *(a)* 1, 2 and 4 only

- **Statement 1 is correct:** Bio NPK fertilisers are biofertilisers composed of beneficial bacteria that facilitate the uptake of nitrogen, phosphorus, and potassium, which are essential nutrients for plant growth. These bacteria help in converting these nutrients into forms that can be easily absorbed by the plants, thereby enhancing their availability in the soil.
- **Statement 2 is correct :** Bio NPK fertilisers are known to promote better seed germination, early crop emergence, and enhanced root development. The beneficial bacteria produce plant growth hormones and vitamins, which stimulate root growth, leading to better establishment of young plants.
- **Statement 3 is incorrect :** Bio NPK fertilisers do contribute to increasing plant resistance to diseases and drought conditions. The bacteria present in these biofertilisers improve root health and nutrient uptake, which can make plants more resilient to both biotic (disease) and abiotic (drought) stresses. By promoting stronger root systems, these fertilisers enhance the plant's overall health and resistance.
- **Statement 4 is correct :** The use of Bio NPK fertilisers has been shown to increase crop yield and quality by 20 to 30 percent. This increase is attributed to better nutrient availability, enhanced plant growth, and improved resistance to environmental stresses, which collectively contribute to higher crop productivity and quality.

**Thus, option (a) is the correct answer.**

**16.** *(b)* 2 and 3 only

- **Statement 1 is incorrect:** While India is a leading producer of organic products, it does not have the largest area under organic farming globally; other countries surpass it in terms of the organic area.

  In 2022, Australia was ranked first with an organic agricultural land area amounting to about 53 million hectares. The land area used for organic agriculture in Australia is thus larger than the acreage of all the other leading countries combined.
- **Statement 2 is correct:** The Indian government provides incentives, such as financial aid for organic certification, to encourage farmers to adopt organic farming methods.
- **Statement 3 is correct:** Organic farming is widely adopted in states like Sikkim, which was declared a fully organic state, and in other states like Uttarakhand and Madhya Pradesh, known for high organic farming rates.

**Thus, the correct answer is (b) 2 and 3 only.**

**17.** *(b)* Only two

Organic farming emphasises sustainable agricultural practices that avoid synthetic inputs. Its core components aim to enhance soil health, promote biodiversity, and reduce environmental impact.

- **Statement 1 is correct**: Crop rotation is a fundamental practice in organic farming that prevents soil depletion, manages pests naturally, and enhances soil fertility by alternating crops.
- **Statement 2 is incorrect**: Genetic modification is not permitted in organic farming, as organic standards require crops to be non-GMO.
- **Statement 3 is incorrect**: The use of chemical fertilisers is prohibited in organic farming, as they can harm soil microbes and disrupt ecosystem balance.
- **Statement 4 is correct**: Biological pest control is a core organic practice, involving natural predators and biocontrol agents instead of synthetic pesticides.

**Thus, the correct answer is (b) Only two.**

***18.*** *(a)* 1-C, 2-D, 3-A, 4-B

- **Principle of Health**: Enhances the health of soil, plants, animals, humans and the planet
- **Principle of Ecology**: Balances ecological systems and cycles, works with them, and sustains them.
- **Principle of Fairness**: Ensures fairness in relationships and environment
- **Principle of Care**: Considers future generations and the environment

**Thus, option (a) is the correct answer.**

***19.*** *(b)* 1 and 3 only

- **Statement 1 is correct**: Paramparagat Krishi Vikas Yojana (PKVY) indeed promotes organic farming using a cluster-based approach, where groups of farmers collectively adopt organic practices, typically across 20 hectare clusters. This approach enhances community-driven organic farming and helps maintain large areas under organic cultivation.
- **Statement 2 is incorrect**: PKVY provides financial assistance to small and marginal farmers, not only large-scale commercial farms. It focuses on making organic farming accessible and viable for small landholders.
- **Statement 3 is correct**: PKVY includes support for organic certification, assisting farmers in obtaining certification for their organic produce. This labelling aids in market recognition, ensuring that farmers can sell their produce at a premium as certified organic.

**Thus, the correct answer is (b) 1 and 3 only.**

***20.*** *(b)* 2 and 3 only

- **Statement 1 is incorrect**: PKVY does not encourage crop residue burning, as this practice leads to soil degradation and air pollution. Instead, the scheme advocates for sustainable soil management practices.
- **Statement 2 is correct**: PKVY promotes the use of vermicompost, a nutrient-rich organic fertiliser, to enhance soil fertility naturally without the need for synthetic chemicals, aligning with organic farming principles.
- **Statement 3 is correct**: Intercropping with leguminous crops is encouraged under PKVY to improve soil nitrogen content naturally, as legumes help fix nitrogen in the soil, enhancing its fertility.

**Thus, the correct answer is (b) 2 and 3 only.**

***21.*** *(b)* It involves community-based verification, where farmers collectively certify each other's organic practices.

PGS allows small-scale farmers to verify organic standards through peer review within the community, offering an accessible alternative to third-party certification, which can be costly and complex. This peer-to-peer approach builds trust within communities and is suited to smallholder farmers, emphasising transparency and mutual accountability.

**Thus, option (b) is the correct answer.**

***22.*** *(a)* Organic farming allows the use of off-farm inputs like compost, while natural farming prohibits all external inputs.

**Organic farming** involves using natural inputs like compost, manure, and biological pest control instead of synthetic chemicals to grow crops, promoting soil health, biodiversity, and sustainability. It avoids the use of chemical fertilisers, pesticides, and genetically modified organisms (GMOs), emphasising eco-friendly practices.

**Natural farming,** on the other hand, goes a step further by minimising external inputs altogether. It follows principles like **zero-budget farming**, relying on natural processes such as soil fertility and local biodiversity without fertilisers, pesticides or even tilling. Both approaches aim for sustainable agriculture, but natural farming emphasises complete harmony with nature's ecosystems.

- **Option (a) is correct:** Organic farming permits the use of **off-farm organic inputs** like compost and vermicompost, whereas **natural farming** does not allow any **external inputs.**
- **Option *(b)* is incorrect: Natural farming** prohibits the use of minerals, while organic farming allows for **micronutrient correction** using minerals.
- **Option (c) is incorrect: Natural farming mimics ecosystems**, which means it avoids practices like **ploughing** and **soil tilling**, while **organic farming** may involve these practices.
- **Option (d) is incorrect: Natural farming** avoids synthetic inputs altogether, unlike organic farming.

**Thus, option (a) is the correct answer.**

***23.*** *(d)* All four pairs

Natural farming promotes soil health and biodiversity through the use of traditional, organic techniques rather than chemical inputs. Each of the following principles aligns with a specific goal in natural farming practices:

- **Pair 1 - Jeevamrutha: Correct.** Jeevamrutha is a biofertiliser created from ingredients like cow dung, cow urine, and other natural materials. It enriches soil microbial activity, providing essential nutrients for plant growth.
- **Pair 2 - Mulching: Correct.** Mulching involves covering the soil with organic matter, such as leaves or straw, to retain soil moisture, suppress weeds, and improve soil fertility by decomposing over time.
- **Pair 3 - Intercropping: Correct.** Intercropping is the practice of growing multiple crop types together, which aids in natural pest control and enhances soil fertility by creating a balanced ecosystem.
- **Pair 4 - Seed Treatment with Beejamrutha: Correct.** Beejamrutha is a natural treatment applied to seeds to protect them against soil-borne diseases, strengthening their resilience and encouraging healthy germination.

**Thus, the correct answer is (d) All four pairs.**

***24.*** *(a)* 1, 2 and 3 only

Zero Budget Natural Farming (ZBNF) offers several cost-effective benefits for farmers by promoting natural inputs and reducing dependency on external resources.

- **Statement 1 is correct:** ZBNF encourages the elimination of chemical fertilisers, which are costly. Instead, it relies on natural fertilisers, significantly lowering input expenses.
- **Statement 2 is correct:** The approach reduces the need for expensive hybrid seeds, allowing farmers to use native seeds or seeds from previous harvests.
- **Statement 3 is correct:** ZBNF leverages locally available resources, such as cow dung and urine, for creating organic fertilisers like Jeevamrutha, minimising reliance on expensive inputs.
- **Statement 4 is incorrect:** ZBNF avoids synthetic pesticides, favouring natural pest control methods, which further reduces costs associated with farming.

**Thus, the correct answer is (a) 1, 2 and 3 only.**

***25.*** *(b)* To support natural farming practices that rely on locally available, eco-friendly resources

The **Bhartiya Prakritik Krishi Padhati** (BPKP) focuses on natural farming techniques, which emphasise the use of locally sourced organic inputs rather than chemical fertilisers or pesticides. This approach aligns with India's goals of sustainability and reducing farming costs while maintaining soil health. By promoting indigenous practices like the use of organic compost and biofertilisers, BPKP aims to support farmers in sustainable agriculture that benefits both the environment and agricultural productivity.

**Thus, option (b) is the correct answer.**

***26.*** *(b)* Only two pairs

- **Crop Rotation is incorrectly matched:** Crop rotation involves growing different types of crops in succession on the same land to maintain soil fertility and reduce pest and disease cycles.

- **Inter-Cropping is incorrectly matched:** Inter-cropping is correctly described as the practice of growing two or more crops simultaneously in the same field, often to make better use of available resources and to provide mutual benefits to the crops.
- **Relay Cropping is correctly matched:** Relay cropping is the practice of planting a second crop before the first crop has been harvested. This technique allows for efficient use of the growing season and provides continuous crop cover.
- **Mixed Cropping is correctly matched:** Mixed cropping involves planting different crops together in no specific arrangement, typically to minimise risks related to crop failure and to improve biodiversity in the field.

**Thus, option (b) is the correct answer.**

**27.** *(d)* 1, 2, 3 and 4

An Integrated Farming System (IFS) aims to optimise resource use and enhance sustainable agricultural productivity by integrating various farm activities that complement one another.

- **Statement 1 (Crop production) is correct:** Crop production forms the core of IFS, providing food and fodder resources.
- **Statement 2 (Animal husbandry) is correct:** Adding livestock generates manure for soil health and diversifies farm income.
- **Statement 3 (Fish farming) is correct:** Fish farming provides food and an additional revenue stream.
- **Statement 4 (Water harvesting) is correct:** Efficient water management is vital for sustaining IFS, especially in water-scarce regions.

**Thus, the correct answer is (d) 1, 2, 3 and 4.**

## Past Learning (Answers)

| | | | | | | | | | |
|---|---|---|---|---|---|---|---|---|---|
| 1 (a) | 2 (d) | 3 (c) | 4 (a) | 5 (d) | 6 (b) | 7 (d) | 8 (c) | 9 (d) | 10 (d) |
| 11 (b) | 12 (c) | 13 (c) | 14 (c) | 15 (b) | 16 (b) | 17 (c) | | | |